Wolfram's Parzival. On the Genesis of it

MIKROKOSMOS
BEITRÄGE ZUR
LITERATURWISSENSCHAFT UND
BEDEUTUNGSFORSCHUNG
Herausgegeben von Wolfgang Harms

BAND 9

Marianne Wynn

Wolfram's Parzival
On the Genesis of its Poetry

Verlag Peter Lang
Frankfurt am Main · Bern · New York · Nancy

Marianne Wynn

Wolfram's Parzival
On the Genesis of its Poetry

Verlag Peter Lang
Frankfurt am Main · Bern · New York · Nancy

CIP-Kurztitelaufnahme der Deutschen Bibliothek

Wynn, Marianne:

Wolfram's Parzival : on the genesis of its
poetry / Marianne Wynn. - Frankfurt am Main ;
Bern ; New York ; Nancy : Lang, 1984.
  (Mikrokosmos ; Bd. 9)
  ISBN 3-8204-8050-1
NE: GT

ISSN 0170-9143
ISBN 3-8204-8050-1
© Verlag Peter Lang GmbH, Frankfurt am Main 1984

Druck und Bindung: Weihert-Druck GmbH, Darmstadt

TABLE OF CONTENT

Preface

I owe many debts, so many, that were I to mention them all, this would become a very long preface indeed. I am grateful to the editors of the Modern Language Review, of Speculum and of the Beiträge zur Geschichte der deutschen Sprache und Literatur for giving me permission to republish here as chapter III articles which had appeared in their pages. They are: Geography of Fact and Fiction in Wolfram von Eschenbach's 'Parzivâl', MLR, 56 (1961), 28-43; Scenery and Chivalrous Journeys in Wolfram's Parzival, Speculum, 36 (1961), 393-423, and Parzival and Gâwân - Hero and Counterpart, PBB (Tübingen), 84 (1962), 142-172. I benefited enormously from the hospitality of many universities, of Cornell, Yale, Princeton, Bryn Mawr, Indiana, Munich, Hamburg, Giessen, Marburg, Frankfurt, Bonn, Copenhagen, and Wrocław, and of the London Institute of Germanic Studies. I wish to record my thanks here to all those colleagues, far too numerous to mention, who organized my visits and who played host to me. The audiences with whom they provided me listened patiently to parts of chapter IV. Discussions arising out of these lectures helped to clarify for me many ideas and often suggested to me new avenues of investigation. Without the unfailing helpfulness and courtesy of librarians, and in particular without their resourcefulness, this book could never have been written. I relied on the British Library, Senate House Library of the University of London, the Institute of Germanic Studies, the German Historical Institute, and above all on my own college library, the Caroline Skeel Library of Westfield College, whose invaluable Interlibrary Loan Service has spared me stress and saved me many hours. I was also fortunate in having been able to solicit advice from medieval historians with the greatest of ease. Over the years Rosalind Hill, Christopher Brooke, and Henry Loyn, all members of the Westfield Senior Common Room, have supplied me with references and have made valuable suggestions. The manuscript itself was put into proper shape for production by the devoted labours of one of my postgraduate students, Janet Wharton, and of Karl Toth, one-time Foreign Language Assistant in the Department of German at Westfield College. Throughout the writing of this book I have been accompanied, helped, and supported by the friendship and encouragement of Dennis Green and Wolfgang Harms. With the utmost patience and the greatest generosity they have listened and commented, discussed and counselled. I am grateful to all who have helped me in the preparation of this book, but my deepest gratitude must go to my parents who first introduced me to the infinite pleasures of poetry and the arts.

The Wolfram scholar needs an iron self-discipline for calling a halt. Wolfram criticism has begun to stretch into infinity. The Wolfram bibliography of 1968 by Ulrich Pretzel and Wolfgang Bachofer listed 1062 items and was described as a select bibliography by its editors. The research report of 1970 by Joachim Bumke on Wolfram research since 1945 reviewed circa 700 contributions and ran to more than 400 pages. Since then books, ar-

ticles, and dissertations on Wolfram have continued to pour off
the presses, not to mention commentary on his work in histories
of literature, and translations of his poetry. Where secondary
literature has exploded in such a manner, it is inevitable that
much which is important will slip through the critic's net. In
some ways this may be fortunate, for at a certain stage he must
no longer permit himself to be tempted along new paths of interpretation and to be swayed by new views. In the end he must have
the courage of his convictions, or else these convictions will
never reach print. In the one hundred and fifty years of Wolfram
scholarship 'Parzival' has become one of the most controversial
works of European literature. Every observation that the critic
makes is felt by others as a challenge, often even as a provocation. Every comment stimulates discussion. It may indeed be
said, with apologies to Dr. Johnson: "Every other author may
aspire to praise: the Wolfram scholar can only hope to escape
reproach - and even this negative recompense has been yet granted to very few."

Westfield College   Marianne Wynn
University of London
August 1983

I. Introduction

This study seeks to capture aspects of the creation of poetry
as they manifest themselves in the composition of a great work -
of the 'Parzival' of medieval imperial Germany.[1] Facets of the
poetic process come to be outlined as its author recasts, and
fundamentally re-creates, the French 'Contes del Graal'. His
response to the received narrative gives impetus to a literary
activity which fans out in seemingly countless directions: He
expands and condenses, embellishes and prunes, adds and suppresses, accepts and changes, re-aligns, re-interprets, and altogether re-conceives. These features of the making of poetry as
they become crystallized in the regeneration of the French work
- whether they be attributed to consciously developed literary
expertise, or to the repercussions of chance inspiration of
which the poet himself was not aware, is immaterial within this
context - these features combine to characterize specifically
and significantly Wolfram von Eschenbach working on 'Parzival'.
At the same time they represent a pattern of poetry in the
making and are indicative of the poetic process as such. They
are, moreover, of particular interest to the comparatist of
literature providing him as they do, with a unique amalgam of
possible classifications. For while the French and German works
may be seen on one level as the independent results of the
imagination and industry of two poets widely separated in time,
place and language - the baseline of the comparative proposition
- on another they are also in a state of dependence, and of

---

1 The most recent sustained view of the actual genesis of 'Parzival', of Wolfram in his workshop while composing it, is
Karl Bertau's. He states it at length in his Deutsche Literatur im europäischen Mittelalter, vol. II: 1195-1220, Munich,
1973. Vid. in particular chapter 26: Literatur als Erkennt-
nisrahmen für eine ungeborgene Welt, p. 774ff.; chapter 27:
Die Scherben des Reiches, p. 815ff., and chapter 31: Abstrakt-
werden des Stofflich-Konkreten. Abschluss des 'Parzival',
pp. 966-1019. In outlining his proposals regarding the stages
of composition of the work he comments also on aspects of its
poetry. His perspective differs fundamentally from the one
offered above in that his main interest is centred upon the

highly specific dependence at that. Not only does the German
work derive directly from its French counterpart, but bearing
in mind the quality of Chrestien de Troyes as a writer, it may
also be considered the sum of collaboration of two poets of
quite unusual distinction. Admittedly, the 'Contes del Graal'
is not held in the same high critical regard as Chrestien's
other narratives, and in the corpus of his works it undoubtedly
represents a lesser one. Nevertheless, there are passages of
brilliant psychological insight, and of superb realistic description which betray unequivocally the characteristic view
and presentation of the human condition by Chrestien at his
best. The comparatist thus has before him the challenge of sep-
arating independence from dependence, of assessing them both
individually and of considering in addition the unusual circum-
stance of the convergence of two immensely gifted minds. The
eternally fascinating aspect to the critic of Wolfram's 'Parzival' is that the work is not so different in plot from the
original which inspired it, but totally different in character.
Some of these differences in character are due, to be sure, to
those of time, place and language. The French work was written
a generation before Wolfram von Eschenbach and in and for an
environment other than his. The major differences, however, the
new spirit which infuses it, its vision, its pathos, its powerful appeal to the emotions, are due to the remodelling forces
of his poetic genius and of his literary craftsmanship. It is
these latter differences which in the end override the concrete
similarity between the two works. The two narratives may indeed
share most of the same episodes and motifs, but in the German
work different themes have been grafted on to them and a new
symbolism has been developed for them. In this way the same

---

question of how the whole work came into being, upon its
total genesis in fact. The focus here is rather on details
of Wolfram's poetic craft, on his independence of Chrestien,
on his originality as it declares itself in specific stylistic features and their poetic efficacy.

scenes and motifs, mostly even appearing in the same chronological sequence, take on new meanings. Tracing and understanding
this corpus of distinctions - isolating them, describing and
analyzing them, accounting for the reasons of their existence,
following the course of their genesis, assessing their poetic
significance within the work, and finally apprehending their
nature as poetry, all this, though much, seems on the face of
it an easy, because straightforward critical task. The formula:
'Parzival' minus 'Contes del Graal' equals the creation of great
poetry, looks manageable.[2] It firmly focusses the question and
clearly circumscribes the area for investigation. Its simplicity

2   The proposition from which the above discussion proceeds, and
    on which the whole book is indeed based, namely that the
    'Contes del Graal' forms the blueprint of the German 'Parzi-
    val',is not intended to mean that Wolfram made use of no other
    ready-made fiction. It does mean, however, that the author
    considers it an established fact that the 'Contes del Graal'
    represents the chief source for 'Parzival', and the longest
    connected account which Wolfram followed in detail for the
    bulk of his work, and carefully adapted. No other additional
    and coherent source for those parts of the plot which are
    not congruent with Chrestien's narrative has ever been proved
    conclusively for 'Parzival'. Nevertheless, the 'Contes del
    Graal' cannot be called its only source. All literature,
    heard and read, is source-material to the poet, and Wolfram
    might easily have incorporated descriptions, episodes, even
    series of scenes from other works into his own, in a more or
    less modified form. This still leaves the 'Contes del Graal'
    as his major, and only proven source. To look for yet another
    for the main body of the work, where the plot so closely
    tallies with the French narrative, seems unnecessary, to say
    the very least. The researches of Mary A. Rachbauer, Wolfram
    von Eschenbach. A Study of the Relation of the Content of
    Books III - VI and IX of the 'Parzival' to the Crestien
    Manuscripts, The Catholic University of America, Studies in
    German, 4, New York, 1934, Jean Fourquet, Wolfram d'Eschen-
    bach et le Conte del Graal. Les Divergences de la Tradition
    du Conte del Graal de Chrétien et leur Importance pour
    l'Explication du Parzival. Publication de la Faculté des
    Lettres de Strasbourg 1938, Friedrich Panzer, Gahmuret, Quel-
    lenstudien zu Wolframs Parzival. Sitzungsberichte der Heidel-
    berger Akademie der Wissenschaften, philosophisch-historische
    Klasse, Jahrgang 1939/40. Abh. I, Heidelberg, 1940, Bodo
    Mergell, Wolfram von Eschenbach und seine französischen
    Quellen. II. Teil. Wolframs Parzival, Forschungen zur deut-
    schen Sprache und Dichtung, 11, Münster, 1943, and Hermann

and all-inclusiveness, however, are apparent only and misleading.
Poetry cannot be quantified. It resists comprehensive description
even when relation and dependence throw it into relief as here.
The finer its quality, the more elusive its nature; for the
greater its merit, the larger the number of levels on which it
exists. All the critic can hope to do is to uncover aspects of
its totality in a given work. This limitation to individual
critical discovery explains the present study. For 'Parzival'
and its model have been under comparative scrutiny times without number both for specific topics and wider themes. The comparison has formed the subject of countless investigations of
restricted scope and also on a larger scale. Yet because of the
vast spectrum of poetic effects and meanings in a work as outstanding as 'Parzival' there is always room for more analyses
of the same or similar type.

The most important account to date of Wolfram's relation to
Chrestien is that by Bodo Mergell.[3] It is the only comprehensive investigation of the connection between the 'Contes del
Graal' and 'Parzival', commenting in detail on Wolfram's translation and adaptation of Chrestien's text from beginning to end.
The purpose of the analysis is to resolve the question whether
the 'Contes del Graal' is the major source for the German work,
or not. Mergell's study presupposes his earlier investigation
of the links between Wolfram's 'Willehalm' and the 'Bataille
d'Aliscans'.[4] If - this is his proposition - identical features

---

Schneider, Parzival-Studien, Sitzungsberichte der Bayerischen
Akademie der Wissenschaften, philosophisch-historische Klasse,
Jahrgang 1944/46, vol. 4, among others, have confirmed this
view. Yet the question of Wolfram's source or sources for
'Parzival' seems fated to remain a matter of schools of
thought. Other major sources continue to be postulated for
it, vid. in particular Herbert Kolb, Munsalvaesche. Studien
zum Kyotproblem, Munich, 1963.

3 Op. cit.

4 Bodo Mergell, Wolfram von Eschenbach und seine französischen
Quellen, 1. Teil: Wolframs Willehalm, Forschungen zur deutschen Sprache und Dichtung, 6, Münster, 1936.

of literary transformation can be isolated for both of Wolfram's
verse narratives, their demonstration may be accepted as evidence
that the 'Contes del Graal' provided the chief source for 'Parzival'. His enquiry thus has a dual aim: the definitive establishment of the main source material for 'Parzival', and the recognition of Wolfram's characteristic manner of reworking a received
narrative, as it manifests itself in both his major works.[5] The
method whereby he pursues this double objective is the chronological juxtaposition of individual terms, descriptive phrases,
and whole sentences and passages in 'Parzival' with their counterpart in the French work, choosing as his points of departure
complexes of thought and units of description as they appear in
narrative sequence. The present study shares neither aims nor
method with Bodo Mergell's analysis.[6] Its purpose is to observe

_____

5   Wolframs Parzival, pp. 11,12: "Lässt der zwischen Chrestien
    und Wolfram zu beobachtende Wandel der Parzivaldichtung eine
    einheitliche Linie künstlerisch planvoller Umgestaltung aller
    Teile erkennen, die ihrem Wesen nach mit der Wandlung der
    Willehalmdichtung übereinstimmt? Kann diese Frage eindeutig
    beantwortet werden, so darf die Kyotfrage in dem Sinne als
    gelöst gelten, dass nur Chrestiens Percevalroman dem deutschen
    Dichter als Hauptquelle vorlag ... Falls sich für Parzival
    und Willehalm eine tiefere Verwandtschaft der Umwandlung
    ihrer Vorlagen nachweisen lässt, kann diese Gemeinsamkeit
    weder Zufall sein noch auf einer imaginären Nebenquelle -
    etwa Kyot - beruhen, sondern wir haben in beiden Dichtungen
    Wolframs eigene, schöpferische Leistung zu erkennen."

6   Even though this is so, it would be churlish not to acknow-
    ledge emphatically the very considerable debt which any Par-
    zival specialist whose project involves the detailed consi-
    deration of Chrestien's work owes to this milestone of Wolf-
    ram scholarship. Patiently and meticulously assembled, the
    material in correlation still represents one of the basic
    aids in Wolfram research. Much may be criticized, it is true,
    notably the nebulous terminology of the general conclusions
    (e.g. the use of 'Romanik' and 'Gotik' for works of literature,
    pp. 11, 12 and 354ff.) and the occasionally hyperbolical
    style in which they are cast (vid. e.g. pp. 239 and 349/50).
    Both serve to obfuscate rather than define. Moreover the
    book resists consecutive reading, wearying as it is with a
    syntax based predominantly on co-ordination, (there is a
    recurrent scheme of 'while Chrestien does this, Wolfram does
    that'). This is a pattern of style, however, which is rooted
    in the subject-matter. The constant parallelism of German

a poet at work. Its objective is to record aspects of the construction of the poetic fabric as its author follows a borrowed
plot, solicits stimulus from a brilliant story-teller and learns
from his literary technique, only to leave him behind entirely
in a masterful transformation of his work. A further aim is to
try and define features characteristic of the poetry of 'Parzival' in those parts of the narrative where its author may be
deemed to be working on his own, without his collaborator, but
still responding to him. For 'Parzival' offers the rare opportunity of studying a poet in detailed dependence upon a coherent work of fiction and at the same time in almost total independence of it. On the one hand it shows a poet using the
poetry of another for his own ends, and on the other, that same
poet freely inventing his own at the prompting of his model
author, both processes outlining themselves in the same work.
In order to describe a variety of features of poetry-making,
different work-areas of the poet have been chosen for analysis.
Thus his treatment of the background to the plot is considered
under three headings: His extension of scenery and arrangement
of itineraries, his creation of a closely knit fictional geography embedded in the world of fact, and his use of the description of place for the typecasting of hero and counterpart. Independent organization of a narrative unit is discussed in a
study of the form and substance of Book IX. The introductory

---

text and French source hardly allows of any other form of
presentation. These are minor objections considering the
lasting achievements of the book: its author demonstrates
convincingly the intimate proximity of German work to French
text, thereby proving conclusively that Chrestien is Wolfram's main source. He is often brilliantly evocative of
meaning in the consideration of detail, and illuminating
with reference to Wolfram's aims. He isolates the decisive
importance of genealogical connections as a major theme in
the work. He shows on the basis of abundant evidence that
the predictive and preparatory manner of description is a
characteristic of Wolfram's art of composition. He throws
into relief the significance of the relationship between
the plot centred upon Gawan and that centred on the hero.

components leading to the target-scene are subjected to close
reading, analyzed, and related to the great dialogue. The dialogue itself is examined in detail and read primarily and predominantly from the vantage-point of the hero. In the course of
the investigation links with, echoes of, and pointers to, other
parts of the romance reveal themselves tellingly, showing with
crystalline clarity Wolfram's genius for poetic design, his
phenomenal memory and controlled foresight, and his intensely
vivid, but also wayward fancy. His style of presentation and
the manner of his thought as a poet in independence, unaccom-
panied by a pattern of suggestions by Chrestien, is considered
in an analysis of Books I and II. His endeavour to motivate
the story which he had received and transformed, declares itself in the precision with which he uses the principle of contrast as an instrument of description. He is seen to deploy it
in the chronological account of two marriages. His expertise
with this type of technique proves quite as dazzling here as
in the juxtaposition Parzival/Gâwân. In both cases he establishes major ideas with unswerving firmness and renders the
figures and situations involved memorable. Independent as a
poet, independent as a thinker, Wolfram's stature as an artist
grows step by step in the analyses of Books I, II, and IX.

Three major and constant points of reference dominate this
study: The poet's audience, his hero, and his reality. Poetry
of all forms and at all times is consumer-orientated, even if
that consumer is only the self. It therefore must inevitably
bear the marks of that orientation. A listening and watching
audience requires for its reception of poetry stylistic techniques different from those of a reading-public. Wolfram, alert
to these specific needs, developed, perfected, possibly even
invented, modes of expression which would assist his audiences.
Like later playwrights he may be said to have had the closest
possible audience-involvement in mind. He gave his listeners a
hero whom he kept firmly in focus throughout his long narrative,
a hero with whom they could identify, someone assailed by the

dominant problem of the age, the relationship between man and God. Sin, fall from Grace, suffering in its wake, and the ultimate demand - the conquest of self-will - all form part of his experience of life. His dilemma and the forms in which it manifests itself would not have appeared as remote theorizing to his listeners, but would have touched their deepest concerns. The central position which the poet accords his hero, characterizing him into individuality, constructing an elaborate kinship background for him, and including him in the poetic perspective during the Gâwân-story, make it imperative for any critical evaluation of the work to take particular cognizance of his role. The emotive load with which the poet charges his hero's career and his experiences makes it doubly so.

The appeal to the emotions issuing from the portrayal of the hero's life is powerful and profound now, but the poet's contemporaries must have felt particularly deeply engaged in the predicament of Wolfram's hero. They lived in a religious age, at a period when faith was a burning issue, not merely debated by the experts, by churchmen, but discussed and pondered by everyone. It occupied the minds of all. In this sense, as in many other respects, Wolfram's work is intimately linked with, and responds to, the spirit of his time. To evoke the age, and to recreate aspects of the poet's practical reality therefore seemed a desirable, even essential task that should precede a critical assessment which takes into account meaning. It is salutary for the critic of medieval literature to be reminded that the framework of ethical reference which dominated the middle centuries is no longer so all-pervasive. Intermittent glances at the historical, social, and personal context of the work can prove a necessary corrective to aesthetic judgement. Reflections of this kind prompted the first chapter and also the many references to contemporary reality throughout the book.

Despite these reservations, despite the awareness of all manner of obstacles, despite the time-gap, despite the difference in

emotional, intellectual and spiritual premisses, the work has
a miraculous universality that speaks across nearly a millennium.
What is its magic? No one can account for it exhaustively. Part
of it lies undoubtedly in Wolfram's outstanding capacity for the
recognition of pathos in human life, in his intuitive grasp of
the precarious balance that governs many human situations, and
in his unerring sense of drama. Many scenes of the work imprint
themselves indelibly upon memory because of the combination of
these three features in their poetic projection. Wolfram is the
poet of compassion. His understanding of the 'conditio humana'
is profound and his range of responses to human suffering immense.
A powerful mechanism to move animates his poetry. What this
mechanism is, what its infinitesimal parts may be is the enduring
mystery of his and any poetry.

II. The Work in its Context

A work of art, however timeless its appeal, is intimately linked
with the context in which it was engendered. Wolfram's 'Parzival' is no exception to this rule. Reaching out far beyond its
contemporary context in the wide applicability of its story,
and the universality of its theme, it is nevertheless the product of a particular period, bearing a vast number of the marks
of its own time, and of the historical, everyday personality of
its author. Some of these features are so obvious that they
require neither elucidation, nor comment. Others, probably an
equally great, or even greater number are hidden to the reader
of later centuries. Wolfram's contemporary audience, who inhabited and experienced the same reality as he, would have been
intuitively alive to the work in all its allusiveness to a present which they shared with it. To Wolfram's later public, however, such as the twentieth century reader, this present has
become a distant past. Their reality has shifted, its visual
aspect has changed, its hidden world has come to be differently
conditioned. The context within which 'Parzival' came into
being, is no longer readily accessible to us. Yet for the recognition of what constitutes the poetry of 'Parzival', and for
the description and assessment of it, an awareness of the work's
context in the widest possible sense is of considerable importance. This is not to say that the aesthetic qualities and the
meanings of 'Parzival' cannot be made apparent without reference
to its context. Most of them can be isolated from within, and
through a comparison with its model and source. A grasp of context, however, may on occasions not only corroborate such re-
cognitions, but will also illuminate attitudes of the poet and
those of his public. Insights such as these cannot but enhance
the understanding of the work's poetic fabric and assist substantially in its critical evaluation. Not too many expectations
must be brought to bear on an adumbration of this context and
the attempt to link it with the work. All too little is known
of Wolfram himself, and about figures like him, to allow of

any consequential definitive conclusions. Yet even questions merely asked, and then left open, will enlarge our range of responses to the work and contribute fundamentally to the critical appreciation of it.

The context of a medieval verse narrative like 'Parzival' has many layers. First and foremost there is the background of contemporary historical events to which it must react, either by relating to it, or by remaining deliberately severed from it. There is furthermore the social environment in which and for which it was developed. And there is also the personal nexus, the network of impressions received and absorbed by the author during his everyday pursuits, which would feed and condition his poetic imagination. The literary tradition in which the work stands, the history of ideas in which it has a place, and its medium, language, are further examples of contexts, and more could still be listed. No single commentator could do justice to them all; he must select. Chosen here for purposes of evoking the poet's immediate reality are facets of the historical, social and personal contexts. They will throw into relief characteristics of the poet's interpretation of life, outline some of the approach-roads he is likely to have followed towards his problems, and demonstrate the relationship he had with his public.[1]

---

1 Two authors have recently concerned themselves with the problem of linking the literary interpretation of a medieval German verse-narrative with its contemporary historical background. Both, Walter Falk, Das Nibelungenlied in seiner Epoche. Revision eines romantischen Mythos, Heidelberg, 1974, and Rudolf Rosskopf, Der Traum Herzeloydes und der rote Ritter. Erwägungen über die Bedeutung des staufisch-welfischen Thronstreites für Wolframs 'Parzival', Göppinger Arbeiten zur Germanistik, 89, Göppingen, 1972, proceed specifically from the central notion of a political, social and moral crisis within the Empire. Rudolf Rosskopf sees Wolfram as a prophetic poet who issues condemnation and warning, but also a message of hope, in Herzeloyde's apocalyptic dream vision. According to him the dragon of her dream has a three-fold significance: It stands for her son Parzival, for the contemporary nobility in its moral decline, and for the

The wider historical background to 'Parzival' hardly presents
any problems. Its details may be followed in most standard history books on the period.[2]. The time during which 'Parzival'
was being conceived and composed - at some stage after 1197
and before 1222 -[3] was one of tremendous social and political
turmoil in the Empire. The death of the Emperor Henry VI in
1197 plunged Germany into civil war. It revived the struggle

'apocalyptic' dragon whose coming heralds the end of an age,
but also the beginning of a new epoch. An early attempt to
define connections between poetic creation in 'Parzival'
and historical fact was made by Friedrich Panzer, Gahmuret,
Quellenstudien zu Wolframs Parzival, Sb. d. Heidelberger
Akad. d. Wiss., philos.-hist. Kl., Jg. 1939/40, Abh. 1, Heidelberg, 1940. He took the view that Richard Lionheart had
stood model for Gahmuret, and generally stressed the importance of the house of Anjou for the opening sections of the
work. On this latter topic vid. also W. Snelleman, Das Haus
Anjou und der Orient in Wolframs Parzival, Diss. Amsterdam,
Nijkerk, 1941.

2　As for example in The Cambridge Medieval History, vol. VI:
Victory of the Papacy, ed. by J. R. Tanner, C. W. Prévité-
Orton, Z. N. Brooke, Cambridge, 1929; G. Barraclough, The
Origins of Modern Germany, Oxford, [2]1947; Bruno Gebhardt,
Frühzeit und Mittelalter, Handbuch der deutschen Geschichte,
vol. I, Stuttgart, [9]1970; Karl Hampe, Germany under the
Salian and Hohenstaufen Emperors, Oxford, 1973, (transl.
from the twelfth German edition of Deutsche Kaisergeschichte
in der Zeit der Salier und Staufer, ed. by Friedrich Baethgen, Heidelberg, 1968); Th. Toeche, Kaiser Heinrich VI,
Jahrbücher der deutschen Geschichte, Leipzig, 1867; Eduard
Winkelmann, Philipp von Schwaben und Otto IV. von Braun-
schweig, 2 vols., Jahrbücher der deutschen Geschichte, 1873
and 1878, (reprint Wissenschaftliche Buchgesellschaft, Darmstadt, 1968), Kaiser Friedrich II., 2 vols., Jahrbücher etc.
1889 and 1897 (reprint WBG, 1967); Ernst Kantorowicz, Kaiser
Friedrich der Zweite, Berlin, [4]1936 and Ergänzungsband, Quel-
lennachweise und Exkurse, Berlin 1931. Vid. also J. B.
Gillingham, The Kingdom of Germany in the High Middle Ages
(900-1200), Pamphlet No. 77 of the Historical Association,
London, 1971, with an excellent map, and Die Zeit der Staufer,
Geschichte-Kunst-Kultur, Katalog der Ausstellung, 5 vols.
(Württembergisches Landesmuseum), Stuttgart, 1977-1979, in
particular vol. III: Aufsätze, and vol. IV: Karten und Stammtafeln. In the latter volume maps VII and IX show the itineraries of Philip II, Otto IV and Frederick II, and map VIII
indicates the places where Philip II and Otto IV sealed.

3　Joachim Bumke, Die Wolfram von Eschenbach Forschung seit

for dynastic power between the two great families, the Hohenstaufen on the one hand and the Welf dynasty on the other. The
shifting fortunes of the two factions as they rallied and lost
supporters, tried to guard against and fell victim to conspir-
acies, created widespread unrest, moral uncertainty and immense
hardship. In the twenty-five years into which the composition
of 'Parzival' falls, Germany was ruled over by three different
kings in succession, and for more than half of that time by two
of them simultaneously. For the period 1198 to 1208, and then
again from 1211 to 1218, Germany had two rival kings, one Welf,
one Hohenstaufen. The deadlock was broken for a few years after
the Hohenstaufen had been murdered, and then finally after the
Welf had died. A measure of the general confusion which prevailed in the Empire and of the unabating tug-of-war between
the factions was that each one of their candidates was acclaim-
ed king several times over. Philip, the Hohenstaufen, brother
of Henry VI, was elected king at Mühlhausen on March 8th, 1198,
crowned at Mainz on September 8th of the same year, and crowned once more at Aachen on January 6th, 1205. Otto the Welf,
youngest son of Henry the Lion, was elected King at Cologne on
June 9th, 1198, crowned one month later at Aachen on July 12th,
and elected again at Frankfurt on November 11th, 1208. Frederick,
son of Henry VI, was elected 'in imperatorem coronandus' in Nuremberg in September 1211, elected again on December 5th, 1212, in
Frankfurt, crowned four days later in Mainz on December 9th
1212, and crowned again at Aachen on July 25th, 1215. In addition both Otto IV and Frederick II were crowned emperor at
Rome on October 4th, 1209 and 22nd November 1220 respectively.
Germany was thus subjected to the aftermath of twelve different
instances of an election or coronation, royal or imperial, during this relatively brief span of time. Twice the head of state

---

1945. Bericht und Bibliographie, Munich, 1970, p. 68: "Nach
allem, was wir wissen, ist der Parzival nach 1197 und vor
1222 entstanden."

was excommunicated, Philip II in 1201 and Otto IV in 1210, for
another power-struggle cut across the ambitions of Hohenstaufen
and Welf, that between Emperor and Pope. The data of imperial
history are readily available, and from them one may deduce a
gigantic and sustained upheaval. What is less easy to establish
is the immediate historical and social context of the work. What
were the precise repercussions of this large-scale political
havoc on the locality in which the poet lived, and on the areas
where he travelled and found his daily livelihood? Did the effects of the chaos percolate at all times to those regions of
Germany in which he moved, even down to the last hamlet? Did
the individual remote from the scenes of decision come to be
involved in the tumult? What were the practical day-to-day
implications of the anarchy for him? How did the storm at the
apex of the hierarchy affect those in the lower echelons of
society, for this is where the poet was? Linked though he was
with families of influence and power, the sensation of the chaos
would have been of a quality different for him, from what it was
for them. What precisely was at stake for him in social and
personal terms? Did he experience the major events of his time
as cataclysmic? - None of these questions can be answered in
detail, for we are spectacularly lacking in historical documen-
tation for the lives of ordinary people during this period, and
for behaviour in general through all strata of society.[4]

---

4   This is the conclusion which the non-specialist must inevit-
    ably reach when sifting the relevant literature. Collections
    and studies devoted to the questions of practical day-to-day
    living, and of attitude, behaviour and manners in the Middle
    Ages fall largely into three categories, in accordance with
    the method of investigation and type of coverage chosen.
    Some are restricted geographically as e.g. L. F. Salzmann,
    English Life in the Middle Ages, London, 1926; Joan Evans,
    Life in Medieval France, London, [2]1957, (revised and newly
    illustrated edition); Adolf Waas, Der Mensch im deutschen
    Mittelalter, Graz, [2]1966, and Dietrich W. H. Schwarz, Sach-
    güter und Lebensformen. Einführung in die materielle Kultur-
    geschichte des Mittelalters und der Neuzeit, Grundlagen der
    Germanistik, 11, Berlin, 1970. Other are restricted tempor-
    ally such as Wolfram von den Steinen, Der Kosmos des Mittel-
    alters von Karl dem Grossen zu Bernhard von Clairvaux, Berne/

Moreover we possess only the sketchiest biographical information
about Wolfram himself. Nevertheless, it is possible to go some
way towards answering them, even if only in a tentative and specu-
lative manner. By relating the few personal data we do have to
the general historical background, it is possible to project a
reflection at least of the immediate social climate which informed the genesis of 'Parzival', and of the likely emotional situation of its author.

Munich, [2]1967, or Jacques Le Goff, Das Hochmittelalter, Fi-
scher-Weltgeschichte, vol. 11, Frankfurt, 1965. Either group
takes into consideration evidence spread over centuries,
rather than decades. The third category takes in an even
wider perspective of the Middle Ages than the first two, in
that it ranges in the selection of source-material not only
over the whole of Europe, but draws into its enquiry an even
greater stretch of time, than the second group of studies,
by beginning with the early Middle Ages, or even earlier, and
ending with the late medieval period. Examples of this kind
are: Life in the Middle Ages, selected, translated and annotated by G. G. Coulton, 4 vols., Cambridge, [2]1928-30; The
Flowering of the Middle Ages, ed. by Joan Evans, London, 1966;
Medieval Culture and Society, ed. by David Herlihy, London,
1968, and Jeremy du Quesney Adams, Patterns of Medieval Society, Englewood Cliffs, 1969. The wealth of publications
concerned with the social history of the Middle Ages tends
to give a false impression of an abundance of data for any
part of this period. Texts and objects furnishing documentary evidence on which to base conclusions may indeed be
plentiful, but they constitute an evidence which is very
thinly spread in relation to time and space. Even the ambitious and impressive work by Arno Borst, Lebensformen im Mittelalter, Frankfurt/Main, 1973, which sets out by deliberately attempting to overcome the restrictions of the first
two categories of studies mentioned here, still falls squarely into the third. Examples are drawn from the whole of
Europe, and range from the early to the late Middle Ages.
The number of texts chosen from the early and late Middle
Ages outweighs those selected from the Central Middle Ages
by one seventh, and those taken from the Central Middle Ages
cover two centuries. The reason given for the choice of this
particular spread of evidence is the especial significance
of existential patterns during peripheral periods: "Doch er-
weist sich erst in Grenzsituationen die Tragweite und Inte-
grationskraft von Lebensformen. Deshalb sind im folgenden
von den hundert Zeugnissen immerhin drei Siebtel dem Hochmittelalter vom 11. bis 13. Jahrhundert gewidmet, je zwei
Siebtel dem frühen und dem späten Mittelalter" (p. 24). Yet
one wonders whether the structure of this study, as that of

Many of the important events of the time, both political and
military, took place within or near the bounds of Wolfram-
country, that is according to the testimony of a handful of
place-names which he mentions, within or near the confines of
parts of Thuringia, Franconia, Swabia, Bavaria and Styria.[5]
Thus he had knowledge, or even personal experience, of the
dreadful devastation of Thuringia in the Hohenstaufen campaigns of the years 1203 and 1204, an area which suffered
particularly and tragically in the civil war from friend and
foe alike. Not only did the raids of Philip II lay waste vast
tracts of the countryside, but the Bohemian troops whom the
landgrave had called in for his defence added to the horror.
Returning to their homeland they plundered and terrorized the
inhabitants wherever they went. Sixteen religious houses were
stripped of their possessions and three hundred and fifty
townships and villages razed to the ground.[6] Wolfram makes ref-

all its predecessors, was not unwittingly dictated by the
dearth of data for single regions at periods of obvious historical interest or importance, during this vast span of
time which we call the Middle Ages. One such place and time
would be Germany during the civil war. Yet there is, to my
knowledge, no detailed study of the anarchy in Germany during the civil war and of its social repercussions on Wolfram's generation, nor of the practical circumstances of
life at all levels at that time. If no such investigation
has as yet been made for so important a period of German
history, and of German literary history, the non-historian
must indeed conclude that there cannot be sufficient data
available to enable an historian to undertake such a study.

5 Albert Schreiber, Neue Bausteine zu einer Lebensgeschichte
Wolframs von Eschenbach, Deutsche Forschungen, 7, Frankfurt
a. M., 1922, pp. 2 and 3, and passim; Joachim Bumke, Wolfram
von Eschenbach, Stuttgart, [4]1976, pp. 1-14, and op. cit.,
chapter I,4; Leben, Bildung, Wirkung, literarische Beziehungen. Vid. also the useful map in Karl Bertau, Deutsche Literatur im europäischen Mittelalter, 2 vols., Munich, 1972
and 1973, vol. 2, p. 792 and the accompanying text.

6 Eduard Winkelmann, Philipp von Schwaben, vol. 1, p. 287ff.

erence to the siege of Erfurt of 1203 and its resultant destruction.[7] The allusion means that he was either an eye-witness, or
that the plight of Thuringia had become a bye-word. Whichever
it is, he was clearly familiar with large-scale devastation;
it was part of life. As a soldier he must in any case have been
involved himself in the almost ceaseless fighting throughout
the civil war, although in whose private army he saw active
service, where he did so, and in which campaign, it is impossible to tell. The type of warfare which he knew and which undoubtedly marked and marred most of his life, was of the most
brutal kind. It gave no quarter to the civilian population.
Towns and villages were sacked, crops destroyed, booty taken
and every imaginable cruelty committed. Even among the military
men themselves life was cheap. The only prisoners-of-war who
could expect to survive were those who were able to command a
large ransom. Nevertheless there were periods during the civil
war, when the poet must have remained shielded from the strife;
when it had moved to areas remote from where he happened to be.
Thus for example the fighting by the Rhine when both Remagen
and Bonn were burnt in 1198, and the Rhenish campaigns of 1199,
1205, and 1206 when Cologne capitulated, need not have concerned the poet much, unless, of course, he was riding in one of the
armies. Similarly, he is not likely to have been affected by
Otto IV's raids into the Magdeburg region in 1213 and 1217.
Distant sieges like those of Brunswick and Goslar of 1200 and
1206 respectively, and others more, may also have passed him by,
not only because these towns are far away from the localities
where he might be expected to be most frequently, but because
he, as a mounted soldier, even if he did take part in any of
these campaigns, may not have stayed for the sieges.[8] Soldiers

---

7   P. 379.18 (Bk. VII): Erffurter wîngarte giht/von treten noch
    der selben nôt:/maneg orses fuoz die slâge bot.

8   Winkelmann, op. cit., vol. 1, pp. 139-153, 183ff., 368ff.,
    and 392-400; vol. 2, pp. 345ff. and 460ff.

on horseback, such as himself, were vital as shock troops in
open country, but they were of limited usefulness in a siege.[9]
So there were times while 'Parzival' was taking shape when the
actual war was far off and when its effects had been toned down
by distance.

Apart from the civil war which affected the poet's life on many
levels, impinging on his consciousness and absorbing his physical energies, there were occasions of political significance
which must have brought home to the poet the political uncertainty of the time and the veering fortunes of the great particularly sharply. When Philip the Hohenstaufen was murdered
in the episcopal palace at Bamberg on the 21st of June 1208,
history moved close to Wolfram. The murder was no political
assassination, but had sprung from a private quarrel, and as
such the act of individual violence held out, quite paradoxically, the promise of an end to general violence. One of the
rival kings was dead, and in his death there lay a promise of
peace. The non-political killing of the Hohenstaufen king may
be seen as the most unlikely and least expected occurrence of
the civil war, an event beyond conjecture. And again when a
mere six months later Otto the Welf held court in Augsburg on
the 6th of January 1209, history had remained near homeground,
both Bamberg and Augsburg being approximately equidistant from
Eschenbach. The Welf king presided over an impressive assembly
which the whole of the Bavarian nobility, both secular and ecclesiastical, attended without exception. It is hard to image
that Wolfram was not especially sensitive to the wider implications of these two events, near as they were to him. He may

---

9   That Wolfram was a mounted soldier, and not a footsoldier,
    is an assumption, but a reasonable one. In the first place
    he refers to himself as a mounted soldier by circumlocution.
    In the second place footsoldiers were drawn from the artisan
    class. The education which Wolfram betrays in his work,
    sketchy though it may be, clearly assigns him to a social
    group above the fullers, lorimers, smiths and others. He
    therefore cannot have been a member of the infantry. Cf.
    John Beeler, Warfare in Feudal Europe 730-1200, Cornell

even have been a witness to the Welf king standing on the thresh-
old to ultimate political triumph, to his final preparations on
German soil for his journey to Rome in order to be crowned Holy
Roman Emperor. For a little later in that same year of 1209
Otto IV returned to Augsburg in July and gathered around him
an expeditionary force which was to accompany him to Italy.
Among the dignitaries who formed the king's immediate entourage
was Hartwig, Bishop of Eichstätt, in whose diocese Eschenbach
lay. The leaders and their followers were encamped on the great
plain by the river Lech in the vicinity of Augsburg before they
set out on their road to Italy. Less than three months later
Otto managed to have himself crowned emperor. But the glory was
not to last long, within a year he was excommunicated, and by
the end of 1211 the civil war had resumed.[10] These are only
three examples of historical moments picked at random, which
because they happened within the orbit of the poet's personal
geography may be expected to have had a particularly emotive
effect on him. There were others like them which must have
stirred his imagination equally, and many more at greater distance from his immediate environment which did likewise. One
further occasion which involved his neighbourhood and its peripheral regions, both intimately and extensively, deserves
specific consideration within this context, and that is the
proposed crusade of 1217. It was in the south-east of Germany
that a particularly large contingent of nobles had decided to
take the cross. Among the prominent men who were making preparations for their expedition to Outremer were the Bishop
Ekbert of Bamberg, Duke Otto of Andechs-Meran, and also Hartwig,
the Bishop of Eichstätt.[11]

Paperbacks, 1972, (first published 1971), pp. 247/8.

10 Winkelmann, op. cit., vol. 1, pp. 464ff.; vol. 2, pp. 134ff.,
   161-201 and 248-282.

11 Winkelmann, op. cit., vol. 2, p. 447ff.

Isolated incidents such as these may have imprinted themselves
on the poet's consciousness and met his bent for uncovering
the core of symbolism in human events. More important, however,
than single instances of historical significance was, where
the moulding of a view of the world was concerned, the temper
and quality of those twenty-five years during which, at some time,
'Parzival' was in the making. The keynote of the period was instability. Confusion and violence reigned, and the future was
uncertain. The civil war, no doubt, brought to the fore fine
qualities in individuals who found themselves in challenging
situations, but on the whole, like any other civil war, it is
a story of crass ambition, weather-vane allegiance, opportunism,
treachery, and brutality. The misery which it brought was sharpened by the effects of the twofold excommunication of the crown
and by famine. On the 3rd of July 1201 the Hohenstaufen king
was excommunicated; the anathema was announced from the pulpit
in Cologne. Nine years later, on the 18th of November 1210 the
Welf king met with the same fate. On the 31st March 1211 the
excommunication was made public, and all places which the
emperor chose to visit were placed under interdict.[12] What
the excommunication meant in practical terms to their subjects
was further disruption of an already dislocated society. The
whole social edifice threatened to collapse. Excommunication
of the head of the state absolved from the oath of allegiance
to him. All contracts with the crown were void. It opened the
gates wide to general lawlessness and total anarchy. Under the
twin pressures of civil war and royal excommunication 'pax et
iustitia' could hardly be expected to have existed. In 1217,
just before the Welf king's death and thus the ultimate end
of the civil war, Germany was in the grip of famine. It raged
in the north-German regions, spread as far afield as Austria,
Bohemia and Hungary, and in its course took in Bavaria, so that
it engulfed part of Wolfram-country. The pattern of medieval

---

12 Winkelmann, vol. 2, pp. 249-260.

famines was relatively static. Starving peasants left their
homesteads and roamed the countryside in search of food. Villages and farms were abandoned in panic, and forests and open
country ransacked for whatever was edible. Paupers wandered
about aimlessly and helplessly begging for food, falling prey
in their debility to unidentified diseases. In their desperate
and ceaseless journeying they carried infection from place to
place, until it reached epidemic proportions. In the end vast
numbers of them were carried off, either by pestilence or starvation. Corpses on the roads and in towns as well as in the
open country were a familiar sight during a time of famine,
and the stench of rotting human carcases filled the air.[13]
What was familiar to most during the hungry years of 1217 and
1218, must have been familiar to Wolfram too.

It is pertinent to recognize that destruction, death and violence were a tangible reality to the poet. It is relevant to
understand that he could not have escaped observing their inevitable consequences among his fellow-men, of stunted emotions,
brutalized behaviour, and diminished morals. Different from many
a modern author and from the vast majority of his twentieth-
century readers he did not experience such a reality at one
remove, via the press or the television screen, but was deeply and personally involved in it. The world he portrays - or
to define it accurately - the world which he projects - is very
different from the one he knew. This tension between the two,
between the vision and the lived reality from which it springs,
illuminates features both of the work itself and of the poetic
personality which created it. It indicates unequivocally that
the gloss of idealization in much of his character-portrayal,
however great its debt may be to literary tradition, both ver-

---

13 Fritz Curschmann, Hungersnöte im Mittelalter. Ein Beitrag
    zur deutschen Wirtschaftsgeschichte des 8. bis 13. Jahrhun-
    derts, Leipziger Studien aus dem Gebiet der Geschichte, 6,
    Leipzig, 1900, p. 42ff.

nacular and rhetorical, is prescriptive. It shows indubitably
that the utopian treatment of manners and social intercourse
in many scenes emanates from a perceptive intent. Nor is the
establishment of a pronounced element of didacticism in the
work the sole critical gain which derives from the recognition
of this tension. The gap between contemporary reality and the
fictional world of 'Parzival' lends Wolfram's technique of
idealization a poignancy which - were we unaware of the nature
of the gap - would elude us. For his idealization of behaviour
testifies to a belief in human potential which - all things
considered - is as astonishing as it is admirable. In a similar
fashion the gap gives particular point to the optimism expressed in the work on many levels, and notably in the conclusion
which, as the received narrative breaks off before, is entirely
Wolfram's own and can be held to represent succinctly his view
of life at that point in time. His major characters, and many
of his minor ones, experience achievement in this conclusion.
The main plot centred upon the hero opens out into the future,
and most of the subsidiary narratives are finalized in a like
manner. In this last part of the work the poet formulates for
his audience the perspective of a well-ordered world in which
nothing is out of joint. His confident idealism bears witness,
in view of the gap, to an outstanding, and rarely equalled gift
to transcend the tangled mass of human suffering in poetic vision, to a supreme effort of volition, and to a exceptional
degree of spiritual courage.

But the background to 'Parzival' was not only destruction, death
and violence at home, there was holocaust abroad as well. In
1209 the Albigensian crusade began with the unspeakable brutality of the massacre at Béziers, where the entire population was
slaughtered. When Carcassonne fell shortly afterwards, all its
citizens were driven out empty-handed. When Minerve was captur-
ed 140 'Perfecti' were put to the stake, and after the fall of

Lavaur between 300 and 400 Cathars were burned.[14] Just when the civilization of Languedoc had reached its apogee, it was crushed. When Provençal poetry had come to be widely celebrated and copied, its patrons were persecuted, dispersed and decimated.[15] For the writers of profane literature in imperial Germany a model and a source of inspiration had gone.

In the wider world too, in Christendom at large, there were events taking place which mirrored the cruelty, the treachery, and the cynical disregard of right and wrong with which the poet had come to be familiar during the civil war in Germany. At the turn of the century the crusading movement suffered a sea change. It erupted in open crisis in the latter part of the Fourth Crusade which had begun to be preached as early as 1198, and which ended in 1204. Indifference towards the crusading ideal, and towards the standards of behaviour required to uphold it, had indeed already shown itself in the temporal leaders of Western Christendom before. The Third Crusade in particular had furnished notable examples of it, two of them at the very top of the social hierarchy. Neither the German emperor, nor the king of France, appears to have felt any qualms at enriching himself at the expense of a prominent crusader. Henry VI had held Richard Lionheart captive and had extorted the highest ransom in history. In order to raise the 150,000 Cologne marks which he demanded, heavy taxes had had to be imposed on Richard's subjects. Philip Augustus, on the other hand, had raided the English king's territories during his absence with impunity. Actions such as these were in direct contravention of the apostolic promise that the person and the

---

14 Bernard Hamilton, The Albigensian Crusade, Pamphlet of the Historical Association, G. 85, London, 1974, in particular pp. 8 and 12ff.; also Walter L. Wakefield, Heresy, Crusade and Inquisition in Southern France 1100-1250, London, 1974, chapter VI: The Albigensian crusade, invasion and conquest 1209-1215, p. 96-113.

15 L. T. Topsfield, Troubadours and Love, Cambridge, 1975, p. 2ff.

lands of a crusader would be inviolate until his return home.
They made a mockery of the protective powers of the Church,
and of the respect due to all those who had taken the cross
in sincerity, dedication and faith. However, this was a mere
faint foretaste of what the future held in store. The whole-
sale perversion of the crusading ideal to political ends, the
manipulation, deception and coercion of crusaders for purposes
of political expediency, and the subsequent unleashing of greed
on the grand scale were yet to come. The story of the Fourth
Crusade is one of intrigue and escalating corruption. The crusaders never reached the Holy Land, and instead of fighting
the Moslems, they fought and massacred Christians.

In 1202 part of the crusading army had assembled in Venice,
among them a contingent from Germany, for embarkation to
Outremer. Almost at once the crusaders ran into serious fi-
nancial difficulties. Their advance treaty with Venice for the
supply of ships and provisions had placed them heavily in debt
to the Venetians who pressed to be paid. They were unable to
raise the money and unable to leave. At this point the doge
stepped in with diplomacy and blackmail: The crusaders could
set sail and postpone the settlement of their debts, if they
would join an expedition to reconquer Zara for the Venetians.
Zara was a town on the Dalmatian coast which Venice had lost
to Hungary, whose king was at that very moment preparing to go
on crusade himself. Briefly - in order to have their credit
extended, the crusaders were expected to sack a Christian city.
There were some who rebelled against such a monstrous proposal,
but the remainder of the army complied. They felt they had
little choice. So Zara was reconquered with fierce and speedy
efficiency. The city capitulated after five days, and was then
given over to looting.

This deliberate diversion of a crusade from religious to political objectives, which was exemplified at Zara, was to be exploited further, this time, so it appears, by Philip II, the Hohenstaufen king. Early in 1203 envoys arrived in Zara from Germany

with an offer similar to that which the doge of Venice had made.
The crusaders' debts would be cleared, if they would continue
on to Constantinople and restore Philip II's father-in-law, the
rightful ruler of Constantinople, to the Greek imperial throne.
Alexius, the pretender and Philip's brother-in-law, had guaran-
teed the monies which the crusaders still owed the Venetians.

Whether the plan originated with Philip II, or whether he was
the victim of a series of chance events, has never been entirely resolved. Historians are still divided on this point today,
and Philip II's contemporaries presumably also hotly debated
the question. Yet where general opinion and the emotional atmosphere within Germany at the time is concerned, it matters
little whether he engineered the scheme, merely went along with
it, or came willy-nilly to be involved in it. It suffices that
he was associated with it. The Hohenstaufen king had somehow
come to be implicated in the disastrous transformation of the
crusading movement which was to culminate in the brutal tragedy
of Constantinople in the following year. Again there were those
among the crusaders who protested, in fact half the army rebelled on reaching Corfu. But in the end they acquiesced, many of
them having been led to believe that Byzantium would actively
contribute to the crusade, once they had helped to reinstate
its legitimate ruler. After they had arrived at Constantinople
it only took the crusaders a month to accomplish what they had
set out to do, but they were soon to be disillusioned where
the reward for this service was concerned. Their debts to the
Venetians remained unpaid. Throughout the latter part of 1203
the crusading army was seething with dissatisfaction, and the
atmosphere in the city was smouldering. In January 1204 a palace revolution once again removed the rightful ruler from the
Greek throne, and the crusaders, prompted by the Venetians,
finally decided to dismember Byzantium, install an emperor of
their own choosing, and to take the city by storm. After this,
there was no further thought of a crusade.

The horror which was perpetrated then, has reverberated down the centuries. The sack of Constantinople has no equal in history as regards the magnitude of the destruction of both art and life, and the concentration of violence into a brief span of time. On the 12th of April 1204 the crusaders stormed the walls of Constantinople, on the next day they entered it. And for three days the greatest, richest, most civilized and sophisticated city of the time, the great metropolis of Eastern Christendom, an incomparably beautiful town, became an open city. Soldiers went on a rampage of rape, murder, plunder and destruction. Their barbarity knew no bounds. Men, women and children were killed indiscriminately. Countless works of art were looted, exquisite masterpieces wantonly destroyed. Drunken soldiers hunted for relics, jewels, gold and silver, and treasure of any kind. Tapestries and books were torn up, paintings defaced, statuary mutilated, churches and palaces wrecked. For three days bloodshed and brutality alternated with pillage and destruction. The account of the sack of Constantinople still makes awesome reading to-day. How much greater must have been the impact of the horror when the description of it reached contemporaries! Anyone dedicated to civilization and humaneness, any believer in man and his achievement, any lover of the arts and of beautiful objects - anyone like Wolfram - must have stood aghast.[16]

---

16 There is a vast literature on the crusades. For details of the Fourth Crusade vid. in particular A History of the Crusades, ed. by Kenneth M. Setton, Medieval Academy of America, University of Pennsylvania Press, Philadelphia 1955 -, then University of Wisconsin Press 1969 -, vol. I: The First Hundred Years (1955) [2]1969; vol. II: The Later Crusades 1189-1311 (1962) [2]1969; Steven Runciman, A History of the Crusades, 3 vols., Cambridge University Press, 1951, (reissued in Pelican Books 1971); Hans Eberhard Mayer, The Crusades, Oxford University Press 1972 (transl. from Geschichte der Kreuzzüge, Stuttgart 1965); H. Roscher, Papst Innozenz III. und die Kreuzzüge, Göttingen 1969; E. Winkelmann, Philipp von Schwaben etc.; Adolf Waas, Geschichte der Kreuzzüge, 2 vols., Freiburg 1956; James A. Brundage, The Crusades. A documentary Survey, Wisconsin 1962; H. Grégoire, The Question of the Diversion of the

So the temper and quality of those crucial twenty-five years
into which the composition of 'Parzival' falls, were characterized by social and spiritual turmoil, moral decline and
widespread despair. They were not of the kind which would pro-
mote easily an affirmative view of life; any such perspective
would have to be considered hard won. Wolfram was no direct
commentator on the contemporary scene, no Walther von der Vogelweide, but he cannot be said to have stood aloof from it
in his 'Parzival'. For commentary there is here in his sharp
reaction to the turbulent times in which he lived, expressed
indirectly. There is a distinct inverse echo to the instability
which was their dominant characteristic: His central figure is
an agonized seeker groping for stable values in a problematic
world. Dogged perseverance helps him in his fight for spiritual survival. His central theme is the quality which bonds
human beings together stably and permanently, both on the level
of society at large, and on that of the intimate unit of single
individuals, and of man and God. The keyword for this theme,
'triuwe', covers the whole range of meanings from feudal surety,
that basic contract which held society together, the pledge
of loyalty which could only be broken 'in extremis', so self-
denying love and deep compassion, and to faith. Is it chance
that such a leading theme was formulated, and such a hero developed at a time of near-anarchy and ceaseless civil war,
when law and order could not be upheld at home, when barbarity

---

Fourth Crusade. An Old Controversy solved by a Latin Adverb,
Byzantion, 15 (1940), 158-166; J. Folda, The Fourth Crusade.
Some Reconsiderations, Byzantinoslavica, 26 (1967), 277-290;
D. E. Queller and S. J. Stratton, A Century of Controversy
on the Fourth Crusade, Studies in Medieval and Renaissance
History, vol. 6, 1969, 235-277; Donald E. Queller, The
Fourth Crusade. The Conquest of Constantinople, 1201-1204,
Leicester, 1978. For further references vid. Hans Eberhard
Mayer, Bibliographie zur Geschichte der Kreuzzüge, Hannover,
[2]1965, entries 2119-59, and the bibliography in Donald E.
Queller, The Fourth Crusade etc.

triumphed abroad, and when life was precarious on every level, and from every point of view? For none of this may be said of the work as he found it, so extensively and fundamentally did he rethink and remould it in accordance with his experience of his own time.

A context even more tightly surrounding the work than the immediate historical situation, is that represented by the poet's everyday personality. The everyday individual cannot be equated with the poet, for it is likely that in the manner of most artists, the two were linked in a schizophrenic existence in Wolfram also. The relevance of the routine person to the poetic self in this duality is obvious: The amalgam of day-to-day experiences and impressions, absorbed by the routine individual, forms the background to the poet's creativity. It stands at the back of the creative process, influencing poetic imagination by offering it material to which it must react. This knowledge continuum, this blend of day-to-day awareness, is made up of the outward circumstances of the poet's life, of his standard of living, his daily pursuits and duties, his practical and personal problems, and of the people he meets. All of this will have a bearing on his poetic individuality.

When trying to distinguish between poet and person, and to define their separate entities, the consideration of the poetic 'persona' must not be omitted. For the poet creates a specific narrator for the work, a poetic 'persona', a make-believe figure, which releases its identity on examination of the style and structure of 'Parzival', and also on the co-ordination of direct statements about a self. Conversely, the narrator, or poetic 'persona', as a conceptual instrument, serves to isolate features of narrative technique and viewpoints characteristic of 'Parzival'.[17] At the same time it allows tantalizing glimpses

---

17 For analyses of the figure of the narrator in both Wolfram's 'Parzival' and 'Willehalm' vid. Michael Curschmann, Das Abenteuer des Erzählens. Über den Erzähler in Wolframs 'Parzival', DVJ, 45 (1971), 627-667, and The French, the

of what could be, but need not be true, of Wolfram, the poet,
and Wolfram, the routine person. The narrator is thus a character in a given work, a product of the poet's manufacture, as
well as a self-portrait. In him three figures are merged: the
artist, the everyday individual, and a poetic self especially
formulated for the work. The degree of density to which these
three overlap is such that separation is very nearly impossible.
One can never be quite certain of what is autobiographical in
this self-portrait, and what is conscious role. The complicat-
ing factors here are Wolfram's humour and the immense range of
his histrionic gifts. His humour, which stretches from subtle
wit to bawdiness, goads him into ridiculing himself, his talent
for mimicry into playing games. He can present himself on the
one hand as a virtuoso poet of extreme sophistication, and on
the other as a country bumpkin of proverbial oafishness.[18] The
result is a poetic 'persona' of chameleon-like qualities, and
a shadowy and elusive self-portrait. Wolfram is not to be trusted in his statements, both direct and indirect, about the self,
both poetic and everyday. His untrustworthiness in this respect
makes the business of identifying the day-to-day individual
doubly difficult. For there is nothing to hand on which to base
an outline of the routine ego beyond Wolfram's own references
to a self. There is no autobiography, no correspondence, no
biography by someone who knew him, no contemporary documenta-
tion of any kind.[19] The critic can therefore do no more than

---

Audience, and the Narrator in Wolfram's Willehalm, Neophilo-
logus, 59 (1975), 548-562; Eberhard Nellmann, Wolframs
Erzähltechnik. Untersuchungen zur Funktion des Erzählers,
Wiesbaden, 1973; Uwe Pörksen, Der Erzähler im mittelhoch-
deutschen Epos. Formen seines Hervortretens bei Lamprecht,
Konrad, Hartmann, in Wolframs Willehalm und in den Spiel-
mannsepen, Philolog. Studien und Quellen, 58 (1971); also
Bumke, op. cit., chapter: Syntax, Metrik, Stil, Wortschatz.

18 P. 4.2ff. and 121.5ff.

19 The only contemporary reference by Wirnt von Gravenberg:
"... her Wolfram, ein wîse man von Eschenbach; sîn herze
ist ganzes sinnes dach; leien munt nie baz gesprach", (ed.
Kapteyn, lls. 6343-46), does not take us very far in this
direction.

scrutinize these few direct statements by the poet for their
possible veracity. He can then combine what he considers to
be of likely truthfulness in this self-portrait, with what is
generally known of similar persons in the Middle Ages.

Wolfram names himself three times in the course of 'Parzival',
linking himself each time with Eschenbach.[20] He calls himself
a Bavarian, although the village lies in Franconia and his
language has East Frankish characteristics, a paradox which
is not easily explained.[21] He describes his poverty as bordering on penury,[22] and once in a striking phrase, redolent of
pride and pleasure, he announces that soldiering is his profession.[23] The poverty-stricken soldier is unlikely to have
been a role which Wolfram created specifically for the poetic
'persona' of 'Parzival'. It would be absurd for a poet who is
also a performer, to present himself as a particular social
type to his audience, when he was patently something else.

---

20 P. 114.12; 185.7; 827.13. He does it again in 'Willehalm'
   4.19.

21 It has given rise to endless speculation and argument. One
   suggestion has been that the region changed hands, and
   from being Bavarian became Frankish, cf.e.g. Hanns Fischer:
   'Die Schwierigkeit, dass Wolfram sich einen Bayern nennt
   (Parzival 121.7: ein prîs den wir Beier tragen ...),
   während sein Herkunftsort Eschenbach (östlich Ansbach)
   doch auf fränkischem Boden liegt und seine Sprache ganz
   entsprechend ostfränkisches Gepräge zeigt, löst sich wohl
   am einfachsten mit Hilfe der Annahme, dass das Geschlecht
   des Dichters der bayerischen Ministerialität der Grafen
   von Hirschberg angehörte, jedoch mit dem Besitz um Plein-
   feld und Eschenbach an die Grafen von Wertheim überging.'
   (Die mittelhochdeutsche Literatur, pp. 521-536; In: Handbuch
   der bayerischen Geschichte, ed. by Max Spindler, 4 vols.
   Munich, 1969-75, vol. I, [3]1975, p. 531).

22 184.29ff.

23 115.9: "schildes ambet ist mîn art"; 'art' has a dual semantic
   value. Its meaning can be either 'hereditary nature, destiny', or 'inclination, ambition'. The statement could
   thus mean either 'I have been destined by birth for a
   career of fighting', or, 'fighting is my vocation'. Whichever it is, either meaning indicates that he followed the
   profession of soldiering.

Moreover, at the point where he describes himself as a soldier
he draws a distinction between his everyday person and his
poetic self, thereby giving the routine individual, at least
on this one occasion, a quite clear-cut silhouette.[24] There
seems no reason therefore for not taking this description of
his everyday self at face-value, but quite the contrary, there
are good grounds for accepting it as the autobiographical truth.

If he then was a soldier - a cavalryman presumably, judging by
his education, although he himself does not say so in precise
terms[25] - what kind of a soldier was he? There appear to have
been three possibilities.[26] Was he a mercenary, i. e. was he

---

24 114.12,13 and 115.11ff.

25 Wolfram refers once to his 'word of honour as a soldier',
    (mîn ritterlîchiu sicherheit, 15.12), but never calls him-
    self 'ritter' which in view of the present controversy
    surrounding both term and concept may be just as well.
    Nevertheless it is a curious circumstance that he defines
    himself socially by circumlocution, and not by what we are
    inclined to accept as the then standard term for what he
    was and did. It is at present not possible to decide,
    whether this is to be attributed to chance, or to deliber-
    ate avoidance.

26 On the question of soldiering in the Middle Ages, and on
    the problems associated with it of feudalism and chivalry
    vid. in particular Charles W. C. Oman, A History of the
    Art of War in the Middle Ages, 2 vols., London, [2]1924, and
    the same work abridged and under the title: The Art of
    War in the Middle Ages. A. D. 378-1515, revised and edited
    by John H. Beeler, Ithaca, New York, 1953; John Beeler,
    Warfare in Feudal Europe 730-1200; Ruth Harvey, Moriz von
    Craun and the Chivalric World, Oxford, 1961; Sally Harvey,
    The Knight and the Knight's Fee in England, Past and Pre-
    sent, 49 (1970) 3-43; J. F. Verbruggen, The Art of Warfare
    in Western Europe during the Middle Ages. From the Eighth
    Century to 1340, Europe in the Middle Ages. Selected Studies,
    vol. 1, Amsterdam-New York-Oxford, 1977, (transl. from De
    Krijgskunst in West-Europa in de Middeleeuwen, IXe tot
    begin XIVe eeuw, Verhandelingen van de Koninklijke Vlaamse
    Academie voor Wetenschappen, Letteren en Schone Kunsten
    van België, Klasse der Letteren, 20, Brussels, 1954, re-
    vised by the author for the English edition; Ferdinand
    Lot, L'Art Militaire et les Armées au Moyen Âge en Europe
    et dans le Proche Orient, 2 vols., Paris, 1946; Hans
    Delbrück, Geschichte der Kriegskunst im Rahmen der politi-

an itinerant soldier who hired himself out for a variety of
campaigns to a series of noblemen? As a hireling he might have
received an advance payment and been given horses, equipment,
and also clothes. He would then have been paid per day and been
compelled to move on once the fighting was over. As a mercenary
he could equally well have been a member of a semi-permanent
troop of soldiers who all travelled together under the command
of a captain following the scent of rumours of war. His existence would have been nomadic, his income hazardous, with occasional affluence punctuating long periods of hardship.

---

schen Geschichte, vol. III: Das Mittelalter, Berlin, [2]1923,
(reprint Berlin, 1964); Eugen von Frauenholz, Das Heerwesen
der germanischen Frühzeit, des Frankenreiches und des rit-
terlichen Zeitalters, Munich, 1935; Wilhelm Erben, Kriegsgeschichte des Mittelalters, Munich-Berlin, 1929; Gustav
Köhler, Die Entwicklung des Kriegswesens und der Kriegsführung in der Ritterzeit, 6 vols., Breslau, 1886-93; Das
Rittertum im Mittelalter, ed. by Arno Borst, Wege der Forschung, 349, Darmstadt, 1976. (This contains the most extensive bibliography to date on the areas of medieval soldiering, feudalism, and chivalry prepared by Arno Borst);
Joachim Bumke, Studien zum Ritterbegriff im 12. und 13.
Jahrhundert. Mit einem Anhang: Zum Stand der Ritterforschung 1976, Heidelberg, [2]1977; – Ministerialität und Ritterdichtung. Umrisse der Forschung, Munich, 1976; – Parzivals 'Schwertleite', in: Fs. Taylor Starck, ed. by Werner
Betz, Evelyn S. Coleman, Kenneth Northcott, Den Haag, 1964,
235-245; Carl Stephenson, Medieval Feudalism, Cornell,
1942, (Great Seal Books, Paperback, 1956); F. L. Ganshof,
Feudalism, London, 1952, (Longman Paperback, [3]1964), (transl.
from Qu'est-ce que la féodalité? Brussels, [2]1947; all English
editions revised by the author); Marc Bloch, Feudal Society,
London, [2]1962, (Routledge Paperback, 1965, 2 vols., reprint
1975), (transl. from La Société Féodale, 2 vols., Paris,
1939/40); Chivalry. A series of studies to illustrate its
historical significance and civilizing influence, ed. by
Edgar Prestage, London, 1928; Sidney Painter, French
Chivalry, Ithaca, N.Y., 1957.
The distinction drawn above between the three types of
mounted soldiers in the Middle Ages follows in the main
Joachim Bumke's lucid account given in the chapter: Der
Ritter als Soldat in: Studien zum Ritterbegriff, and also
John Beeler's description in his: Warfare.

He could have been a vassal, i.e. he could have been allotted
a portion of land for his own use by an owner of extensive estates, in return for which he paid partly in military service.
If so, he would have enjoyed a certain measure of independence,
and his income would have been adequate to permit him to buy
and maintain his own horses and equipment. Under these circumstances he would have owed no more than forty days of military
service per annum, and would have farmed for the rest of the
year.

Was he a permanent soldier, i. e. was he a member of a land-
owner's garrison troop, on constant call, economically entirely dependent upon him, and living on the estate? In this case
he could be considered as being 'in service', as being 'in
employment'. Suitable horses and equipment would have been on
loan to him for his military duties.[27]

Of the three groups of men who made up the mounted shock-troops
of medieval warfare, this latter category was the most highly
esteemed. A military leader could not command absolute loyalty
from his mercenaries. An opponent might outbid his offer of
wages and thus spirit away from him a whole detachment of men,
or at least seriously erode it. Their 'mercenary' concerns made
them unreliable. Unreliability also characterized the soldiering of vassals, though for different reasons. They were frequently reluctant to answer a summons to a campaign, claiming
either privileges of exemption, or opting to pay scutage, or
quite simply ignoring it in open defiance, when their political
and economic power permitted it. Moreover, the time-limit of
their service, the contract for a mere forty days, made it
impossible for any general to consider them as anything else

---

27 Bumke, Ritterbegriff, pp. 41ff.; Beeler, Warfare, pp. 247ff.

but temporary reinforcements.[28] No matter which way the campaign
was going, whether it was likely to be successful, or whether
it looked like failing, once their forty days were over, they
were entitled to head off home, and often did. Household troops,
on the other hand, laboured under no such odium of uncertain
service in the field. Their loyalty to their commander, and in
consequence their reliability under conditions of war were beyond question. Also as permanent, and not occasional soldiers
like vassals, they could be expected to be in better fighting
trim than they. Thus they were looked upon in the Middle Ages
as the cream of the cavalry.

It is this high reputation that the cavalrymen of a magnate's
'familia militaris' enjoyed, which is a forceful argument in
favour of considering Wolfram one of their kind. He very clearly saw himself as a member of the fighting élite of his day.
His "schildes ambet ist mîn art" is no mere descriptive statement,
but an assertion of professional pride which presupposes membership of a group of military men, whose fighting qualities were
prestigious. The ring of pride is secured by the context into
which the phrase is set. He is no scholar, he says, and does
not wish to be taken for one.[29] A woman who prefers the poet in
him to the soldier, appears to him dim-witted.[30] Soldiering may
not have meant more to him than his poetry, but he certainly
rated it more highly socially than his literary pursuits and
achievements.[31] The distinction he saw in it, reveals the form
in which he must have practised it.

---

28   Bumke, op. cit., pp. 53 and 54; also Charles W. C. Oman
     (rev. by John H. Beeler), op. cit., p. 57ff., and Charles
     W. C. Oman, A History of the Art of War in the Middle Ages,
     2 vols., London, 1924, vol. I, in particular Book V: The
     Crusades, A. D. 1097-1291, and Book VI: Western Europe from
     the Battle of Hastings to the Rise of the Longbow.

29   115.25ff.

30   115.12-14.

31   On the attitude of medieval German poets generally towards
     their literary work vid. Fritz Tschirch, Das Selbstverständ-
     nis des mittelalterlichen deutschen Dichters, in: Miscellanea

Neither the poverty he parades, nor the near-certainty that he was a mounted soldier in permanent private service are any indication of his social origins. His poverty does not automatically label him a commoner. There were many petty nobles in twelfth-century Germany who were desperately poor, bastard sons, and younger sons for example, who had not received a portion of their father's wealth, and who had to make shift as best they could. Being a member of an equestrian troop, on the other hand, is no pointer to aristocratic birth. The system of service by 'ministeriales' in medieval imperial Germany put even the unfree serf on horseback.[32] It is highly unlikely though that he was well connected. Aggressively self-confident, as he so often shows himself in his work, he would scarcely have omitted mentioning his station, if it had been in any way exalted.

If one accepts on internal evidence that Wolfram was a member of a household troop, it is difficult to escape the conclusion that he was a 'ministerialis'.[33] Yet there is no external evidence to support it.[34] Definitive classification of Wolfram as

Mediaevalia, Veröffentlichungen des Thomas-Instituts an der Universität Köln, vol. III: Beiträge zum Berufsbewusstsein des mittelalterlichen Menschen, Berlin, 1964, pp. 239-285.

32 The phrase is borrowed from John Beeler, op. cit., p. 248. vid. also Arno Borst, Das Rittertum im Hochmittelalter. Idee und Wirklichkeit, Saeculum, 10, (1959), pp. 213-231; reprinted in: Das Rittertum im Mittelalter: pp. 212-246: 'Ritters Art ist keineswegs an adlige Abkunft gebunden.' (p. 213).

33 Cf. on the other hand Josef Fleckenstein's view 'dass ein Ritter zwar nicht ohne weiteres ein Ministeriale, ein Ministeriale aber in der Regel ein Ritter /ist/.' Review of: Hans Georg Reuter, Die Lehre vom Ritterstand, Zum Ritterbegriff in Historiographie und Dichtung vom 11. bis zum 13. Jahrhundert, Neue Wirtschaftsgeschichte, 4, Cologne/Vienna, 1971, in: Blätter für deutsche Landesgeschichte, 108 (1972), p. 526.

34 Cf. Joachim Bumke, Ministerialität, p. 59: 'Die Anerkennung des Ministerialenstatus muss von zwei Voraussetzungen abhängig gemacht werden: 1. muss eine Ministerialenfamilie desselben Namens für die Zeit des Dichters eindeutig nachgewiesen sein; 2. muss es gute Gründe dafür geben, dass der Dichter dieser Familie zuzurechnen ist ... In mehreren Fällen ist die erste Voraussetzung nicht erfüllt: es gibt keine

a 'ministerialis' would tell us a good deal about his legal
status, his rights as an individual, and his possible duties
other than military ones. Altogether the immediate personal
and professional world which he inhabited would be thrown into
considerable relief for us. For although status and function
of a 'ministerialis' varied enormously according to period and
area, there are certain key features which characterized all
of them. Thus the 'ministeriales', that class of civil servants peculiar to medieval Germany, were in service to the
crown and to great landowners, performing military and administrative duties for emperor and barons.[35] Common customs and

---

Ministerialenfamilie gleichen Namens aus der Zeit des Dichters. Das gilt für Wolfram von Eschenbach... An Wolframs
Ministerialenstatus zu zweifeln, ist beinahe ein Sakrileg.
Meistens wird schon der Vers 'schildes ambet ist mîn art'
(Parz. 115.11) als ausreichender Beweis für seine 'Ritter-
bürtigkeit' betrachtet. Tatsache ist jedoch, dass im frän-
kischen Wolframs-Eschenbach erst seit 1268 eine Familie
von Eschenbach bezeugt ist; und nicht einmal für diese späten Eschenbacher ist der Ministerialenstatus sicher.'

35 The 'ministeriales' have remained a vexed problem for historians. Discussion of them as a curious social phenomenon,
of the variability of their rights, of their relation to
the nobility proper, and of a host of other aspects connected with them, has continued unabated. Only a selection
of references can be given here; full bibliographies will
be found in Timothy Reuter and Gert Kaiser, vid. infra;
G. Bossert, Die Ministerialen der Staufer in ihrer schwäbischen Heimat und in Franken, Württembergische Vierteljahreshefte für Landesgeschichte, 13 (1890) 76-80; H. Brunner,
Deutsche Rechtsgeschichte, 2 vols., Munich, ²1928; Friedrich
Keutgen, Die Entstehung der deutschen Ministerialität, Vierteljahrsschrift für Sozial- und Wirtschaftsgeschichte, 8
(1910), 1-16; 169-195, 481-547, - Bürgertum und Ministerialität im 11. Jahrhundert, Vierteljahrsschrift für Sozial-
und Wirtschaftsgeschichte, 18 (1925), 394-396; B. S. Philpotts, Kindred and Clan in the Middle Ages, Cambridge, 1913;
O. von Dungern, Adelsherrschaft im Mittelalter, Munich, 1927,
(reprint Darmstadt 1967, Libelli, 198); Geoffrey Barraclough,
op. cit., passim; K. Schmid, Zur Problematik von Familie,
Sippe und Geschlecht, Haus und Dynastie beim mittelalterlichen Adel, Zeitschrift für die Geschichte des Oberrheins,
105 (1957), 1-62; J. K. Campbell, Honour, Family and Patronage, Oxford, 1964; Marc Bloch, A problem in comparative history; the administrative classes in France and in Germany,
in: Land and Work in Mediaeval Europe. Selected Papers,

traditions seem to have united them all, and they formed a

London, 1967, pp. 82-123, translated and extracted from
Mélanges Historiques, École Pratique des Hautes Etudes, 1966;
Lordship and Community in Medieval Europe, ed. by F. L.
Cheyette, New York, 1968; D. A. Bullough, Early medieval
social groupings. The terminology of kinship, Past and Present 45 (1969/70), 3-18; Karl Bosl, Die Reichsministerialität
der Salier und Staufer, 2 vols., Schriften der Monumenta
Germaniae Historica, 10, Stuttgart, 1950/51; - Herrscher und
Beherrschte im deutschen Reich des 10.-12. Jahrhunderts, pp.
135-55; Über soziale Mobilität in der mittelalterlichen Gesellschaft. Dienst, Freiheit und Freizügigkeit als Motive
sozialen Aufstiegs, pp. 156-179; Freiheit und Unfreiheit.
Zur Entwicklung der Unterschichten in Deutschland und Frankreich, pp. 180-203; all in: Frühformen der Gesellschaft im
mittelalterlichen Europa. Ausgewählte Beiträge zu einer Strukturanalyse der mittelalterlichen Welt, Munich/Vienna, 1964;
Hans Georg Reuter, Die Lehre vom Ritterstand. Zum Ritterbegriff in Historiographie und Dichtung vom 11. bis zum 13.
Jahrhundert, Neue Wirtschaftsgeschichte, 4, Vienna, 1971;
Günther Flohrschütz, Der Adel des Wartenberger Raums im 12.
Jahrhundert, Zeitschrift für bayer. Landesgesch., 34 (1971),
85-164, 462-511; J. Fleckenstein, Friedrich Barbarossa und
das Rittertum. Zur Bedeutung der grossen Mainzer Hoftage
von 1184 und 1188, in: Festschrift für H. Heimpel, vol. 2
Göttingen, 1972, pp. 1023-1041; Karl Bosl, Die Grundlagen
der modernen Gesellschaft im Mittelalter, 2 vols., Stuttgart,1972; - Soziale Mobilität in der mittelalterlichen Gesellschaft. Soziale Aufstiegsbewegungen im europäischen Mittelalter, pp. 44-60; Die aristokratische Struktur der mittelalterlichen Gesellschaft, pp. 25-43, both in Die Gesellschaft
in der Geschichte des Mittelalters, Göttingen, [3]1975; E.
Warlop, The Flemish Nobility before 1300, 4 vols., Kortrijk,
1975/76; J. B. Freed, The origins of the European nobility:
the problem of the ministeriales, Viator, 7 (1976), 211-242;
La noblesse au moyen âge, XI-XVe siècle. Essais à la mémoire
de Robert Boutruche, ed. by P. Contamine, Paris, 1976;
Georges Duby, The chivalrous society, London, 1977; K. F.
Werner, Adel, in: Lexikon des Mittelalters, vol. 1, Munich,
1977, pp. 118-128; The Medieval Nobility. Studies on the
ruling classes of France and Germany from the sixth to the
twelfth century, edited and translated by Timothy Reuter,
Europe in the Middle Ages. Selected Studies, 14, Amsterdam-
New York-Oxford, 1979. Vid. also the eminently readable
account of the rise of the 'ministeriales' by Gert Kaiser,
Zur Ministerialität: Der Widerspruch zwischen sozialer Bedeutung und rechtlichen Beschränkungen, chapter III, in:

clearly marked out group within the German social hierarchy.[36]
Their most striking characteristic was their curious half-free-
dom reflected in their extraordinarily equivocal and uncertain
legal position; they were, in fact, technically unfree. Thus
while they were able to hold hereditary fiefs, they could not
subinfeudate them. Although they had property and possessions,
their ownership was not always deemed to be total. Some of them
managed to take freeborn women as wives, but as a general rule
they were debarred from marrying into the nobility proper. Many
of them rose to great prominence through merit, yet the shadow
of servitude was always upon them. If there was a sale of land
a 'ministerialis' and his family could be sold along with it.
He and his dependants could also be given away, or exchanged
for other 'ministeriales', and their children could be shared
out among different squires. It is precisely this indefinite

Textauslegung und gesellschaftliche Selbstdeutung. Die Ar-
tusromane Hartmanns von Aue, Wiesbaden, [2]1978, pp. 56-100.
He discusses their political significance and their equivocal legal position, and tries to assess their status and
function within society.

36 Gert Kaiser, op. cit., p. 71 refers to the 'Sonderstellung
und Eigenart dieser sozialen Schicht', and points out that
the 'ministeriales' are persistently characterized in contemporary documents as an 'abgegrenzte Schicht oder Ge-
meinschaft' (p. 75). Vid. also Otto Brunner who describes
their situation thus (Sozialgeschichte Europas im Mittelalter, Kleine Vandenhoeck-Reihe, 1442, Göttingen, 1978,
first published as Inneres Gefüge des Abendlandes, Historia
Mundi, 6 (1958), p. 38): 'Die Ministerialen sind Unfreie,
die im Dienst des Königs oder grosser Herren stehen, am
Hof oder in den grossen Grundherrschaften als Beamte, auch
als Kriegsleute dienten. So erscheint mit dem 11. Jahrhundert neben den freien Vasallen eine Schicht von Ministerialen, von Dienstmannen, deren Dienstpflicht aus ihrer Unfreiheit erwuchs, aus einer Unfreiheit allerdings, von der
wir ja wissen, dass sie längst nicht mehr Rechtlosigkeit
war. Mochten die Ministerialen landrechtlich als unfrei
gelten, so bildeten sie in den grossen geistlichen und welt-
lichen Herrschaftskomplexen, denen sie zugehören, doch ge-
nossenschaftliche Verbände und formen ein eigenes Ministe-
rialenrecht aus. Sie sind ja Krieger, Vollkrieger, die sich
gegebenenfalls selbst zu schützen wissen und selbst gegenüber ihren Herren zur Gewalt greifen.'

nature of their legal and civic status, the shifting pattern
of their civil rights, the vague freedom which they enjoyed and
which could be underminded, or clipped at any moment, which
makes them into an especially interesting and problematic group
in medieval Germany. Social ambition must have been boundless
among them at all times, and social resentment no less great.

So knowledge that Wolfram was a 'ministerialis' would define
for us the actual limits of his social mobility, and the precise hurdles set for his social aspirations. It would in consequence indicate to us the possible hopes that he might have
entertained, and the likely frustrations he would have suffered.
Against such a background of social precariousness coupled with
a particular kind of personal predicament his work might take
on aspects of meaning which are concealed to us now. Attitudes
and views might come to outline themselves which we do not even
suspect for the moment. Even so, even if it could be proved
that he was a 'ministerialis', this would still leave the questions of his social origin, and of his standing within the community wide open. For a 'ministerialis' could be a commoner, a
bondsman even, recently recruited to the class of 'ministeriales',
or he could be a noble who had given up his freedom in order to
join a social group where the career prospects were considerable.
He could be rich and powerful, or he could be poor and insignifi-
cant. The mere description of 'ministerialis' is no indication of
either birth, or social importance.

Fighting on horseback, mounted military attack and defence, was
thus Wolfram's job and his vocation. He seems to have practised
it as a member of a magnate's household troop. It has been said
that for the society and time in which he lived, war was normal,
peace abnormal, so that one may conclude that most of his life
was spent in the saddle, enduring privations, physical and emotional, which would be considered intolerable in Western Europe
to-day. Much of the year he was presumably under arms, campaigning and raiding in all weathers. As he insists on his military
duties only, and mentions no administrative ones, one may infer

from this that these, even if they do not represent his sole
responsibilities, were at least his dominant assignment. Military duties, however, then as now, consisted not only of fighting, but included also ceremonial and security work, and the
training of juniors and novices. A cavalry soldier in permanent
service would normally be present at formal functions, such as
an enfeoffment, a tournament, an accolade, or a wedding, and
might assist in them. He would go on night-watch and day-patrol.
Every now and then he would provide armed escort for important
personages, or the transport of valuables. In the yard he would
instruct beginners in the use of weapons and the care of horses,
and in the open country he would teach horsemanship, fighting
techniques, and types of assault. On occasions he might be invited to accompany the noble in whose service he was on hunting
and hawking expeditions.[37] Sometimes he would join him in his
peripatetic existence as he moved from manor to manor, vassal
to vassal, policing and demanding his seignorial rights.

While day-to-day life may have been exacting, tough and even
humdrum for much of the time, there was compensation for it in
the field. The cavalry made up the core of a fighting force,
and in a battle the cavalry soldier found himself to be part
of a select group, of a contingent far smaller then the host
of foot-soldiers, and tactically of immense importance. Thus
in the battle of Bouvines on the 27th of July 1214, through
the defeat in which Otto IV. ultimately lost the empire to
Frederick II., the cavalry accounted for only 18% of the total
combined armies.[38] So the mounted soldier enjoyed an exposed
as well as an exalted position in the field. Here at least he
would have a sense of privilege, a feeling of being one of the
few.

---

37 Bumke, Ritterbegriff, p. 56.
38 Verbrugge, op. cit., p. 220ff.

He had to pay for it in exceptional bravery. Instant death was
less likely for him than a lingering one, for on the whole only
foot-soldiers killed, while cavalry men took captives.[39] The
casualties among the mounted shocktroops of the Middle Ages
were generally low.[40] There was every likelihood that he might
perish in a prison, not being able to raise the ransom, and
waste away through starvation, disease and neglect. Similarly,
serious injury in the field, being maimed or wounded, would
lead to the same kind of slow and agonizing death, the sort of
torture that Wolfram describes with such compassion and evident
empathy in Anfortas. There was no medical aid, no nursing care,
no rescue of any kind in the field. The only hopes that a severely injured man might have was that a friend would dispatch
him, or that he would have the strength and the limbs to do it
himself.

Wolfram's range of experience therefore encompassed life in a
feudal establishment, and expert knowledge, both general and
detailed, associated with soldiering, including front-line
service. When he then describes manorial households and great
courts, and single and massed armed encounters as he does in
'Parzival', although he has the blueprint from Chrestien for
most, but not all, of these situations and themes, he may be
held to have considered, handled, translated and recast
Chrestien's descriptions and comments against the background
of firsthand experience. His professional military knowledge,
his insight into feudal affairs, and his acquaintance with the
style of manorial living would have affected his own additions
to the narrative under these headings equally. In both cases,
in adaptation as well as in free composition in 'Parzival',
the poet's opportunities for firsthand observation and the
likely consequent use of it must be taken into account. For if
Wolfram is found to deviate in the delineation of factual cir-

---

39 Verbrugge, op. cit., pp. 157-159.
40 Ibid., p. 236, also Sidney Painter, Mediaeval Society,
    Ithaca, New York, 1951, p. 29.

cumstances from realistic description, - i. e. if the poet is
seen to be acting at variance with the routine person, - it is
well to consider whether implausibilities of this nature are
not to be attributed to a deliberate distortion of such circumstances, rather than to an ignorance of them. Distortion of a
reality he knew need represent neither an error, nor an over-
sight. It could signify a conscious contravention of this reality for the sake of poetry. It could be dictated by the desire
to establish a specific viewpoint via idealization, symbolism,
or irony.

It would be of very considerable critical import to have certain
knowledge of the actual circumstances of feudal living as Wolfram encountered them, and of the specific personalities that
played a part in his life. Both are likely to have influenced
his reworking of Chrestien's narrative, and to have suggested
to him situations, themes, and possibly characters for his free
composition. They may have directly conditioned, or even prompted, departures from descriptions in Chrestien, as also his additions to the French text. For the recognition of the poetic
processes at work in the composition of 'Parzival' such knowledge would be invaluable. Yet we possess little information on
these subjects, and none which may be considered proven fact.
Wolfram must have been familiar with many manorial establish-
ments, and have come into contact with a considerable number
of aristocratic families. His travels seem to have led him
through Thuringia, Franconia, Bavaria, Styria, and the Rhine-
land. Yet of all the families settled in these parts, he can
be linked only with three of them, and only on his own testimony, which in one case is quite vague. He knew that great
court of the Landgrave of Thuringia, the household of the Lords
Durne, and apparently also that of a Count Wertheim.[41] The re-

---

41 He makes highly suggestive mention furthermore of the
    châtelaine of the castle Haidstein in Bavaria (430.29ff.),
    and refers also to a nobleman named Heinrich von Reisbach
    (297.29), a placename which seems to point to Upper Germany

lationship in which he stood to these families is not certain.
He may have been attached to one or other in his capacity as a
soldier, he may have merely visited them on a military mission,
or an administrative errand, or been their guest as a follower
in the military escort of a visiting nobleman, or in his own
right as an entertainer. Two of them certainly were rich families, well able to afford luxuries, which would include a wide
spectrum of entertainment. The Durnes had sufficient funds
available to build for themselves an impressive stronghold in
a commanding position on a spur in the Odenwald. They added to
it and improved it over decades, and the residential quarters
in particular with their many windows, their enormous fireplace,
and also the two separate keeps, testify to the affluence of
this family.[42] It will never be established even remotely at
what stage of its construction Wolfram had come to know Wildenberg castle, and thus with which parts of its imposing architecture he was familiar. What can be said, however, is that at
the very point of the narrative when he claims to be at Wildenberg, and to be reciting his work there, his hero is introduced
into a castle of staggering splendour.[43] Its riches leave him

---

as well. It could indicate Reisbach an der Vils between
Landshut and Passau. (Vid. Joachim Bumke, Wolfram von Eschenbach, p. 5). The latter cannot be identified with any historical personage, and whether Wolfram knew the irresistible lady and her household personally, or only by hearsay,
is not possible to decide.

42 Walter Hotz, Burg Wildenberg im Odenwald. Ein Herrensitz
der Hohenstaufenzeit, Amorbach (Emig), 1963; William Anderson, Castles of Europe. From Charlemagne to the Renaissance,
photographs by Wim Swaan, London, 1970, p. 158ff., plate
194. Friedrich Neumann, Wolfram von Eschenbach auf dem Wildenberg, ZfdA, 100 (1971), 94-110. Vid. the latter also for
the relevant bibliography. A large fireplace at Wildenberg
seems implied in P. 230.6ff.

43 230.12ff.

44 It is possible that the concept of a 'mountain of salvation', a 'mons salvationis', has also played its part in
the coinage of this placename. Cf. e. g. W. Deinert, Ritter
und Kosmos im Parzival. Eine Untersuchung der Sternkunde
Wolframs von Eschenbach, Münchener Texte und Untersuchungen
zur deutschen Literatur des Mittelalters, 2, Munich, 1960,

dumbfounded, so much so that consciousness of all else is shut
out, and he misses his mission. The name which Wolfram invents
for this fictitious castle, 'Munsalvaesche', represents a manipulation of a French 'mont' and 'sauvage', and is thus an echo of
'Wildenberg'.[44] Is the overpowering impact of the riches on his
hero a reflection of a personal experience? Did the formal magnificence of the Durne household embarrass and shock newcomers
into silence, in the manner in which Parzival was silenced at
Munsalvaesche? The theme of failing to speak at the crucial
moment is, to be sure, found at this same narrative juncture in
the French source. But was the poet's motivation of this failure,
and his re-formulation of the type of question required, perhaps
suggested by the overpowering effect of the wealth and circum-
stance of the Durne household? Are motivation and re-formulation
echoes of the dehumanizing and alienating effect of excessive
display, of the resultant emotional discomfort once felt by
himself?

The rich Durnes were neighbours of the Wertheim family. These
seem to have been lesser folk. They certainly left no architectural trace of a dazzling living-standard as did the Durnes.
Their castle on the river Main lay approximately twenty kilo-
metres north-east of the Durne stronghold. But they also had
property in Eschenbach which they held as a fief from the bishop
of Eichstätt.[45] Wolfram makes mention of a Count Wertheim, and
this reference together with the family's geographical links,
both with the poet himself, and with his hosts, the Durnes,

p. 94, and Herbert Kolb, Munsalvaesche, Studien zum Kyotproblem, Munich, 1963, p. 129ff.

45 Joseph Aschbach, Geschichte der Grafen von Wertheim, von
den ältesten Zeiten bis zu ihrem Erlöschen im Mannsstamme
im Jahre 1556, 2 vols., Frankfurt a.M., 1843; Joachim Bumke,
Wolfram von Eschenbach, p. 2.

make it more than likely that he was personally acquainted with
the Wertheim household. He may even have been connected with it
in an official capacity.[46]

Both the Wertheims and the Durnes pale into insignificance
beside the Ludovings of Thuringia. Having been raised to the
rank of landgraves they ultimately built themselves no mere
castle, but a palace. The Wartburg at Eisenach is one of the
few princely examples of a palace at that period, most of the
others being owned by the emperor.[47] The landgraves were meant
to provide a bulwark of power for the crown against the might
of the territorial magnates, and were therefore of immense importance in the political and social fabric of the Holy Roman
Empire. Wolfram entered the world of the great when he went to

---

46 Wolfram's reference is not unequivocal by any manner of
    means. His statement "mîn herre der grâf von Wertheim/waer
    ungern soldier dâ gewesn:/ er möht ir soldes niht genesn"
    (184.4-6),- 'my lord, the count Wertheim, would not have
    liked to be a mercenary there. He could not have survived
    on their pay,' - comes during a description of a famine
    caused by a siege. It could represent respectful teasing.
    It could also be a bitingly derisory remark exposing a
    well known weakness on the part of a count Wertheim for
    habitual overeating. The phrase has to my knowledge never
    been expounded in this way. On this latter reading the
    form of address is seasoned with a sardonic note - 'my
    noble lord' - and indicates a distant relationship, to say
    the least, between the poet and the baron. Even on the
    other reading, that of respectful teasing, the title 'mîn
    herre', need not mean 'my liege'. Neither interpretation
    makes personal knowledge of the Wertheim family certain.
    Cf., however, Friedrich Neumann, Wolfram auf der Burg zu
    Wertheim, in Mediaevalia litteraria, Festschrift für Hel-
    mut De Boor, edited by Ursula Hennig und Herbert Kolb,
    Munich, 1971, pp. 365-378 (p. 372): "Ein Wertheimer wird
    von Wolfram als Lehnsherr angesprochen." It is the combi-
    nation of this reference with the geographical links out-
    lined above, not the reference on its own, which makes the
    poet's formal connection with the Wertheim family highly
    likely.

47 William Anderson, op. cit., p. 153. Also S. Asche, Die
    Wartburg und ihre Kunstwerke, Eisenach, 1954.

the court of Thuringia. Hermann, the landgrave, became his patron for his later work 'Willehalm', but Wolfram already knew
both, the Wartburg and its master, while he was working on 'Parzival'.[48] In Hermann he met one of the most colourful men of
action of his time. Hermann was a scoundrel in his public deal-
ings, and probably also in his private affairs. He was a political turncoat of the first order, forever manoeuvring his advantage this way and that between the two parties of the Hohenstaufen and the Welfs. When he succeeded to the lordship in 1190,
his cousin, the Emperor Henry VI, tried to withhold the enfeoffment of Thuringia from him, and to consider the district as
escheated to the Empire. It was only after Hermann had made
certain concessions that he was able to wrest the province from
the grasp of the emperor. His early bitter experience of the
duplicity of those in power, and of even his own kith and kin,
may in part account for a lifetime of double-dealing. Whatever
the reasons for it were, no one could count on his allegiance
for any length of time. He received fiefs from Otto IV in 1198,
and in 1199 he accepted them also from Philip II, but by 1203
he was back in the Welf camp. He came to grief, crashing with
princely magnificence, bringing his whole territory on the verge
of total ruin. His Pyrrhic victory over Philip II in 1203 was
followed by defeat and disgrace in 1204. Yet he managed to obtain a royal pardon in the peace of Ichtershausen on the 17th
of September of that same year. For some time after he stayed

---

48 Lls. 3.8-9 of 'Willehalm' acknowledge Hermann as Wolfram's
   patron. His description in Book VI of the landgrave and his
   court cannot but be read as claiming personal acquaintance
   with both: "von Dürgen fürste Herman,/etslîch dîn ingesinde
   ich maz,/daz ûzgesinde hieze baz./dir waere och eines Keien
   nôt,/sît wâriu milte dir gebôt/sô manecvalten anehanc,/
   etswâ smaehlîch gedranc/unt etswâ werdez dringen" etc.
   (297.16-23), - 'I took the measure of some members of your
   household, quite a few ought to have been put out of the
   door. You would need a good majordomo, since genuine generosity has wished on you such an uneven crowd of petitioners,
   some worthless, some possessed of real dignity.' Further
   links with Thuringia are suggested in Book XIII (niwer tänze
   was dâ wênc vernomn,/ der uns von Dürngen vil ist komn,
   639.12), and in Book VII in the reference to Erfurt (379.18/

with the Hohenstaufen cause, but not for long, soon he was
embarked once again on his round of political gambling. In
1208 he supported Otto in his election as king, but by 1211
he had become one of the ringleaders of the revolt against
him, and by 1212 he had done a complete volte-face, support-
ing now the election of the Hohenstaufen Frederick. Before
his death in 1217 he was said to have been planning yet another change of sides.[49] He was incorrigible. His restlessness,
his eternal plotting, and his addiction to walking the political tightrope presumably left him far too busy and too preoccupied to take much notice of the artists, entertainers, and
craftsmen with whom his establishment was teeming. His interest
in literature and in the arts in general, is attested by his
patronage.[50] Yet no one can tell how deep and how probing that
interest may have been. The princely way of life demands the
nimbus of the arts, and it is likely that one poet was to him
much like another, so that Wolfram was presumably never more

---

19) already quoted.

49 Allgemeine Deutsche Biographie, vol. 12, 1880, p. 155ff.;
    Neue deutsche Biographie, vol. 8, Berlin, 1969, pp. 642/
    643; Eduard Winkelmann, Philipp von Schwaben, 2 vols.
    passim; Th. Knochenhauer, Geschichte Thüringens zur Zeit
    des ersten Landgrafenhauses (1039-1247), Gotha, 1871,
    pp. 222-296; C. Polack, Die Landgrafen von Thüringen. Zur
    Geschichte der Wartburg, Gotha, 1865.

50 Martin Lintzel, Die Mäzene der deutschen Literatur im 12.
    und 13. Jahrhundert. Thüringisch-Sächsische Zeitschrift
    für Geschichte und Kunst, 22 (1933), 47-77; E. Schröder,
    Der Anteil Thüringens an der Literatur des deutschen Mit-
    telalters, Zeitschrift des Vereins für thüringische Ge-
    schichte und Altertumskunde, 39 N.F. 31, (1934/35), 1-19;
    Judy Mendels und Linus Spuler, Landgraf Hermann von Thürin-
    gen und seine Dichterschule, DVJ, 33 (1959), 361-388;
    Willibald Sauerländer, Die bildende Kunst der Stauferzeit,
    in: Die Zeit der Staufer, vol. III, Aufsätze, pp. 205-229;
    Joachim Bumke, Mäzene im Mittelalter, Die Gönner und Auf-
    traggeber der höfischen Literatur in Deutschland. 1150-1300,
    Munich, 1979, pp. 159-169.

at his court than one of a crowd. Hermann was surrounded by a
large family, four sons and four daughters, and he was reck-
lessly free-spending, as he could well afford to be. Changing
sides had proved a lucrative business. His household was huge
and lavish, rowdy and disorganized,[51] yet even though Wolfram
may have merely existed on its periphery, and at great distance
from its master, life at the Thuringian court must still have
been an experience of lasting imprint for him. This was a place
where action was bundled, where events crowded, and where
throngs of individuals moved in and out. While no direct repercussions of all this can be traced in 'Parzival', Wolfram
must nevertheless have assembled here a storehouse of impressions that served him as a quarry for his work for ever after.[52]

Soldiering in the twelfth and thirteenth centuries meant constant travelling, as the poet himself emphasizes[53]. His travels
in service, his visits to households such as these, and when
campaigning, would take him through country vastly different
from what it is now. The world which surrounded him was predominantly rural, and between eighty and ninety per cent of
the population of Europe were settled on the land as peasants[54].
The countryside was chiefly forestland, much of it mountainous,
while the smaller part of it, cleared for cultivation, consisted of farmland of no more than average quality[55]. In the year

51 Cf. Walther von der Vogelweide, (Lachmann 20,4) and also
    Wolfram's own description, 297.16ff.

52 For a different viewpoint on this question vid. Judy Mendels
    and Linus Spuler, op. cit. The authors try to demonstrate
    that certain aspects of Hermann's life are echoed in 'Par-
    zival'. The parallels quoted, however, are of so general a
    nature as to constitute no proof of tangible narrative in-
    terference.

53 P. 499.9: swer schildes ambet üeben wil,/der muoz durch-
    strîchen lande vil.

54 Richard Roehl, Patterns and Structure of Demand 1000-1500 in:
    The Fontana Economic History of Europe, ed. by Carlo M.
    Cipolla, vol. 1: The Middle Ages, London and Glasgow, 1972,
    (pp. 107-142), p. 119.

55 Josiah Cox Russell, Medieval Regions and their Cities,

1200 Germany was a medium-sized country by the standards of
the Middle Ages. It had approximately eight million inhabitants,
and was thus smaller than France with a population of twelve
million, but much larger than England which cannot have had
more than two and one half million people[56]. There were few
large cities in Germany. Cologne seems to have been its big-
gest urban settlement at the turn of the twelfth and thirteenth
centuries, with at least 32.000 citizens in 1180, but Magdeburg, Augsburg, and Prague were also important. Of these, Augsburg, the nearest to Eschenbach, appears to have been half the
size of Cologne[57].

Studies in Historical Geography, Newton Abbot, 1972, p. 75.

56 V. H. H. Green, Medieval Civilization in Western Europe,
London, 1971, p. 15; Josiah Cox Russell, Medieval Regions,
estimates the population of Germany for the period 1248-1348
at between 9.3 millions and 12.2 millions (p. 78). This
would place the figure for 1200 somewhat higher than eight
million. The total population of Europe in 1300 has been
estimated at about seventy-five million people (J. C. Russell,
Population in Europe 500-1500 in: The Fontana Economic History,
pp. 25-70; p. 40). Vid. also Erich Keyser, Bevölkerungsgeschichte Deutschlands, Leipzig, [3]1945.

57 Josiah Cox Russell, Medieval Regions, pp. 76ff. and p. 82,
Fig. 4; N. J. G. Pounds, An Economic History of Medieval
Europe, London, 1974, chapter 6: The development of the
medieval Town, pp. 223-278; also Erich Keyser, Deutsches
Städtebuch. Handbuch für städtische Geschichte, 5 vols.
(10 parts) Stuttgart, 1939-1974; Hans Planitz, Die deutsche
Stadt im Mittelalter. Von der Römerzeit bis zu den Zunftkämpfen, Vienna-Cologne-Graz, [4]1975; Die Stadt des Mittelalters, 3 vols., ed. by Carl Haase, WdF, 243-245, Darmstadt,
1969-1973, and Henri Pirenne, Medieval Cities. Their Origins
and the Revival of Trade, Princeton, 1925.
For the economic history of medieval Europe in general vid.
among others The Cambridge Economic History of Europe, vol. 1:
The Agrarian Life of the Middle Ages, ed. by M. M. Postan,
[2]1966, vol. 2: Trade and Industry in the Middle Ages, ed.
by M. Postan and E. E. Rich 1952; Josef Kulischer, Allgemeine Wirtschaftsgeschichte des Mittelalters und der Neuzeit,
vol.1: Das Mittelalter, Darmstadt, [4]1971; Gerald A. J.
Hodgett, A Social and Economic History of Medieval Europe,
London, 1972; Georges Duby, Rural Economy and Country Life
in the Medieval West, London, 1968 (transl. from L'Économie
Rurale et la Vie des Campagnes dans l'Occident Médiévale,

The fact that it had its own mint would not have made it especially remarkable in the poet's eyes. For there were well over four
hundred different currencies in circulation in the 'regnum Teuto-
nicum' at the time, and even Eichstätt struck its owns coins in
its episcopal mint.[58] What would have been of interest to him,
however, was the silver shrine which was being fashioned in Augsburg in 1205 for the purpose of housing, and also of displaying
the host.[59] Fine though the Augsburg monstrance may be, both in
design and workmanship, it could not compare in magnificence with
the giant shrine that was being made in Cologne during the years
1180 and 1210. Its size alone would have proved a magnet to any
traveller, - it became the largest of all medieval shrines - but
it must have been a breathtaking sight chiefly because of the

---

2 vols., Paris, 1962); Henri Pirenne, Economic and Social
History of Medieval Europe, London, 1936 (transl. from the
French; first appeared in Histoire du Moyen Âge by Henri
Pirenne, Gustave Cohen and Henri Focillon), and J. W. Thomson,
Economic and Social History of the Middle Ages (300-1300),
(The Century Historical Series) London, 1928. For the econ-
omic history of medieval Germany in particular vid. Handbuch
der deutschen Wirtschafts- und Sozialgeschichte, 2 vols.,
ed. by H. Aubin und W. Zorn, Stuttgart, 1971 and 1976,
vol. 1: Von der Frühzeit bis zum Ende des 18. Jahrhunderts;
F. Lütge, Deutsche Sozial- und Wirtschaftsgeschichte, Berlin-
Heidelberg-New York, [3]1966; Heinrich Bechtel, Wirtschaftsgeschichte Deutschlands, vol. 1: Von der Vorzeit bis zum
Ende des Mittelalters, Munich, [2]1951.

58 Elisabeth Nau, Münzen und Geld in der Stauferzeit, in: Die
Zeit der Staufer, vol. III (pp. 87-102), p. 87; ibid., vol.
IV, Map XIV, Münzstätten der Stauferzeit (Bearb.: U. Klein).
Cf. also Norbert Kamp, Moneta Regis. Beiträge zur Geschichte
der königlichen Münzstätten und der königlichen Münzpolitik
in der Stauferzeit. Diss. Göttingen, 1957, (Typescript), and
A. Suhle, Deutsche Münz- und Geldgeschichte von den Anfängen
bis zum 15. Jahrhundert, Berlin, [2]1964.

59 Hermann Tüchle, Die Kirche der Christenheit, in: Die Zeit
der Staufer, vol. III (pp. 165-175), p. 174; Tilmann Breuer,
Kunst, in: Handbuch der bayerischen Geschichte, vol. III,
Part 2 (pp. 896-899), p. 899.

60 Willibald Sauerländer, Die bildende Kunst der Stauferzeit
in: Die Zeit der Staufer, vol. III (pp. 205-229), pp. 226f.;
Hugo Kehrer, Die Heiligen Drei Könige in Literatur und Kunst,
2 vols., Leipzig, 1908/09, vol. II, p. 142ff. Hermann Schnitzler

dazzling splendour of its adornment. Lavishly decorated with
pearls, precious stones, cameos and gold, notably three gold
crowns, - much of which has now been lost, - it must have
presented the medieval beholder with a near unearthly vision.
Among the contributors towards these riches was Otto IV, hoping
thereby to secure for himself the support of the see of Cologne
against Philip II. Yet it was not only dimensions, radiance, and
play of colour that would have riveted the contemporary gaze,
a startling visual impact would have emanated also from the
particular presentation of the figures on the shrine. A fluid-
ity and mobility governs them, still highly unusual and novel
at the time, and which, though harking back to the models of
classical antiquity, would have appeared exhilaratingly futur-
istic. Their style bears the unmistakable imprint of that leading master craftsman of the age, Nicholas of Verdun, and of his
workshop. Moreover, the immensely important content of the
shrine, the skeletal remains of the three Magi, made it into
the most prominent reliquary in medieval Germany.[60] Objects
such as these would infallibly have drawn Wolfram to the bigger
towns. Art treasures were as yet not plentiful, and the visual
stimulus to the imagination which they provide, had to be sought
out laboriously. Nevertheless, Eichstätt already possessed a
representation of the Holy Sepulchre at this period.[61] Wolfram's
interest in precious and intricately fashioned artifacts is
attested at several points of his work, and it is more than
likely that he would eagerly have seized every opportunity for
visiting places where they might be found, if such a chance
presented itself. Altogether the visible world mattered to Wolf-

Der Dreikönigsschrein, Bonn, 1939; Percy Schramm/Florentine
Mütherich, Denkmale der deutschen Könige und Kaiser. Ein
Beitrag zur Herrschergeschichte von Karl dem Grossen bis
Friedrich II. 768-1250, Veröffentlichungen des Zentral-
instituts für Kulturgeschichte in München, 2, Munich, 1962,
pp. 187, 188, 191, 192.

61 Hermann Tüchle, op. cit., p. 171.

ram, the castles and manors, the roads and pathways leading to them, and the countryside with its forests and fields, rivers and streams. More than Chrestien he endows the background and the localities of the 'Parzival'-narrative with inviduality. The fictional landscape specifically created for 'Parzival' discloses aspects of the visual reality that the poet himself experienced, even if it does so only marginally and fleetingly. There were few roads, and with the exception of those which had survived from Roman times, they were in an appalling state. Unmade, deeply furrowed in dry weather, flooded when it rained, they were mere mud-tracks. A soldier on horseback would frequently be riding cross-country. Bridges were a rarity so most waterways had to be forded, unless there was a ferry.[62] Some of this is reflected in descriptions in 'Parzival'. The great forests Wolfram knew were leaf-forests, and in these the beech-tree predominated. Forests composed of coniferous trees were rare in Germany during his life-time,[63] so that the vast and impenetrable forest of symbolic connotation to which his hero is persistently drawn, must be imagined as a beech forest.

---

62 Hedwig Heger, Das Lebenszeugnis Walthers von der Vogelweide. Die Reiserechnungen des Passauer Bischofs Wolfger von Erla, Vienna, 1970, p. 149. Cf. also W. Schadendorf, Zu Pferde, im Wagen, zu Fuss. Tausend Jahre Reisen, Bibl. d. Germanischen National-Museums Nürnberg, 11, Munich,²1961, and J. W. Thompson, Economic and Social History, p. 565ff.

63 Horst Fuhrmann, Deutsche Geschichte im hohen Mittelalter. Von der Mitte des 11. bis zum Ende des 12. Jahrhunderts, Deutsche Geschichte, ed. by Joachim Leuschner, vol. 2, Kleine Vandenhoeck-Reihe, 1438, Göttingen, 1978, p. 18: "Die Waldgebiete, die damals (from the turn of the 11th to the 12th century) urbar gemacht wurden, bestanden nahezu ausschließlich aus Laubbäumen. Wenn man einer Statistik der ältesten Ortsnamen Glauben schenken darf, so lässt sich an ihnen ablesen, dass Laubholzareale gegenüber Nadelwäldern stark überwogen: 6115 dieser ältesten deutschen Ortsnamen weisen auf Laubholz und nur 790 auf Nadelholz. An der Spitze der Laubbäume wiederum stand die Buche. Ausser im Harz, im Thüringerwald, im Böhmerwald, in den Alpen und im Schwarzwald gab es kaum irgendwo Nadelwälder, die als 'arbores non fructiferae' für wenig wertvoll angesehen wurden ... Eine hohe Bedeutung hatte der Wald als Viehweide, für die Schwei-

Many of the errands on which the poet was sent he may have carried out on his own, but when travelling to a campaign it was
usual for a cavalryman to have a personal escort, and to be in
charge of three, or even four, horses. A knight, when setting
out for the business of war, was deemed to need two horses for
himself, the palfrey for taking him to the place of battle, and
the charger for fighting in it. He was generally accompanied
by a squire, also on horseback, who would carry the knight's
shield and lance, and would lead the charger. Frequently another
horse was added to this unit of two men and three horses, a sump-
ter which carried the equipment.[64] A military unit such as this
might be sent by itself on a special mission, or else it would
be joined to a baron's following. The distance which a mounted
soldier would be able to cover in a day varied according to
season, weather-conditions, and topography of the route. It
depended also upon the quality of his horses, and whether he
had to adjust his speed to any accompanying contingent of foot-
soldiers. On an average a soldier managed to ride forty kilo-
meters, and sometimes even more than fifty, in one day.[65]

---

nehaltung, aber wegen weithin fehlender Wiesen auch für die
Rinder, Pferde und Ziegen; mastfördernde Bäume wie Eichen,
Buchen, und Waldobstbäume waren eigens geschützt; ..."

64 Josef Fleckenstein, Das Rittertum der Stauferzeit, in: Die
Zeit der Staufer, vol. III, p. 103; Horst Fuhrmann, op. cit.,
p. 196.

65 Harry Kühnel, Die materielle Kultur Österreichs zur Babenbergerzeit, in: Tausend Jahre Babenberger in Österreich.
Stift Lilienfeld. Katalog der Ausstellung, Vienna, [3]1976,
p. 101: "Am Beispiel des Kaplans Odo von Deuil vermögen wir
zu ermitteln, dass zu Pferd täglich eine Strecke zwischen
38 und 55 km. zurückgelegt werden konnte". Hedwig Heger,
op. cit., calculates an average speed of 39 kms per day for
Wolfger von Erla, Bishop of Passau, for his journey from
Germany to Italy and back in the year 1204. This must be
considered an ideal average speed, as Wolfger was travelling at the best time of the year, from the beginning of
April to the end of July. Moreover, it seems that he was
able to make use of relatively good roads. Cf. also F.
Ludwig, Untersuchungen über die Reise- und Marschgeschwindigkeit im XII. und XIII. Jahrhundert, Berlin, 1897, pp.
101-104, and W. Schadendorf, op. cit.

The villages through which he passed would for the most part be
no more than a collection of huts put up by the villagers, and
made from wood, thatch, and mud or dung mixed with straw, with
not a stone-building among them, except perhaps for the parish-
church.[66] The people who sheltered here, and who represented
the vast majority of the population of medieval Germany, were
desperately poor,[67] existing merely on the subsistence level,
with an average life-span of less than thirty years, and still
less for women.[68] Exploited for heavy labour, tied to the soil,

---

66 Edward Miller/John Hatcher, Medieval England. Rural society
    and economic change 1086-1348, Social and economic history
    of England, ed. by Asa Briggs, vol. 2, London, 1978, p. 156ff.
    For the social conditions relating to the medieval peasantry
    vid. in particular chapters 4, 5 and 6.

67 Edward Miller and John Hatcher paint a grim picture of peas-
    ant poverty in medieval England, op. cit., p. 158: "To modern
    eyes even the richest peasants had a very narrow range of
    possessions. The most essential and most costly items in
    peasant houses were bronze cooking pots and pans: well-used
    pots of one or two gallons capacity, were often valued at
    2s or more. Iron hearth equipment - tripods for holding pots
    over the fire, andirons, gridirons, trivets and the like -
    were likewise essential and expensive. They were frequently
    valued at from 6d to 1s each. There is less information about
    furnishings, but we can assume that most cottages had a bed,
    a bench or chair or stool or two, and perhaps a trestle table,
    generally home-made like the cottages in which they found a
    place. Chests are sometimes recorded in peasant inventories,
    especially if they had locks. Commoner but seldom mentioned
    because no value could be placed on them, were dishes, mugs,
    platters and bowls made of wood or earthenware. The poorer
    peasantry probably made their own wood utensils, but table-
    ware made of wood or clay fit even for the king's household
    could be bought for a shilling or less per hundred pieces.
    Clothing is mentioned only where it was unusually plentiful
    or fine; but most peasants appear to have possessed no more
    than a single outfit and little or no cloth or bedlinen or
    window curtains in their houses. The reason is simple: cloth,
    like metalware, was relatively very expensive. ... Some
    families, indeed, were too poor to own a metal cooking pot."
    Although this description is based on English records, there
    is no reason to assume that different circumstances prevail-
    ed on the Continent.

68 An average life-span of thirty years has been postulated
    for the inhabitants of Central Europe between the tenth and
    twelfth centuries. The estimate, however, takes into consi-

and endowed with negligible rights, they were also physically
defenceless, and dependent for refuge upon the lord's manor,
keep, or castle, and for protection upon him personally, or
his men-under-arms. As such, as a soldier, and in particular
as one of the élite equestrian kind, Wolfram would have earned
their respect, if also their mistrust. For Wolfram, the poet,
on the other hand, they would have had no use whatsoever. They
sought their entertainment, if any of it ever came their way -
music, song and dance, poetry of a kind, juggling and tricks -
in the market-square, at fairs, and on the periphery of tour-
naments from itinerant performers. Despite Gottfried von Strassburg's offensively phrased insistence that Wolfram belonged to
this group of vagabond entertainers, it is clear from the style
of his work, the manner of his thought, his knowledge, and his
self-portrayal that he did not.[69] This is not to say that he
may not have been intimately familiar with village life, life

---

deration all strata of society. There is evidence that
members of the lower social groups died earlier. Cf. Horst
Fuhrmann, op. cit., p. 21ff.; J. C. Russell, Population in
Europe 500-1500. Length and Expectation of Life, in: The
Fontana Economic History, pp. 41-50; David Herlihy, Life
Expectancies for Women in Medieval Society, in: The Role
of Woman in the Middle Ages, Papers of the sixth annual
conference of the Center for Medieval and Early Renaissance
Studies, State University of New York at Binghamton 6-7 May
1972, ed. by Rosmarie Thee Morewedge, London, 1975, pp. 1-20.

69 It is now generally accepted that lls. 4638-4690 of Gottfried's 'Tristan' have Wolfram as their target. However,
proof cannot be absolute, and the specific relevance of
these lines to Wolfram has been disputed by Peter F. Ganz,
Polemisiert Gottfried gegen Wolfram? Zu Tristan Z. 4638f.,
PBB (Tübingen), 88 (1967), 68-85. For a bibliography on the
subject of the disagreement and hostility between the two
poets vid. Joachim Bumke, Die Wolfram von Eschenbach Forschung, pp. 81-88; also Gerhild Geil, Gottfried und Wolfram
als literarische Antipoden. Zur Genese eines literaturge-
schichtlichen Topos, Cologne, 1973, and Gottfried Weber,
Wolframs von Eschenbach Antwort auf Gottfrids von Strassburg 'Tristan', Zur Grundstruktur des 'Willehalm', Sitzungsberichte der Wiss. Gesellschaft an der Johann Wolfgang
Goethe-Universität, 12, Frankfurt a.M., 1975.

at its lowest level, and may indeed have shared in it at one
time. For Eschenbach, the hamlet with which he links himself,
was at the turn of the twelfth to the thirteenth century in
all likelihood no more than a handful of wattle and daub cot-
tages, like any other village in medieval Europe.[70] Some of
these would have huddled around the church which stood on a
rise, and which had been consecrated in the eleventh century,
some may have stood further afield. Their inhabitants would
have gone about the business of life in much the same way as
all peasants of medieval Europe - providing farm labour for
the local magnate, cultivating their own strips of land in the
little spare time they had, and living in fear of harsh winters,
drought, famine, pestilence, and armed attack. There was nothing
in that village that might have given anyone a notion that life
could have a content other than labouring for one's daily needs
while most of the time not even being able to meet those. The
only stimulus to thought and imagination would have been the
services held in the church. But though the poet's origins may
have lain in deprivation of all kinds, in squalor, hunger, and
poverty, by the time he came to compose 'Parzival' he had raised himself above them and left them behind. His work as regards
subject-matter is clearly aimed at the interests of the gentry
and the nobility, and the treatment of it betrays knowledge of,
and easy familiarity with, their ways.

How he managed to raise himself in this way is entirely a matter
of speculation. What may have helped was the link between Eschenbach and Eichstätt.[71] The territorial rights over the region in

---

70   Vid. the information, scanty though it may be, in Erich
     Keyser, Deutsches Städtebuch; also vol. 5, Bayerisches
     Städtebuch, ed. by Erich Keyser and Heinz Stoob, Teil II,
     1974, p. 583ff., and Fr. X. Buchner, Das Bistum Eichstätt.
     Historisch-statistische Beschreibung, auf Grund der Litera-
     tur, der Registratur des Bischöflichen Ordinariats Eichstätt
     sowie der pfarramtlichen Berichte, 2 vols., Eichstätt, 1937/
     38, vol. 2, p. 801.

71   For an assessment of the possible connections of Wolfram
     with Eichstätt, which differs substantially from the above,

which Eschenbach lay were held by the bishops of Eichstätt who
before 1215 enfeoffed the counts of Rieneck and Wertheim with
parts of it, including the parish church and all its appurten-
ances.[72] It is possible that this connection may have brought
Wolfram to Eichstätt, although in what capacity and on how many
occasions we cannot tell. During the years of 1195 to 1223, under
the episcopate of Hartwig (or Hertwig), Count of Sulzbach and
Dollstein, Eichstätt became a place of some consequence in the
Empire. The bishop seems frequently to have been in close contact with Philip II. He attended his court and accompanied him
on his travels, and was thus often found in the king's entourage.
In 1202 Philip appointed Hartwig vice-chancellor of the realm.
More important still where Wolfram is concerned was that on the
19th of September 1199 Philip granted the bishop the privilege
of holding an annual fair in Eichstätt. It was to last fourteen
days, and all merchants travelling to and from the fair were
given safe conduct.[73] Such fairs were important events in the
Middle Ages; they drew large crowds and attracted people from
far-away places. Tariffs and tolls were sometimes reduced to
bring in as many travellers as possible, and all manner of con-
veniences for sale and purchase was provided. Special courts
were set up for the settling of disputes and the collection of
debts. Goods came in on loaded carts and on mule-back in a far
greater variety than on ordinary market-days, not just corn,
wine, fruit and honey, but cloth, maybe silk, embroidered stuff,

---

vid. Johann B. Kurz, Wolfram von Eschenbach und seine Be-
ziehungen zum Hochstift Eichstätt, Historische Blätter für
Stadt und Landkreis Eichstätt (Beilage zum Donau Kurier),
Jahrgang 3, Eichstätt, 1954, No. 10,4pp.

72 Keyser/Stoob, op. cit., p. 584 and 585, also F. X. Buchner,
op. cit., p. 801.

73 Julius Sax, Versuch einer Geschichte des Hochstiftes und
der Stadt Eichstätt, Nuremberg, 1858, p. 69ff.; - Die Bischöfe und Reichsfürsten von Eichstätt 745-1806. Versuch einer
Deutung ihres Waltens und Wirkens, 2 vols., Landshut, 1884,
pp. 83-94, also Keyser/Stoob, op. cit., p. 174.

leather, trinkets precious and trivial, feathers, ornaments
perhaps, dyes and spices, and delicacies. Dialects from different regions would be heard, foreign languages possibly, and
there would be side-shows - acrobats and conjurers, knife-throwers
and fire-eaters, singers and fiddlers, buffoons, male and female,
with their performing animals, and every now and then undoubtedly, a minstrel who deserved an attentive hearing.[74] So at least
once a year the horizon waas briefly extended for the curious
and the imaginative who lived in Eichstätt, or within reasonable reach of it. Apart from this one short but striking burst
of activity every year Eichstätt possessed other features of
note from which the poet could have, and may have, profited.
Not only was there an episcopal court and a cathedral close with
the usual concentration of lettered and learned men, but it had
a cathedral school of long tradition. This had been founded as
early as in the middle of the eighth century by an Anglo-Saxon,
Willibald, monk from Wessex and kinsman of St. Boniface, whose
German mission he had joined. He became the first bishop of
Eichstätt and was later canonized. There are signs also that
Eichstätt had a tradition of practical charity. An almshouse
for strangers and for the poor is recorded there which had been
in existence since about the year 900. And in 1210 Donat, Abbot
of the Church of the Holy Cross, gave an order that seven loaves
were to be given every week to the lepers, and seven loaves likewise to the paupers, and that on the two saint's days of Willibald and Martin fifty-two denarii should be distributed among
them.[75]

---

74 J. W. Thompson, Economic and Social History, p. 586ff.;
    Eileen Power, Medieval People, London, 1924, p. 21ff., E. K.
    Chambers, op. cit., vol. 1, p. 42ff.; John F. Benton, The
    Court of Champagne as a literary Centre, Speculum, 36 (1961),
    551-591.

75 Keyser/Stoob, op. cit., p. 179; Julius Sax, Versuch einer
    Geschichte des Hochstiftes, pp. 72 and 73. Vid. also Lexi-
    kon für Theologie und Kirche, hrsg. v. Josef Höfer u. Karl
    Rahner, Freiburg, ²1959, entry Eichstätt, column 724ff.,
    and Mittelalterliche Bibliothekskataloge Deutschlands und
    der Schweiz, hrsg. v. d. Bayerischen Akademie der Wissen-

What Wolfram's later career was, once he had moved on from the
locality centred upon Eschenbach, and whether he returned to
it periodically, or regularly, is as obscure as the circumstances
surrounding his childhood and adolescence. No one can account
for the reasons which put him on horseback, whether this was a
foregone conclusion, or the result of mere chance, or the consequence of someone's interest and goodwill. How in addition he
became a poet is almost equally mysterious, although here one
would think that he must have had the early stimulus and encouragement of an environment where literature was not only welcome,
but fostered. He must have come into early contact with a variety of manorial families for whom poetry as entertainment was an
established aspect of their life-style.

The opportunities for the recitation of poetry in the hall of
manor or castle were indeed becoming manifold during his lifetime. Already the twelfth century had witnessed extensive castle-
building. Promoted first by the Hohenstaufen family as an ef-
ficient means of enforcing, securing and demonstrating political
power, it was soon adopted by the nobility, secular and ecclesiastical alike, by the princes, dukes, and bishops. At the beginning of the thirteenth century, however, a second phase of
castle-building set in, in which this time the gentry, and also
the 'ministeriales', participated. Every family that could afford it, moved away from the valleys to the heights, away from
the proximity to peasants, to fortified isolation, thus visibly
proclaiming their social superiority. And there were many who
could afford it, so many that the landscape of medieval Germany
came to be studded with castles.[76] The social prestige, the aura

---

schaften in München, vol. 3, part. 3: Bistum Eichstätt, bearbeitet von Paul Ruf, Munich, 1933.

76 Hans-Martin Maurer, Burgen, in: Die Zeit der Staufer, vol.
    III (pp. 119-128), p. 121: "Zu Beginn des 13. Jahrhunderts
    setzte dann eine neue Welle des Burgenbaus ein. Nun erfasste
    auch die unterhalb des Grafenstandes stehenden Adligen, die
    Reichsministerialen, Fürstenministerialen und die kleineren
    Edelherren der Ehrgeiz, Burgherren zu werden, und viele von

of might, which derived from the ownership of a castle is exemplified in the description of a royal alliance of the time. When
in 1209 Beatrice, elder daughter and heiress of the murdered
Hohenstaufen king, Philip II, was betrothed to Otto IV, it was
mentioned specifically and precisely that she brought into the
marriage as part of her dowry, a string of three hundred and
fifty castles.[77]

While the need for military defence, the urge to display might
and wealth, and the desire to create a tangible symbol of social
prominence played a major part in the planning and construction
of castles, the comfort of the living-quarters too was beginning to receive an increasing degree of attention. Their centre
was the main hall where the lord's family gathered, met with
those members of the manorial community who were in residence,
sat at meals with them, received visitors, conducted business,
and arranged entertainment. The main hall was the hub of feudal
living, and it was here that Wolfram would be called upon to
recite from his work.

The recipients of Wolfram's 'Parzival' were members of audiences,
were listeners in groups both large and small, occasionally no
doubt single listeners, and every now and then presumably also

---

ihnen besassen die Mittel, ihr Vorhaben zu verwirklichen.
Es begann ein neues Werken, Roden, Graben, Planieren und
Bauen auf den Bergen, und in allen Landschaften zogen weitere
Ritterfamilien von den Dörfern auf die Höhen. Das 13. Jahrhundert wurde zur Hauptphase des deutschen Burgenbaus." Vid.
also Fritz Arens, Die staufischen Königspfalzen, in: Die Zeit
der Staufer, vol. III, pp. 129-142. On castles in general vid.
Otto Piper, Burgenkunde. Bauwesen und Geschichte der Burgen
zunächst innerhalb des deutschen Sprachgebietes, 3rd rev. ed.,
Munich, 1912, and Curt Tillmann, Lexikon der deutschen Burgen und Schlösser, 4 vols., Stuttgart, 1958-1961.

77 Arnold von Lübeck (chronicler): "Er nahm sie als Gattin auf
mit ihrem väterlichen Erbe, mit vielen Reichtümern und mit
dreihundertfünfzig Burgen;" quoted by Hans-Martin Maurer,
op. cit., p. 119.

individual readers. But predominantly they listened and were
not members of a reading public. The core of these audiences
consisted of men and women of a social group, richer and pol-
itically far more powerful than the section of society to which
the poet belonged. He probably had no more than a wretched croft
whose uncertain and poverty-stricken produce would have represented part-remuneration for a life of permanent soldiering. If
indeed he had even that.[78] They, on the other hand, were settled
on fortified manors surrounded by large estates, and in military
strongholds, and could afford entertainment of which poetry
formed only a part. They might pay a poet in kind or money for
a few hours or days, or might even board him for a season or
more, and even commission work from him. Their standard of education varied from illiterate - which does not mean that they
were ignorant either of literature, or of certain types of spe-
cialized knowledge - to highly literate, i. e. they were versed
in works written in German, French and Latin, and possibly also
in other languages. These formed the core of the audience, the
landed group which paid the piper, and their kinsfolk, visitors,
and friends. For the poet they represented beyond doubt, and
for obvious reasons, the most important social unit among his
listeners. A curious feature of this dominant inner circle, and
one which the poet could hardly afford to ignore, was that its
lettered members would for the most part be women. They were
the ones who, trained on the psalter, would be able to read.

---

78 It is also perfectly possible that Wolfram was totally land-
    less, in the sense that he was merely able to accommodate
    his family somehow, somewhere on the estate to which he was
    attached, and had no land, not even of even modern allotment-
    size, to till. Cf. the discussion of landownership in the
    Middle Ages by Edward Miller and John Hatcher, op. cit.,
    p. 168: "The word 'knight' was ... variably used. From one
    point of view it described any member of the feudal military
    class, baron or tenant of a baron; and it was a personal
    label which carried no implications of landowning. The Abbot
    of Abingdon at first defended his abbey with a force of
    stipendiary knights and the knights quartered by the Con-
    queror on Ely Abbey received their daily rations at the
    hand of the cellarer ... landless knights were regularly

62

The men in this group, on the other hand, may be deemed to have
possessed such a skill only rarely. Two distinct types of literary expectation thus prevailed in his core audience, strangely differentiated according to sex, one based on watching and
listening, the other based on watching and listening as well,
but also on reading. 'Parzival' contains a series of powerful
portraits of masterful and highly individualized women, greatly
changed and elaborated as against the corresponding portrayals
in Chrestien. One wonders whether these changes and elaborations
are not a highly articulate and practical acknowledgement of
the presence of lettered noblewomen in the audience. They were
the ones who would be able to read 'Parzival' at leisure, after
hearing and watching the work recited. They were the ones who
would be able to immerse themselves privately in it, and to
take critical account of the veracity of description in detail.[79]

But there were other challenges to be taken into consideration
by the poet as well, for the land-owning families of the Middle
Ages were surrounded by a 'familia', the size of which was governed by their capital assets. Thus a socially prominent household
invariably included priests, a large number of mounted soldiers,
and a chancellor together with members of his chancery i. e.
lawyers, administrators and scribes. It would embrace chamberlains and stewards, bailiffs and almoners, and many other offi-
cials. Apart from these a host of attendants of all kinds would
wait upon the family. Some were charged with general duties like
companions, male and female, and men-servants and maid-servants;

found in baronial households in the twelfth and thirteenth
centuries alike."

79 On the importance of women for the development of literature
in medieval Germany vid. Joachim Bumke, Mäzene im Mittelalter, chapter V: Die Rolle der Frau im höfischen Literatur-
betrieb, pp. 231-247 and Herbert Grundmann, Die Frauen und
die Literatur im Mittelalter, Archiv für Kulturgeschichte,
26 (1936) 129-161.

others had specific functions to perform, like armourers and
huntsmen, falconers and dog-handlers, and pages who ran errands.
In addition, entertainers, such as musicians and minstrels of
either sex, generally formed part of the 'familia' as well,
either as permanent, or as temporary members. Finally, a great
household always attracted a motley crowd of paupers, waifs
and itinerants, and of all manner of hangers-on. A large household of the Middle Ages therefore represented an impressive
cross-section of medieval society, and in consequence the social,
educational, and intellectual spectrum of the poet's potential
audience could be very wide indeed. Moreover, it was likely to
contain a great many age-groups. This broader audience among
his listeners, the 'familia', did not matter to the poet economically. Its members were not the ones who had commissioned
work, or were paying for it in any way. They were not likely to
give bonuses, or to offer future engagements. Nevertheless, they
were of very considerable consequence to him. For it was in this
broader audience that he would find acute observers and alert
critics with specialist knowledge. Foremost among them would be
the lettered clerks who had undergone an academic discipline,
and who knew literature. They may be expected to have known
some of the best, Latin literature certainly, Roman authors,
the songs of the Vagantes, chronicles, the Vulgate, and the
whole panoply of sacred poetry. Some of them must have been
familiar also with literature in German and French, and even
perhaps in other languages. In these listeners the poet faced
a discriminating public of connoisseurs, well able to assess his
stature. In addition legal, theological and military expertise
would be represented in this wider audience, together with the
skills of a host of craftsmen. Specialists such as these are
likely to have been watchful and would therefore have been a
spur to both accuracy and plausibility in those parts of the
poet's narrative which touched upon their particular fields of
knowledge. He thus had to meet challenges on a variety of levels,
or at any rate be prepared for them. Not least among them was
the challenge of the face-to-face confrontation with listeners

who even if they did not voice criticism openly, could show
displeasure and boredom by lack of attention and restlessness.
Furthermore, the sheer size of an audience at one of the great
courts of the Empire would be daunting to a poet who was also
a performer. Even if one takes into account that the numbers of
some of the groups mentioned are quite indefinite and could be
very small, and that not all of them were present at all times,
a poet entertaining at a large household, a ducal or episcopal
establishment, could at a conservative estimate, count on an
audience of between eighty and one hundred listeners.[80]

---

80 The above brief sketch is based among others on the following: E. K. Chambers, The Medieval Stage, 2 vols., Oxford,
1903, pp. 419 and 480; Martin Lintzel, die Mäzene der deutschen Literatur im 12. und 13. Jahrhundert, Thüringisch-
Sächsische Zeitschrift für Geschichte und Kunst, 22 (1933),
47-77; Albert Schreiber, op. cit., pp. 1-9; Werner Fechter,
Das Publikum der mittelhochdeutschen Dichtung, Deutsche
Forschungen, 28, Frankfurt a.M., 1935, repr. WBG 1972;
Herbert Grundmann, Die Frauen und die Literatur im Mittelalter; - Literatus-illiteratus. Der Wandel einer Bildungsnorm vom Altertum zum Mittelalter, Archiv für Kulturgeschichte, 40 (1958), 1-65; Ruth Crosby, Oral Delivery in
the Middle Ages, Speculum, 11 (1936), 88-110; H. J. Chaytor,
From Script to Print. An Introduction to Medieval Vernacular Literature, Cambridge, 1945; Ritchie Girvan, The Medieval Poet and his Public, English Studies To-day, Oxford,
1951, pp. 85-97; Erich Auerbach, Literatursprache und Publikum in der lateinischen Spätantike und im Mittelalter,
Berne, 1958; James W. Thompson, The Literacy of the Laity
in the Middle Ages, New York, 1960; Helmut Brackert, Rudolf
von Ems: Dichtung und Geschichte, Heidelberg, 1968, Chapter
I: Mäzene, Gönner, Adressaten, Kritiker, pp. 25-33; Hedwig
Heger, op. cit., p. 227ff.; Michael Curschmann, Waltherus
cantor, Oxford German Studies, 6 (1972), 5-17; W. C.
MacDonald and U. Goebel, German Medieval Literary Patronage
from Charlemagne to Maximilian I: A Critical Commentary
with Special Emphasis on Imperial Promotion of Literature,
Amsterdamer Publikationen zur Sprache und Literatur, 10
(1973); Karl Bertau, op. cit., passim, in particular pp.
791ff., 858, 861, 891, 908, 966. The outline also makes use
of information inferred from the poets themselves, notably
Walther. We know lamentably little about medieval poets and
their public. In 1976 Joachim Bumke was still compelled to
say: 'Unsere Kenntnis von den Höfen und literarischen Zentren,
von den fürstlichen Gönnern und Auftraggebern, von den Wegen
der literarischen Verbreitung, von der Zusammensetzung des

Such was the public Wolfram had to entertain.[81] These were the

---

Publikums, für das diese Literatur bestimmt war, ist leider allzu fragmentarisch, jedenfalls für die deutschen Verhältnisse im 12. und 13. Jahrhundert.' (Ministerialität, p. 9) His recent book (Mäzene im Mittelalter. Die Gönner und Auftraggeber der höfischen Literatur in Deutschland 1150-1300, Munich, 1979) has gone a long way towards making good this deficiency in our knowledge by giving detailed account of the families of patrons of medieval literature, and also of their family connections. It throws into decisive relief the vastly important role which patronage played in the development of vernacular literature in medieval Germany. It does not, however, concern itself with speculation on the subject of who the members of a poet's public might have been during actual recitation of his work. As regards Wolfram the problem remains a thorny one, - even after Joachim Bumke's very precise investigations, - since he names neither a patron, nor a court, that could be linked with the commission to compose 'Parzival'. What one would wish for ideally would be a roll-call of persons, - at different dates, perhaps at different seasons of the year, - to be found at the manorial households with which we <u>know</u> he came into contact, like those of the Lords Durne and of Hermann of Thuringia, and of those families in Upper Germany with whom he <u>might</u> have come into contact. We need to know the composition of these households, the number of individuals involved, their standard of education, their day-to-day pursuits, and the languages with which they were familiar. Even if only a limited number of relevant data can be assembled, it should be possible to construct a series of models which could provide a working basis for the formulation of generalizations as regards medieval audiences. One such model is supplied by Joseph Gottschalk in his description of the Piast household of Silesia of the late 12th and early 13th century (St. Hedwig. Herzogin von Schlesien. Forschungen und Quellen zur Kirchen- und Kulturgeschichte Ostdeutschlands, ed. by Bernhard Stasiewski, vol. 2, Cologne/Graz, 1964). The immediate family of Henry I. and Hedwig embraced seven children, a daughter-in-law, ten grandchildren, Henry's sister and five nephews. Their entourage included among others, a chancellor and members of the ducal chancery, a series of chaplains some of whom had legal and administrative duties in addition to their religious ones, Father Confessors who had a further function of being general counsellors, soldiers, chamberlains, bailiffs and almoners. There was a group of women in personal attendance on the duchess prominent among whom was a close friend Demundis, a godchild named Catherine, and one Adelheid who had twice been on a pilgrimage to Rome. There was also a jester called Quetiko.

81 Clearly, Wolfram did not only recite to audiences on such a grand scale. The sample described above would by no means

individuals with whom he had to establish a rapport in order
to succeed as a poet, to achieve the satisfaction of being
heard and applauded as an artist, and possibly also in order
to supplement his livelihood. He had to appeal to their tastes,
pander to their preferences, interest them, amuse them, introduce subjects of topicality for them, show himself versed in
their specialist knowledge, keep them in suspense, cajole their
attention, and jog their memory. The composition of 'Parzival'
exhibits the marks of efforts in all these and in similar directions. Altogether the work bears the distinctive stamp of a poet
wooing his public with all the tricks of a literary trade which
involved recitation. Wolfram possessed a high degree of audience-
awareness. He cultivates in 'Parzival' an immediacy of style
which is akin to that of a speaker with a watchful eye on his
audience. It manifests itself most strikingly perhaps in the
frequently used form of direct address whereby he endeavours to
enlist audience-participation, and in an often emotional syntax
suggestive of the spoken language.[82] Thus he made calculations
as to audience-reaction, and language and narrative structure
of 'Parzival' show the indelible imprint of his businesslike
craftsmanship. In this way the contemporary audience has been
drawn into the work extensively. A direct and non-anonymous re-

---

be the norm, rather the exception. The pattern, one imagines,
approximates to that of the court of Hermann of Thuringia.
Other manorial households where he entertained might have
consisted only of the squire's family and a handful of re-
tainers. The great variation in the size of audiences would
be have been yet another challenge to the poet.

82　On the closeness of Wolfram's style to the spoken language
vid. Blanka Horacek, 'Ichne kan deheinen buochstap', in:
Festschrift Dietrich Kralik, Horn, N.-Ö., 1954, pp. 129-
145, who sees Wolfram as a near-oral poet with only minimal
skill in reading and writing. In particular p. 145: "Er
konzipiert seine Dichtung nicht von der Buchlektüre ausgehend
wieder für das Auge, ... sondern ... für das Ohr, das unmittelbar an das Gefühl appelliert. So stellt sich manches aus
seinem Mund verworren dar, ... Wolframs sogenannter "dunkler
Stil", seine "asianische" Sprachbehandlung haben hier ihre
Wurzeln. Seine Syntax ist reine Sprechsyntax, Redesyntax,
mit allen ihren Vorteilen und Mängeln. Erst nach ihm wird

lationship between poet and public permeates it.[83] This particular link must therefore enter all critical considerations of
'Parzival' as poetry. It is likely to have affected the poetic
fabric not only on the surface, but also on less obvious levels.
That despite this highly professional attitude towards literature Wolfram was no mere entertainer is a point which need hardly
to be laboured. What must be stressed, however, is that although
he was a poet of deep seriousness, with a pronounced sense of
mission, he nevertheless clearly recognized the importance and
advantage of being an entertainer, and took pains to act upon it.

What he thought of his audience is thus plain enough, but what
his audience thought of him is quite another matter. The standing
a poet had in the society of medieval Germany is very much a matter of speculation.[84] It is difficult enough to draw general conclusions on the standing a poet enjoys within twentieth century
society. Much depends upon his personality, his success, and
upon the company he keeps. His social standing is not fixed but
variable, and relative to the individual and to his specific cir-

---

diese Art der Darstellung als besondere Kunstform auch von
literarischen Dichtern bewusst gepflegt."

83 Cf. E. Nellmann, op. cit., who argues convincingly that Wolfram creates for his works not only a fictitious narrator, but
also a fictitious audience whom this narrator addresses. By
so doing the poet, in his view, manages to establish a close
relationship with his real listeners; p. 8: "Durch seinen
Erzähler schmeichelt er den realen Hörern (die sich bemühen,
den fiktiven ähnlich zu werden) und so gewinnt er sie. Er
lässt sie den Abstand, der sie von den Protagonisten trennt,
für kurze Zeit vergessen und hebt sie scheinbar auf dieselbe
Ebene, auf der diese agieren. Mit dieser Form der Publikums-
beeinflussung durch Schaffung eines fiktiven Idealpublikums
ist Wolfram innerhalb der erzählenden deutschen Dichtung
bahnbrechend."

84 Arno Borst, op. cit., sections: Hofpoeten, Vaganten, Dichter,
(pp. 538-549), discusses only the examples of Theodulf of
Orléans and the Archpoet, leaving out the type of poet who
interests us here, the poet around 1200 who composed in the
vernacular.

cumstances.[85] The one common denominator which poets may share
may be that they are looked upon as outsiders. It is always
only a small circle of 'cognoscenti' who holds them in high regard. Is it not likely that the attitude towards them was no
different at the turn of the twelfth to the thirteenth centuries?[86] A horseman who wrote poetry, would have been forgiven
his eccentricity because of his horsemanship by the many, he
would have been highly respected for the quality of his poetry
by the few.

---

85 Vid. e.g. Erich Köhler, Zur Selbstauffassung des höfischen
    Dichters, 1962; W. H. Bruford, Der Beruf des Schriftstel-
    lers, 1963; William Jackson Lord, Die finanzielle Lage der
    amerikanischen Schriftsteller, 1962, and Dietrich Strohmann,
    Die Regie des Autoreneinsatzes, [2]1963, all conveniently re-
    printed as Chapter V: Rolle und Status des Schriftstellers,
    pp. 245-331, in: Wege der Literatursoziologie, hrsg. und
    eingeleitet von Hans Norbert Fügen, Berlin, 1968; also
    Levin Schücking, Soziologie der literarischen Geschmacks-
    bildung, Berne, [3]1961 (revised edition), in particular
    chapter III: Die Verschiebung in der soziologischen Stel-
    lung des Künstlers, pp. 24-35, and Hans Erich Nossack, Die
    schwache Position der Literatur, pp. 7-27, in: Die schwache
    Position der Literatur. Reden und Aufsätze, edition suhr-
    kamp, 156, [2]1967.

86 Cf. on the other hand Hans Joachim Gernentz (Die gesell-
    schaftliche Stellung des Künstlers in Deutschland um 1200,
    Wissenschaftliche Zeitschrift der Universität Rostock, 9
    (1959/60), Gesellschafts- und Sprachwissenschaftliche Reihe,
    Heft 1, 121-125), who arrogates to the poet around 1200 a
    social position of almost dizzy heights. He claims an im-
    portant ideological role for him (p. 125) and sees him as
    exercising considerable influence on the aristocracy (p. 122).
    It is a moot point how effective such influence, if poets
    indeed possessed it, was at the time. Walther von der Vogel-
    weide's songs addressed to Otto IV, which are cited here as
    examples of influence and high position, are not a happy
    choice as evidence. The songs did not make Otto IV change
    his policies, and the stance which the poet adopts in them
    is no indication of exceptional position, but suggests mere
    brazenness. That writing poetry in medieval imperial Germany
    did not confer social status has been argued lucidly by
    Michael Curschmann in his article Waltherus cantor, Oxford
    German Studies, 6 (1972), 5-72.

In the Middle Ages, even more than in the later centuries, a
poet needed a patron in order to be able to practise his art.
The patron provided the source-book, the text to be adapted,
the expensive vellum, a scribe or two for dictation, revision
and copying, and board and lodging for the period that the work,
or part of the work was in progress. It is unlikely that the
circumstances surrounding the genesis of 'Parzival' differed
from the usual pattern, Wolfram vaguely claims a patron for
his work, a woman whom he does not name (827.27-30). The woman
patron may be fiction, but patronage for 'Parzival' cannot but
be a fact. The quality of the patronage would in some measure
circumscribe the poet's social position. The more elevated the
patron's status within society, the higher the poet would be
lifted at least within the group of his peers. It clearly must
have led to greater social acclaim to have been invited to
write and recite for a time at a ducal or episcopal court, or
better still at the royal or imperial court, than at the manor
of a rear-vassal. Wolfram, we know, spent some time among the
entourage of the Landgrave Hermann of Thuringia, recited, and
most likely also composed, at Castle Wildenberg, the family-seat
of the rich Lords Durne, and seems to have had links with the
Counts Wertheim. From this type of patronage one may conclude
that he occupied a fairly exceptional position among the literary artists of his time, but not a striking one. The prize
stages appear to have eluded him, the royal or imperial court,
a ducal establishment, an episcopal household, to all of which
Walther von der Vogelweide found easy access. It is a pity that
we cannot identify the woman patron at whom Wolfram hints in
the last lines of his work. It might help us to see his social
silhouette as a poet in a sharper light than we are able to do
without this knowledge. However, had she possessed a status of
surpassing consequence, her name, title, and territorial possessions would have been assigned a place of note in the work.
We therefore cannot but conclude that this was not so.

Whether or not a poet was able to attract patrons of high prestige would partially depend upon the reputation he enjoyed among
other poets, and among men and women of letters. The esteem in
which he was held by them, or the lack of it, would have spread
beyond their small circle, and affected his chances of entrée
to a prominent public. The opinion which contemporary poets and
intellectuals had of Wolfram is too sparsely documented to allow
of a rounded picture of his reputation among them. We only know
the extremes of the spectrum of views; there is nothing to hand
apart from Gottfried von Strassburg's savage criticism and Wirnt
von Gravensberg's enthusiastic praise. Two comments of this nature form too slender a basis for reliable general conclusions
to be drawn about his standing in this group.[87] Nothing in turn
can therefore be said about its influence on a possible public.

Whether Wolfram received from his patrons anything more than
board and lodging, and the usual facilities offered to poets,
we do not know. Whatever it was, it did not make him into a
rich man.[88] Like the vast majority of poets in the Middle Ages
he relied for his living, such as it was, on his main occupation
which in his case was soldiering.[89]

---

87 The question of Wolfram's position among contemporary and
    later poets is discussed by Hedda Ragotzky, Studien zur
    Wolfram-Rezeption. Die Entstehung und Verwandlung der
    Wolfram-Rolle in der deutschen Literatur des 13. Jahrhun-
    derts, Studien zur Poetik und Geschichte der Literatur,
    20, Stuttgart, 1971.

88 On the impecuniousness of poets in the Middle Ages vid.
    Ernst Robert Curtius, The Mode of Existence of the Medieval
    Poet, Excursus VII, pp. 468-473, in: European Literature
    and the Latin Middle Ages, (transl. by Willard R. Trask),
    London, 1953.

89 Vid. e.g. Karl Julius Holzknecht, Literary Patronage in
    the Middle Ages, London, 1966, (Originally published 1923
    by The Collegiate Press), p. 236: "The Middle Ages were
    content to allow literature to be the occupation of an idle
    hour rather than a profession to which a man might devote
    all his talents and his life. The practice of letters as a
    profession, therefore, was highly impractical unless the
    author had other means of support, and many of the medie-
    val poets had remunerative positions which supplied their

A host of questions involving both patron and poet surrounds
the choice of Chrestien de Troyes's 'Contes del Graal' as the
first work to be translated and adapted by Wolfram. Was the
choice his, or was it the patron's? Was it a deliberate choice
by one or the other, or did a manuscript containing Chrestien's
verse narrative happen to be available somewhere where Wolfram
happened to be? Neither the fact that he does not name his patron specifically, nor the extreme liberties which he takes
with the received narrative, rule out a deliberate choice by
a patron. The pseudo-patroness may have been someone of unusual
modesty, or she may have had good reason for not wishing to ad-
mit that she owned a manuscript of the French work. The poet may
have had a particular brief to complete Chrestien's unfinished
story and to extend it. He may in addition have been asked to
make all manner of changes to conform with the patron's tastes
and ideas. There is a possibility that he is hinting at such a
directive before a major narrative switch to a different tone.
When moving on to the career of his second hero, he lists five
of his women characters claiming that he has portrayed them in
a favourable light, thus demonstrating his ability to do so,
and at the same time making amends for former adverse criticism
of a particular woman. In view of this he asks for a patroness's
encouragement to continue his version. While these statements
are couched in general terms and are seemingly addressed to
women in general, they could imply a patroness at whose bidding
these five character portrayals had been slanted in a certain
direction.[90] Conversely, the poet may have been given a totally
free hand, or may have done the initial choosing of the text to
be adapted himself, so that every single alteration and ampli-
fication represents the poet's personal choice. If it was a deliberate decision on the poet's part to adapt Chrestien's last

---

needs and yet gave them leisure in which to write."
90   337.1 - 30.

work, then it was an incredibly shrewd one. Two of Chrestien's
romances had already been reworked for German audiences by
Hartmann von Aue, a cavalryman like Wolfram, yet exceedingly
unlike him in other respects, - a lettered 'ministerialis' who
confessed himself to be proud of his unusual standard of education, and whose scholarly bent made him handle Chrestien's
work with greater restraint than Wolfram was ever willing to
practise. Wolfram had acquainted himself carefully with Hartmann's versions of the two celebrated works by the widely renowned French poet. Accomplished and polished they mark, despite an earlier attempt by Eilhart von Oberg to introduce the
Arthurian utopia to German audiences, the true beginning of
Arthurian literature in Germany. They launched it on its course
of popularity. Was it this potential of popularity which induced Wolfram to take up another work by Chrestien? Was the
young poet sufficiently calculating to try and follow in the
wake of Hartmann's achievement, and to profit from it? Was he
at the same time fired with the ambition to improve upon it by
planning to be bolder with the French text than Hartmann had
allowed himself to be, bolder by far, and hoping to create a
new type of Arthurian romance? By choosing a work by Chrestien
for his first adaptation from the French, was he moreover swayed by the thought that with Chrestien he had selected a brilliant and established author whose reputation provided him with
a highly respectable source? What was it that commended itself
in 'Li Contes del Graal' over and above 'Cligés' and 'Lancelot',
neither of which had been turned into German, and both of which
were complete? Was it perhaps the very incompleteness of this
apparently last, and for Wolfram then latest, work of Chrestien's
which made it attractive to him? Was he sensitive from the start
to an overriding advantage for him in the fact that it was unfinished? Incomplete as it was it offered a far better chance
of intensive remoulding of themes and extensive elaboration of
subject-matter than had it been complete. The lack of a conclusion made it a more promising vessel for the poet's own ideas,
for his untrammelled imagination, and for his particular brand

of imperious originality than had it already been concluded and
thought out. Was he aware of his powers at the moment of choice?
- There are no answers to this jungle of questions. And anyone
of them would bring us closer to Wolfram's identity as a poet.

Uncertainty also obscures the way in which he obtained the manuscript. 'Li Contes del Graal' is the only one of Chrestien's
verse narratives to have been composed for Philip, count of
Flanders, most of the others, it would seem, having been commissioned by Marie de Champagne[91]. In the summer of 1190 Philip of
Flanders, so it appears, escorted the Emperor Henry VI from
Wimpfen into Lombardy. One of the Lords Durne, Rupert, was also
a member of the imperial retinue. Did a Chrestien manuscript
pass from one to the other, and thence to Wolfram?[92] Or did he
obtain the work in some other way? Troubadours, and French minstrels in particular, travelled widely throughout Europe, some
of them reaching as far as the Holy Land.[93] There is every reason to believe that Wolfram came into contact with foreign poets
and performers as they visited and entertained German manorial
households. Such entertainers from abroad could easily have been
the source for a copy of Chrestien's last work.

Once such a copy was in his possession, what did he do with it?
How did he set about working on it? One would like to know something of the practical day-to-day circumstances under which the
work came into being. Could he read Chrestien's narrative, or

---

91 Stefan Hofer, Chrétien de Troyes. Leben und Werke des alt-
    französischen Epikers, Graz/Cologne, 1954, p. 42; also Karl
    Otto Brogsitter, Chrétien de Troyes, in: Enzyklopädie des
    Märchens. Handwörterbuch zur historischen und vergleichenden
    Erzählforschung, ed. by Kurt Ranke et al. Berlin, 1979,
    p. 1366-1379.

92 Albert Schreiber, op. cit., pp. 56/57; also Karl Bertau,
    op. cit., p. 793.

93 L. T. Topsfield, op. cit., pp. 4 and 5.

was he dependent upon others reciting and reading it to him?
Was he able to write down his adaptation himself, or did he
have to rely on a scribe to take it down from dictation? It
was by no means usual for a man who was neither monk nor clerk
to be able to read and write, and trying to pinpoint the exact
degree of the poet's literacy is an elusive undertaking. He himself may maintain in a famous and hotly debated passage that he
cannot make out a single letter, yet within its particular context the claim looks more like a hyperbole than a statement of
sober fact, more like a deliberate provocation, whereby he
scornfully distances himself from other authors who relied for
their art on book-learning. No pen-pusher he![94] The proposition
of not being able to read and write at all becomes ludicrous,
when one considers how many times he would have needed to have
heard the work recited in toto, and how often parts of it would
have had to be read and reread to him, in order to enable him
to make the enormous number of intricate changes which he made.
Adaptation, as he understood it, involved him in a complex programme of literary operations. Apart from the basic, and by no
means easy business of translating, there were also the tasks
of establishing a leading theme, of developing major concepts,
of adjusting the narrative weighting of episodes in accordance
with new thought, of structuring the subject-matter so that it
would bear it out, of linking aspects of the plot with one an-

---

94 The trend of scholarly consensus on 115.27 "ine kan de-
    cheinen buochstap" is at present towards interpreting it as
    an exaggeration prompted by disdain and arrogance, vid. J.
    Bumke, Die Wolfram von Eschenbach Forschung, p. 72ff. Yet
    there will always be voices of dissent and doubt as e.g.
    that of Blanka Horacek, op. cit. Nor is it likely that
    agreement will be reached on the reading of this line in
    detail, vid. e.g. the contrast in the interpretations of
    Hans Eggers, Non cognovi litteraturam. Zu Parzival 115.27,
    in: Festgabe für Ulrich Pretzel zum 65. Geburtstag darge-
    bracht von Freunden und Schülern, ed. by Werner Simon
    Wolfgang Bachofer, Wolfgang Dittmann, pp. 162-172, Berlin,
    1963, reprinted in Wolfram von Eschenbach, Wege der For-
    schung, 57, ed. by Heinz Rupp, Darmstadt, 1966, pp.
    533-548, and Edwin H. Zeydel, Wolfram von Eschenbach und
    diu buoch, Euphorion, 48 (1954) 210-215.

other, of inventing and creating new figures, of recasting characters, of reformulating scenes of action, of eliminating detail on the one hand and of adding it on the other, of introducing and motivating the received narrative and of concluding
it, - and of a host of other similar assignments. Even if he
knew Chrestien's work off by heart, as he most likely did, even
if we make allowance for the fact that he lived in an unletter-
ed world, a world in which few could read and write, and where
the printed word was not obtrusively ever present - even so, it
is unthinkable that he would have been able to compose his version of the Parzival-story without a modicum of literacy. We
must imagine him with a (to us) phenomenal memory which relied
on the ear rather than the eye, with considerable skill in reading, and some facility in writing.[95]

The only way whereby he could have learnt these skills would
have been via Latin, and there is some evidence that he knew it.[96]

---

95 Herbert Grundmann in a seminal essay (Dichtete Wolfram von
Eschenbach am Schreibtisch?, Archiv für Kulturgeschichte,
49 (1967), 391-405) in which he draws attention to the fact
that ease in reading and writing among the lay public around
1200 was the exception rather than the rule, concedes to
Wolfram only a minimal ability to read: "... dass auch Wolfram ... etwas lesen konnte und einige Psalmen kannte ..."
(p. 401). Vid also Litteratus - illitteratus. Der Wandel
einer Bildungsnorm vom Altertum zum Mittelalter, Archiv für
Kulturgeschichte, 40 (1958), pp. 1-65, by the same author.
Further on the subject of Wolfram's literacy cf. Friedrich
Ohly, Wolframs Gebet an den Heiligen Geist im Eingang des
'Willehalm', Zeitschrift für deutsches Altertum und deutsche
Literatur, 91 (1961/62), 1-37, (reprinted with Nachtrag 1965
in: Wolfram von Eschenbach, edited by H. Rupp, and more
recently H. Bernard Willson, Literacy and Wolfram von Eschenbach, Nottingham Medieval Studies, 14 (1970) 27-40, also Fritz
Peter Knapp, Der Lautstand der Eigennamen im 'Willehalm' und
das Problem von Wolframs Schriftlosiqkeit, in: Wolfram-Studien,
vol. II, 1974, pp. 193-218.

96 Wilhelm Deinert, op. cit., passim.

Knowledge of Latin at the turn of the 12th to the 13th centuries
was rare among laymen, and he is unlikely to have had more than
a smattering of it. He had certainly never received any formal
education in it; there is no evidence in his work that he had
been trained on the 'auctores'. Yet he was impressively literate where the writings in the vernacular are concerned. He knew
the 'Nibelungenlied'[97], the early Tristan-version by Eilhart von
Oberg[98], the work of Henric van Veldeken,[99] Hartmann von Aue[100],
Gottfried von Strassburg, and the songs of Walther von der Vogelweide[101], and Neidhart von Reuenthal[102]. He shows familiarity
with heroic poetry other than the 'Nibelungenlied' and also knew
the important historical fiction of his time - the 'Kaiserchro-

---

97 Friedrich Panzer, Vom mittelalterlichen Zitieren, Sitzungs-
    berichte der Heidelberger Akademie der Wissenschaften. Phi-
    losophisch-historische Klasse, Jahrgang 1950, Heft 2, Heidel-
    berg, 1950, pp. 1-44, in particular pp. 5-14 and 37-44, also
    Emil Ploss, Die Datierung des Nibelungenliedes, Beiträge zur
    Geschichte der deutschen Sprache und Literatur, Tübingen, 80
    (1958), 72-106.

98 Hans Eggers, Literarische Beziehungen des 'Parzival' zum
    'Tristrant' Eilharts von Oberg, Beiträge zur Geschichte der
    deutschen Sprache und Literatur, Tübingen, 72 (1950), 39-51.

99 Henric van Veldeken is mentioned twice in 'Parzival' (292.18
    and 404.29) and once in 'Willehalm' (76.25). On the links
    between Wolfram and Henric van Veldeken vid. James F. Poag,
    Heinrich von Veldeke's minne; Wolfram von Eschenbach's liebe
    und triuwe, Journal of English and Germanic Philology, 61
    (1962), 721-735, and Wolfram von Eschenbach's Metamorphosis
    of the Ovidian Tradition, Monatshefte für deutschen Unter-
    richt, deutsche Sprache und Literatur. A Journal Devoted to
    the Study of German Language and Literature, 57, Madison,
    Wisconsin, 1965, pp. 69-76.

100 Hartmann receives mention in 143.21 and his characters at
    several points of Wolfram's work. Wolfram's debt to Hartmann
    has been investigated among others by Hermann Schneider (Par-
    zival-Studien, Sitzungsberichte der Bayerischen Akademie der
    Wissenschaften, Philosophisch-historische Klasse, Jahrgang
    1944/46, Heft 4, Munich, 1947) and Peter Wapnewski (Wolframs
    Parzival. Studien zur Religiosität und Form, Heidelberg, 1955).

101 Wolfram refers to Walther once in 'Parzival' (297.24) and
    once in 'Willehalm' (286.19). The relationship between the
    two poets has been covered in detail by Manfred G. Scholz,
    Walther von der Vogelweide und Wolfram von Eschenbach. Lite-

nik', the 'Rolandslied', and the 'Alexanderlied'.[103] He probably
knew a good deal else besides, but this is all we can identify.
Even so it can be said that he was intimately acquainted with
the total spread of all that was significant in the vernacular
literature of his time. Nothing noteworthy in the German literary scene had escaped him, everything that was new and challenging, creative and stimulating had claimed his attention, - love-
songs and dancing-songs, political and gnomic poetry, the revival
of classical antiquity, Arthurian utopia, pseudo-historical narrative, the versions of an immortal story of legendary lovers,
and antiquarian adaptation of historical subject-matter with
heroic themes. He had watched innovations being made and con-
ventions forming themselves, and consciously and critically
profited from both. He was fortunate in that he lived at a time
of brilliant literary experimentation and achievement, and he
was sensitive and acute enough to make use of this good fortune.
To what extent he had already done so when he first embarked on
the initial version of 'Parzival' is impossible to tell. However,
it is clear that he was immensely receptive to the new writing
in Germany, and keenly interested in it. That he knew French
literature in addition is obvious, apart from adapting 'Li Contes del Graal' and later 'Li Bataille d'Aliscans', he betrays
knowledge of the subject-matter of 'Lancelot' and 'Cligés', and
was very likely familiar with other works in French as well.[104]

---

rarische Beziehungen und persönliches Verhältnis, Diss.
Tübingen, 1966.

102 Willehalm 312.12; Karl Bertau, Neidharts 'bayrische' Lie-
     der und Wolframs 'Willehalm', Zeitschrift für deutsches
     Altertum, 100 (1971), 296-324.

103 Joachim Bumke, Wolfram von Eschenbach, pp. 8 and 98; also
     Friedrich Maurer, Wolfram und die zeitgenössischen Dichter,
     in: Typologia litterarum, Festschrift f. Max Wehrli, Zürich,
     1969, pp. 197-204; reprinted in Friedrich Maurer, Dichtung
     und Sprache des Mittelalters, Berne, ²1971, pp. 447-453.

104 Bumke, ibid., pp. 46 and 96ff.

His awareness of the dazzling efflorescence of vernacular verse, both recent and contemporary, did not daunt him. Quite the contrary, young as he must have been, and handicapped by multifarious duties, both disruptive and time-consuming, he set out on an ambitious scheme of remodelling the work of a well-known author. He seems to have begun at the beginning, first working on the material now contained in Book III and continuing until he had concluded Book VI. He thus dealt first with that part of the received subject-matter which holds within it the major propositional elements of the total narrative - the impact upon the hero of the demands of civilized society, of career, marriage, ethos, and faith. Up to here he appears to have based himself on a single copy of Chrestien's work.[105] Having got as far as this he lost heart, or got bored, or simply ran out of commission. At any rate, in the closing lines of Book VI he declares in a spirit of either insouciance, or irritation, that someone else can carry on, although he himself would be willing to do so, were his anonymous patroness to ask him.[106] There is a possibility also that he may have lost the manuscript on which he was working, or that it was taken away from him, or that he had to return it to its owner. In any case the work of adaptation was interrupted, and he turned for a time to free composition, occupying himself now with the hero's parental history, i.e. with the construction of Books I and II.[107] He then appar-

---

105 J. Fourquet, Wolfram d'Eschenbach et le Conte del Graal. Les divergences de la tradition du Conte del Graal de Chrétien et leur importance pour l'explication du 'Parzival'; Publications de la Faculté des Lettres de Strasbourg, 1938, and the revised version, in: Publications de la Faculté des Lettres et Sciences humaines de Paris-Sorbonne, Série 'Études et Méthodes' 17, Paris, 1966; also Die Entstehung des 'Parzival', in: Wolfram-Studien III, Schweinfurter Kolloquium 1972, ed. by Werner Schröder, Berlin, 1975, pp. 20-27.

106 337.23-30. For a discussion of a further aspect of importance of this particular passage vid. p. 71.

107 J. Fourquet, Die Entstehung, p. 24ff. The break in the narrative here was discovered already by Konrad Zwierzina, Beobachtungen zum Reimgebrauch Hartmanns und Wolframs, in:

ently managed to obtain a second manuscript of 'Li Contes del Graal' and continued the work of translation and adaptation.[108] He used for it the rhymed couplet with lines of either three or four beats, but at some stage decided to introduce a form of strophic organisation into the lengthy narrative, and made the unit of thirty lines the chief technical element of his composition.[109] He first applied this technique haphazardly, but then evolved it as a regular method. Passages worked early, were later revised to conform.[110] How he originally structured the narrative in its major outlines is a question which has never been answered, and probably never will be. Does the form of sixteen chapters, or books, in which we read it today, come in any way close to his personal view of the logic of the plot? Or does this particular division merely reflect the perspective of those who committed the work to vellum? Is the sixteen-part

---

Abhandlungen zur germanischen Philologie. Festgabe für Richard Heinzel, Halle, 1898, p. 437-511. The later date of Books I and II in the chronology of composition was proposed also by Albert Schreiber, Die Vollendung und Widmung des Wolframschen 'Parzival', Zeitschrift für deutsche Philologie, 56 (1931), 14-37, and Elisabeth Karg-Gasterstädt (Zur Entstehungsgeschichte des 'Parzival' Sächsische Forschungsinstitute in Leipzig, Forschungsinstitut für neuere Philologie I, Altgermanistische Abteilung, H. 2, Halle, 1925), both scholars arriving at this conclusion independently of one another, and by different methods.

108 Cf. on the other hand Joachim Heinzle (Gralkonzeption und Quellenmischung. Forschungskritische Anmerkungen zur Entstehungsgeschichte von Wolframs 'Parzival' und 'Titurel', in: Wolfram-Studien III, pp. 28-39), who rejects J. Fourquet's thesis of Wolfram's use of two manuscripts as not proven.

109 It is now generally accepted that Wolfram deliberately composed on this principle; cf. e.g. Bernd Schirok, Der Aufbau von Wolframs 'Parzival', Untersuchungen zur Handschriftengliederung, zur Handlungsführung und Erzähltechnik sowie zur Zahlenkomposition, Diss. Freiburg i.Br., 1972.

110 Joachim Bumke, Die Wolfram von Eschenbach Forschung, p. 180ff.

organisation, promoted by his nineteenth-century editor, to be
attributed solely to scribal tradition, or was the pattern already intended by Wolfram, and made manifest by him explicitly?
Any system of division is interpretative, and it may well be
that the poet's narrative weighting differs from the manner in
which the modern reader of the work now habitually sets his accents, accustomed as he is to the sixteen-section grid.[111] Wolfram may have planned the plot in instalments, in manageable, and
reasonably equal portions for public recitation. He may have
recognized an exigency inherent in the particular circumstances
in which poetry reached its public during his lifetime, and he
may have tried to contend with it by composing to a pattern of
a series of intermediate conclusions, each of which marking an
excerpt for performance. Yet whether these portions correspond
to the sixteen books of the modern 'Parzival' edition is by no
means certain.

On all levels of the practical process of composition we must
reckon with revision, whether this concerns the metrical form,
the overall structure, or the subject-matter itself. There can
be little doubt that Wolfram constantly revised, interpolated
here and there, amplified, compressed, elaborated, deleted, connected, and made all manner of changes. Long-term as the process
of reworking the French original was, it must, in the course of
time, have proved a discipline beyond price, a cumulative experience of poetic technique and of the powers of language,
which actively contributed to the development of his own method
of expression. How often he revised certain parts, and how many
versions he composed of the initial adaptation, we shall presumably never know. Nor can we ever know anything of his actual
practice of writing, or indeed how it came to the genesis of

---

111 How interpretative such division can be is shown admirably
by Karl Bertau (op.cit., pp. 782-787). His discussion of
the structure and genesis of the work takes into detailed
account the most recent major study of the manuscript tradition of 'Parzival' by Gesa Bonath, Untersuchungen zur
Überlieferung des Parzival Wolframs von Eschenbach, 2 vols.,

'Parzival' at all, if we wish to take account of the emotional
and intellectual mainsprings of the poet's creative energy. How
authors write their books is so very varied, and how they solicit inspiration, or are visited by it, suggests so wide a
spectrum of chance and behaviour, that no two seem to be alike
on either of these counts.[112] Moreover, where medieval authors
are concerned we possess little information on these points.
When Laȝamon composed his 'Brut' in the 1180s, he set out in
front of himself the three books in Latin, French, and English
from which he worked, putting the French book in the middle.
Comparing the texts he turned over the pages and wrote down a
condensed version of the three on parchment.[113] While Laȝamon
evidently pursued his chosen task on his own, Bernard of Clairvaux dictated to secretaries, discussed ideas, and asked for
conclusions to be taken down.[114] Wolfram gives no description
of how he went about the business of writing. Nor does he say
anything in detail about inspiration, mentioning it only in his
later work in a general and seemingly conventional way.[115] Yet

---

Germanische Studien, H. 238 and 239, Lübeck and Hamburg,
1970 and 1971.

112   The series, Writers at Work. The Paris Review Interviews,
      (First series edited, and with an introduction, by Malcolm
      Cowley, second series edited by George Plimpton and intro-
      duced by Van Wyck Brooks, third series edited by George
      Plimpton and introduced by Alfred Kazin, fourth series
      edited by George Plimpton, introduced by Wilfrid Sheed,
      London, 1958-1977) offers fascinating insight into the
      varied manner in which authors go about their work.

113   Laȝamon, Brut, ed. by G.L. Brook and R.F. Leslie, vol. 1:
      Text (Lines 1-8020), Early English Text Society, 250,
      Oxford, 1963; l. 16ff.

114   Jean Leclercq, Bernard of Clairvaux and the Cistercian
      Spirit, Cistercian Studies Series, 16, Kalamazoo, Michigan,
      1976, p. 30ff. (Originally published in French as S. Bernard
      et l'esprit cistercien, Editions du Seuil, Collection
      Maîtres spirituels, Paris, 1966).

115   "wan hân ich kunst, die gît mir sin" (Willehalm, 2.22). The
      line has been glossed in detail by Bruno Boesch, Die Kunst-
      anschauung in der mittelhochdeutschen Dichtung von der Blü-
      tezeit bis zum Meistergesang, Berne and Leipzig, 1936,
      p. 118ff., and Friedrich Ohly, Wolframs Gebet an den Heili-

in a work on so large a scale as 'Parzival', with so compelling
and sustained a vision, and shot through with so intense a
quality of pathos, it is difficult to imagine that the poet was
a stranger to recurrent and powerful visits of inspiration.[116]

Any attempt to place the work into the context of its distant
period, its alien locality and remote civilization, and into
that of the poet's everyday individuality must perforce remain
incomplete. The absence of documentary evidence relating to
biographical details forms a formidable barrier. The consequence
of such an exploration in a strait-jacket are its limited results. Neither the personal context of the work, nor its social
one, nor the historical background to it, have left broader
tangible traces in 'Parzival', none, at any rate, that we can
detect with our hampered vision. There is nothing here of which
it can be said definitively that it was prompted by certain
isolated experiences, or specific single events, or derived
from particular personal knowledge. To the latecomers to Wolfram's work these contexts are pervasive, and no more. Nevertheless their reconstruction is an essential concern. It serves as
a reminder that 'Parzival' is inextricably linked to a time, a
place, and an individual, all trivial facts which are only too
easily forgotten. For the very universality of the work which
lifts it beyond its contemporary reality, makes such contexts
appear irrelevant. There is a powerful temptation to disregard

---

gen Geist im Eingang des 'Willehalm', Zeitschrift für deutsches Altertum und deutsche Literatur, 91 (1961), 1-37;
reprinted in: Wolfram von Eschenbach, Wege der Forschung,
with Nachtrag 1965, pp. 455-518.

116 The question of poetic inspiration in relation to a longer
work is discussed by C. M. Bowra in: Inspiration and Poetry:
(Rede lecture delivered in Cambridge on 1 Mai 1951 and
reprinted in the volume of the same title London), 1955,
pp. 1-25, here p. 17ff. The nature of inspiration, the
forms in which it makes its appearance, and the ways in
which it is experienced by a number of writers, poets,
musicians, painters, and scientists has been described by
Rosamund E. M. Harding, An Anatomy of Inspiration and an
essay on the creative mood. With an Appendix on The Birth

them altogether which emanates directly from its greatness. Yet
to neglect them represents a loss in aesthetic responses and a
part-shuttered perspective. The temper of the age, its emotional
climate and atmosphere of thought, and the social circumstances
in which the poet found himself, all combined to create a particular texture of life, which, through his awareness of it,
entered his work. The contexts of history, society, and everyday routine may indeed be merely pervasive where 'Parzival' is
concerned, and no more, but as such they condition the work in-
asmuch as they represent the realities experienced by the poet.
It is from the sum of his reactions to these realities that he
would formulate ideas, articulate emotions, and develop attitudes,
ultimately to evolve poetic techniques in order to express them.[117]

---

of a Poem by Robert Nichols, Cambridge, [3]1948.

117 Jean Fourquet's observations on the critical analysis and
     assessment of medieval poetry must be mentioned here, be-
     cause they run counter to the premisses of the literary in-
     terpretation implicit in this study and outlined explicitly
     in the above chapter. In his view a medieval work cannot be
     held to represent the expression of an individual eschatol-
     ogical vision, nor can it ever be interpreted as a work in
     which the received subject-matter has been made to serve
     governing concepts: 'Das Modell des dichterischen Werkes
     als Ausdruck einer individuellen Anschauung der letzten
     Dinge, wobei ein überlieferter Erzählstoff souverän der
     Idee dienstbar gemacht wird, wie dies in Goethes 'Iphigenie'
     oder 'Faust' der Fall ist, ist irreführend. Das Verhältnis
     des mittelalterlichen Dichters zum Stoff, die Wege, auf
     denen er seine Kunst manifestieren will, verlangen andere,
     grundverschiedene Modelle, ... Wer das Modell, das die Gei-
     steswissenschaft mit Recht aus Goethes Schöpfungen erschlos-
     sen hat, auf den 'Parzival' anwendet, begeht einen Irrtum
     ...' (Die Entstehung des 'Parzival', in: Wolfram-Studien III,
     pp. 20-27; p. 27). It is interesting to note that Jean
     Fourquet seems to have committed that self-same error him-
     self in an illuminating contribution in which he tried to
     show how Wolfram remodelled the received narrative in accord-
     ance with his notion of three different worlds, that of the
     Grail, of King Arthur, and of the Orient (La structure du
     'Parzival', in: Les romans du Graal aux XIIe et XIIIe
     siècles. Paris, 1956, pp. 199-209). Vid. also Michel Huby,
     Wolframs Bearbeitungstechnik im 'Parzival', Buch III, in:
     Wolfram-Studien III, pp. 40-51, who is at pains to outline
     an entirely mechanical practice of transposition on Wolfram's
     part.

III. Adaptation of a Continuous Theme -
Reworking the Background

1. Scenery and Chivalrous Journeys

Description of background in 'Parzival' is sparse, mostly ab-
breviated, generally couched in conventional language and seemingly incidental to the action. Small wonder, therefore, that in
the course of Wolfram scholarship it has attracted little notice.[1]

---

1   Otto Unger's dissertation, Die Natur bei Wolfram von Eschenbach, Greifswald, 1912, offers little beyond a collection of
relevant references. Nothing is said about the narrative significance of the natural background.
Joachim Schildt in a more recent paper (Zur Gestaltung und
Funktion der Landschaft in der deutschen Epik des Mittelalters,
PBB, Halle, 86 (1964), 279-307, based on his Berlin dissertation of 1960, Gestaltung und Funktion der Landschaft in der
deutschen Epik des Mittelalters (1050-1250)), although drawing
most of his evidence from Wolfram's 'Parzival' is nevertheless not primarily concerned with Wolfram's work, but rather
with the whole complex of medieval German verse narratives.
He seeks to classify types of landscape in this literature,
and to demonstrate their function. The author, incidentally,
is not aware that Wolfram has created a coherent landscape
for 'Parzival'. When discussing the function of a 'Landschafts-
bild in zusammenhängend gestalteter Form', he adds - "für die
die Epik Wolframs von Eschenbach kein treffendes Beispiel bie-
tet."
Marion Gibbs, Wrong Paths in 'Parzival', MLR, 63 (1968), 872-
876, gives brief consideration to the function of misdirec-
tion in Parzival's travels.
Wolfgang Harms in his exhaustive and broad-based investigation
of the symbol Y and its meanings in pictorial presentation,
and its significance as crossroads in literary portrayal,
(Homo viator in bivio. Studien zur Bildlichkeit des Weges,
Munich, 1970), includes a chapter on Wolfram's 'Parzival':
Die Situation des homo viator in bivio im 'Parzival' Wolframs
von Eschenbach, (pp. 221-249). He here concerns himself predomi-
nantly with the type of road taken by the hero and sums up:
"Nimmt man alle Hinweise auf die Eigenschaften von Parzivals
Weg vor seiner Ankunft bei Trevrizent zusammen, so findet sich
kein Attribut aus dem Bedeutungsbereich des breiten Weges,
sondern nur solche des schmalen Weges. Wenn Parzival also im
Gralsbereich zwischen zwei Wegen zu wählen hat, so kann dar-
aus nur eine Modifizierung des Bedeutungsbereichs des schmalen
Weges resultieren. Die Zeit und der Ort, in denen auch für
Parzival breite Wege wählbar waren - vor seiner Ankunft am

Wolfram does not linger descriptively over landscape in response
to its beauty. Only where the treatment of scenery involves portrayal of architectural marvels is the usual brevity of description occasionally abandoned for enthusiastic elaboration. Aesthetic wonder is not extended to the natural scene but reserved
for the inanimate world of artifacts. These few more detailed
passages are placed at significant points of the narrative and
form an exception to the general technique of presenting background in 'Parzival'. Full treatment of scenery in the manner
of post-medieval artists there is none in 'Parzival', and even
where it is more specific, it retains its character of a brief
indication of the setting.

Certain aspects of the portrayal of background reveal techniques
of presentation which later authors in particular have exploited

---

Artushof in Nantes -, sind vorüber. Im Gralsbereich geht es
für ihn darum, nachzuweisen, dass er ein würdiger viator des
schmalen, schwierigen Weges, der zum Ziel führt, geworden
sei." (p. 243). He adds an important observation on Wolfram's
poetic craft: "Wir sehen im 'Parzival', wie Wolfram ein Wählen
zwischen Wegen zwar immer wieder darstellt, dass er aber nirgends auf die traditionellen Formen der Zweiwegsituation so
unmittelbar zurückgreift, dass man von einem Motivzitat oder
auch nur von einer einfachen Übertragung eines Komplexes be-
deutungstragender Bildelemente sprechen könnte. Die Vorstellung von der starren Alternative einer bivium-Entscheidung
löst Wolfram immer wieder auf in eine Abfolge differenzier-
ter Situationen, Vorgänge, Reflexionen, dinglicher Zeichen,
je nach den Anforderungen des erzählerischen Kontexts."
(p. 241).
Ernst S. Dick, Katabasis and the Grail Epic: Wolfram von
Eschenbach's Parzival, Res Publica Litterarum, vol. I, University of Kansas, 1978, pp. 57-87, has drawn attention to
the mythical/folkloristic background to the hero's travel-
history. The vocabulary associated with the description of
journeys in 'Parzival' has been assembled and analyzed together with the same terminological complex in 'Erec', 'Iwein',
'Lanzelet', 'Wigalois', and 'Jüngerer Titurel' by Ernst
Trachsler, Der Weg im mittelhochdeutschen Artusroman, Studien
zur Germanistik und Komparatistik, 50, Bonn, 1979.
So altogether the scenery in 'Parzival' has on the one hand
received scholarly attention in passing only as it were, in
connection with other works of literature, and on the other
has merely had certain aspects of it examined, no more. The
only full investigation of the intrinsic and structural significance of the scenery in Parzival is the one offered above.

to the full. Of these - the association of sentiment with scenery, the development of atmosphere, and the connection of events with background - Wolfram makes only limited use.

There are suggestions that landscape can shift in accordance with the mood of his characters. Brief though these allusions may be, they clearly attempt to establish a relationship between sentiment and setting.

Herzeloyde, in her grief for Gahmuret, ceases to take note of the external world:

> 117.3 ein nebel was ir diu sunne.
> si vlôch der werlde wunne.
> ir was gelîch naht unt der tac:
> ir herze niht wan jâmers phlac.
>   Sich zôch diu frouwe jâmers balt
> ûz ir lande in einen walt,
> zer waste in Soltâne;
> niht durch bluomen ûf die plâne.
> ir herzen jâmer was sô ganz,
> sine kerte sich an keinen kranz,
> er waere rôt oder val.

To Parzival, regretfully thinking of Lîâze, Nature has shed all attractiveness:

> 179.18 im was diu wîte zenge,
> und ouch diu breite gar ze smal:
> elliu grüene in dûhte val,
> sîn rôt harnasch in dûhte blanc:
> sîn herze d'ougen des bedwanc.

The technique of linking emotion with scenery is clearly perceptible in these paragraphs. Wolfram, however, does not consistently rely on it, either for delineation of background or for portrayal of character.

Similarly, the use of the development of atmosphere in the setting is much restricted in the work. It is only to certain parts of the background that atmosphere is imparted. Individual characteristics and consequently distinctive atmosphere are clearly created for both Terre de Salvaesche and Terre Marveile. On the remaining parts of the background less care of this sort is ex-

pended; Bertâne, e.g., does not exhibit a set of consistent
features and consequently lacks atmosphere altogether.

But the technique of creating atmosphere is not merely limited
by its desultoriness, it is also severely restricted by the means
on which it relies. Specific atmosphere is here not achieved by
detailed descriptive passages. It is not conveyed by direct
statement and elaborately varied insistence on its characteristic aspects, nor is it powerfully developed, but largely implicit and almost incidental.[2]

Finally, this technique of relating events to the background is
employed only occasionally and by no means fully developed. At
some points of the narrative the specific meaning of an event
may be underlined by its location. Thus Parzival's first meeting with Sigûne stands in contrast to his second and third meetings with her, a contrast which is reinforced by the change of
location from Bertâne to Terre de Salvaesche.

The restricted use of these three techniques and the general
brevity of description as related to scenery would seem to indicate that Wolfram attached little importance to the background
of his narrative. When comparing 'Parzival' with its French
source, however, it becomes immediately obvious that he made a
large number of striking and consistent changes in the treatment of background which establish beyond doubt his concern with
the style of its presentation, and with its function within the
narrative.

Two of the three techniques described above represent additions
where the style of Chrestien de Troyes is concerned. There is
no counterpart in 'Li Contes del Graal' for either the association of sentiment with scenery, or the connection of events
with background. Concise description too forms a departure from

---

2 Cf., e.g., the references to the setting of Parzival's third
  meeting with Sigûne, 434.11ff.

Chrestien's poetic technique which relies on greater detail and
a wider range of terminology. But the most conspicuous change
of all is the increase in the number of place-names involved in
the main action. Where Chrestien has, in chronological order,
Valdone (Pass of), Carduel, Goort, Belrepeire, Dinasdaron an
Gales, Carlion, Tintaguel, Escavalon, Galvoie, La Roche de
Chanpguin, Le Grué Perilleus, Orquelenes, and Orcanie, Wolfram
allots to the corresponding section of his epic Soltâne, Brizljân,
Bertâne, Nantes, Grâharz, Pelrapeire in Brôbarz, Karminâl in
Brizljân, Dîanazdrûn in Löver, Terre de Salvaesche, Lake Brumbâne,
Munsalvaesche, Fontâne la salvâtsche, Karidoel, Plimizoel, Bêâ-
rosche, Laehtamrîs, Schanpfanzûn in Ascalûn, Karnant, Barbigoel,
Lôgroys, Terre Marveile, Schastel Marveile, Li Gweiz Prelljûs
in River Sabîns, Rosche Sabbîns, and Bems bî der Korcâ in Löver.[3]

This profusion of place-names is used by Wolfram with extraordinary skill and subtlety to invest the background of his narrative with a significance never intended by Chrestien. On the
basis of these place-names he develops symbolic aspects of the
setting which elucidate the meaning of a number of episodes,
help to define the relationship between Parzival and Gâwân,
establish the function of the Arthurian court in the work and
contribute to narrative unity. With the assistance of these
names, further increased in Books I, II, IX, and XIII to XVI,
he elaborates forms of the presentation of scenery already employed by Chrestien, to immense complexity and new significance.
As in Chrestien's work, the scenery here too is conceived as
the background to a travel-history, is represented as a geographical scheme and divided into two distinct parts - the background to the Parzival story and the setting of the Gâwân narrative. With the use of specific names for certain locations,
however, through their extension, and by a host of consistent

---

3 The orthography of place-names and proper names is based on
   the Verzeichnis der Eigennamen appended to Lachmann-Hartl,
   Wolfram von Eschenbach, 7th ed., Berlin, 1952.

minor changes connected with them, Wolfram not only achieves
a much more clearly defined background than Chrestien, but
greatly intensifies its importance. This particular and unexpected emphasis by Wolfram on the setting of 'Parzival'
emerges with indubitable clarity in an analysis of the chivalrous journeys of the romance.[4]

The setting throughout is presented as a background to chivalrous travels in search of âventiure. It is thus never static
but seen as a series of constantly shifting pictures. The listener mowes along the changing scenery first with Gahmuret, subsequently with Parzival and Gâwân. The illusion produced is
that of a vast journey across continents, exploring large tracts
of the world of actual reality (the East, Africa, and Europe)
with excursions into fabulous regions, and ending at Munsalvaesche of mysteriously indefinable location.

In Books I and II the background to Gahmuret's exploits bears
the character of introduction. The course of his travels is only
briefly indicated in broad outline, Wolfram merely supplying
the geography of his journeys. It is not until we proceed to
the central narrative, i.e., Book III, that the treatment of
the background changes from the general to the specific and
is made more clearly visible through descriptive detail and geographical connection. In Books I and II it consists almost
purely of place-names.

The action opens in Anschouwe. Gahmuret leaves for Baldac to
assist the bâruc in a campaign. Neither the voyage to the East
nor Baldac is described. Wolfram states briefly: "dar kom der
junge Anschevîn" (14.8). After the Baldac venture Gahmuret's

---

4   An admirable account of these journeys is to be found in
    M.O.'C. Walshe's "Travel Descriptions in MHG Arthurian Epics"
    (unpublished M.A. diss., London, 1935). Vid. in particular
    the section, "The Fabulous Geography of Lanzelet", published
    in London Medieval Studies, 1 (1937-39), pp. 93-106.

travels take him over wide stretches of the East and Africa.
The countries and towns visited are enumerated - Marroch, Persîâ,
Arâbîe, Dâmasc, Hâlap, Arâbî, Alexandrîe. Thus Gahmuret establishes his chivalrous fame throughout the East and Africa before
the meeting with Belakâne. He then sails for Zazamanc arriving
at Pâtelamunt, the residence of the queen. Neither his voyage
there nor Pâtelamunt itself is described in detail. He leaves
Pâtelamunt by night and sails the seas for over a year (57.29-
58.4). He finally arrives at an unnamed port (58.21: "daz mer in
truoc in eine habe") and from there journeys to Sibilje. In Spain
he visits Dôlet (58.27-30) and then continues his journey to
Wâleis where he makes his way to Kanvoleis (59.21-25). Shortly
after his marriage to Herzeloyde he leaves again for the East to
offer the 'bâruc' his assistance.

We are thus merely given a brief report of Gahmuret's travels,
no more in fact than a list of place-names. This list, however,
does not seem to have been composed in a haphazard fashion. Geographical fact and fiction are freely mingled in it, purposely
so, no doubt, for the effect is striking. Two of the names, Pâtelamunt and Kanvoleis, refer to fabulous places. They appear to
be "constructed" names or else they have been purposely so cor-
rupted that they can no longer be related to geographical reality.[5] Two others, Wâleis and Zazamanc, suggest the borderline
between reality and fairyland, echoing the real world of Valois,
Wales,[6] and possibly Salamanca.[7] The remainder of the list con-

---

5 Pâtelamunt = Mont de Bataille. Parz., ed. Ernst Martin, Ger-
manist. Handbibliothek, IX, 2, Halle, 1900-1903, Vol. 2, Kommentar 17.4.
Jean Fourquet, Les Noms Propres du Parzival, in: Mélanges de
Phil. Rom. et de Litt. Méd. offerts à Ernest Hoepffner, Publications de la Faculté des Lettres, Strasbourg, 113, Paris
1949, pp. 245-260, p. 256: "Patelamunt signifie sans doute
Schiffsberg."
Kanvoleis-E. Martin. op.cit., 59.24: "... erscheint etwa Camp
Valois sein zu sollen, ist aber in der Wirklichkeit nirgends
nachzuweisen.

6 E. Martin, op.cit., 59.23: "... gemeint ist wohl Le Valois ...
zugleich aber spielt die Vorstellung von Wales in Großbritan-
nien hinein, s. zu 103.9, 121.7.

sists of place-names which are part of actual geography. These
refer to all continents of the known world. Europe is represented by Anschouwe (Anjou), Sibilje (Seville), and Dôlet (Toledo);
Africa by Marroch (Marocco) and Alexandrîe (Alexandria), and Asia
by Baldac (Bagdad), Persîâ (Persia), Arâbîe (Arabia), Dâmasc
(Damascus), Hâlap (Aleppo), and Arâbî.[8] Gahmuret in his pursuit
of chivalrous fame has thus not only travelled the world but has
ventured into such distance as to have entered fabulous regions.
His extraordinary endeavour and outstanding achievement as a
knight are conveyed by the simple device of linking actual with
fictious place-names.

Wolfram attached considerable importance to this travel-history
of Gahmuret; in Book IX we are reminded of it again by Trevrizent.
Trevrizent gives an account of his own journeys pointing out that
his path crossed that of Gahmuret, a feature by which Wolfram
invites comparison between the two. Chivalrous exploits, so he
tells Parzival, have taken him to all three continents:

> 496.1 Sus pflac ichs durch die werden
> ûf den drîn teiln der erden,
> ze Eurôpâ unt in Asîâ
> unde verre in Affricâ.

Leaving Munsalvaesche, he first came to the port of Karcobrâ in
Barbigoel where the Plimizoel flows into the sea (497.6-10)[9]. In
Sibilje he met Gahmuret who was then returning to the East after
his marriage to Herzeloyde (496.22-30). They parted company after
a short while, Gahmuret leaving for Baldac and Trevrizent making
his way towards Zilje (Celje, Yugoslavia) via Frîûl (Friuli) and
Aglei (Aqueileia) (496.19-21). From Zilje he rode out to the

---

7 Gerhart Eis, Zur Datierung des Nibelungenliedes, Forschungen
  und Fortschritte, 27(1953), 48-51. Cf. also Friedrich Panzer,
  Gahmuret. Quellenstudien, etc. p. 14: Zazamanc and Azagouc =
  "geographisch undefinierbare Länder"

8 Unidentified Eastern town.

9 Cf. E. Martin, op.cit., on 497.9.

Rôhas (Rogatec, Yugoslavia),[10] where he fought for some time
against a Slav tribe (498.21-23; 496.15-18). After the adventure
at Mount Rôhas Trevrizent rode into Gandîne (Haidin[11]), a large
town situated at the meeting of the two rivers Greian (Grajena)
and Trâ (Drava). The waters of the Trâ carry gold (498.29-499).
Zilje, Mount Rôhas, Gandîne, and the two rivers Greian and Trâ,
Trevrizent assigns to Styria - "so istz lant genennet Stîre."
In addition he mentions frequent rides to Mount Gauriûn in order
to exercise his skill at arms and to Fâmurgân for the same purpose. He recalls chivalrous deeds at Agremontîn against burning
men on one side of the mountain and ordinary mortals at the other
(496.5-14). In conclusion he stresses the importance of these
journeys as an essential part of chivalrous education and service:

> 499.9   swer schildes ambet üeben wil,
>   der muoz durchstrîchen lande vil.

The account of Trevrizent's travels again exhibits those features
already noted in Gahmuret's travel-history. Factual and fabulous
geography overlap in actual and fictitious place-names. His journeys too have taken him extraordinarily far afield. Like Gahmuret
he has visited all three continents and has penetrated to mythical
regions. In his case, however, the fabulous aspect of the travel-
history is elaborated by the addition of descriptive features, and
emphasized by the inclusion of Munsalvaesche, the Grail territory
and its precincts. Trevrizent, we must conclude, has covered
greater distance, visited countries more fantastic, and has incurred greater dangers than Gahmuret. He is therefore the more
illustrious knight of the two. As he is a member of the Grail kinship, his chivalrous deeds must surpass those of Gahmuret, and
his travel-history in consequence reveals greater wonders than
Gahmuret's journeys. This same technique of indicating disparity
of knightly renown by extending one travel-history as opposed to

---

10 But cf. also E. Martin, op.cit., 496.15: "Hier aber liegt wohl
    Verwechslung mit Roha, dem arabischen Namen von Edessa vor";
    and B. Mergell, who believes that the confusion was inten-
    tional: Der Gral in Wolframs Parzival. Entstehung und Ausbil-
    dung der Gralssage im Hochmittelalter, PBB, 73 (1951), 1-94,
    and 74 (1952), 77-159; p. 142, footnote.

the other, and including Terre de Salvaesche in one but not in
the other, is employed by Wolfram again for his differentiation
between Parzival and Gâwân.

With the beginning of the Parzival story proper in Book III, the
treatment of background changes from an outline of geography to
a description of natural scenery. While in Books I and II Wolfram's account of Gahmuret's exploits moved rapidly from one
country to another and even from continent to continent, without pausing to record distinctive detail, large parts of the
area over which Parzival and subsequently Gâwân travels are
clearly specified. Descriptive features are added which occasionally become sufficiently detailed to individualize a setting.
The character of the travel-history is, however, retained throughout. Parzival and Gâwân are forever moving, arriving, departing,
never remaining. The background shifts with each episode.

In Book III Parzival leaves Soltâne,[12] a stretch of wild, open
country in the midst of a forest where he has spent his childhood (117.7ff.). He turns towards the forest of Brizljân[13] (129.5,
6), the enchanted wood in Arthurian country. Here the encounters
with Jeschûte and Sigûne take place on the following day (129.22
ff.). Leaving Sigûne, he takes a road leading to King Arthur's
court (142.3-5). He spends the night in a fisherman's cottage
and reaches Nantes, the capital of Bertâne, the next morning
(144.5-8). After the slaying of Ithêr, Parzival sets out again
and reaches Grâharz[14] in the evening. Only a brief description

---

11 Cf. J. Weiss, Gandîne, ZfdA, 28 (1884), 136-139.

12 Evidently developed from "la gaste forest soutainne" (R shows
    variant "soltaine"). Chrestien, 75.

13 Brizljân was already known to Wolfram's audience as the magic
    forest of Arthurian kinghts through Hartmann's 'Iwein'. Nei-
    ther Soltâne nor Brizljân are named in Chrestien; see 75 and
    628-634.

14 Chrestien, 1548: Goort and variants. Is Wolfram's version
    not an obvious pun on grâ and hâr? Cf. Parzival's first words
    to Gurnemanz (162.29): "mich pat mîn muoter nemen rât/ze dem
    der grâwe locke hât".

of the castle is given (161.23, 24; 162.7-11).[15] After his departure from Grâharz Parzival rides through wild country, over
mountains and through forests across uninhabited land until he
comes to the kingdom of Brôbarz (unnamed in Chrestien). Arriving
at a waterfall he follows it down into the valley where he finds
Pelrapeire,[16] its capital (180.3-25). The next stage of his wanderings takes Parzival to Terre de Salvaesche (unnamed in Chrestien). One evening he arrives at Lake Brumbâne[17] (unnamed in the
French epic, where the lake is a river; cf. 2985ff.), where
Anfortas directs him to Munsalvaesche (unnamed in Chrestien).

Of all the places Parzival visits, Terre de Salvaesche is the
most clearly individualized. It is thus marked out as the most
important station of Parzival's travels. Description remains
brief, incidental, and indirect, but the single features, sparsely distributed and frequently only implied, attain to a coherence.
Specific, repeatedly stressed qualities of the forest setting,
its wildness, loneliness, and isolation link up to a homogeneous
scheme of landscape of characteristic aspect[18]. Its emergence as
a clearly defined setting is assisted by its recurrent use in the
epic. Its repetition represents an important departure from 'Li
Contes del Graal'. While Chrestien shows Perceval against the
background of the Grail territory only three times - during his
single ride to the castle, his meeting with his kinswoman and
his encounter with Orguelleus de la Lande - and in all probabil-
ity intended to do so only once more - at the conclusion, Wolfram uses Terre de Salvaesche as setting for eight different episodes: Parzival's first and second visit to Munsalvaesche, his

---

15 Chrestien's treatment is more elaborate, 1321-1350.

16 Chrestien, 2386; Belrepeire.

17 B. Mergell, op.cit., p. 141: "Der Name Brumbane stammt aus
    Honorius Augustodunensis." footnote: "Er ist entwickelt aus
    Tabrobane in dessen Imago mundi I. Cap. II und erscheint in
    Rudolf von Ems Weltchronik ... als Probane zur Bezeichnung
    einer Insel ..."

18 Cf. 224.19,20; 225.19-21; 250.3ff.; 282.6ff.; 435ff.; 446.6ff.
    etc.

second and third meeting with Sigûne, his joust with Orilus,
extended in the German epic by a visit to Fontâne la salvâtsche,
his trance of longing for Condwîrâmûrs, his joust with a Grail
knight, and his encounter with Trevrizent.

With the visit to Munsalvaesche the first part of Parzival's
travel-history comes to an end. Until now, the various stages
of his journey have been linked in a way which suggests logical
sequence, guidance even, along a correct and prearranged route.
In his subsequent travels Parzival does not lose this guidance
altogether, with this difference, however, that he must suppli-
cate for it, whereas before, until his first visit to Munsalvaesche, it had been granted to him as a natural privilege. He
pleads for it, or rather provokes it in Book IX:

> 452.1 Er sprach 'ist gotes kraft sô fier
> daz si beidiu ors unde tier
> unt die liut mac wîsen,
> sîn kraft wil i'm prîsen.
> mac gotes kunst die helfe hân,
> diu wîse mir diz kastelân
> daz waegest umb die reise mîn:
> sô tuot sîn güete helfe schîn:
> nu genc nâch der gotes kür.'
> den zügel gein den ôren für
> er dem orse legte,
> mit den sporn erz vaste regte.
> gein Fontân la salvâtsche ez gienc, ...

and Parzival is led to Trevrizent.[19] The unerring direction
becomes exceptional after Parzival's failure at Munsalvaesche;
guidance does not occur again in unbroken sequence as before,
until Parzival is called to the Grail.

---

19 Commenting on 'Parzival', 224.19ff., Bodo Mergell (W.v.E. und
seine französische Quellen, II: Ws. Parz., Münster, 1943,
note 6 to p. 116) also refers to this change without, however, drawing the necessary conclusions: "An diese vertiefte
Schilderung des Reitens - die ohne die Erweiterung der epischen Bewegung in den vorausgehenden Büchern nicht zu denken
ist - wird an entsprechender Stelle im IX. Buch erinnert,
wenn Parzival nach dem Kampf mit dem Gralritter, noch umfan-
gen vom zwîvel, eine ähnliche Gebärde bewusst vollzieht (Parz.
452,1ff.)."

Wolfram makes this purposeful direction of Parzival's early
travels clear by emphasizing Parzival's single-minded effort
which propels him along the right road. From the moment of
leaving Soltâne Parzival is in constant haste. On the morning
of his departure he is already eager to reach Arthur's court
as soon as possible:

> 128.13   des morgens dô der tag erschein
>   der knappe balde wart enein,
>   im was gein Artûse gâch.

He hurries along the road, having just left Jeschûte:

> 138.2   dem knappen vorn ouch was vil gâch.
>   doch wesse der unverzagte
>   niht daz man in jagte.

In the fisherman's cottage he can hardly wait until daybreak
and rides off in great haste:

> 143.15   Die naht beleip der knappe dâ:
>   man sah in smorgens anderswâ.
>   des tages er kûme erbeite.
>   der wirt ouch sich bereite
>   und lief im vor, der knappe nâch
>   reit: dô was in beiden gâch.

On Ithêr's horse he can ride at even greater speed: "er lie'z
et schûften, selten drabn" (161.21). Parzival thus speeds along
without deviating right or left. He never loses his way, not
even in wild country:

> 180.15   Doch reit er wênec irre,
>   wan die slihte an der virre
>   kom er des tages von Grâharz
>   in daz künecrîch ze Brôbarz ...

The certainty of the direction of Parzival's travels is further
reinforced by Wolfram's use of the familiar medieval technique
of gradation.[20] This principle of composition is already clearly recognizable in Chrestien's work. Wolfram, however, elaborates

---

20 Cf., e.g., the sequence of episodes in the inner story of
    Hartmann's 'Erec'; Erec's deeds of valour during his travels
    with Enîte are arranged according to their difficulty and in
    order of importance.

and perfects it with painstaking thoroughness.[21] The four experiences of Nantes, Grâharz, Brôbarz, and Munsalvaesche are arranged in order of importance. The distance and difficulty of approach increase according to the degree of significance of each episode. The logical sequence of the rising importance of these four events is reflected in the successively expanded travel-description. The road to Nantes, although pursued with great urgency, does not tax Parzival's powers unduly. The way to Arthur from the forest of Brizljân is comparatively simple; Parzival rides along a main highway:

> 142.3 eine strâze er dô gevienc,
> diu gein den Berteneysen gienc:
> diu was gestrîcht unde breit.

Afterwards, although hurrying, he must adjust his speed to that of his guide on foot:

> 143.18 der wirt ouch sich bereite
> und lief im vor, der knappe nâch
> reit: dô was in beiden gâch.

It is not until after he has been to Nantes and taken possession of Ithêr's horse that his outstanding effort commences, the quality of the knightly horse providing him with the means of realizing his latent strength (161.9-16).[22] The approach to Grâharz shows Parzival's extraordinary endurance and capacity for covering great distance:

> 161.17 gewâpent reitz der tumbe man
> den tac sô verre, ez hete lân
> ein blôz wîser, solt erz hân geriten
> zwêne tage, ez waere vermiten.
> er lie'z et schûften, selten drabn:
> er kunde im lützel ûf gehabn.

---

21 M. O'C. Walshe, The Fabulous Geography, p. 98; also, Travel Descriptions, p. 71.

22 Cf. B. Mergell, op.cit., p. 47: "Als Parzival nach dem Tode des Roten Ritters zum ersten Male ein ritterliches Ross reitet, verdoppelt Wolfram die Mächtigkeit der Bewegung des jugendlichen Reiters."

When he tells Condwîrâmûrs that his journey from Grâharz to
Brôbarz has taken him one day, she marvels at his tremendous
speed:

> 189.22 hetz anders iemen mir gesagt,
> der volge wurde im niht verjehn,
> deiz eines tages waere geschehn:
> wan swelch mîn bote ie baldest reit,
> die reise er zwêne tage vermeit.

Finally, on his way to Munsalvaesche Parzival surpasses all
previous accomplishments in travelling great distance in a short
time. He rides further and faster than ever before:

> 224.22 uns tuot diu âventiure bekant
> daz er bî dem tage reit,
> ein vogel hetes arbeit,
> solt erz allez hân erflogen.
> mich enhab diu âventiure betrogen,
> sîn reise unnâch was sô grôz
> des tages do er Ithêren schôz,
> unt sît dô er von Grâharz
> kom in daz lant ze Brôbarz.[23]

All these features - Parzival's haste, his capacity for finding
the right way out of wild uninhabited country, his single-minded
pursuit of the roads leading to the scenes of experiences ever
increasing in importance - intensify the impression of supernatural guidance through a pattern pre-ordained. Active, outside guidance becomes conspicuous in Parzival's journey to
Munsalvaesche:

> 224.19 mit gewalt den zoum daz ros
> truog über ronen und durchez mos:
> wandez wîste niemens hant.

Neither Parzival nor anyone else directs the horse, but it is
led through virgin country and over immense distance straight
to Lake Brumbâne - Parzival is guided by the hand of God.[24]

---

23 Chrestien mentions Perceval's speed and endurance on horse-
    back only once (3120-3129).

24 M. O'C. Walshe in Notes on Parzival, Bk. V, London Mediaeval
    Studies, 1 (1937-39), 340-352; here p. 343, suggests that
    "the sense here is probably rather that there was nobody
    to show Parzival the way:" but adds - "this does not exclude

This guidance makes itself felt particularly in the treacherous
stretch of country between the lake and the Grail castle. Anfortas warns:

> 226.6 hüet iuch: dâ gênt unkunde wege:
> ir muget an der lîten
> wol misserîten, ...

but Parzival immediately and without effort finds the right
path:

> 226.10 Parzivâl der huop sich dan,
> er begunde wackerlîchen draben
> den rehten pfat unz an den graben.

After his failure at Munsalvaesche, however, he loses this capacity for finding the right road and is lost; he cannot follow
the tracks of the Grail knights:

> 249.5 do begunde krenken sich ir spor:
> sich schieden die dâ riten vor.
> ir slâ wart smal, diu ê was breit:
> er verlôs si gar:daz was im leit.

The loss of this gift marks the beginning of suffering:

> 249.9 maer vriesch dô der junge man,
> dâ von er herzenôt gewan.

and the rides at random begin.[25] Parzival's travels from now
on assume a different character, they become âventiure proper:
hazardous, chivalrous existence, deliberately seeking out
danger. Divine protection is withdrawn after the visit to
Munsalvaesche and Parzival's travel-history changes into that
of a traditional chevalier errant of the medieval romances:

> 249.3 sîn scheiden dan daz riwet mich.
> alrêrst nu âventiurt ez sich.

---

the possibility that Parzival allowed the horse to take its
own road ..." Even this interpretation would lend support
to the point made above - no human hand, neither that of
Parzival nor anyone else's, leads Parzival's horse either
by controlling its reins or (as here) by pointing out the
way.

25 Chrestien does not employ the motif of the lost tracks.
Perceval finds not only a path but also hoofmarks of horses

In the meantime riding further and further away from Munsalvaesche and ultimately leaving Terre de Salvaesche, Parzival
comes upon Sigûne in the Grail forest, about a mile away from
the castle (250.13-15). He meets her early in the morning (249.
13) and, considerably later in the day, Orilus, whose tracks
he discovers (256.5ff.). After the joust, all three - Orilus,
Jeschûte, and Parzival - ride on to Fontâne la salvâtsche (452.
13, 14), where Parzival takes the oath. Up to this point the
travel-history is to be imagined as spread over a period of
more than a year (139.20,21). From Fontâne la salvâtsche Parzival continues through the Grail forest, reaches its outskirts,
and finally arrives in a field by the Plimizoel (281.10-282.11).[26]

After Cundrîe's curse, Gâwân temporarily becomes the hero of the
narrative, and it is essentially his travel-history with which
the poet is concerned from Book VII onwards. In 'Li Contes del
Graal' Perceval appears only once more, when confessing his sins,
after Gauvain's travels have begun. There is no suggestion of a
journey parallel to that of Gauvain. In Wolfram, however, Parzival's travel-history continues in the background, and the two
journeys are obviously meant to be compared. Parzival follows
largely the same route as Gâwân and visits all the scenes of
Gâwân's exploits with the exception of Schanpfanzûn (Book VIII)
und Barbigoel (Book V). Occasionally he visits these places
before Gâwân's arrival, as Terre Marveile[27] (559.9, 10), sometimes
after, as Li Gweiz Prelljûs[28] (701.1-4) and at Bêârosche[29] their
presence is simultaneous (392.20-393.2). Beginning with the departure from Arthur's camp by the Plimizoel and ending with
Gâwân's and Parzival's meeting near Jôflanze, their travels are

---

which lead him straight to his cousin (3422-3431).

26 No river mentioned in Chrestien; cf. 4160ff.
27 No equivalents in Chrestien. Bêârosche, as Gâwân's first
    adventure, corresponds to Tintaguel.
28 Chrestien, 8495: Le Guê Perilleus.
29 No equivalent in Chrestien.

spread over almost five years (646.14-18). During this time
Parzival manages to travel far more extensively than Gâwân, for
not only does he appear in all the places visited by Gâwân, except the two already mentioned, but in addition returns to Terre
de Salvaesche twice (Book IX), rides to Karnant (434.25-30), and
journeys in parts unknown and unnamed, as his long recitation of
exploits in Book XV reveals (772.1-23). His travels have taken
him so far afield that he no longer has a clear recollection of
the number of countries through which he has passed, nor of their
names:

> 772.24 diz ergienc dâ turnieren was,
> die wîle ich nâch dem grâle reit.
> solt ich gar nennen dâ ich streit,
> daz waeren unkundiu zil:
> durch nôt ichs muoz verswîgen vil.
> swaz ir mir kunt ist getân,
> die waene ich genennet hân.

Wolfram thus clearly differentiates between the relative significance of Gâwân's and Parzival's travels in the same way as in the
travel-histories of Gahmuret and Trevrizent. The travel-history
of the more significant character in the narrative is considerably extended, Trevrizent's as against Gahmuret's, Parzival's
as compared with that of Gâwân. The emphasis is primarily achieved by an extension of the geography, although the addition of
more detailed descriptive features plays its part as well, as
has been shown in the case of Trevrizent. This latter point
hardly applies, however, to the travel-description of the section comprising Books VII-XIII, as (with the exception of Book
IX, solely devoted to the exploration of Terre de Salvaesche
by Parzival) they are concerned with Gâwân's travel-history
and not with that of Parzival. The features of natural description, therefore, elaborated in this section are linked with
Gâwân, Parzival only borrowing, as it were, the geography of
Gâwân's travels but not sharing in their setting. In spite of
this disadvantage, then, of not being able to associate the
occasionally clearly individualized background with Parzival's
travel-history, Wolfram still manages to retain its character as

the more illustrious quest of the two by the skilful introduction of Parzival's own summary of his additional travels in Book
XV and the return to Parzival's travel-history in Book IX.

This extension of geography, with its implication of greater
distance and wider chivalrous experience, is a means by which
Wolfram expresses a differentiation in degree between the two
travel-histories. Another by which he distinguishes in kind
takes again the same form as in the comparison of Gahmuret with
Trevrizent - one travel-history includes Terre de Salvasche,
the other does not. In the case of Parzival and Gâwân, however,
this motif is heavily emphasized. Parzival has complete and
free access at all times to Gâwân's stations of knightly exploits. Gâwân, on the other hand, cannot encroach upon certain
parts touched by Parzival's travels and indeed cannot even
approach them: Terre de Salvaesche remains beyond Gâwân's travel-
experience. It is made clear that this is by no means accidental,
for from Book VIII onwards Gâwân is actively engaged in the
search of the Grail. King Vergulaht exacts this promise from
him:

> 428.19 ich verkiuse ûf iuch mîn herzeleit,
> welt ir mir geben sicherheit
> daz ir mir werbet sunder twâl
> mit guoten triwen umben grâl.

Gâwan accepts and immediately sets out on the quest (428.23-26).
The closing lines of Book VIII repeat the purpose of his journey
and in their subtle suggestiveness make the audience expect to
see Gâwân approaching Terre de Salvaesche in Book IX:

> 432.29 nâch dem grâle im sicherheit gebôt:
> er reit al ein gein wunders nôt.

Instead, however, the story of Gâwân's travels breaks off, and
the narrative returns to Parzival, who is once again in Terre
de Salvaesche (435.2ff.). The change at this characteristic point
strikingly illuminates the difference between the two travel-
histories. While Parzival has constant access to Grail territory,
Gâwân seems to be striking off in an entirely different direc-

tion. In the beginning of Book X his search for the Grail is
mentioned again (503.21-30), but his travels take him to different parts. This particular feature of the geographical
limitation of Gâwân's travel-history, the exclusion of the
Grail territory, thus serves to demonstrate the dissimilar nature of the two quests. The differentiation in degree is linked
with a differentiation in kind.

With the beginning of Gâwân's travels in Book VII the background
continues to be represented as shifting scenery. From the
Plimizoel Gâwân sets out for Ascalûn (335.1-3). He interrupts
his journey to take part in the fighting at Bêârosche (350.16)
which Parzival reaches slightly earlier than he (383.23-29). The
next stage of his travels takes him to Schanpfanzûn in Ascalûn
(398.18ff.).[30] Parzival does not appear here but shares indirectly in this particular episode through the king of Ascalûn,
Vergulaht, who relates how he was defeated by him in the forest
Laehtamrîs (424.15ff.). Book IX returns to Parzival's travel-
history.

At the beginning there is brief indication that Parzival's travels
have not been confined to his visits to Bêârosche and the forest
Laehtamrîs since his departure from the Plimizoel, but have been
spread over a far wider area:

> 434.11 nu tuot uns de âventiure bekant,
> er habe erstrichen manec lant,
> zors, unt in schiffen ûf dem wâc.

He has been to Karnant (434.29) and now finds himself in Terre
de Salvaesche by Sigûne's anchorhold (435.2ff.). After the joust
with the Grail knight, he rides away from Munsalvaesche without
realizing it (445.28-30).

The brief transition passage linking this and the subsequent
scene indicates that some considerable time has elapsed since
this joust:

---

30 Escavalon in Chrestien, 5315ff.

446.3   desn prüeve ich niht der wochen zal,
        über wie lanc sider Parzivâl
        reit durch âventiure als ê.

He is next shown approaching a forest (446.9: "ez was ûf einem
grôzen walt"), the Grail forest, as becomes clear from the events
that follow. He meets Kahenîs and his company, and learns that
it is Good Friday (448.7: "ez ist hiute der karfrîtac"). After
their parting he decides to call upon God for guidance in his
travels (451.13-452.9).[31] Characteristically, it is now his
Grail horse which, as the instrument of divine assistance, leads
Parzival to Trevrizent, he himself having lost the power of finding the right way since his failure at Munsalvaesche:

452.9   'nu genc nâch der gotes kür.'
        den zügel gein den ôren für
        er dem orse legte,
        mit den sporn erz vaste regte.
        gein Fontân la salvâtsche ez gienc, ...

He is carried along the tracks left by Kahenîs and his company
(455.23, 24), thus penetrating deeper into the Grail forest. In
spite of thick snow, he recognizes the mountainside as the place
of his joust with Orilus (455.25-30). His horse continues and
halts at Fontâne la salvâtsche (456.1-14).

The space accorded to direct description of Fontâne la salvâtsche,
so important a stage in Parzival's travel-history, is as for
other parts of the background, exceedingly small. In spite of
this brevity, however, a clear picture of the setting emerges,
and its unrelieved austerity sets it apart. It is in particular
one aspect which compels attention and singles it out as being
of especial significance in the narrative - that of the snowfall.

In Wolfram's work the natural setting is twice presented as a
winter-landscape - once at the beginning of Book VI after Parzival's first visit to Munsalvaesche and again in Book IX when

---

31 The concept of supernatural guidance does not enter into
    Chrestien's description. Perceval follows a carefully marked
    path to the hermit (6318ff.).

Parzival seeks out Trevrizent. On both occasions the scene is laid in Terre de Salvaesche. In Chrestien only the first episode is envisaged as a snow scene, and there is no reason to suppose that either takes place on Grail territory. Wolfram's changes establish a link between the two scenes indicating an inner connection.

Moreover, turning to his audience, he pointedly emphasizes the rarity of snow scenes in contemporary Arthurian literature:

> 281.10 welt ir nu hoeren war sî komn
> Parzivâl der Wâleis?
> von snêwe was ein niwe leis
> des nahtes vast ûf in gesnît.
> ez enwas iedoch niht snêwes zît,
> istz als ichz vernomen hân.
> Artûs der meienbaere man,
> swaz man ie von dem gesprach,
> zeinen pfinxten daz geschach,
> odr in des meien bluomenzît.
> waz man im süezes luftes gît!
> diz maere ist hie vast undersniten,
> ez parriert sich mit snêwes siten.

His insistence suggests that specific meaning attaches to the appearance of a winter-landscape, which indeed it does, as the examination of the relevant passages shows.

The unusual snowfall in Book VI is explained by Trevrizent in Book IX: with the rise of Saturn, Anfortas's pain increases, and snow falls during the following night:

> 489.24 dô der sterne Sâturnus
> wider an sîn zil gestuont,
> daz wart uns bî der wunden kuont,
> unt bî dem sumerlîchen snê. 32

The wintry landscape through which Parzival rides in Book VI, and again on Good Friday in Book IX (446.6-8), is the visible reminder of Anfortas's continued and, on these two occasions, severely aggravated suffering. Parzival's failure at the Grail

---

32 Cf. B. Mergell, op.cit., pp. 179-180, and Hermann J. Weigand, Die epischen Zeitverhältnisse in den Graldichtungen Chrestiens und Wolframs, PMLA, 53 (1938), 917-950, here p. 937ff. Both

castle is foreshadowed by Anfortas's unparallelled physical anguish:

> 492.23 der wirt sprach 'neve, sît noch ê
> wart dem künige niht sô wê,
> wan dô sîn komen zeigte sus
> der sterne Sâturnus:
> der kan mit grôzem froste komn.
> drûf legen moht uns niht gefromn,
> als manz ê drûffe ligen sach:
> daz sper man in die wunden stach.
> Sâturnus louft sô hôhe enbor
> daz ez diu wunde wesse vor,
> ê der ander frost koem her nâch.
> dem snê was ninder als gâch,
> er viel alrêrst an dr andern naht
> in der sumerlîchen maht.

The rise of the planet, Anfortas's racking pain, the snowfall, and Parzival's sins are closely linked. With Parzival's sin of omission at Munsalvaesche, Anfortas's agony is continued, snow falls, and Parzival rides across frost-covered country. Just before the full extent of his sins is revealed to him by Trevrizent, snow falls again, symbolizing Anfortas's torment. On both occasions Anfortas's physical anguish and Parzival's utter desolation are intertwined, Anfortas's suffering echoes in Parzival, it becomes cosmic suffering - a feature underlined by the connection of Anfortas's pain with the ascent and decline of the planet - and the world is transformed into a wintry landscape.

In Book VI Parzival's difficulties in snow-covered country, his physical discomfort (282.1ff.), his bewildered search for a way out of the forest, are his own doing. Divine guidance is withdrawn immediately after his failure to ask the question, but in addition this failure means continued agony for Anfortas. As no healing question intervenes, there is the inevitable fall of snow, and the setting of Parzival's travels is transformed into cold and inhospitable landscape.

---

comment on the connection of the summer snow in Bk. VI with Anfortas's pain and the rise of the planet, but neither links these three features with Parzival's guilt. In Chrestien, incidentally, there is no relation between the suffering of the Fisher King and the planets.

In the same sense, he is equally responsible for his trance
following the vision conjured up by the blood on the snow. His
misery, through a complex, interrelated chain of events, is self-
inflicted.

The connection between the two snow scenes of Books VI and IX
is demonstrated furthermore by their stylistic interdependence.
Various aspects of the scene in Book VI reappear as elaborated
and extended in Book IX. The physical discomfort to which Parzival is subjected in Book VI appears as a more painful experience
in Book IX. In Book VI it is mentioned only briefly that Parzival suffered from intense cold while spending the night in the
forest:

> 282   Die naht bî Parzivâle er[33] stuont,
> da in bêden was der walt unkuont
> und dâ se bêde sêre vrôs.

In Book IX the cold is so severe that the stranger knight in his
armour excites the pity of Kahenîs's daughters:

> 448.28   'was wilt du, vater, rechen?
> sô boese weter wir nu hân,
> waz râts nimstu dich gein im an?
> Wan füerstun da er erwarme?
> Sîne gîserten arme,
> swie rîterlîch die sîn gestalt,
> uns dunct doch des, si haben kalt:
> er erfrüre, waern sîn eines drî.'

At Fontâne la salvâtsche he suffers pathetically from the frost:

> 459   Parzivâl stuont ûffem snê.
> ez taete eim kranken manne wê,
> ob er harnasch trüege
> dâ der frost sus an in slüege.

Whereas the harshness of the winter setting of Book VI is only
briefly sketched, the austere background to Fontâne la salvâtsche
is stressed repeatedly, Parzival now sharing in Trevrizent's self-
imposed hardship. Again, while in Book VI the withdrawal of di-

---

33   King Arthur's falcon.

vine guidance had only recently occurred, the rides at random,
when Parzival appears at Fontâne la salvâtsche for the second
time in Book IX, have lasted for approximately four and one half
years.[34] Parzival himself exclaims at the immense amount of time
spent in aimless wandering:

> 460.28 alrêrst ich innen worden bin
> wie lange ich var wîselôs
> unt daz freuden helfe mich verkôs.

Finally, in Book IX, the cosmic significance of the pattern,
the interrelation of the ascent of the planet, Anfortas's pain,
the snowfall and Parzival's sins and suffering, is deepened,
reiterated as it is on Good Friday against the background of
Christ's Passion. Thus the second snow scene in Book IX may be
taken as the logical counterpart to the similar scene in Book
VI and as its concluding climax.

That the snowfall and Parzival's sinfulness are linked in this
symbolic fashion can be seen further in Book XVI, where the pattern of the four features is broken. Had Parzival asked the
fateful question at Munsalvaesche, the snowfall would not have
occurred. For in Book XVI, when Anfortas's increased pain recurs,
this time associated with the rise of Jupiter or Mars (789.4-17),[35]

---

34 The day after his failure at Munsalvaesche Parzival takes
the oath for Jeschûte at Fontâne la salvâtsche. He notices
a lance in Trevrizent's cell (268.29: "ein gemâlet sper
derbî dâ lent") and takes it with him. (271.10: "Parzivâl
diz sper von Troys/ nam und fuortez mit im dan.") This lance
is mentioned again in Book IX and Parzival asks, how long it
is that he took it:

> 460.5 ein gemâlt sper derbî ich vant:
> hêr, daz nam al hie mîn hant;
> ....
> 17 wie lanc ist von der zîte her,
> hêr, daz ich hie nam daz sper?

Trevrizent calculates the exact lapse of time for him:

> 460.22 'fünfthalp jâr unt drî tage
> ist daz irz im nâmet hie.
> welt irz hoern, ich prüeve iu wie.'
> ame salter laser im über al

snow does not follow, as Parzival, vindicated by his conduct,
absolved from his sins, and already called to the Grail, is on
his way to Munsalvaesche, ready to ask the required question
and thus releasing Anfortas from his suffering (789.18, 19).
By allotting a specified location to two episodes, by emphasizing, repeating, and explaining one single feature - the snowfall - and by introducing the significance of the planets, Wolfram achieves a pattern of symbolic connections which elucidates
his theme and greatly enhances its poetic impact.[36]

After the episode at Fontâne la salvâtsche the narrative again
takes up Gâwân's travel-history in Book X. He has been to
Barbigoel (503.5-20), and has continued from there in search
of the Grail (503.21-30). He next reaches Lôgroys, and then, in
company with Orgelûse, Terre Marveile (507.29ff. and 534.20ff.).[37]
From Plippalinôt, the ferryman with whom he lodges for one
night, he learns the name of the magnificent castle nearby,
Schastel Marveile (557.1-9).

> diu jâr und gar der wochen zal,
> die dâ zwischen wâren hin.

35 The change of the planet here from Saturn to Jupiter or Mars
    may be to indicate the dissimilar course of events to follow.
    For while Wolfram and his contemporaries looked upon Saturn
    as wholly evil, Mars was perhaps slightly less so, and Jupi-
    ter was considered good. Cf. Hasting's Encyclopaedia of
    Religion and Ethics; entry: Sun, Moon and Stars.

36 Alain Renoir, Gawain and Parzival, Studia neophilologica,
    31 (1959), 155-158, would cast doubt on the originality of
    the motif of the snowfall in Book IX, and wonders whether
    it might not be traced back 'to a lost manuscript tradition
    of Chrestien's Perceval', (p. 157ff.).

37 The corresponding places in Chrestien are Galvoie (6600ff.)
    and La Roche de Chanpguin (8813-8817). Lôgroys is based on
    Logres, the birthplace of l'Orguelleuse de Logres (8637-
    8640). It is mentioned also in connection with the bleeding
    lance (6166-6171).

Although Gâwân's journeys do not end at Schastel Marveile and
although his chivalrous exploits continue after his success
here, Schastel Marveile assumes the central position in Gâwân's
travel-history. It is to Schastel Marveile that he returns after
Li Gweiz Prelljûs (615.12ff.) and again at the end of his travel-
history.[38] It represents the climax of his chivalrous endeavour,
just as Munsalvaesche represents the high mark of Parzival's
achievement. He becomes lord of the castle, and over Terre
Marveile, just as Parzival will be crowned king at Munsalvaesche.
The parallel features of Schastel Marveile and Munsalvaesche are
manifold, but there are two which particularly concern the question of the travel-history.

Both Schastel Marveile and Munsalvaesche are placed at the conclusion of the first part of the respective strands of the narrative. Their position is carefully marked by the technique of
gradation, which is discontinued in the subsequent episodes. In
Parzival's travel-history Nantes, Grâharz, Brôbarz, and Munsalvaesche are arranged in order of rising significance. This same
pattern is repeated in the Gâwân narrative, in the sequence,
Bêârosche, Ascalûn, Lôgroys, and Schastel Marveile. Gâwân, it
is true, visits Barbigoel as well (503.5-20), before reaching
Lôgroys. However, his visit to Barbigoel appears as a mere digression in the course of his travel-history, and is consequent-

---

38 It is not specifically stated that he returns to Schastel
    Marveile in the end, but it may be inferred from a passage
    in Book XVI. When Feirefîz returns to Jôflanze on his home-
    ward journey, he finds it almost deserted, most of the
    knights, among them Gâwân, having returned to their own
    countries:

           822   Liute ein teil si funden.
                 an den selben stunden
                 Feirefîz frâgete maere,
                 war daz her komen waere,
                 ieslîcher was in sîn lant,
                 dar im diu reise was bekant:
                 Artûs was gein Schamilôt.

ly not included in the scheme of gradation. It is not presented
in full as a separate episode, as are the other four. Wolfram
contents himself with a passing mention of Barbigoel, thus re-
moving the initial cause of Gâwân's travels (320.22ff.) and clear-
ing him of a false accusation. At the same time he renders Gâwân
free for greater and more important exploits, ultimately allowing
him to fulfil Cundrîe's second challenge.[39] The parallelism of
the two quests, already evident in the partial congruence of the
travel-histories and the combined search for the Grail, is reinforced from a new angle after Barbigoel. Both Gâwân and Parzival in the end answer the challenges uttered by the same messenger. Both are urged to their finest achievement by Cundrîe.[40]

The pattern of gradation which links the stations of Gâwân's
travels was noted long ago from the point of view of content.[41]
As in the corresponding sequence of Parzival's travels, this is

---

39 Immediately after her condemnation of Parzival in Book VI
    Cundrîe speaks of Schastel Marveile:

    318.13 si sprach 'ist hie kein rîter wert,
            des ellen prîses hât gegert,
            unt dar zuo hôher minne?
            ich weiz vier küneginne
            unt vier hundert juncfrouwen,
            die man gerne möhte schouwen.
            ze Schastel marveil die sint:
            al âventiure ist ein wint,
            wan die man dâ bezaln mac,
            hôher minne wert bejac.

40 Wolfram has here fully elaborated a motif suggested in the
    French text. The ugly messenger in Chrestien mentions, apart
    from the Grail castle, the Chastel Orguelleus (4689) and
    the damsel at Montescleire (4706-07). Gauvain vows to set
    her free (4718-4720), but never reaches Montescleire. In the
    same way Wolfram has followed up the motif of a combined
    search of the two heroes. In Chrestien both Perceval and
    Gauvain are pledged to seek the bleeding lance; Perceval
    accepts the messenger's challenge (4727-4740) and Gauvain
    follows the King of Escavalon's bidding (6110ff.).

41 G. Ehrismann, Gesch. d. dtsch. Lit. bis z. Ausgang d. Mittel-
    alters: D. mhd. Lit. Blütezeit. Vol. 2, II, 1, Munich, 1927,
    p. 231: "Die Erzählungskunst Chrestiens und der Artusdichter
    ist stark in Steigerungen und Kontrastwirkungen. Die Gawan-
    handlung als ein Stück Artusroman ist nach dem Gesetz der

supported by the progressively expanded use of a certain theme.
In Parzival's travel-history it is his mounting physical endurance,
the rising speed with which he conquers greater and yet greater
distance. With Gâwân it is the steadily increasing elaboration of
description relating to the castle he is about to visit. The excellence of the castles visited is a <u>sine qua non</u>. The last three,
however, are given individual features by which each surpasses
the previous one. For the first, Bêârosche, the customary hyper-
boles suffice:

> 350.17 burg und stat sô vor im lac,
> daz niemen bezzers hûses pflac.
> ouch gleste gein im schône
> aller ander bürge ein krône
> mit türnen wol gezieret.

Schanpfanzûn in Ascalûn on the other hand, is more imposing than
Carthage:

> 399.11 disiu burc was gehêret sô,
> daz Enêas Kartâgô
> nie sô hêrrenlîche vant,
> dâ froun Dîdôn tôt was minnen pfant.

Its dimensions are extraordinary, and it has as many towers,
turrets and buildings as Acratôn[42] (399.15ff.). Its great height
and position by the sea afford it ample protection against attack:

> 399.21 si was alumbe wol sô hôch,
> und dâ si gein dem mer gezôch:
> decheinen sturm si widersaz,
> noch grôzen ungefüegen haz.

The field before it measures a league (399.25). Its size and
architecture are so remarkable that Wolfram feels compelled to
mention it once again, as Gâwân rides into Schanpfanzûn:

Steigerung aufgebaut: Drei Damenverhältnisse, die von blosser
Spielerei (Obilot) und sinnlicher Reizung (Antikonie) zu
ernster Verliebtheit (Orgeluse) aufsteigen, drei Tapferkeits-
proben (Bearosche, Ascalun, Schastelmarveil), deren letzte
die schwerste Leistung ist."

42 E.Hartl, Verzeichnis: "Acraton - vielleicht Acra, Accaron-
Acon, heute Akka" = Acre.

403.15 swer bûwes ie begunde,
        baz denne ich sprechen kunde
        von dises bûwes veste.
        dâ lac ein burc, diu beste
        diu ie genant was ertstift:
        unmâzen wît was ir begrift.

Lôgroys, the next castle visited by Gâwân, has two characteristic
and highly prized features which render it unique. It stands on
a steep, terraced mount which makes it invincible, as it is in-
accessible to the enemy from three sides:

508.1   An der bürge lâgen lobes were.
        nâch trendeln mâze was ir berc:
        swâ si verre sach der tumbe,
        er wând si liefe alumbe.
        der bürge man noch hiute giht
        daz gein ir sturmes hôrte niht:
        si forhte wênec selhe nôt,
        swâ man hazzen gein ir bôt.

It also boasts an unusual, exotic orchard:

508.9   alumben berc lac ein hac,
        des man mit edelen boumen pflac.
        vîgen boum, grânât,
        öle, wîn und ander rât,
        des wuohs dâ ganziu rîcheit.

Schastel Marveile, finally, appears to Gâwân as the paragon of
castles (534.20-30). Its fortifications defy any attack:

564.27 er vant der bürge wîte,
        daz ieslîch ir sîte
        stuont mit bûwenlîcher wer.
        für allen sturm niht ein ber
        gaeb si ze drîzec jâren,
        op man ir wolte vâren.

Marvel after marvel is revealed. The roof of the main building
has the appearance of a peacock's plumage, dimmed by neither
rain nor snow (565.7ff.). The interior reveals exquisite orna-
mentation (565.13ff.). Its intricate and highly ornamental
architecture is described in detail after Gâwân has made himself master of Schastel Marveile. It displays a richness such
as he has never seen before:

588.28   sînen ougen wart nie bekant
            rîchheit diu dar zuo töhte
            daz si dem glîchen möhte.

A spiral archway rises high in the hall, crowned by the marvel-
lous pillar:

589   ûf durch den palas einesît
               gienc ein gewelbe niht ze wît,
               gegrêdet über den palas hôch:
               sinwel sich daz umbe zôch.
               dar ûffe stuont ein clâriu sûl.

It is round as a tent - 'sinwel als ein gezelt ez was' (589.13).
The windows and roof are fashioned from all manner of precious
stones:

589.18   adamas und amatiste
            (diu âventiure uns wizzen lât),
            thôpazje und grânât,
            crisolte, rubbîne,
            smârâde, sardîne,
            sus wârn diu venster rîche,
            wît unt hôch gelîche
            als man der venster siule sach
            der art was obene al daz dach.

In addition to this untold treasure Schastel Marveile boasts
the 'Lît marveile' (566.11ff.) and the 'Krâmgewant' (562.22ff.).

Thus the rising significance of each experience, at Bêârosche,
Ascalûn, Lôgroys, and Schastel Marveile, is reflected in the ever
increasing beauty and excellence of the background against which
each episode is enacted. Schastel Marveile surpasses them all in
exotic splendour, in importance and the difficulty of the test.
It becomes the focal point of Gâwân's travel-history, for it is
at Schastel Marveile that he establishes himself in his proper
sphere, making himself master of its riches. The remainder of his
travel-history is mere sequel to the great exploit of Schastel
Marveile. The scheme of gradation in the travel-history ceases
as soon as the hero arrives at the location of his highest
achievement. For Gâwân it is Schastel Marveile, for Parzival
Munsalvaesche. That the last part of Gâwân's travel-history is
to be understood as being sequel only to Schastel Marveile is

unequivocally stated by Wolfram himself. For, when Wolfram, at
the beginning of Book XII, compares Gâwân's conquest of Schastel
Marveile with other deeds of valour famous in contemporary literature, dismissing them one by one as not requiring the supreme
prowess necessary for the adventure at Schastel Marveile, he
includes Li Gweiz Prelljûs, the next station of Gâwân's travel-
history:

> 583.25 Li gweiz prelljûs der furt,
> und Erek der Schoydelakurt
> erstreit ab Mâbonagrîn,
> der newederz gap sô hôhen pîn,
> ....

In spite of the continuance of Gâwân's travels after Schastel
Marveile, this particular adventure retains its central position.

After the conquest of Schastel Marveile Gâwân is led by Orgelûse
to Li Gweiz Prelljûs in the river Sabîns[43] (602ff.). He refuses
to accompany Gramoflanz to Rosche Sabbîns[44] (610.26), where the
river is bridged, and regains the opposite shore by taking a
flying jump on horseback. Both he and Orgelûse then return to
Schastel Marveile (615.12, 13). After a brief stay here, Gâwân
and his retinue proceed to Jôflanze (667.9ff.). Here Gâwân's
and Parzival's travels converge. Their presence is not merely
simultaneous as at Bêârosche; they meet at the river Sabîns
(678.18ff.), near Jôflanze. Gâwân's journeys are at an end.
From Jôflanze he returns again to Schastel Marveile (822.1-6).

Parzival's parallel movement has continued after the break of
Book IX. In Book XII, after her reconciliation with Gâwân,
Orgelûse recalls Parzival's appearance before Lôgroys:

---

43 Unnamed in Chrestien.
44 Rosche Sabbîns corresponds to Orquelenes (Chrestien, 8626).

618.19 mînen lîp gesach nie man,
        ine möhte wol sîn diens hân;
        wan einer, der truoc wâpen rôt.
        mîn gesinde er brâht in nôt:
        für Lôgroys er kom geritn ...

In the same way as Gâwân, he proceeded from Lôgroys to Terre
Marveile:

618.27 zwischen Lôgroys unde iurm urvar,
        mîner rîtr im volgeten fünfe dar:
        die enschumpfierter ûf dem plân
        und gap diu ors dem schifman.

In Book XI Gâwân had already been informed of Parzival's earlier
visit to Terre Marveile by Plippalinôt:

559.9   der Ithêrn vor Nantes sluoc,
        mîn schif in gestern über truoc.
        er hât mir fünf ors gegebn
        (got in mit saelden lâze lebn),
        diu herzogen und künege riten.
        swaz er hât ab in erstriten,
        daz wirt ze Pelrapeire gesagt:
        ir sicherheit hât er bejagt.
        sîn schilt treit maneger tjoste mâl.
        er reit hie vorschen umben grâl.

His visit to Lôgroys must therefore also have preceded Gâwân's.
Contrary to Gâwân, Parzival does not remain in Terre Marveile,
but continues on his way immediately after the defeat of
Orgelûse's followers. Neither does he learn of the secrets of
Schastel Marveile from Plippalinôt (559.19-26). Li Gweiz Prelljûs
is finally reached by Parzival after Gâwân's visit. When they
meet by the river Sabîns near Jôflanze, Gâwân notices a branch
from Gramoflanz's tree in the stranger knight's possession:

679.14 er hêt ouch gebrochen
        von dem boum, des Gramoflanz
        huote, ein sô liehten kranz
        daz Gâwânz rîs erkande.

After their joust Parzival confirms this:

701   der dâ heizt rois Gramoflanz
        von sînem boume ich einen kranz
        brach hiute morgen fruo,
        daz er mir strîten fuorte zuo.

With Parzival's arrival at Jôflanze the narrative once again
returns to his travel-history proper. Its third and last part
is taken up largely with Parzival's return to Munsalvaesche.
There is only one brief interlude, a journey out of and back
to Jôflanze, before he is readmitted to Grail territory. He
leaves Jôflanze at dawn (733.30) and meets Feirefîz in open
country near a forest (735.5-8). Their encounter takes place
in Terre Marveile, within six miles or less of Schastel Marveile
(755.16-21; 759.21-23). Both ride back to Arthur's camp at
Jôflanze (753.25ff.). Here Parzival is given the opportunity
of reciting a long list of knights defeated by him during his
travels (772.1-23). It is not clear where the majority of these
encounters occurred; Parzival himself is not certain of the
great variety of countries visited by him (772.24-30). A number
of these knights were overcome by him away from their own countries. Thus he captures Schirnîel and Mirabel at Bêârosche
(384.7-9), as well as Marangliez (384.11, 12). Vergulaht he
meets in the forest of Laehtamrîs (424.15-26). The rest do not
appear elsewhere in the work. All the countries mentioned except
two, Arl (Arles) and Jeroplîs,[45] belong to Wolfram's fabulous
geography,[46] indicating by their very names and profusion the
mysterious distance into which Parzival was drawn during his
travels.

After having been called to the Grail, he and Feirefîz depart
for Munsalvaesche, led by Cundrîe (786.30). They penetrate into
Terre de Salvaesche without difficulty (792.10-13), and ride
straight to Munsalvaesche (793.29, 30). From here Parzival sets
out again to meet Condwîrâmûrs. A number of Grail knights lead
him to Fontâne la salvâtsche (797.17, 18), and then through the
forest to the Plimizoel, where Condwîrâmûrs is waiting (799.9-
17). On their return to Munsalvaesche Parzival asks to be shown

---

45 E. Hartl, Hierapolis in Mesopotamia.

46 The remainder of these place-names cannot be identified.
    Cf. J. Fourquet, op.cit., p. 252.

to Sigûne's anchorage (804.8ff.) His journey ends at Munsalvaesche (805.16, 17).

In this brief description of the third and last part of Parzival's travel-history, one significant feature clearly emerges
- as soon as he is called to the Grail, he is again assisted
in his travels. His rides are once again marked by speed, ease,
certain direction, and definite aim. Guidance now appears in
concrete form; the servants of the Grail serve Parzival, and
so Cundrîe leads him from Jôflanze to Munsalvaesche, and the
Grail knights guide him through the forest to Fontâne la salvâtsche and the Plimizoel, to Sigûne's anchorage and back to
Munsalvaesche. The gift, temporarily in abeyance through his
own doing, is restored to him in greater power than ever before.

This vast travel-history of Parzival, although beyond the reach
and capacity of the ordinary and even the excellent knight, and
unique in the resultant sum of experience, is never permitted
by Wolfram to dissociate itself entirely from the world of
chivalry, represented in this work, as in others, by the
Arthurian court. Parzival's road, although lonely, is not
isolated from the normal chivalrous world; it is not pursued
in forgetfulness of the Arthurian scene.

His travel-history throughout remains firmly linked, indeed
anchored, in the Arthurian setting. This close connection is
exemplified by the role played by the Arthurian court in the
structure of the travel-history and by the repeated reminders
of King Arthur's court which occur at several points.

The scenery of the Arthurian court is as mobile as that of
Parzival's and Gâwân's travel-histories; it is, in fact, a
travel-history in nucleus itself. In spite of its mobility,
however, the Arthurian court remains a constant for both Parzival and Gâwân. It is never withdrawn beyond their reach; its
changing location can always be easily traced.

Structurally Parzival's travel-history falls into three distinct
sections, the first embracing his departure from Soltâne, his
entry into the world of chivalry at Nantes and his first unsuc-
cessful visit to Munsalvaesche. The second part covers his
journeys parallel to Gâwân's travel-history, and the third, his
final and successful return to Munsalvaesche. In the course of
his travels he joins the Arthurian court three times, first at
Nantes, then by the Plimizoel, and finally at Jôflanze. Each
of these three visits is placed at a strategic point of the
narrative; they mark the beginning of each section of the
travel-history.[47] It is true that Nantes does not stand at
the very beginning of his travels. After his journey from
Soltâne, there follow his wanderings in the forest of Brizljân

---

47 It is interesting to note in this connection that Wilhelm
    Kellermann, Aufbaustil und Weltbild Chrestiens von Troyes
    im Percevalroman, Zeitschrift für romanische Philologie,
    Beihefte, 88 (1936), attaches great importance, from the
    point of view of composition, to the Arthurian episodes in
    four of Chrestien's verse narratives. He refers to them as
    "die tragenden Pfeiler der Romanarchitektur" (p. 12). He
    distinguishes four such episodes of which a central one is
    singled out as being of particular structural significance
    (pp. 11ff.): "Die Romane Chrestiens bestehen aus zwei mehr
    oder minder eng miteinander verbundenen Teilen. Lose ist
    ihr Zusammenhalt im Cliges, wo Chrestien das im Mittelal-
    ter so geläufige genealogische Schema verwendet und so die
    oströmische Atmosphäre mit der Artuswelt koppelt. Im Erec
    und Yvain ist die Gewinnung Enidens bezw. Laudinens abge-
    setzt vom eigentlichen Romangeschehen. Der Percevalroman
    ist durch die Scheidung in Perceval- und Gauvainepisoden
    am schärfsten getrennt. In allen vier Werken erfolgt nun
    diese wichtigste Handlungsgliederung in unmittelbarem epi-
    schem Zusammenhang mit der wegen ihrer kompositionellen
    Bedeutung so zu nennenden Haupt-Artusszene. Sie beginnt
    an folgenden Stellen: Erec V 2135 (Beginn des Hochzeittur-
    niers), Cliges V 2383 (Ende der Vorgeschichte), Yvain V 2639
    (Yvain vergisst die Heimkehrverpflichtung), Perceval V 4603
    (Ankunft der hässlichen Botin). In allen Fällen ist das
    Romangeschehen bereits vor dieser zentralen Szene längere
    Zeit im Bann der Artusatmosphäre. Das Mittelstück des Artus-
    rahmens trennt ja nicht nur, sondern es verbindet auch nach
    vorne und rückwärts. Es befindet sich im Yvain an der Stel-
    le, da der Held nach der Gewinnung Laudinens, der Besiegung
    Keus und der Anerkennung Gauvains auf dem Gipfel seines
    Glückes steht, im Erec, wo Erec Enide heimgeführt hat und

and only then does he reach Nantes. It is, however, immediately
after he has left the forest of Brizljân that his single-minded
effort is no longer allowed to be side-tracked. After his departure from the forest the scheme of gradation sets in, leading
him from Nantes to Grâharz, to Pelrapeire in Brôbarz and to
Terre de Salvaesche in a direct line characterized by speed,
ease, certain direction and supernatural guidance. In the light

---

das Ziel des Romans sich scheinbar erfüllt hat. Im Perceval
ist die grosse mittlere Artusszene von grösster komposi-
neller Wichtigkeit. Der Held ist nach langem Suchen von Artus
gefunden und geehrt worden. Hier liegt also ein Handlungs-
einschnitt vor, der in diesem Roman deswegen erhöhte Bedeutung
besitzt, weil sich unmittelbar darauf die Handlung durch die
parallele Beschuldigung der beiden Helden gabelt. In allen
drei Fällen hat das Geschehene mit einer Auszeichnung der
Titelgestalt einen Ruhepunkt erreicht. Zwei weitere Beobachtungen erhärten die Übereinstimmung in den betrachteten Mit-
telszenen zum Gesetz. Der entscheidende Konflikt, der die
Handlung von neuem in Gang setzt, befindet sich jedesmal
am Beginn des zweiten Romanteiles ... Ausserdem aber ist
die Bedeutung dieser Angelpunkte der Handlung episch dadurch
wirkungsvoll unterstrichen, dass vor oder unmittelbar nach
ihnen eine Zeitspanne liegt ..."
According to Kellermann this central episode represents the
second of the Arthurian episodes in the four works. There
follows a third "die einen Teilungspunkt von untergeordne-
ter Bedeutung darstellt und deren Platz weniger fest ist."
This third episode is missing in 'Perceval': "Im Perceval
bricht der Dichter unmittelbar vor dieser dritten wichtigen
Teilungsszene ab." And in the completed epics there is finally a fourth episode: "Der Anfangsszene am Artushofe ent-
spricht schliesslich in jedem der vollendeten Romane eine
ebensolche Schlusszene, auf der die Handlung wiederum in
die Rahmenatmosphäre einmündet. Wichtig ist hier, dass auch
im Cliges (V 6673ff.) und im Yvain (V 5872-6527) der Erle-
digung aller äusseren und seelischen Konflikte eine Artusszene vorgelegt ist. Es besteht keine Veranlassung, daran
zu zweifeln, dass das im ausgeführten Percevalroman anders
gewesen wäre."
A shadow of this fourth Arthurian episode of Chrestien's
romances is left in Wolfram's 'Parzival' in the form of
Parzival's second visit to Jôflanze in Book XV. As a result
of the changed rôle of the Arthurian court in the Parzival
story compared with its usual position in the verse narratives, the episode has not only lost its structural importance but even its narrative independence, and appears
as repetition.

of the scheme of gradation, Soltâne and the forest of Brizljân become introductory stations, the exposition to the travel-history.

Arthur's camp by the Plimizoel stands at the beginning proper of the second section. Both Parzival and Gâwân set out from here on their respective travels. Jôflanze, finally, is placed at the commencement of the third and last part of the travel-history. Parzival sets out from here to return to Munsalvaesche.

A notable feature of this arrangement is that all three points - Nantes, the Plimizoel, and Jôflanze - constitute a beginning for further travels. Parzival's journeys do not end at Arthur's court; they begin here. Thus, although his life is shown as intimately associated with the world of Arthurian chivalry, the relationship appears as being of a specific and, within court literature, of an unusual kind. For Parzival's travel-history or, in a wider sense, for his life, the Arthurian setting provides points of departure, not the ultimate aim. It is interpreted merely as a temporary, though nevertheless important, end in itself in the very early stages of the travel-history; hence the position of Nantes at the beginning of the scheme of gradation in Part I of the travel-history, but after an exposition. Had it been incorporated into this scheme of gradation at a later point, its place within it would have totally changed the significance of Arthur's court for Parzival's development.

Three times in the course of his travels Parzival is drawn into the Arthurian setting, only to be propelled onwards almost immediately by the events which befall him there. At Nantes, the slaying of Ithêr provides him with the material necessities of knighthood - armour, horse, and arms, and he sets out at once to try them in further deeds of valour. By the Plimizoel, Cundrîe's curse compels him to rehabilitate himself, and he takes leave immediately in order to search for the Grail. At Jôflanze, his proclamation as king of the Grail demands his instant departure. Thus, although these three momentous happenings occur while Parzival is part of the Arthurian scene, he is drawn away each time in order to transcend it.[48]

This peculiar function, as point of departure, which the Arthurian setting performs within Parzival's travel-history, becomes still clearer, when compared with the role it is permitted to play in Gâwân's travel-history. For Gâwân's travel-history the Arthurian scene is beginning and end. Gâwân sets out from the Arthurian court by the Plimizoel and returns to it at Jôflanze. His travel-history does not fall into distinct

---

48 Luise Lerner in Studien zur Komposition des höfischen Romans im 13. Jahrhundert, Diss., Frankfurt, 1936, distinguishes a double structure in 'Parzival', two parts of the story: Parzival's journey to Munsalvaesche and its repetition, and three parts of the theme: the development of Parzival's faith (p. 11): "Die Gliederung der inneren und äusseren Handlung überschneidet sich. Die äussere Handlung zerfällt in zwei Teile: Parzivals doppelter Weg zum Gral. Parzivals religiöse Entwicklung zerfällt in drei Abschnitte - kindlich naive Gottesvorstellung, konventionell-höfischer Glaube, wahre Gotteserkenntnis -, deren entscheidende Gelenke, Parzivals Einkehr bei Gurnemanz und Trevrizent sind."
Neither of these divisions takes comprehensive account of the details of the narrative and the development of the theme. The interpretation of the story (die äussere Handlung) as being composed of two parts, fails to consider its form as a travel-history, the Gâwân narrative, the schemes of gradation, and the part played by the Arthurian court in the narrative structure. All of these features contribute towards establishing three clearly recognizable parts of the narrative beginning with Book III.
The triple division of the theme into naive piety, conventional belief, and true faith overlooks a vital part of Parzival's development, in fact, a major point of the whole - Parzival's rejection of all faith. Three major stages may, indeed, be distinguished in Parzival's development; they are, however, not those set out by Miss Lerner. For the first part, naive piety as fostered by Herzeloyde, and conventional belief as taught by Gurnemanz, may be grouped together, the latter arising as logical consequence out of the former. Parzival's rejection of God, and his ultimate arrival at true faith, form Parts 2 and 3 respectively. These three stages of Parzival's development correspond to the three sections of his travel-history. The evolution of the theme is harmoniously fitted into the narrative structure.

sections but is all of one piece, and its beginning and end lie
within the Arthurian setting. His final merging with the Arthurian scene is complete, so much so, that his return to
Schastel Marveile, subsequent to his appearance at Jôflanze,
receives no separate treatment. Only a general allusion to the
breaking-up of Arthur's court at Jôflanze permits the reader
to assume that Gâwân too departed for his own territories.

Nor is Gâwân ever drawn beyond the Arthurian domain of fabulous
geography as Parzival is. Indeed, the major stations of his
travel-history are accessible to Arthur's court, as its movements, retracing part of Gâwân's road, show. After having received Gâwân's message at Bems bî der Korcâ (644.11ff.), Arthur
and his court make their way to Lôgroys (664.18-665.24) and
from there to Schastel Marveile (661.10ff.), whence they depart
again for Jôflanze (667.1-5).

Gâwân's connection with the Arthurian scene is thus shown to
be of a different kind from Parzival's, according to the part
played by Arthur's court in Gâwân's travel-history. The Arthurian court here is not used to punctuate changes and fresh
beginnings but to illustrate an inseparable relationship - Gâwân throughout remains an integral part of the Arthurian scene.

Parzival's connection with the Arthurian scene, although not
manifesting itself in the absorption of Gâwân, is still close,
in particular during the first part of his travel-history. He
sets out from Soltâne with the express purpose of seeking
Arthur (126.9-14). And after his visit to Nantes he maintains
this link with the Arthurian setting by sending to Arthur's
court three knights overcome in battle. From Pelrapeire in
Brôbarz Parzival sends first Kingrûn to King Arthur's court
at Karminâl in Brizljân (206.5-11), and then Clâmidê, who finds
the king at Dîanazdrûn in Löver (214.29-216.8). From Terre de
Salvaesche Orilus is despatched to Arthur's court after his
defeat in the joust (267.9-268.6), and he joins Arthur's camp
by the Plimizoel (273.1ff.). Thus, between the two appearances

of Parzival at Arthur's court, first at Nantes and then by the
Plimizoel, a triple narrative thread in the form of messengers
links his travel-history with the Arthurian setting. After the
episode by the Plimizoel Parzival's connection with the Arthurian world becomes less close. There are no longer any direct threads running between his movements and Arthur's. Nevertheless, the link is maintained, but it is now carried on by
Gâwân. There are two reasons for this change. The obvious technical one is that Gâwân has now temporarily taken over the
role of the hero, and as such it has fallen to him to continue
the pattern of narrative structure as evolved previously. The
second reason is more important and goes deeper; it is concerned with the transformation of Parzival after Cundrîe's accusations. Realizing that he has brought disgrace to Arthur
and his knights, he now dissociates himself voluntarily from
them until such time, if it ever does occur, as his transgressions will have been rectified, and he will once again feel free
to ask to be admitted to their company:

> 330.7 vil werder rîter sihe ich hie:
> durch iwer zuht nû râtt mir wie
> daz i' uwern hulden naehe mich.
> ez ist eine strenge schärpf gerich
> gein mir mit worten hie getân:
> swes hulde ich drumbe vloren hân,
> daz wil ich wênec wîzen im.
> swenne ich her nâch prîs genim,
> sô habt mich aber denne dernâch.
> mir ist ze scheiden von iu gâch.
> ir gâbt mir alle geselleschaft,
> die wîle ich stuont in prîses kraft:
> der sît nu ledec, unz ich bezal
> dâ von mîn grüeniu freude ist val.

After this, any direct link between Parzival and Arthur's court
would be out of place. From now on, the knights suffering defeat
at his hands are no longer bidden to seek out Arthur, but are
sent to Pelrapeire instead. For in the place of God, whom he
rejects, Parzival now puts love and Condwîrâmûrs, as his parting
words to Gâwân reveal:

> 332.9   friunt, an dînes kampfes zît
> dâ nem ein wîp für dich den strît:
> diu müeze ziehen dîne hant;
> an der du kiusche hâst bekant
> und wîplîche güete:
> ir minn dich dâ behüete.

Shortly afterwards Wolfram formulates the implications of this
passage for the subsequent narrative:

> 333.23   Condwier âmûrs,
> dîn minneclîcher bêâ curs,
> an den wirt dicke nu gedâht.
> waz dir wirt âventiure brâht!

Thus Parzival sends three knights to Pelrapeire from Bêârosche,
the king of Avendroyn, Schirnîel von Lyrivoyn and Marangliez
(388.15-389.14). Vergulaht, whom he meets in the forest Laehtamrîs, is also despatched to Pelrapeire (424.15-425.14). Finally,
five of Orgelûse's knights are sent to Pelrapeire from Terre
Marveile (599.9-18).[49]

Simultaneously the connection with Arthur's court is continued
through Gâwân, who first sends his retinue back from Schanpfanzûn to Dîanazdrûn (432.14-22) and then despatches a messenger
from Schastel Marveile to the king and queen at Bems bî der
Korcâ (626.12-18). After this, Arthur himself follows part of
Gâwân's road from Lôgroys to Terre Marveile and to Jôflanze.

The travel-histories of Parzival and Gâwân must therefore be
understood not only as being closely linked with one another
but also as being firmly connected with the Arthurian scene.
The relation of Parzival's travel-history with that of Gâwân,
the connection of the journeys with Arthur's court, the threads
running between the three, the arrangement of the complexity
of these movements and the structure imparted to the narrative
by the interrelation of the major travel-histories, and thus
of the component parts of the background, can be shown clearly
in a comparative table of the place-names and locations involved.

---

49   This change in the hero's relationship with the Arthurian
    court does not occur in Chrestien. During the period spent
    without prayer Perceval despatches sixty knights to King
    Arthur (6217-6235).

The Travel Histories of Parzival and Gâwân and the Movements of Arthur's Court

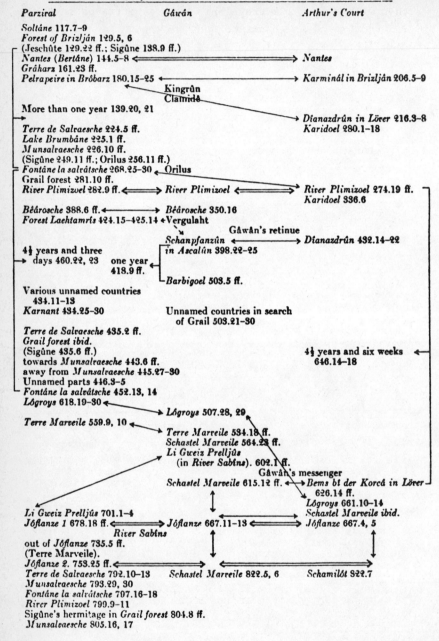

Parzival	Gâwân	Arthur's Court

Soltáne 117.7–9
Forest of Brizlján 129.5, 6
(Jeschûte 129.22 ff.; Sigûne 138.9 ff.)
Nantes (Bertáne) 144.5–8 ⟸⟹ Nantes
Gráharz 161.23 ff.
Pelrapeire in Bróbarz 180.15–25 ⟵ ⟶ Karminál in Brizlján 206.5–9

Kingrûn
Clamide

More than one year 139.20, 21
⟶ Dianazdrûn in Löver 216.3–8
Terre de Salvaesche 224.5 ff. Karidoel 280.1–18
Lake Brumbâne 225.1 ff.
Munsalvaesche 226.10 ff.
(Sigûne 249.11 ff.; Orilus 256.11 ff.)
Fontáne la salvátsche 268.25–30 ⟵ Orilus
Grail forest 281.10 ff.
River Plimizoel 282.9 ff. ⟸⟹ River Plimizoel ⟸ ⟶ River Plimizoel 274.19 ff.
Karidoel 336.6

Bêârosche 388.6 ff. ⟵⟶ Bêârosche 350.16
Forest Laehtamrîs 424.15–425.14 ⟵ Vergulaht
Gâwân's retinue
Schanpfanzûn ⟵ ⟶ Dianazdrûn 432.14–22
in Ascalûn 398.22–25
4½ years and three
days 460.22, 23 one year
418.9 ff.
Barbigoel 503.5 ff.

Various unnamed countries
434.11–13
Karnant 434.25–30 Unnamed countries in search
of Grail 503.21–30
Terre de Salvaesche 435.2 ff.
Grail forest ibid.
(Sigûne 435.6 ff.) 4½ years and six weeks ⟵
towards Munsalvaesche 443.6 ff. 646.14–18
away from Munsalvaesche 445.27–30
Unnamed parts 446.3–5
Fontáne la salvátsche 452.13, 14
Lôgroys 618.19–30 ⟵
⟶ Lôgroys 507.28, 29
Terre Marveile 559.9, 10 ⟵
⟶ Terre Marveile 534.18 ff.
Schastel Marveile 564.23 ff.
Li Gweiz Prelljûs
(in River Sabîns). 602.1 ff.
Gâwân's messenger
Schastel Marveile 615.12 ff. ⟵ ⟶ Bems bî der Korcâ in Löver
626.14 ff.
Lôgroys 661.10–14
Li Gweiz Prelljûs 701.1–4 Schastel Marveile ibid.
Jôflanze 1 678.18 ff. ⟸⟹ Jôflanze 667.11–13 ⟸ ⟶ Jôflanze 667.4, 5
River Sabîns
out of Jôflanze 735.5 ff.
(Terre Marveile).
Jôflanze 2. 753.25 ff. ⟸
Terre de Salvaesche 792.10–13 Schastel Marveile 822.5, 6 Schamilôt 822.7
Munsalvaesche 793.29, 30
Fontáne la salvátsche 797.16–18
River Plimizoel 799.9–11
Sigûne's hermitage in Grail forest 804.8 ff.
Munsalvaesche 805.16, 17

This skeleton outline of the triple movement within the narrative,
together with Gahmuret's travel-history as portrayed in Books I
and II, represents the basis of the background in 'Parzival'. In
Gahmuret's travel-history, where the setting bears the character
of an introduction, little has been added to this basis. In the
movements of the Arthurian court there is a total absence of descriptive features relating to scenery, with the exception of
those points which are also part of either Parzival's or Gâwân's
travel-history. Throughout the epic the portrayal of the setting
is characterized by economy of description; and even where elaboration occurs, it is brief, frequently incidental, and largely
implicit. For this sparing use of descriptive features the background in 'Parzival' has been compensated by the meaning it
derives from its form. Dissolved into a travel-history portraying one vast movement, its structure rests on the arrangement of
a long series of place-names.[50] Some of these, as has been seen,

---

50 The question of narrative structure in 'Parzival', has been
    considered by a number of scholars from various aspects. As
    the narrative structure of a work can reveal itself on many
    levels, interpretations will vary in accordance with the
    particular level chosen, and with the specific technique of
    isolating that level. Illuminating contributions have been
    made, among others, by the following: Hildegard Emmel, Form-
    probleme des Artusromans und der Graldichtung. Die Bedeutung
    des Artuskreises für das Gefüge des Romans im 12. und 13.
    Jahrhundert in Frankreich, Deutschland und den Niederlanden,
    Berne, 1951, examines the function of the Arthurian figures
    in relation to poetic form and concludes that 'Parzival'
    shows the pattern of the traditional Arthurian romance as
    developed by Chrestien (pp. 70ff.); W. J. Schröder, Der
    dichterische Plan des Parzivalromans, PBB, 74 (1952), 160-
    192 and 409-453, proceeding from the idea that the main
    action of 'Parzival' corresponds to the pattern of the
    Redemption (p. 170), illustrates the narrative structure
    by diagrams (pp. 426ff.) and finds parallel forms in the
    passion-play and ecclesiastical architecture (pp. 435ff.);
    H. de Boor, Die höfische Literatur. Vorbereitung, Blüte, Aus-
    klang. 1170-1250, Munich, [9]1974, draws attention to the
    significance of the Arthurian world and the world of the
    Grail which to him causes the 'Zweisträngigkeit der Hand-
    lungsführung' (p. 96). He also stresses the importance of
    the various encounters and of the threefold division of
    Parzival's journey for the composition of the epic (pp. 95ff.).
    Hans Eggers, Strukturprobleme mittelalterlicher Epik, darge-
    stellt am Parzival Wolframs von Eschenbach, Euphorion, 47

represent actual geography, others are adaptations from the French source, a considerable number of them are presumably borrowings from other sources which can no longer be traced, others again are clearly Wolfram's coinage. Their tremendous increase over the limited number employed by Chrestien points to their newly allotted and important function in the German work. The manner in which they are assembled, grouped, and repeated imparts to them a poetic reality of unflagging consistence.

The structure assumed by the background from Book III onwards derives largely from the interdependence of the three movements represented by Parzival, Gâwân, and Arthur's court. Through partial parallelism, occasional convergence, and frequent cross-connections, they are balanced against one another, thus dividing a travel-description of great length into clear-cut sections. Parzival's journeys, far from becoming a mere rambling progress

---

(1953), 260-270, investigates the numerical aspect of composition, similarly Peter Wapnewski, Wolframs Parzival. Studien zur Religiosität und Form, Heidelberg, 1955, pp. 115ff.; Jean Fourquet, La Structure du Parzival, discusses the nature of Wolfram's source and sees in the introduction of the Orient and the creation of a world of the Grail the poet's characteristic contribution towards structural balance; Dagmar Hirschberg, Untersuchungen zur Erzählstruktur von Wolfram's Parzival. Die Funktion von erzählter Szene und Station für den doppelten Kursus, Göppinger Arbeiten zur Germanistik, 139, Göppingen, 1976, tries to elucidate the structure of meanings and for this purpose distinguishes between 'narrated scene' and 'narrative complex', a unit of description, coherent in both time and space.
A number of investigations have also been devoted to the narrative structure of Wolfram's source. The basic work here is that by W. Kellermann, op.cit. The problem has also been treated by Erich Köhler, Ideal und Wirklichkeit in der höfischen Epik. Studien zur Form der frühen Artus- und Graldichtung, Beihefte zur Zeitschr. f. roman. Philologie, 97 (1956), who considers the appearance of plot and fully-fledged parallel plot in 'Li Contes del Graal' to be an expression of the tension between individual and society (pp. 240ff.). Stefan Hofer, La Structure du Conte del Graal, in: Les Romans du Graal, pp. 15-26, after emphasizing Chrestien's careful manner of composition as manifest in his other romances, postulates the hypothesis that the Gauvain section is the work of a continuator.

in space, fall into a pattern of three parts, through the insertion of Gâwân's travel-history and the contacts with Arthur's
court. This pattern is further sustained through the change in
cross-connections after the episode by the Plimizoel. Between
Nantes and the Plimizoel Parzival's messengers link his movements with Arthur's court. Between the Plimizoel and Jôflanze
they are sent to Pelrapeire instead, the change illustrating
the beginning of a new phase. Furthermore, Parzival's travel-
history moves three times in the direction of Munsalvaesche. In
the first part the Grail castle is reached, in the second section the attempt takes Parzival only into the vicinity of
Munsalvaesche, and in the third part the initial journey is
successfully repeated.

Several definitions of time also assist this pattern of three
parts. It would seem that Parzival's travel-history, beginning
at Soltâne and ending at Munsalvaesche, is to be understood
as being spread over a period of approximately six years. The
first part of Parzival's travels takes up more than a year.
Between his meeting with Jeschûte in the forest of Brizljân and
his encounter with Orilus near Fontâne la salvâtsche, over a
year has elapsed (139.20-21). The second part represents the
longest period. The rides at random extend over a span of well
over four years. Between Parzival's first and second visits to
Fontâne la salvâtsche, four and a half years and three days
have passed (460.22, 23). Between his appearance by the Plimizoel and the arrival of Gâwân's messenger at Bems bî der Korcâ
in Löver, four and a half years and six weeks have gone by
(646.14-18). The last section appears to cover the shortest
period. Its length is not stated, but the certainty with which
Parzival and Feirefîz, led by Cundrîe, make their way towards
Munsalvaesche, without delay, suggests a minimum of time spent
on their journey.

The three sections of Parzival's travel-history are thus differentiated by the varying time limit allotted to each. These
definitions of time, however, not only underline the tripartite

scheme of the journey; they also serve to consolidate its coherence by limiting its duration to a specified period.[51] The
travel-history is thus outlined in time as well as in space.
The scheme of gradation employed for the first part of the
travel-history further emphasizes its divisions. It presents
four major stations of Parzival's travels in closely knit narrative, marking out Munsalvaesche as their focal point. The conclusion of the carefully dovetailed narrative core signals a
new beginning, another phase, a second part.

Gâwân's travel-history derives its form and effect of close
continuity from the same narrative principles that shape the
pattern of the description of Parzival's travels. Shorter,
simpler, and less ambitious than Parzival's travel-history,
it does not show a pattern of three sections, and its cross-
connections on the one hand with Parzival's movements, and on
the other with the Arthurian court, do not undergo a sudden
change. The links remain of the same type throughout. But it
too receives its outward form through its contacts with the
Arthurian setting which represents the framework into which
it is set. A time-limit is imposed here as well; between Gâwân's
departure from the Plimizoel and his return to Schastel Marveile
after the adventure of Li Gweiz Prelljûs, four and a half years
and six weeks have passed (646.14-18). A similar gradation scheme
of four parts unites individual episodes in a closely woven narrative, and singles out one point, Schastel Marveile, as the most
important. For Gâwân, however, this scheme is interrupted by the
sudden return of the story to Parzival in Book IX. The unexpected break in the narrative lends emphasis equally to the events
befalling Parzival and those concerning Gâwân. For Parzival an
episode of momentous importance must be anticipated, as its insertion rends the context of the Gâwân-story immediately after

---

51 For Wolfram's treatment of time as compared with that of
   Chrestien, see H. J. Weigand, op.cit.

suspense has been expressly directed towards Gâwân's travel-
history by the closing lines of Book VIII.[52] For Gâwân this
rift in the story separates his first minor adventures from
the more important experiences to come: Lôgroys and Terre Marveile. The short introductory section to Book X finishes off
the narrative set in motion by Kingrimursel's challenge, by
dealing briefly with his presence at Barbigoel, and shows him
in pursuit of the Grail, which leads him in the course of Book
X to Lôgroys and Terre Marveile.[53] Gâwân, too, like Parzival,
is drawn three times to the scene of his highest achievement;
after his conquest of Schastel Marveile he returns to it again
from Li Gweiz Prelljûs and withdraws to it finally after Jôflanze.

The triple movement portrayed by the three strands of the travel-
history produces an illusion of simultaneous developments at
the three centres of the work. This illusion is achieved by the

---

52   432.29   nâch dem grâle im sicherheit gebôt:
                   er reit al ein gein wunders nôt.

Although following Chrestien's narrative closely at this
point, Wolfram makes this break much more dramatic than
the French poet. In the first place anticipation is emphatically directed towards Gâwân, a feature missing in
Chrestien, cf. 6199-6216; in the second, Wolfram immediately shows Parzival on Grail territory where Gâwân is now expected to be. In Chrestien Perceval does not appear in the
Grail forest at this point, cf. 6217ff.

53 There is additional indication towards the end of Book VIII
that Gâwân's future experiences will be of different, more
serious nature than the previous episodes. At the end of
Book VI Gâwân sets out on his travels most luxuriously
equipped. In striking contrast to the simplicity of Parzival's preparations for the journey (332.19-333.15), Gâwân
takes with him three shields, seven horses, twelve lances,
an escort of eight pages and squires (429.1-30) and rich
treasure granted by King Arthur (335.10-30). All this accompanies him to Bêârosche and Schanpfanzûn. At Schanpfanzûn,
however, having pledged himself to the quest of the Grail,
Gâwân suddenly rids himself of his lavish equipment and
retinue, and sets out unencumbered and alone, like Parzival
(432.14-30). These features of Gâwân's elaborate preparations
and sudden decision to continue without followers and equipment Wolfram has taken from his source. However, by intro-

links which gather the Arthurian scene into the main plot at
frequent intervals, and by the parallelism of Parzival's and
Gâwân's journeys, which are worked into one another by the
contrapuntal movement of the two heroes. It is underlined by
the simultaneous presence of all three at three different
places at significant stages of the narrative.

The various means by which this vast movement through space is
separated into introduction and main action, cut into a triple
line of independent and individual progress and then linked
again, divided into various sections and connected once again
by repetition, balanced by parallelism and schemes of gradation and held together in every possible way, concrete and
obvious or implied, reveal characteristic aspects of Wolfram's
manner of composition. His narrative technique shows itself
primarily as a process of ordering, not by ruthless elimination, for Wolfram is loath to reject anything and anxious to
conserve throughout as much as possible of whatever his source
suggests, but by patiently arranging, skilfully connecting, and
subtly elaborating details, thus imparting a coherence to his
work which compels admiration. The urge to retain is matched
by the painstaking concern for unity of form. They are the hall-
mark of his poetic technique. The detailed genealogical bonds
which unite his characters in kinship, the schemes of gradation,
the complex patterns of ownership of possessions, the parallelism of characters and situations, the links between single
episodes and whole sections of the narrative, the systems of
contrasts and similarities, the setting in the form of geographical schemes and travel-histories, all answer to this same
formula. Even Time is subjected to this unifying process, as
past and future are drawn into the present by reminiscence and
anticipation.[54] Wolfram's treatment of chivalrous journeys and

---

ducing the contrast of Parzival these aspects become poetically more effective in Wolfram.

54 Past events, e.g., are constantly drawn back into the plot
by reminders, unexpected connections, and sudden appearances.

their scenery, so intricate, yet so brilliantly evolved and so triumphantly mastered, adds immeasurably to the poetic efficacy of the whole work. For his technique of presentation not only aids the visual impact of the action, but also vitally assists the compactness of plot and the narrative unity of the epic.

Thus Trevrizent's description of his travels in Book IX recalls Gahmuret's travel-history at the beginning of the romance, and Feirefiz's account of his deeds of valour in Book XV once again unfurls the exotic scene of far-off pagan lands which Books I and II had portrayed. Earlier developments are recapitulated, as when Guinevere recalls Parzival's and Gâwân's departure from the Plimizoel at Bems bî der Korcâ or when Orgelûse describes Parzival's travels through Lôgroys and Terre Marveile in Book XII.

2. Geography of Fact and Fiction

The scenes of action in 'Parzival' and the places of origin of
characters and their possessions, as mirrored in the place-
names employed, form a curious hybrid of actual and fabulous
geography. This fusion of fact and fiction in geography is not
Wolfram's invention. Chrestien already intersperses his descriptions of the fabulous localities in 'Li Contes del Graal' with
allusions to the real world. Both poets thus link their imagin-
ary world with the world of reality.

In Chrestien's work this link is tenuous. The appearance of
factual place-names is rare, and they are, moreover, introduced
haphazardly and not presented as geographically coherent. Twice
actual place-names are incorporated into a description of gifts.
From Gornemant de Goort Perceval receives a tunic made of silk
woven in India (1604); at the Grail castle he is presented with
a sword whose pommel is fashioned of gold from Arabia or Greece
and whose sheath consists of gold-work from Venice (3162f.). In
addition there are references to Beirut (3052), Limoges (3076),
Lombardy (5947), Pavia (6662), Rome (2689) and the Loire (1316).
All these were clearly identifiable for Chrestien's audience as
part of the real world. Whether this same recognition extended
to four further actual place-names which Chrestien introduced
into the epic background is problematic. Carlion (4003, etc.),
Galvoie (6602, etc.), Tintaguel (4835, 4884) and Gales (2753,
etc.) used by Chrestien as scenes of action, have been identified
by his modern editors as Caerleon-on-Usk, Galloway, Tintagel and
Wales.[55] With the exception of Wales, in connection with which
Chrestien betrays a knowledge of the patron saint St David,[56]

---

55 Cf. ed. Alfons Hilka, Namenverzeichnis; Berichtigungen und
    Anmerkungen, Halle, 1932. Also ed. William Roach. Index des
    Noms Propres, Geneva/Lille, 1956.

56 Chrestien, 4134, 4135.

it seems unlikely that any of them would have been accepted by
Chrestien's audience as representing reality. They may have been
recognized as real places, but it is highly probable that they
were primarily looked upon as part of the mythical Arthurian
geography which had been progressively unfolded in Chrestien's
previous romances.[57] Taking this into account we may conclude
that the references to the world of fact in 'Li Contes del Graal',
scanty and casual as they are, hardly play a prominent part in
the work.

In the German version we are presented with an entirely different
picture. References of this kind abound and, in comparison with
Chrestien's romance, we are plunged into a veritable welter of
them. Some may be casual; others are deliberately placed to
provide points of comparison with fictitious places; others again
are named as the places of origin of either characters or certain
objects; and most important of all, Wolfram claims parts of the
real world as scenes of action for some of his characters. By
multiplying the references to the world of fact, and particularly
by drawing it into the narrative as a component of the epic background, Wolfram considerably strenghtens the link with reality
which his source merely adumbrated.

The allusions to the world of common knowledge are especially
numerous in Books I and II. In connection with the episode of
Pâtelamunt Wolfram mentions the king of Scotland (16. 16) and
his Scotsmen (27. 18), Gaschier of Normandy (25. 14) whose
kinsman Killirjacac describes how he left his native Champagne
to join the host at Rouen in Normandy (47.10-17), Kaylet, the
king of Spain (48.7), the king of Gascony (48.10) and Hiutegêr
of Scotland (52.18). Among the knights appearing before Kanvoleis
are Schîolarz of Poitou (68.21), the duke of Brabant (73.30),
Portuguese (66.26), Provençals (66.29), Germans (67.22), the
king of Aragon (67.14), Môrholt of Ireland (67.19) and again the

---

57 Gales had appeared already in 'Cligés', 'Erec' and 'Yvain';
   Carlion in 'Lancelot'; and Tintaguel in 'Erec'.

kings of Gascony and Spain (72.25; 64.13). Gahmuret, closely
associated with Anjou and frequently described as the Angevin
(11.1; 14.8; 17.9; 40.1; 98.18, etc.), is wooed by the queen
of France (76.13) and his brother Gâlôes dies in the service
of the queen of Navarre (91.23).

Further references showing the connection of characters with
the real world are scattered throughout the epic. Kyôt, uncle
to Condwîrâmûrs, appears as duke of Catalonia (186.21). Lysa-
vander, a vassal of Meljanz, is count of Beauvais and described as a Frenchman (348.15-17). Liddamus, one of King Vergulaht's
vassals, mentions his estates in Spanish Galicia (419.19). One
of Gâwân's squires, cons Lîâz fîz Tînas, comes from Cornwall
(429.18), Orilus comes from Burgundy (545.29); Parzival defeats
a Provençal knight from Arles (772.22) and Feirefîz the king of
Arabia (770.19). There are Saracens in Gahmuret's retinue (18.
28), and Saracens and Frenchmen at Arthur's court at Jôflanze
(699.29; 702.23).

A number of references indicate the origin of certain possessions
in the real world. Orilus's shield has been fashioned in Toledo,
his breastplate in Soissons and his surcoat and mantle have been
cut from silk woven in Alexandria (261.2f.). Cundrîe wears cloth
from Ghent (313.4) and a hat from London (313.10) and some of
the Grail bearers wear silk from Nineveh (235.11). Gramoflanz's
horse has been imported from Denmark (605.18) and his headgear
from Chichester (605.8). Gahmuret's surcoat is ornamented with
gold from the Caucasian mountains (71.18). King Vergulaht rides
a horse from Spain (400.4).

On several occasions the real world is drawn in for comparison.
The bazaar at Schastel Marveile is worth far more than all the
treasures of Greece (563.8) and Thasmê is larger than Nineveh
(629.22). There are more tents at Dîanazdrûn than fallen trees
in the Spessart (216.12). The forest of lances led by Poydicon-
junz is vaster than the Black Forest, even if it were extended
(379.6). The Lechfeld is rather larger than the meadow at

Schastel Marveile (565.4).

Apart from these there are references to England (735.16), Erfurt (379.18), Hainault (89.16), Capua (656.19), Cologne (158.
14), Naples (656.17), Regensburg (377.30), Paris (761.28), Rome
(13.27), Sicily (656.25), the Rhine (285.6) and many more.

This list, though not complete, suffices to show, when compared
with the small number of similar references in the French source,
that Wolfram pursued the objective of forging a link with reality
with a tenacity and exuberance not equalled by Chrestien. It
seems that he was intent on developing to the utmost the possibilities of a device indicated by his source. He appears bent
on establishing more securely than Chrestien, and on sustaining
more effectively than he, a definite connection of his fabulous
world with this world, here and now. His purpose might be considered to have been achieved with a flourish simply by the remarkable increase in the number of references to the actual world.
But far from being content with mere multiplication, Wolfram
buttresses this link with reality still more firmly by presenting the real world, on two occasions, in geographical coherence
and by attaching it as background to the actions of three major
characters, Gahmuret, Trevrizent and Feirefîz, and one subsidiary
figure, Loherangrîn.

Loherangrîn is described as having been sent to Brabant (824.1f.),
Feirefîz takes possession of India (822.21f.), Gahmuret and
Trevrizent visit a number of places in the real world. These latter appear as geographically coherent through their enumeration
in plausible sequence. As the place-names are correctly grouped,
they become credible and coherent itineraries. We can thus readily
accept that Gahmuret left Anjou (6.27) for Baghdad (13.16f.),
established his chivalrous fame in Morocco and Persia, that is,
throughout pagandom,[58] distinguished himself at Damascus and

---

58   15.15   ... sîn manlîchiu kraft
                behielt den prîs in heidenschaft,
                ze Marroch unt ze Persîâ.

Aleppo, in Arabia (15.19-21) and at Alexandria (18.14), and returned to Europe reaching the coast of Spain and travelling north to Toledo via Seville (58.21f.). Equally coherent is Trevrizent's itinerary in the world of fact. After meeting Gahmuret in Seville he embarked on a long voyage in the direction of Celje, and having sailed all round the sea finally reached it via Friuli and Aquileia. From here he rode to Rogatec and thence to Haidin where the Drava and Grajena meet (496.19f.).

The fact that reality appears in geographical coherence, even though this occurs only twice, and that it provides scenes of action for four characters, three of whom play parts of prime importance in the narrative, throws the real world, and with it the link with reality, into considerable relief. It is given still further prominence through the positions which have been allotted to it in the work. As a background to action reality appears, forming part of Gahmuret's travel-history, in the beginning of the romance, as an interlude in Trevrizent's chivalrous journeys, at the centre of the work, and as a setting for Feirefîz and Loherangrîn, at its conclusion. At these points of the poetic structure, the beginning, middle and end of the narrative, the world of fact cannot fail to claim additional attention, contrasted as it is with a fully developed geography of fiction.

In the first two introductions of the world of reality as background Wolfram quite clearly lays particular stress on extent in space and world-wide connection. He ascribes to both Gahmuret and Trevrizent visits to all three continents, Asia, Africa and Europe, thus drawing the whole of the known world into the narrative and creating the illusion of an immense horizon. He illustrates the vastness of this background furthermore in the description of Gahmuret's choice of a lord. In the bâruc whom Gahmuret decides to serve, the whole of the pagan world is represented. He holds sway over two-thirds of the earth or more:

13.16   im wart gesagt. ze Baldac,
         waere ein sô gewaltic man,
         daz im der erde untertân
         diu zwei teil waeren oder mêr.

He is the pagan equivalent of the pope, and Baghdad the counterpart of Rome:

13.26   seht wie man kristen ê begêt
         ze Rôme, als uns der touf vergiht.
         heidensch orden man dort siht:
         ze Baldac nement se ir bâbestreht
         (daz dunket se âne krümbe sleht,)
         der bâruc in für sünde
         gît wandels urkünde.

This width of background conjured up by such simple means is
recaptured to a certain extent at the conclusion, when the power
of the Grail is shown to reach as far as India, where Feirefîz
proceeds to spread the message of Christianity, and to manifest
itself in as near a place as Brabant, where Loherangrîn has been
sent from Munsalvaesche.

Range is thus seen to be an important attribute of the factual
world in 'Parzival'; even the references previously mentioned
exhibit this feature, in so far as they relate characters and
objects to widely divergent localities.

The illusion of tremendous expanse is increased by combining the
world of fact with fabulous regions. In its four brief appearances
as background, reality is not shown as self-contained, but as being
connected with fictitious countries and places. Gahmuret, after
performing deeds of valour in the real world, sails for Zazamanc
(16.2). Trevrizent, apart from journeying in Styria, rides to
Gaurîûn and Fâmurgân (496.5-8). Feirefîz sets out from Azagouc
and Zazamanc (328.6-10; 771.9-10) and finally departs for India.
Loherangrîn, after fulfilling his mission in Brabant, returns to
Terre de Salvaesche (826.20f.). The vast extent of the factual
background, established by allowing its scope to encompass the
three continents in the travels of Gahmuret and Trevrizent, is
thus extended still further by opening it to the limitless dis-

tance of fabulous territories.[59]

This creation of an immense space may be said to be as important
a result of the elaborated use of the factual world as the
strengthened link with reality. Both these features help to indicate the symbolic significance of the Parzival narrative. By
repeatedly referring to the world of fact and permitting momentary glimpses of it, Wolfram is able to show the story of Parzival as firmly anchored in reality; by opening up an enormous
breadth of horizon he contrives to place Parzival's fate in a
context of world-wide, universal application. The changes Wolfram made in the use of factual geography are, therefore, seen
to have been shrewdly calculated to achieve effects which were
never in Chrestien's mind. The alterations and innovations in
themselves are comparatively simple. Summed up they amount to
no more than an increase in the references to the actual world,
the introduction of reality as a component part of the epic
background, its presentation on two occasions in geographical
coherence, its insertion at prominent points of the narrative,
and the emphasis on its extent. Yet the repercussions of these
changes are complex and the poetic gain astonishing. The link
with reality and the extension of epic horizon which result,
illuminate the meaning of the whole work.

While Wolfram's treatment of the geography of fact thus appears
to have been carefully thought out and to have been guided by
an inspired imagination, his development of a geography of fiction, evolved around Parzival and Gâwân, still surpasses it in

---

59 The various methods whereby medieval poets endeavoured to
    make the transition from the real world to the world of
    fantasy plausible for their audiences, have been analyzed
    by Dennis H. Green, Der Weg zum Abenteuer im höfischen Ro-
    man des deutschen Mittelalters, Veröffentlichung der Joachim
    Jungius-Gesellschaft der Wissenschaften, Göttingen, 1974;
    vid. also its extended form: The Pathway to Adventure,
    Viator, Medieval and Renaissance Studies, 8 (1977), 145-
    188.

laborious planning and imaginative vision. The factual world in
'Parzival', although deliberately rendered significant by various
methods, is, after all, only sketched in, its existence merely
indicated. The fictitious world, on the other hand, in which
Parzival and Gâwân find themselves, is distinctly outlined by
being presented in the form of geographical schemes.[60] The
various parts of this fabulous geography are systematically
linked and co-ordinated, so that continuous landscapes emerge.
Coherence now becomes detailed and perspective in consequence
precise. Here again Wolfram differs conspicuously from Chrestien.
For although Chrestien too seems to have had a scheme of fabulous
geography in mind, the relationship between the various locations
has remained vague and shadowy. It exists mainly by virtue of the
movements of Perceval and Gauvain. Only occasionally is there an
indication of distance or situation. When meeting the Fisher-
King, for example, Perceval is told that he cannot cross the
river with his horse for twenty miles either upstream or down-
stream,[61] and later his cousin refers to twenty-five miles of
lonely country in the direction whence he has travelled.[62] But
as these details are not supplemented by further description,
they are of little use in the construction of a geographical
scheme. Similarly, although three castles visited by Perceval
(Carduel, Goort and Belrepeire) and two visited by Gauvain
(Escavalon and Galvoie) are said to be by the sea,[63] they cannot be co-ordinated into a scheme as the connection between them
is not supported by additional details. Moreover, at one point

---

60 The question of a co-ordinated fabulous geography in Chres-
    tien's works, 'Parzival' and other Middle High German verse
    narratives has been treated fully by M.O'C. Walshe, Travel
    Descriptions etc. The maps in this thesis differ from those
    given here. They have been constructed on the principle of
    itineraries and not, as here, on the basis of perspective.

61 Chrestien, 3017f.

62 Chrestien, 3466f.

63 Chrestien, 843, 1322, 1709, 5755, 6661.

of the narrative, when Chrestien reverts to the story of Perceval, a clear break occurs in his fabulous geography. The forest in which Perceval journeys has no connection with any place previously visited by him.

Chrestien fails to achieve a compact geographical scheme for reasons which come to light when the construction of his fabulous geography is compared with that of Wolfram's. He hardly gives any definitions of time or distance; although he mentions a number of rivers, he does not name them; and finally, he does not reintroduce the different settings sufficiently frequently. All these omissions Wolfram has made good, with the result that there emerges a geography of fiction exhibiting visible coherence and vivid perspective, lucidly organized into continuous landscapes, a feature which, like the arrangement of the travel-histories, contributes to the unity of the work, and assists in its interpretation.

Not all parts of Wolfram's fabulous geography are brought into this scheme. The early stages of Parzival's and Gâwân's journeys are treated merely as itineraries from point to point. Grâharz and Brôbarz do not stand in any clear geographical relation either to one another or any other part of the fabulous geography, and the same applies to Bêârosche and Schanpfanzûn. The link here is provided solely by direct progress from one to the other. When, however, Parzival and Gâwân penetrate to the core of their travels, early enumerative portrayal gives way to coherence, co-ordination and perspective. The landscape in which Munsalvaesche stands, the regions in the vicinity of Terre de Salvaesche, and the parts surrounding Schastel Marveile and bordering on Terre Marveile gradually unfold their continuity.

The exact location of Munsalvaesche within Terre de Salvaesche is never revealed, nor its precise relation to the outside world. All description relating to the surroundings of Munsalvaesche and to its approaches, while disclosing some essential features of the landscape, is purposely vague on the question of its dis-

tance from other points mentioned in the narrative, except in
the case of Lake Brumbâne. It appears as extremely far removed
from Brôbarz. Parzival's journey between Pelrapeire and Munsalvaesche implies extraordinary distance (224.22-30), so does
Condwîrâmûrs's ride from Brôbarz into Terre de Salvaesche:

> 796.28   ine weiz wie mange raste
> Condwîr âmûrs dô was geriten
> gein Munsalvaesch mit freude siten.

It is also remote from Jôflanze, and its actual distance from
it is intentionally obscured:

> 792.10   in Terre de salvaesche ist komn,
> von Jôflanze gestrichen,
> dem sîn sorge was entwichen,
> Parzivâl, sîn bruoder unde ein magt.
> mir ist niht für wâr gesagt,
> wie verre dâ zwischen waere.

In close proximity to it, however, in Terre de Salvaesche, is
the Lake Brumbâne (491.6-8; 225.22), where Parzival sees Anfortas for the first time (225.2-7). A short ride takes Parzival
from here to the Grail castle (225.25f.). Munsalvaesche is surrounded by thirty miles of wild and uninhabited country. Anfortas
first stresses this feature (225.19-21) which is later repeated
by Sigûne:

> 250.22   inre drîzec mîln wart nie versnitn -
> ze keinem bûwe holz noch stein:
> wan ein burc diu stêt al ein.

The wilderness encircling the Grail castle is mountainous and
covered with dense forest. It becomes more dangerous and forbidding as the distance to Munsalvaesche lessens, thus shelter-
ing it by a ring of virtually impenetrable country (224.19, 20;
250.20, 21; 443.11-445.17). The only human being living in the
wilderness immediately surrounding Munsalvaesche is Sigûne. She
is closer to Munsalvaesche even than Trevrizent. Leaving the
Grail castle after his first visit, Parzival comes upon her
shortly afterwards, still very early in the morning (249.11-13).
In Book IX Sigûne appears to have moved, as Parzival, riding up
to her anchorhold, recognizes neither its surroundings nor, at

first, Sigûne herself (435.2f.). She has, however, remained in
close proximity to Munsalvaesche. Cundrîe visits her here regularly (439.1-5), and Parzival, penetrating further into the
wilderness, is immediately attacked by a Grail knight for attempting to approach Munsalvaesche (442.24f.). Her nearness to
the Grail castle may, furthermore, be inferred from the description of Parzival's last ride to Munsalvaesche in Book XVI. He
finds Sigûne in her cell late in the evening (804.21-3) and
reaches Munsalvaesche the same night (805.16f.). In spite of
the short distance lying between her and the Grail castle, Sigûne does not know the way to it, and cannot direct Parzival in
Book IX (442.9-23).

Trevrizent's hermitage is also situated in Terre de Salvaesche.
Fontâne la salvâtsche lies in the Grail forest (268.25-30), but
is considerably further away from the Grail castle than Sigûne.
Apart from Parzival, only the inhabitants of the Grail castle
are familiar with Sigûne's abode. She is well known to the
Grail knights, for when Parzival asks to be directed to her in
Book XVI, they do so immediately:

> 804.13 von sînen geselln wart im gesagt,
> si wisten ein: 'dâ wont ein magt,
> al klagende ûf friundes sarke:
> diu ist rehter güete ein arke.
> unser reise gêt ir nâhe bî.'

No one else, however, ever touches upon these parts.

Fontâne la salvâtsche, on the other hand, is known to and visited by others. Orilus and Jeschûte come here together with Parzival (268.25-30) and Kahenîs and his family make a yearly pilgrimage to Trevrizent (457.5-20). The great distance between
Munsalvaesche and Trevrizent's hermitage is implied as early
as Book V. Meeting Sigûne in the early morning (249.13: "ez was
dennoch von touwe naz") Parzival comes upon Orilus much later
in the day (256.5: "durch klage und durch den tac sô heiz/ begunde netzen in der sweiz"). The joust with Orilus seems to
take place in the vicinity of Fontâne la salvâtsche to which

they proceed immediately afterwards. Though Fontâne la salvâtsche
thus lies closer to the outside world than Sigûne's anchorhold,
the distance by which it is separated from it is still considerable. After his last visit to Trevrizent in Book XVI it takes
Parzival all night to reach the Plimizoeles Plân where Condwîrâmûrs is waiting. He arrives there in the morning:

> 799.14 Parzivâl die naht streich dan:
> sînen gesellen was der walt wol kunt.
> dô ez tagt, dô vant er lieben funt ...

This stretch of country by the Plimizoel, the scene of Parzival's
trance and of his encounters with Keye and Segramors, lies on
the outskirts of Terre de Salvaesche, in the young wood before
the Grail forest (282.9; 797.4-10). Segramors riding towards
Parzival takes his horse at a gallop over the undergrowth:

> 286.25 ûz fuor Segramors roys,
> kalopierende ulter jûven poys.
> sîn ors übr hôhe stûden spranc.

Here Arthur has set up camp (284.21f.). Realizing that he has
crossed into Grail territory and expecting attacks from the Grail
knights defending their forest, he at first refuses Segramors
the boon of the joust:

> 286 Artûs ze Segramorse sprach
> 'dîn sicherheit mir des verjach,
> du soltst nâch mînem willen varn
> und dîn unbescheidenheit bewarn.
> wirt hie ein tjost von dir getân,
> dar nâch wil manc ander man
> daz ich in lâze rîten
> und ouch nâch prîse strîten,
> dâ mite krenket sich mîn wer,
> wir nâhen Anfortases her,
> daz von Munsalvaesche vert
> untz fôrest mit strîte wert:
> sît wir niht wizzen wâ diu stêt,
> ze arbeit ez uns lîhte ergêt.'

Terre de Salvaesche thus embraces at least part of the Plimizoeles Plân and apparently extends even to the Plimizoel itself; the
river seems to form its boundary. Arthur's camp is spread over
both banks of the Plimizoel (273.2-11) and is to be imagined as
being partly on Grail territory, and partly in Bertâne. A ref-

erence to Gâwân in Book VIII as having come to Schanpfanzûn from
Bertâne (419.25 "her ist von Bertâne komn/ gein dem ir kampf hât
genomn") places the site of Arthur's camp as partly in Bertâne.
This is corroborated by Orilus's journey to the camp. He is
bidden by Parzival to seek out Arthur in Bertâne:

> 267.9 Parzivâl der hôch gemuot
> sprach 'liute, lant, noch varnde guot,
> der decheinez mac gehelfen dir,
> dune tuost des sicherheit gein mir,
> daz du gein Bertâne varst,
> unt die reise niht langer sparst, ...

and proceeds to the Plimizoeles Plân. Bertâne must, therefore,
here reach to the Plimizoel and in this way border on Terre de
Salvaesche. Connection between the two countries is illustrated
also by the movements of Orilus and Sigûne. The forest of Brizljân lies in Bertâne (206.5-8). Sigûne moves from here into Terre
de Salvaesche (138.9f.; 252.27-253.4), and Orilus and Jeschûte
also make their way from the forest of Brizljân into the Grail
forest (129.27f.; 256.11f.). The distance between the two, however, is not defined. The only point in Bertâne clearly within
easy reach of the Plimizoeles Plân is Karidoel, one of Arthur's
castles. Arthur sets out from here to seek Parzival (280f.) and
returns again to Karidoel after the camp by the Plimizoel is
broken up (336.4-6).

As in the case of the Grail forest, a young wood lies before the
forest of Brizljân; Schîânatulander is killed here in his joust
with Orilus (271.8, 9; 141.8f.). In Brizljân stands Arthur's
hunting-lodge, Karminâl (206.5-9), and from the forest of Brizljân Parzival rides to Nantes, the capital of Bertâne (142.3-144.8).
Beyond the forest lies Soltâne (129.5, 6).

The river Plimizoel continues as an important landmark in Wolfram's fabulous geography. Apart from establishing a connection
between Bertâne and Terre de Salvaesche, it extends geographical
perspective by linking the latter territory with Karcobrâ, Barbigoel and Lîz. It enters the sea at Karcobrâ in the bishopric

of Barbigoel (497.7-10). Near here lies the forest Laeprisîn
through which Feirefîz and Repanse must pass on their return
from Munsalvaesche to Jôflanze (821.1-13). Barbigoel is the
capital of Lîz, Meljanz's kingdom (385.2, 3), through which
the Plimizoel thus flows. This port in Barbigoel, Karcobrâ, is
the closest point of the outside world in relation to Munsalvaesche. Trevrizent setting out on his travels from Munsalvaesche first comes to Karcobrâ (497.5-10), and so does Feirefîz after his departure from the Grail castle (821f.). The see
of Barbigoel is thus presumably adjacent to Terre de Salvaesche.
Gâwân visits Barbigoel in answer to Kingrimursel's summons; it
represents his closest approach to Grail territory (503.5-13;
646.4, 5).

The geographical scheme built up around Munsalvaesche thus embraces Lake Brumbâne, Sigûne's anchorhold, Fontâne la salvâtsche,
the river Plimizoel, the Plimizoeles Plân, Bertâne, Nantes, the
forest of Brizljân, Karminâl, Karidoel, Soltâne, Lîz, Barbigoel,
the forest Laeprisîn, and Karcobrâ. Neither Grâharz nor Brôbarz
appear to be incorporated into this scheme, for although Grâharz
is linked with Nantes by a definition of time[64] and again with
Brôbarz in the same way,[65] and although a definition of time also
links Brôbarz with Terre de Salvaesche,[66] the geographical connection between Grâharz and Brôbarz, and their position in relation to other places in the narrative, remain obscure.

A similar scheme with considerable detail is evolved around
Schastel Marveile.[67] In contrast to Munsalvaesche its position

---

64 161.23, 24.

65 180.20f.

66 224.22f.

67 The existence of this scheme was pointed out as long ago as
    1850 by F. W. Rührmund, Wolframs von Eschenbach Beschreibung
    von Terre Marveile, ein poetisches Landschaftsgemälde, Ger-
    mania, Jahrbuch f. dtsch. Spr. u. Altertumskunde, 9 (1850),
    12-35. He describes it and appends a map. Unfortunately he
    does not restrict himself to the co-ordination of definite
    details only, but also speculates when they become vague.
    There are several major errors in his account. Karcobrâ and
    the natural harbour are connected; Clinschor's forest, the

within its own territory, Terre Marveile, is <u>not</u> kept strangely undefined. While a fourfold protection shrouds Munsalvaesche - its location is unknown, it is extremely remote from the outside world, it is heavily defended and cannot be found by those who seek it - Schastel Marveile is clearly visible to all who pass through Terre Marveile and easily approachable from other parts. Thus Parzival,[68] Gâwân,[69] Orgelûse,[70] Arthur,[71] Clîas,[72] Orgelûse's 'turkoyte',[73] Lischoys Gwelljus[74] and other knights,[75] all reach Schastel Marveile without any difficulty. This lack of obstacles which permits anyone to enter Terre Marveile and even penetrate as far as the castle, illuminates the difference in character between Schastel Marveile and Munsalvaesche. The quality of otherworldliness which characterizes Munsalvaesche and its territory is missing in the case of Schastel Marveile. The conception of the outside world does not apply here; Terre Marveile and its castle are part of the world. Schastel Marveile is not, therefore, sealed off within its own domain, nor are its approaches veiled in mystery. Terre Marveile is easily reached from Lôgroys which borders on it (661.10-14); Orgelûse, Gâwân,

---

'liehte waste', and the unnamed forest are wrongly placed; and the field of jousts and the field at Jôflanze are taken to be identical. There are a number of minor mistakes as well. He assumes that Terre Marveile borders on the sea (p. 17), that the forest near Lôgroys is part of the un- named forest (p. 20), that the Sabîns is connected with the stream at Lôgroys (p. 23), and others more.

68 618.27-30.

69 662.26, 27.

70 536.10f.

71 534.11-23.

72 334.11-15.

73 618.27-30.

74 Ibid.

75 Ibid.; 593.30f.

Parzival, Arthur, as well as Orgelûse's knights come to Terre
Marveile from Lôgroys. Originally Terre Marveile, which extends
for eight miles around Schastel Marveile, had been part of Irôt's
kingdom, until it came into Clinschor's possession.

> 658.9   ein künec der hiez Irôt,
> der ervorht im die selben nôt,
> von Rosche Sabînes.
> der bôt im des sînes
> ze gebenne swaz er wolde,
> daz er vride haben solde.
> Clinschor enpfienc von sîner hant
> disen berc vest erkant
> und an der selben zîle
> alumbe aht mîle.

Close to Schastel Marveile, on the same side of the river, stands
Plippalinôt's house (548.14f.). On the opposite bank, by the
landing-place of the ferry, is the field of jousts (535.6: "an
dem urvar ein anger lac/ dar ûfe man vil tjoste pflac"). This
river below Schastel Marveile is unnamed, although it is a prominent feature of the landscape. The ferry attended to by Plippalinôt is mentioned many times (535.25-8; 543.30f.; 559.9, 10; 596.
8-13; 621.10f.; 667.27f.). It is, however, most likely that the
river Sabîns is meant, for, not far from Schastel Marveile, Li
Gweiz Prelljûs may be found in the Sabîns (602.1f.; 604.1). Here,
about one 'raste' from Schastel Marveile, and still within Terre
Marveile, is Clinschor's forest (601.7f.). This probably extends
over both banks of the Sabîns. Gâwân reaches it on the bank opposite to Schastel Marveile, having first crossed the river
(595.30-596.12), and then plucks the branch off Gramoflanz's
tree, having recrossed it at Li Gweiz Prelljûs. Gramoflanz's
tree seems to be still in Clinschor's forest (601.13-24). The
river Sabîns fulfils the same function for the geographical
scheme around Schastel Marveile, as the Plimizoel performs for
the similar pattern around Munsalvaesche; it connects various
regions, thus forming a continuous landscape. In this manner
Terre Marveile is linked with the territory inherited by Gramoflanz from his father Irôt, with the royal residence Rosche
Sabbîns, the only place where the river is bridged:

> 610.25   der künec Gâwânn mit im bat
> ze Rosche Sabbîns in die stat:
> 'irn mugt niht anderr brücken hân.'

Rosche Sabbîns is situated by the sea between the mouth of the
Sabîns and that of the Poynzaclîns; Arthur's messengers reach
Gramoflanz -

> 681.6   ûf einem plâne bî dem mer.
> einhalp vlôz der Sabbîns
> und anderhalb der Poynzaclîns:
> diu zwei wazzer seuten dâ:
> der plân was vester anderswâ:
> Rosche Sabbîns dort
> diu houbetstat den vierden ort
> begreif mit mûren und mit grabn
> und mit manegem turne hôhe erhabn.

The course of the Poynzaclîns appears to be partly parallel to
the Sabîns. Bêne carrying a message from Itonjê to Gramoflanz
arrives at Rosche Sabbîns, presumably from Schastel Marveile,
on the Poynzaclîns:

> 686.16   Bêne ûf dem Poynzaclîns
> kom in eime seytiez.
> disiu maere si niht liez,
> 'von Schastel marveile gevarn
> ist mîn frowe mit frouwen scharn'.

Jôflanze too is integrated into this geographical scheme by the
river Sabîns; it continues its course in the vicinity of Jôflanze.
Gâwân riding out of Jôflanze comes upon Parzival by the Sabîns:

> 678.15   al ein reit mîn hêr Gâwân
> von dem her verre ûf den plân.
> gelücke müezes walden!
> er sah ein rîter halden
> bî dem wazzer Sabîns, ...

Jôflanze lies somewhere between Rosche Sabbîns and Terre Marveile,
near the Sabîns. It does not seem to be particularly far removed
from Schastel Marveile, both Arthur and Gâwân reach Jôflanze from
Schastel Marveile in a short space of time (667.4f.). But it is
not on the same side of the Sabîns as Schastel Marveile. Arthur,
who has camped on the field of jousts, can move off straightway
to Jôflanze (662.26-663.14; 667.1-8). Gâwân's retinue must be
ferried across the Sabîns before following the same road (667.27-

668.8). There is no great distance, either, between Jôflanze
and Rosche Sabbîns; Arthur's messengers are despatched from
Jôflanze to Rosche Sabbîns shortly before the encounter between
Gâwân and Parzival takes place (677f.), and return to Jôflanze
while the joust is still in progress (688.4f.).

The scene of Parzival's joust with Feirefîz is also incorporated
into the pattern arround Schastel Marveile. The combat is seen in
the magic pillar at Schastel Marveile (755.16-21) which records
the happenings within a radius of six miles (592.1-13; 759.21-6).
The 'liehte waste' where Parzival meets Feirefîz is not far from
Jôflanze. He reaches it shortly after his departure from Arthur's
camp (733.2Of.) and returns with Feirefîz on the same day (754.
29-755.30). As the magic pillar reflects the events within six
miles, and Terre Marveile extends for eight miles around Schastel
Marveile, the scene of Parzival's joust with Feirefîz is to be
sought in Terre Marveile, no further than six miles from its
castle. Their speedy return from this place of combat to Jôflanze,
consequently suggests a short distance also between Terre Marveile and Jôflanze.

Bordering on the heath where the two brothers meet is a forest
(735.5-8), and beyond it lies the natural harbour where Feirefîz's
fleet has cast anchor (736.25-7; 737.7-9). The harbour is fairly
close to the 'liehte waste' (753.3-7) and easily reached from
Jôflanze (822.8-12).

The geographical scheme dominated by Schastel Marveile thus includes Plippalinôt's house, the rivers Poynzaclîns and Sabîns,
the landing-place with the field of jousts, Clinschor's forest,
Li Gweiz Prelljûs, the scene of Parzival's encounter with Feirefîz, Rosche Sabbîns, Lôgroys, Jôflanze, an unnamed forest and
the natural harbour. The early stages of Gâwân's travels, Bêârosche and Schanpfanzûn, are not linked with this scheme, just as
Grâharz and Brôbarz of Parzival's travel-history are not fitted
into the geographical perspective.

Terre Marveile and its neighbouring regions are as clearly outlined as Terre de Salvaesche and its surroundings. With a mass
of definitions of place, time and direction, all of which aim at
interlocking the various fabulous localities, and by constant re-
association of familiar background with a variety of characters,
Wolfram shapes a geography of fiction impressive in its vividness,
and startling in its precision. The absence of conflicting elements in this poetic cartography is evidence of a definite, exact
and concrete picture of two landscapes in Wolfram's imagination.
It is possible to retrace this picture leaving out of account the
points of the compass. East and west, north and south must remain
interchangeable; Wolfram is silent on this point.

The two schemes around Munsalvaesche and Schastel Marveile are
not linked with one another geographically. The obvious points
from which a spatial relationship might have been developed are
Jôflanze and Barbigoel. Feirefîz returns to Jôflanze from Munsal-

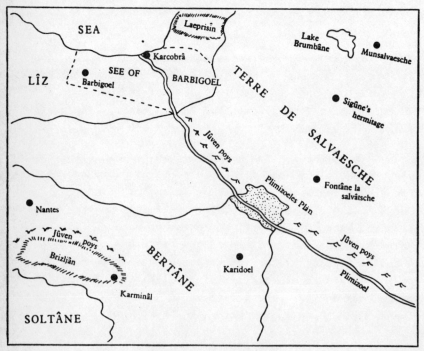

Munsalvaesche and its surroundings

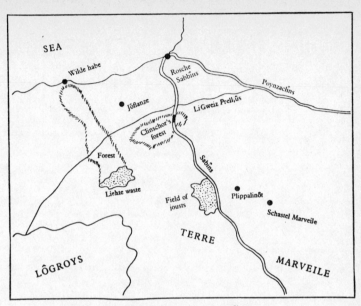

Schastel Marveile and its surroundings

vaesche via Karcobrâ in the see of Barbigoel, and Parzival rides
straight from Jôflanze into Terre de Salvaesche, but in neither
case is there any allusion to direct geographical connection.
On the contrary, Jôflanze is shown to be extremely remote from
both Terre de Salvaesche (792.10-15) and Karcobrâ (821.29, 30).
No link is suggested either between Barbigoel and Lôgroys. At
the beginning of Book X Gâwân's visit to Barbigoel is mentioned
and his subsequent appearance at Lôgroys then treated in detail.
However, he does not reach Lôgroys directly from Barbigoel, but
spends some time in unnamed regions in search of the Grail, before
coming to Lôgroys. The two geographical patterns are not bridged
at any point, and instead of one continuous landscape, they form
two self-contained schemes of fabulous geography. Connection
between them is provided solely by the movements of the various
characters, by Arthur who journeys to the outskirts of Terre de
Salvaesche and to Terre Marveile, by Gâwân who travels to Barbigoel and Terre Marveile, by Parzival who has access to most
stations of Gâwân's travel-history, by Feirefîz who comes to

Terre Marveile and Jôflanze and is then taken to Munsalvaesche, and finally by Cundrîe who is the only one to penetrate into both castles, Schastel Marveile and Munsalvaesche. Cundrîe, the Grail messenger, is in the habit of visiting Arnîve at Schastel Marveile. In Book XI Arnîve explains to Gâwân the origin of the ointment which will help to cure him.

> 579.23   sie sprach 'ich senfte iu schiere.
>   Cundrîe la surziere
>   ruochet mich sô dicke sehn:
>   swaz von erzenîe mac geschehn,
>   des tuot si mich gewaltec wol.
>   sît Anfortas in jâmers dol
>   kom, daz man im helfe warp,
>   diu salbe im half, daz er niht starp:
>   si ist von Munsalvaesche komm.'

But while through her person a connection is woven between Schastel Marveile and Munsalvaesche - one of many, for Schastel Marveile is seen as the counterpart to Munsalvaesche - an allusion of hers establishes their separation in terms of Wolfram's fabulous geography. Schastel Marveile is extraordinarily far removed from Terre de Salvaesche, so much so, that even the Grail messenger has difficulties in reaching it in one day from the Plimizoeles Plân:

> 318.16   ich weiz vier küneginne
>   unt vier hundert juncfrouwen,
>   die man gerne möhte schouwen.
>   ze Schastel marveil die sint:
>   al âventiure ist ein wint,
>   wan die man dâ bezalen mac,
>   hôher minne wert bejac.
>   al hab ich der reise pîn,
>   ich wil doch hînte drûffe sîn.

As striking as the wide separation of the two schemes is the difference in size of Terre Marveile and Terre de Salvaesche. While Schastel Marveile commands a territory of only eight miles' radius, Munsalvaesche dominates a wilderness of thirty miles all round. The implication here is the same as in the travel-histories, where inequality of distance covered is one of the features used to contrast Parzival's travels with those

of Gâwân. Munsalvaesche's superiority over Schastel Marveile
is indicated by its wider territorial power.

One further feature underlines the dissimilarity of the two
schemes. Although a continuous landscape is represented in both,
only one of them is homogeneous in character. The domain of
Gâwân's exploration mirrors the even course of his adventures,
and shows no abrupt division of its component parts. Neither
the geographical pattern centred on Schastel Marveile, nor the
action set against it, know of any sharp distinction between
Terre Marveile and the world at large. The scheme which represents the background to a large part of Parzival's travels,
however, falls by the insistence on the other-wordly quality
of Terre de Salvaesche into two parts, Terre de Salvaesche and
the outside world - Terre de Salvaesche and Bertâne.

The break in the continuity of the landscape illustrates the
contrasting nature of Parzival's experiences in Terre de Salvaesche with those elsewhere. In Bertâne Parzival's prime
concern is with chivalrous life, while in Terre de Salvaesche -
which he reaches considerably later - he is confronted with
values of a different kind.

Bertâne sees the beginning and temporary end of Parzival's
career as an Arthurian knight, at Arthur's court at Nantes and
later at the Plimizoeles Plân. While in Bertâne the pursuit of
chivalry is in the foreground, in Terre de Salvaesche it is
Parzival's sins and errors and their expiation. This change in
the nature of events associated with the change of background
from Bertâne to Terre de Salvaesche emerges with great clarity
in Parzival's first two meetings with Sigûne, of which the first
takes place in the forest of Brizljân in Bertâne and the second
near Munsalvaesche in Terre de Salvaesche. In Bertâne Sigûne
informs him of all those details which are of importance in his
pursuit of knighthood, of his noble origin, his ancestry, his
kingship and his obligations as feudal lord:

> 140.25   dîn vater was ein Anschevîn:
> ein Wâleis von der muoter dîn
> bistu geborn von Kanvoleiz.
> die rehten wârheit ich des weiz.
> du bist och künec ze Norgâls:
> in der houbetstat ze Kingrivâls
> sol dîn houbet krône tragen.
> dirre fürste wart durch dich erslagen,
> wand er dîn lant ie werte:
> sîne triuwe er nie verscherte.
> junc vlaetic süezer man,
> die gebruoder hânt dir vil getân.
> zwei lant nam dir Lähelîn:
> disen ritter unt den vetern dîn
> ze tjostiern sluoc Orilus.

In Terre de Salvaesche Sigûne reveals to Parzival some of the
mysteries of the Grail castle, tells him of the Grail kinship and
of the magic properties of the sword he received at Munsalvaesche,
and is the first to upbraid him for his fatal error at the Grail
castle. Her final words declare his newly won knighthood to be
null and void, foreshadowing Cundrîe's condemnation:

> 255.25   ... mirst wol bekant,
> ze Munsalvaesche an iu verswant
> êre und rîterlîcher prîs.

The changed aspect of events is strangely mirrored in Sigûne's
appearance, altered almost beyond recognition since their meeting
in Bertâne:

> 252.27   ôwê war kom dîn rôter munt?
> bistuz Sigûne, diu mir kunt
> tet wer ich was, ân allen vâr?
> dîn reideleht lanc prûnez hâr,
> Des ist dîn houbet blôz getân.
> zem fôrest in Brizljân
> sah ich dich dô vil minneclîch,
> swie du waerest jâmers rîch.

The unique position which Terre de Salvaesche assumes in Wolfram's fabulous geography as a background charged with symbolic
significance, again shows itself in Parzival's encounter with
Orilus. It is not immediately clear why the setting for Parzival's oath, which brings about the reconcilation between Orilus
and Jeschûte, should be Fontâne la salvâtsche (268.25-30). The
reason becomes obvious, however, in Book IX, devoted to Parzi-

val's second visit to Trevrizent's hermitage. Fontâne la salvâtsche is the background to Parzival's repentance of all his
sins and errors, those of which he accuses himself in Book IX,
those which Trevrizent recognizes, and that very first childish
error which caused Jeschûte's misfortune. As Fontâne la salvâtsche is the setting for Parzival's recognition of guilt, it
is appropriate that his oath concerning Jeschûte's innocence
should also be performed here. The choice of any other background
for this particular scene would deprive it of much of its meaning.

As a feature of composition the development of geographical
schemes also performs a purely technical, but in a medieval work
by no means negligible function: it aids memory. In a work of the
length and complexity of 'Parzival', this constitutes an important
virtue even today; to the contemporary audience, however, it must
have been a boon. For, although the verse narratives of medieval
Germany were to some extent composed with readers in mind, the
relative scarcity and considerable expense of manuscripts necessitated that they were predominantly read aloud to groups of
listeners.[76] The ensuing chiefly auditory reception of this literature taxed the memory of an audience severely. A technique
of presentation therefore, which lightened this burden, would
be of inestimable advantage. The geographical schemes have precisely this merit. Places repeatedly reintroduced become familiar,
and their geographical continuity ensures that few of them fade
from sight. Moreover, place-names become associated with episodes;
their repetition and connection with other place-names will call
to mind scenes otherwise perhaps forgotten. Wolfram sometimes
stresses this link. Thus when Parzival reaches Trevrizent's
hermitage for the second time, we are reminded of his previous
visit to Fontâne la salvâtsche with Orilus and Jeschûte (452.13,
14; 455.25-30). Or when he is to meet Condwîrâmûrs on the Plimizoeles Plân in Book XVI, we find a brief reference to his trance

---

76 Cf. Ruth Crosby, Oral Delivery.

and the joust with Segramors which had taken place here (797.4-10). Parzival remembers the forest of Brizljân when meeting Sigûne in Terre de Salvaesche (253.2, 3), and Guinevere recalls the scene by the Plimizoel while at Bems bî der Korcâ (646.6-22). The mere mention of Karcobrâ during Feirefîz's return to the East conjures up an association with Trevrizent setting out on his travels, as he describes it to Parzival in Book IX. Gâwân's visit to Barbigoel strikes a familiar note, as we know Karcobrâ to be connected with it.

By disciplining the background to Parzival and Gâwân into a geography of fiction, Wolfram has gained some obvious technical advantages over his source. His individual episodes are more firmly connected than in 'Li Contes del Graal', as they do not merely appear in sequence, but are adjusted to a perspective. The division of his fabulous geography into two parts, their separation and contrasting character, sharply underline the difference between Parzival and Gâwân. The fixed geographical distribution of scenes of action assists recollection of past events. But far more important than these technical gains is the poetic spell cast by a background which emerges with visual force as a well-known countryside and familiar geography. The realism of geographical co-ordination creates a world in its own right into which the audience becomes absorbed. It ensures its temporary credibility, the suspension of disbelief, the illusion of a reality.

The analysis of Wolfram's construction of a geography of fiction, and his use of the geography of fact, illuminates features of his craftsmanship and personality as an artist which the investigation into his treatment of chivalrous journeys already brought to light. First and foremost he seems to be moved, even driven by an unabating desire to improve on his source. Although sensitive to its slightest suggestion and faithful to its general outline, he transforms it, readjusting it in accordance with his own idiosyncrasies and reorientating it to his personal vision.

To this task he brings a strange blend of extreme self-confidence
and infinite, almost humble patience. Self-confidently he in-
dulges his extravagant love of complexity and plans on a most
ambitious scale, utterly certain of the vitality of his imagination. Patiently, industriously he attends to the introduction of
details necessary for this transformation, attaining complete
command over a maze of minutiae in which a lesser author would
have become irretrievably lost. The unhesitating choice of the
lavish scale, the magpie zest for collecting a myriad of details,
the obvious delight in the bewildering intricacy of cross-refer-
ences are as characteristic of Wolfram as they are untypical of
Chrestien. His powers of organization, his untiring perfectionism,
his sense of symbolism, his emotional and intellectual depth and
the sweep of his imagination save him. What could so easily have
been a mere corruption of Chrestien's work is by these qualities
raised to the level of a masterpiece.

3. Parzival and Gâwân - Hero and Counterpart

Parzival is the hero of Wolfram's epic - we are not left in any
doubt about the author's intention here. Wolfram repeatedly
assures his audience that Parzival is the main figure of the
work. This occurs in the beginning - "den helt ich alsus grüeze"
(4.19), and before his name is revealed - "nu hoert in rehter
nennen,/ daz ir wol müget erkennen/ wer dirre âventiur hêrre
sî..." (140.11-13). In Book VII, when the narrative changes to
Gâwân, he refers to Parzival as "des maeres hêrre" (338.7), and
before their meeting near Jôflanze, Wolfram states, "an den
rehten stam diz maere ist komn" (678.30).

Wolfram's insistence is by no means superfluous, for he provides
the narrative with a parallel hero, Gâwân, who becomes the
counterpart of the main figure, and whose adventures and conduct
elucidate the career of the hero proper. The two characters,
Parzival and Gâwân, stand side by side in the work as it were,
mutually explanatory of their actions, temperament and fate.
In a variety of ways Wolfram has achieved a narrative reciprocity
between them which forces the audience constantly to compare
them, to measure one against the other and ultimately to assess
their relative significance.

The possibility of developing an intimate narrative connection
between the two main figures of the epic, was suggested to Wolfram by his source, where the basis for such a relationship was
laid, but not fully exploited. 'Li Contes del Graal' provided
Wolfram with the primary elements of a juxtaposition of the two
heroes; the roughly equal distribution of verses between them,[77]

---

77 Chrestien devotes lls. 69-4740 and then again lls. 6217-6518
    to Perceval. The Gauvain-story occupies lls. 4741-6215 and
    lls. 6519-9224. Thus just under 5000 lls. are allotted to
    Perceval, while approximately 4200 are assigned to the
    Gauvain-story.

their meeting at the Arthurian court whence they set out on
their respective journeys,[78] the partial congruence of their
quests[79] and the contrasting types of scenery associated with
them.[80] Wolfram makes use of all these features, but elaborates
them in his usual manner so as to establish a narrative reciprocity between Parzival and Gâwân, so close, subtle and meaningful, that comprehension of the hero's fate is impossible without the foil of Gâwân's career. He, moreover, invests the parallelism of Parzival and Gâwân with a particular significance by
making their relationship symbolic and characterizing them as
representatives of two different forms of existence. By showing
them finally in allegorical combat he neatly concludes the narrative left fragmentary by Chrestien, and also provides the
solution to the problem posed by their juxtaposition.

The distribution of space in the epic between Parzival and Gâwân
is approximately the same as in 'Li Contes del Graal', i.e.
slightly less than half deals with Gâwân. Leaving aside the
introductory sections, Books I and II, six books are devoted
to Parzival (Books III, IV, V, IX, XV and XVI), six to Gâwân,
(Books VII, VIII, X, XI, XII and XIII), and two, Books VI and
XIV are concerned with both characters, with Parzival rather
more in the foreground. Therefore, as in 'Li Contes del Graal',
Gâwân's importance is already evident from the mere arrangement
of material.[81]

---

78 Chrestien 4418ff.

79 Both Perceval and Gauvain seek the bleeding lance. Perceval
    sets out to do so after the ugly damsel's challenge (4727ff.);
    Gauvain undertakes the quest after the episode at Escavalon
    (6110ff.).

80 Chrestien shows Perceval consistently against the background
    of a forest. Perceval's childhood is spent there (75). He
    rides through it on his way to his first adventure (628ff.).
    Between Carduel and Goort he passes through a forest (1305,
    1306). He rides through forests once again before reaching
    Belrepeire (1699ff.). In order to approach the Grail castle
    he must make his way through a forest (3422ff.), and he
    finally finds the hermit in a wood (6320ff.). Gauvain, on
    the other hand, is placed into pleasant scenery. He is seen

This narrative balance between the two characters leaves in Chrestien's unfinished work the impression of a division. He deals with the groups of episodes concerning Perceval and Gauvain consecutively, without indicating either connection or simultaneity of their respective adventures. It is difficult to decide whether this manner of handling the fable represents a major fault of his poetic technique as has been suggested.[82] Had Chrestien completed the romance, this feature of a division might have formed an important principle of composition. Wolfram, however, is intent on close connection of his two main figures. During the sequence of the Gâwân-episodes he therefore allows Parzival to appear in person, frequently refers to him, and shows him as partly following Gâwân's route in the background. Purely consecutive treatment gives way to a dual plot, and the audience never loses sight of the hero, although his counterpart occupies the foreground.[83] This fusion of the two strands of the action decisively furthers the development of narrative reciprocity between Parzival and Gâwân.

---

in meadow (4914ff., 6674ff., 7243ff., 8535ff.), orchard (6741ff.), on a hill (6519ff.), under trees (4914ff., 6519ff., 6828ff., 8470ff.), and only twice is he said to have passed through forests, but is never actually shown in a forest-setting (6657ff., 7224ff.).

81 This arrangement was once considered a fault in the composition of the epic, cf. W. Dilthey, Die ritterl. Dichtung und das nationale Epos, Von dtsch. Dichtung und Musik, Berlin, 1933, p. 121.
The balance Perceval/Gauvain in 'Li Contes del Graal' has recently been analyzed by Keith Busby, 'Gauvain in Old French Literature', Amsterdam, 1980, chapter three: 'The Conte du Graal of Chrétien de Troyes', pp. 83-144.

82 Cf. ed. A. Hilka, Einleitung, XXIX; also St. Hofer, La Structure Du Conte Del Graal; but on the other hand, A. Fierz-Monnier, Initiation u. Wandlung, Berne, 1951, p. 65.

83 Cf. Bodo Mergell, Wolfram von Eschenbach und seine frz. Quellen, vol. 2: Wolframs Parzival, pp. 246/247.

The motif of the combined quest reappears in Wolfram's work
in an amended form, so as to accentuate the parallelism of
the hero and his counterpart. The basic feature - the two
characters ultimately pursuing the same quest - is retained;
Perceval and Gauvain are to find the bleeding lance, Parzival
and Gâwân the Grail. The latter pair, however, are parallelized
also in their final achievement. The same messenger challenges
them to their destination, to Munsalvaesche and Schastel Marveile.[84] The close connection between Parzival and Gâwân is
finally made more visible still by Wolfram's additions to the
basic motif of the trait of partly identical journeys.

With the remaining two features provided by his source of the
juxtaposition of the chief characters, with their meeting and
the contrast in scenery, Wolfram allows himself still greater
scope. He entirely recasts the episode of their encounter and
reshapes the contrast in background, drawing a clearer distinction between the two types than Chrestien.

The scene of their meeting in Arthur's camp in Bk. VI establishes
Gâwân as Parzival's counterpart, sets their parallelism into
motion, illustrates their differing temperaments and motivates
the contrasting nature of their progress through life. Their
future is shown as being determined equally by character and
external forces of destiny.

For the prelude to the decisive occurrences at Arthur's court
which send Parzival and Gâwân about their respective tasks, Wolfram still follows his source fairly closely. It is not until
the accusations are levelled against them, that his departure
from Chrestien's description becomes considerable. Here the

---

84 In Chrestien the possibility for this motif exists as well.
    In addition to the Grail castle the ugly damsel mentions
    the quest of Montescleire which Gauvain takes upon himself,
    but the motif remains a blind one, presumably only because
    the romance was not completed.

differentiation between hero and counterpart sets in, immediately after their parallelism has been established.

As in 'Li Contes del Graal' Gâwân appears as a paragon of breeding and courtesy, and is portrayed as the most distinguished knight of Arthur's entourage.[85] Parzival is familiar with Gâwân's fame and eagerly solicits his friendship which is readily granted.[86] This feature of close companionship is pursued by Wolfram even more insistently than by Chrestien. He shows Parzival and Gâwân sitting side by side at the Table Round (311.7/8). After the challenge they are seen standing together and the court comfort them both (326.11-14). Before exchanging farewells Gâwân kisses Parzival (331.22), and both address one another as "friunt" (331.25; 332.9). The hero and "der tavelrunder hôhster prîs" (301.7) are thus linked in mutual recognition, immediate and firm friendship and are set apart from the crowd. In order to demonstrate their parallelism, this basis for comparison, Wolfram uses one further motif of the French romance - a messenger arrives for each with an accusation. At this point the ways of the two story-tellers part. For while Chrestien draws no particular distinction between Perceval and Gauvain, by the content of the accusations, their form, or Perceval's and Gauvain's reactions to them, Wolfram at once differentiates strikingly, opening a gulf of discrepancy between the hero and his counterpart, directly after placing them into a position of proximity for comparison.[87] Every facet of Wolfram's description is now calculated to show their separation in terms of temperament, outlook, maturity and fate.

---

85   Chrestien 4350ff.; Wolfram 299.13ff.

86   Chrestien 4486ff.; Wolfram 304ff. In Chrestien, Gauvain seeks Perceval's acquaintance with as great an eagerness as he seeks his. In Wolfram, Parzival's acceptance is demonstrated simply by Gâwân's use of du, in answer to Parzival's request.

87   Wolfram makes this shift of emphasis very dramatic indeed. The messengers arrive shortly after Gâwân has led Parzival to Arthur's camp. In Chrestien the court is first moved to

The two speeches by Cundrîe and Kingrimursel immediately reveal
the dissimilarity of their fortune. While Kingrimursel delivers
a challenge still fairly courteously worded in chivalrous tradition, Cundrîe utters a condemnation, outrageous, violent and
deeply offensive not only to Parzival but also to Arthur and his
knights. Gâwân is guilty, so Kingrimursel maintains, of a transgression as a knight (321.8-15) and is unfit for the society of
knights (322.1-6). Parzival's condemnation concerns his failure
as a human being, and his presence at Arthur's court has for

Carlion after Perceval's arrival, and the messengers do not
appear until three days later. There is a change of scene and
a lapse of time. Both are eliminated by Wolfram to make the
action less diffuse.
As regards the difference in treatment of the subsequent
events, Chrestien's description is noticeably more moderate
and consequently far less riveting than Wolfram's. The ugly
damsel's speech, although containing severe strictures, is
by no means as offensive as Cundrîe's (4646ff.). She still
adheres to the normal rules of courtesy by greeting the King
and his court, and merely excludes Perceval from this gesture
of respect. She does not shower abuse on Perceval as Cundrîe
does, and takes formal leave from the King before her departure, which Cundrîe omits to do. In contrast with Wolfram's
portrayal, the damsel's accusations make little impression
upon the court. Interest is aroused only by her mention of
the challenge of Montescleire. Immediately after her departure Gauvain speaks, taking the quest of Montescleire upon
himself. Perceval then vows a life of chivalrous hardship
as penitence for his omission, until he has uncovered the
mysteries of the Grail and the bleeding lance. He does not
labour under a particular sense of disgrace, nor does he
display great contrition. After his speech he drops out of
this scene, and receives no further mention in the romance
until the episode with the hermit. No farewells are exchanged between Perceval and Gauvain, or Perceval and the
court.
Guinganbresil's challenge of Gauvain is also less extreme
than Kingrimursel's accusation of Gâwân. His speech does not
include the avowal of hatred nor the lamentations of Kingrimursel. The whole scene is briefer in Chrestien than in
Wolfram. The King does not speak in Gauvain's defence, nor
do the court comment on the episode. After having accepted
Guinganbresil's summons to Escavalon, Gauvain selects his
equipment and leaves Carlion. A reference to the grief felt
by the court at his departure concludes the scene, and the
poet announces his intention henceforth to deal at length
with Gauvain's adventures.

Cundrîe contaminated the King and his company of knights (314.23-315.15). She therefore refuses to salute Arthur (315.17-19) and accuses him and his court of <u>valsch</u> (314.29/30; 315.6). Kingrimursel opens his speech by greeting the King and his court (320.22-25) and rebukes Gâwân for his audacity in partaking of their fellowship (322.1-6). In the face of Cundrîe's grave insults the court is struck dumb (319.12-18); after Kingrimursel's accusation, however, the King speaks in defence of Gâwân (322.15-30), and Bêâcurs, Gâwân's brother offers to fight for him (323ff.). Kingrimursel's challenge proffers Gâwân the opportunity to justify himself by deed of arms (321.16-22). Cundrîe's condemnation offers Parzival neither the possibility nor even the hope of redress. While a misfortune has thus befallen Gâwân, a catastrophe has struck Parzival.

Parzival is plunged into despair by his public disgrace (329.20-24), the sudden confusion of his values (330.1-6) and the realization of his failure (330.21-30). He rejects all efforts to console him and yields to sorrow and grief (329.18-330.22). This sadness which overcomes Parzival is dwelt upon insistently: "daz er sô trûrec von in reit, / ich waen, daz was in allen leit" (331.9, 10), and "den helt treip von in trûrens not" (331.18).

Nothing approaching this dilemma is felt by Gâwân. Kingrimursel's challenge neither disturbs his self-possession, nor does it upset his judgement. While Parzival is thrown into confusion, Gâwân retains his calmness and the sanity of his outlook. He thus refuses Bêâcurs's offer and merely demurs at the unreasonableness of the accusation, expressing also his dislike of fighting for fighting's sake:

> 323.24 Gâwân sprach 'ich pin sô wîs
> daz ich dich, bruoder, niht gewer
> dîner bruoderlîchen ger.
> ine weiz war umbe ich strîten sol,
> ouch entuot mir strîten niht sô wol:
> ungerne wolte ich dir versagn,
> wan daz ich müesez laster tragn.'

Being <u>wîs</u> becomes the governing feature of Gâwân's subsequent
behaviour.[88] We are left in no doubt as to what Gâwân must do:

>325.7 sie jâhen daz her Gâwân
>des kampfes sorge müese hân
>gein sîner wâren manheit,
>des fürsten der dâ von in reit.

He therefore calmly sets about the task of preparing himself for
the journey (335.1-3) and selects his necessary equipment at
leisure (344.10-23). Far from being annihilated by grief and
aroused by inner confusion like Parzival who spends less time
and thought on his preparations (322.19ff.), Gâwân sets out "mit
unverzagter manheit" (355.25).

This mod of confidence and calm acceptance of his misfortune
gives Gâwân a detachment which permits him to consider Parzival's
predicament rather than his own. Gâwân's first words after Kingrimursel's departure, are adressed to Parzival whom he tries to
console. In his efforts to comfort him, Gâwân reveals his trust
in God to whose grace he commends Parzival:

>331.25 'ich weiz wol, friwent, daz dîn vart
>gein strîtes reise ist ungespart.
>dâ geb dir got gelücke zuo,
>und helfe ouch mir daz ich getuo
>dir noch den dienst als ich kan gern.
>des müeze mich sîn kraft gewern.'

But for Parzival the experience of moral bewilderment has had
disastrous results. He not only despairs of God but rejects and
actively defies him:

>323.1 Der Wâleis sprach 'wê waz ist got?
>waer der gewaldec, sölhen spot
>het er uns pêden niht gegebn,
>kunde got mit kreften lebn.
>ich was im diens undertân,
>sît ich genâden mich versan.
>nu wil i'm dienst widersagn:
>hât er haz, den wil ich tragn.

---

88 Cf. Jost Trier's commentary on the use and meaning of <u>wîs</u>
    in Parzival: Der deutsche Wortschatz im Sinnbezirk des Ver-
    standes, vol.I: Von den Anfängen bis zum Beginn des 13.
    Jahrhunderts, Heidelberg, 1931, p. 260.

The situation which had developed immediately after Parzival's departure from the Grail castle is now dramatically reinforced. After Parzival's visit to Munsalvaesche, supernatural guidance had been withdrawn as a consequence of his failure, and the certainty of direction in his travels was lost. He loses his way as soon as he leaves Munsalvaesche, and continues in the same uncertain manner until he suddenly finds himself in Arthur's camp. Divine assistance which had already ended after his visit to Munsalvaesche is now actively repelled by Parzival by his open defiance. His fall from divine favour which had taken place unknown to Parzival, is now confirmed and strengthened by his own action. Divine hostility towards Parzival is now countered by Parzival's hostility against God. The strained relationship between Parzival and God, now doubly charged, produced intensified results. His short aimless ride which had taken him from Munsalvaesche to the Plimizoel, is now extended into one vast ride at random, leading him through innumerable countries and lasting over a period of many years.

Gâwân, on the other hand, older than Parzival, more mature and richer in experience, is better able to bear the blows of fate. Not only does his faith remain unshaken, but he accepts his misfortune with equanimity. At the very outset of his journey Gâwân is already in possession of that outlook on life which Parzival does not achieve until he returns to the Arthurian court at Jôflanze. Before Parzival departs from the court, the change in him becomes manifest, he acquiesces in his fate, and is ready to accept his singularly harsh destiny, a love without solace, exclusion from the joys of others, and continued grief:

> 733.1 Er dâhte 'sît ich mangel hân
> daz den saeldehaften undertân
> ist (ich mein die minne,
> diu manges trûrgen sinne

> mit freuden helfe ergeilet),
> sît ich des pin verteilet,
> ich enruoche nu waz mir geschiht.
> got wil mîner freude niht.
> diu mich twinget minnen gir,
> stüend unser minne, mîn unt ir,
> daz scheiden dar zuo hôrte
> sô daz uns zwîvel stôrte,
> ich möhte wol ze anderre minne komn:
> nu hât ir minne mir benomn
> ander minne und freudebaeren trôst.
> ich pin trûrens unerlôst.
> gelücke müeze freude wern
> die endehafter freude gern:
> got gebe freude al disen scharn:
> ich wil ûz disen freuden varn.'

On the same day as this change of heart becomes apparent, Parzival is called to the Grail, his rides at random cease, and guidance is returned to him in the form of Cundrîe.

Just as Parzival and Gâwân are differentiated in their reactions
to their experiences, a distinction is also drawn in the reasons
for their departure, in so far as they relate to behaviour. Subsequent events show this, and in retrospect illuminate the contrast in personalities still further. Parzival's and Gâwân's
enforced wanderings are in either case precipitated by failure.
Parzival has failed before the Grail, Gâwân, so Kingrimursel
insists, in his chivalrous integrity. Both set out to rectify
the shortcomings of which they are accused. Where Parzival is
concerned, failure is real; whether it is to be interpreted as
an error of judgement due to immaturity and inexperience, or
actual sin, is immaterial in this context. His behaviour at
Munsalvaesche still represents failure. In Gâwân's case, however,
failure proves to have been fictitious; the accusation has been
false. This is stated first in Book VIII:

> 413.13 unschuldec was hêr Gâwân:
> ez hete ein ander man getân,
> wande der stolze Ehcunat
> ein lanzen durch in lêrte pfat,
> dô er Jofreyden fîz Ydoel
> fuorte gegen Barbigoel,
> den er bî Gâwâne vienc.
> durch den disiu nôt ergienc

and is subsequently acknowledged by his opponents, so that the joust between Kingrimursel and Gâwân never takes place (503.5-20).[89]

An accusation rather similar to that by Kingrimursel is later brought against Gâwân by Gramoflanz, but in this repetition of circumstances the imputed transgression does not even concern his own person, but his father Lôt, for whom he is expected to deputize in a trial by joust (608.9-30). The combat is again prevented (726.8ff.).

In contrast to Parzival, Gâwân appears as being incapable of failure, except later where the Grail is concerned. And here again, failure is not real, in the sense that it does not emanate from behaviour, but represents a restriction imposed by destiny. Throughout the work, Gâwân is characterized as the impeccable knight: "der nie gewarp nâch schanden" (338).

The nature of the two accusations levelled against Gâwân also shows that the conception of 'failure' where it concerns Gâwân is of much narrower connotation than within the Parzival-story. When referring to Gâwân, it applies to a crime within the chivalrous code, whereas with Parzival it is a matter of wider humanity. This does not mean that the latter's failure at Munsalvaesche does not also constitute a transgression against chivalry. On the contrary, Cundrîe specifically castigates the knight in Parzival by extolling the chivalrous virtues of Feirefîz and Gahmuret after her condemnation of him (316.29ff.); but while Gâwân's supposed failure appears in the shape of a formal motif of court literature - "ime gruozer mînen hêrren sluoc" (321.10) - Parzival's failure, inactivity in the face of human misery, has wider implications than purely chivalrous ones.

---

89 This feature does not occur in Chrestien.

Wolfram thus extends this scene in Arthur's camp so that it acts as a major revelation of personality. Through his adjustments it also comes to represent the supreme test of character, the hinge of fate, for both Gâwân and Parzival, for the poet uses it to motivate their divergent future. This discrepancy manifests itself quite concretely in the form and in certain features of their journeys.

Gâwân's quest exhibits throughout precisely that positive feature which Parzival's travels had lost after his first visit to Munsalvaesche - certainty of direction. His travels move along an even course of certain success, uninterrupted by momentary failure. Divine guidance is not in such palpable evidence in Gâwân's journey as in Parzival's early route, but neither is there a conspicuous withdrawal of grace. He is never helped along so firmly and unequivocally as Parzival on his first visit to Munsalvaesche, nor does he ever receive such striking supernatural assistance as Parzival does before Fontâne la Salvâtsche in Book IX. Nevertheless, his road is clearly set out for him as well, and he is drawn along it and cannot deviate. That he is firmly fixed on this predestined route, is demonstrated by his inability to enter Grail territory. The hope of being able to do so, still stirs in Gâwân even after his successful struggle at Schastel Marveile. When Arnîve mentions Munsalvaesche Gâwân eagerly reacts to her words:

> 580.2 dô Gâwân hête vernomn
> Munsalvaesche nennen,
> dô begunder freude erkennen:
> er wânde er waer dâ nâhe bî.

This is the last mention in the work of Gâwân's quest for the Grail. It is not within his power to stray from his course.

Gâwân's even progress is further illustrated by his capacity for constantly pursuing the correct road, i.e. the road which inevitably leads directly to <u>âventiure</u>. Whenever Gâwân sets out anew, he is immediately taken to the scene of his next exploit. No tentative movement delays the steady course of his

travels. Again this feature becomes one of particular significance through contrast with Parzival's quest in which hesitant
and bewildered movement occurs several times. Gâwân is never
lost like Parzival after his first visit to Munsalvaesche, and
before he reaches Arthur's camp by the Plimizoel. Nor is he ever
thwarted in the pursuit of his travels as Parzival is in Book IX,
when attempting to return to the Grail castle. Nor is there ever
any indecision on Gâwân's part of where to turn, as there is
with Parzival, shortly before he is led to Fontâne la salvâtsche.
And finally, he is never compelled to roam at random as Parzival
is for long periods after Cundrîe's curse.

This certainty of direction, so marked in Gâwân's travels does
not even apply to Parzival's when the congruence of their travel-
history begins after Book VI. Parzival who follows Gâwân in the
background, nevertheless does not share in the certainty of his
course. For him, Gâwân's journey, which he retraces, is a ride
at random. For, while Gâwân is here in his proper sphere, Parzival is out of his, temporarily excluded from it and compelled to
roam the world aimlessly. Instead of strictly adhering to Gâwân's
progress, Parzival is shown as travelling more widely and therefore as interrupting his parallel journey. Nor does he touch upon
all the places visited by Gâwân. Finally chronological narrative
is at a certain point suspended for him. For although he arrives
at Lôgroys, in Terre Marveile and at Li Gweiz Prelljûs in the
same order as Gâwân, chronological reference to Parzival is discontinued. In the course of the episode at Lôgroys, no mention
is made of him, and it is not until much later, after Gâwân has
been to Li Gweiz Prelljûs, that we learn of Parzival's appearance
at Lôgroys.[90] His parallel movement must therefore be understood
as being punctuated by interruptions, departures from the course.
One such break, for example, although not elaborated, clearly
occurs after Parzival's departure from Terre Marveile. Orgelûse,
in her description of her meeting with Parzival in Terre Marveile

---

90   618.19-30.

merely says of his departure - "hin reit der ûz erkorne" (619.14).
After this encounter in Terre Marveile, Parzival temporarily dis-
appears from the narrative altogether. It is not until much
later that he comes to Li Gweiz Prelljûs which is only a short
distance from Schastel Marveile, and which he could hardly have
failed to find during the same day, had he continued in Terre
Marveile. The implication is that he immediately left Terre Marveile for other parts.

In this way then, by interruptions, actual and implied, suspension of chronological narrative and elimination of certain points
of the journey, Wolfram achieves the seemingly impossible - the
undeviating, certain course of Gâwân's travels becomes a ride
at random for Parzival, moving parallel in the background.

These differences in outward form of the two chivalrous careers
- the relative ease and certainty of the one and the difficulty
and frustrations of the other - are interpreted by Wolfram as
being the direct outcome of behaviour and of the supernatural
response to it. Not only does Parzival's quest originate in
genuine failure, while Gâwân's journey is urged upon him by a
fabricated fault, but Parzival, in his reaction to the catastrophe, falls into sin. Gâwân's prayer, enshrining his declaration of an unshaken faith is followed by Parzival's blasphemous
outburst in which he denies that God is all-powerful and formally rejects him as his liegelord, thus committing the cardinal
sin of superbia.[91] Divine grace is in consequence for a long
period withdrawn from Parzival, while Gâwân retains it. The

---

91 By rebelling against God and thus making himself independent
   of Him, Parzival follows the promptings of pride, one of the
   Seven Deadly Sins. Vid. its definition in Hasting's Encyclopaedia of Religion and Ethics; entry Pride. N.B. the following interpretation: "Pride is a habit of self-isolation or
   conscious independence, a perversity of will which is indif-
   ferent to the opinions and favours of others". Superbia was
   interpreted by some as the worst and basic of the seven cardinal sins, leading naturally to the other six, vid. op. cit.,
   entries: "Pride; Seven Deadly Sins".

shape of chivalrous progress through life therefore appears as being decided by the faith or the absence of faith of the questing knight, and by the resultant supernatural assistance or its withdrawal.

From the episode in Book VI onwards, Wolfram then concentrates chiefly on delineating the contrast in character and destiny of his two main figures. Nevertheless, he does not omit to remind his audience intermittently that there exists the link of similarity between Parzival and Gâwân, that we are, in fact, witnessing a parallelism. Not only do hero and counterpart set out from similar circumstances to follow partly the same road, but in the course of the narrative, other identical features appear, which stress the close connection between the two characters. Thus both Parzival and Gâwân reach their most important destination on a Grail horse. Parzival acquired the horse which will ultimately take him back to Munsalvaesche in a joust with a Grail knight (455.13-20). Gâwân regains Gringuljete before entering Schastel Marveile (50.17ff.). Gringuljete too is a Grail horse (540.26ff.). Parzival and Gâwân each encounter one of the two singular creatures sent to Anfortas by Queen Secundille, and are both treated by them with offensive disrespect. Cundrîe condemns Parzival, her brother Malcrêatiure abuses Gâwân (520.15ff.).

Munsalvaesche and Schastel Marveile, each representing the climax of the respective quest, show a number of similarities. In both castles the inhabitants are waiting to be delivered from misfortune. In both cases, the one who will ultimately set them free, is closely related to them. In both castles the families released from suffering are eminent in chivalrous society. Parzival saves the Grail kinship, Gâwân part of the Arthurian clan.[92] Both castles possess one unique treasure, Munsalvaesche the Grail, Schastel Marveile Clinschor's magic

---

92 Arnîve is King Arthur's mother, Sangîve his sister, Cundrîe and Itonjê his nieces.

pillar. Both treasures are described as a "stein". Arnîve refers
to the pillar in this manner (592.1-4) and Trevrizent uses the
same expression when speaking of the Grail (469.3ff.). The lords
of both castles are crippled by an almost identical injury.
Clinschor is gelded (657.8) - "zeim kapûn mit eime snite / wart
Clinschor gemachet", Anfortas wounded with the same effect

> 479.8 mit einem gelupten sper
> wart er ze tjostieren wunt
> so daz er nimmer mêr gesunt
> wart, der süeze oeheim dîn
> durch die heidruose sîn.

In both cases the mutilation represents the punishment for an
excess of passion, for Clinschor's adultery with Iblis (656.3ff.),
for Anfortas's desire of Orgelûse (616.11ff.).

The parallelism of Parzival and Gâwân is further reflected in
descriptions of Condwîrâmûrs and Orgelûse. Both are of surpassing
beauty, comparable only to one another:

> 508.22 âne Condwîrn âmûrs,
> wart nie geborn sô schoener lîp.
> mit clârheit süeze was daz wîp,
> wol geschict unt kurtoys.
> si hiez Orgelûse de Lôgroys.

For Guinevere, Orgelûse and Condwîrâmûrs are the measure of
grace and dignity. She refers to their uniqueness when promising
to fulfil Gâwân's request for her presence at Jôflanze:

> 645.23 ich tuon im werden dienst dar
> mit wünneclîcher frouwen schar,
> die für wâr bî miner zît
> an prîse vor ûz hânt den strît.
> âne Parzivâles wîp
> unt ân Orgelûsen lîp
> sone erkenne ich ûf der erde
> bî toufe kein so werde.

Both Parzival and Gâwân are introduced into the epic already
as children. Parzival's childhood is treated in full in Book
III. Gâwân, the child, appears in Book II, with his father
before Kanvoleis, Herzeloyde's residence:

> 66.15 hie ist och Gâwân, des suon,
> sô kranc daz er niht mac getuon
> rîterschaft enkeine
> er was bî mir, der kleine:
> er sprichet, möhter einen schaft
> zebrechen, trôst in des sîn kraft,
> er taete gerne rîters tât.
> wie fruos sîn ger begunnen hât!

In the art of battle both Gâwân and Parzival excel above all others. Their simultaneous fighting at Bêârosche makes this clear:

> 388.6 inrehalp wart ez dâ guot getân
> durch die jungen Obilôt,
> und ûzerhalb ein ritter rôt,
> die zwêne behielten dâ den prîs
> für sie niemen keinen wîs.

Finally both Parzival's and Gâwân's highest achievement pivots upon the necessity of a question. A question bestows the Grail kingship upon Parzival; insistence on asking a question introduces Gâwân to the test of Schastel Marveile. In both cases the vital significance of asking it, is indicated by the striking reiteration of the term "vrâgen" and its derivatives.[93]

Parzival and Gâwân, and their careers, therefore appear as closely linked throughout the work. A number of conspicuous

---

93 The problem of the question begins for Parzival during the Grail banquet, where vrâgen occurs six times; 239.10: "durch zuht in vrâgens doch verdroz"; 239.13: "ich solte vil gevrâgen niht"; 239.16: "âne vrâge ich vernim / wiez dirre massenîe stêt"; 240.3: "ôwê daz er niht vrâgte do!"; 240.6: "dô was er vrâgens mit ermant"; 240.10: "des im von vrâgn nu waere rât". The theme is taken up again at his departure: 247.28: "möht ir gerüeret hân den flans / und het den wirt gevrâget!" and then with Sigûne, when vrâgen is again used six times: 245.29: "hastu vrâge ir reht getân"; 225.1: "... ich hân gevrâget niht"; 255.4: "sît ir vrâgens sît verzagt"; 255.6: "daz iuch vrâgens dô verdrôz"; 255.19: "und het gevrâget sîner nôt"; 256.1: "Daz er vrâgens was sô laz". A similar situation where the hero is expected to ask a question, is created for Gâwân at Plippalinôt's house, near Schastel Marveile. During the conversation with Plippalinôt and his daughter, vrâgen appears ten times: 554.25: "daz waer mir liep durch vrâgen"; 555.3: "... hêr, nu vrâgt es niht"; 555.8: "... vrâget ander maere"; 555.11: "mit vrâge

similarities[94] sustains the intimate connection between them,
established by the description of their first meeting, and symbolized in their spontaneous friendship. The bond of identical
features and the close human contact between Parzival and Gâwân
ensure that Gâwân appears neither as Parzival's opponent nor his
rival, and least of all as the hero's mere reflection, but as a
counterpart in his own right.

Despite these links, the hero and his counterpart are separated
by a fundamental disparity of destiny and personality. The difference between them, already sharply outlined by Wolfram's
revised treatment of the episode at the Arthurian court is made
still more prominent by him as he elaborates Chrestien's technique of contrasted scenery. As in 'Li Contes del Graal', the
natural setting in Parzival resolves itself into two parts -
the background to the Parzival-narrative and the scenery of the
Gâwân-story. Certain motifs of natural background predominate
when the author is concerned with the hero, and others when the
narrative switches to his counterpart.[95] Wolfram does not under-

---

er gienc dem maere nâch"; 556.3: "ich vrâgte dise magt ein
teil"; 556.15: "... vrâgets niht durch got"; 556.19: "war
umbe ist iu mîn vrâgen leit"; 556.21: "kunnt ir vrâgen niht
verbern"; 557.3: "daz iuch des vrâgens niht bevilt"; 559.27:
"het ir selbe vrâgens niht erdâht".

94 Some of the above similarities and their narrative function
    have already been pointed out: cf. G. Keferstein, Die Gawan-
    handlung in Wolframs Parzival, GRM, 25 (1937), 256-274, here
    pp. 265-269; Bodo Mergell, Der Gral in Wolframs Parzival.
    Entstehung und Ausbildung der Gralssage im Hochmittelalter,
    PBB, 73 (1951), 1-94 and 74 (1952), 77-159, here p. 83ff.;
    Werner Wolf, Die Wundersäule in Wolframs Schastel Marveile,
    Festschrift Emil Öhmann, Helsinki, 1954, pp.275-314, here
    pp. 295/296; Wolfgang Mohr, Hilfe und Rat in Wolfram's Parzi-
    val, Festschr. Jost Trier, Meisenheim Glan, 1954, pp. 173-197,
    here pp. 174, 189, 191f., also Parzival and Gâwân, Euphorion,
    52 (1958), 1-22, here pp. 7, 8, 13, the latter reprinted in:
    Wolfram von Eschenbach, ed. by Heinz Rupp, Wege der Forschung,
    57, Darmstadt, 1966, pp. 287-318.

95 Cf. M. O'C. Walshe, Travel Descriptions, pp. 6, 105, 106.
    Also Julius Schwietering, Die deutsche Dichtung des Mittel-
    alters, Handbuch der Literaturwissenschaft, Potsdam, 1941,
    p. 171: "In das Gegenüber von Terre de Salvaesche und Terre

take any major changes here, He, however, defines the contrast
in scenery more clearly than Chrestien, by occasionally sup-
pressing certain descriptive detail which might obscure the
distinction, and at other times adding features which will emphasize it.[96] The distinction already begins with the background to Parzival's childhood. Soltâne is characterized as the
type of landscape which will recur again and again as the setting for Parzival's adventures. It is a wilderness, and before
Herzeloyde withdrew to it, it had been unexplored and untouched
by human hand. When she arrives in the middle of the forest
(117.7-9), it has to be made habitable for her (117.16).

The wilderness she has chosen is so isolated, so far removed
from the civilized world that it is possible for her to bring
up Parzival in complete ignorance of chivalry. Parzival is virtually hidden from civilization (117.30).

Parzival's childhood is thus set against a background of an
isolated landscape, lonely, save for those who immediately surround him, uninhabited, remote from the world of ordinary men,
a wilderness covered with dense forest.

Marveile, von Gral- und Clinsorland ist auch die Natur ein-
bezogen: in ihrer urwüchsigen Wildheit und rauhen Einsamkeit
wie in ihrer Heiterkeit und künstlichen Gepflegtheit wunder-
samer Gärten, je nachdem sie Zurückgezogenheit, Insichge-
kehrtheit und Trauer oder aber höfische Geselligkeit beglei-
tet."

96 Stressing the wild aspect of Parzival's landscape he expands,
for example, the description of the road to Brôbarz as
against Chrestien's portrayal (1703-1709 and 1749-1751) and
suppresses the manor in Parzival's early background (450),
the paved road in the Grail-forest (3644) and the hermit's
chapel (6342). Elaborating the pleasantness of Gâwân's background he extends the description of the garden-setting at
Lôgroys (6715, 6783) and introduces another during the episode with the ferryman where Chrestien has none (7494ff.).
For the same purpose he suppresses Chrestien's adjectives
"gast" and "soutain" (7225) when describing Gâwân's journey
towards Schastel Marveile.

When first setting out from Soltâne Parzival travels towards
similar country. He turns to the forest of Brizljân which, during the early part of his journey, appears as lonely as the one
he has just left. For one whole day and night he meets no one
(129.5-17).

This same picture of a desolate and inhospitable landscape returns in full force when Parzival leaves Grâharz. His road to
Brôbarz takes him through dense forest which betrays no sign
of ever having been penetrated before:

> 180.3   kriuze unde stûden stric,
>   dar zuo der wagenleisen bic
>   sîne waltstrâzen meit.

He rides through wild and untamed country:

> 180.6   vil ungevertes er dô reit,
>   dâ wênic wegerîches stuont.

Fallen trees obstruct his path:

> 180.12   slegels urkünde
>   lac dâ âne mâze vil,
>   sulen grôze ronen sîn slegels zil.

Then a mountainous wilderness opens out before him and he makes
his way to Brôbarz "durch wilde gebirge hôch" (180.19). He finds
Pelrapeire by following the course of steep falls cascading over
rocks (180.21-25).

The same features of loneliness, isolation, dense forest and
high mountains with which Wolfram characterizes a virgin landscape are used consistently for the description of Terre de
Salvaesche. Neither in Book V nor in Book VI does he elaborate
on these basic motifs, or vary the simple paraphernalia with
which he indicates a wilderness - waterfalls, rocks and fallen
trees. Additions occur in Book IX, but the same basic vocabulary is employed also. The consistency with which these bare
descriptive features are used, endow Terre de Salvaesche with
an aspect of unmitigated wildness.

The uniformity with which these motifs are carried on from the description of Soltâne to that of Terre de Salvaesche is indeed striking. When first crossing into Terre de Salvaesche Parzival rides "über ronen und durchez mos" (224.20). From both Anfortas and Sigûne Parzival learns that the country is deserted and uncultivated for thirty miles all round (225.19-21; 250.22-23). The path to Munsalvaesche leads Parzival across rocks (225.25/26). The density and extent of the forest isolate Munsalvaesche from inhabited land (250.20: "iuch möht des waldes hân bevilt,/ von erbûwenem lande her geritn"). Parzival is still lost in the depths of the forest shortly before he stumbles upon the Plimizoeles Plân (282.1-5). The same type of landscape continues to surround him until he emerges at Arthur's camp -

> 282.6 vil ungevertes reit er dan
> über ronen und (über) manegen stein.

During the third meeting with Sigûne and his visit to Fontâne la salvâtsche, i.e. throughout the crucial ninth book, the wildness of the natural background is clearly emphasized. Wolfram introduces new features and is obviously concerned with stressing the austere, inhospitable and hostile character of a wilderness. The same features occur again, the forest-setting (435.1-5), the water-fall (435.6-8), the rocky precipice (444.21-445.7) and the isolation (437.4/5). Parzival finds himself "verre von dem wege" (438.24) and describes the landscape as "dirre wilde" (438.25). He loses the spoor of Cundrîe's mule in the "ungeverte" (422.27-29) and rides across "wilden varm" (444.7). His horse lies dead "in grôzem ungeverte" (445.6) after its fall from giddy heights into the ravine. The forest-setting continues for Parzival's encounter with Kahenîs (446.9) as well as for Fontâne la salvâtsche. Trevrizent's cave lies in the depth of the mountains (445.25-456.3), by a waterfall, in a sombre, rocky landscape (458.27-30). Yew and fern grow here (485.13; 458.16/17) and wild roots form Parzival's and Trevrizent's only nourishment (485.21/22). In Book XVI, concerned with Parzival's return to Munsalvaesche, the forest-setting of Terre de Salvaesche again receives mention several times (797.7; 799.15; 804.8; 820.25-27).

For a large part of his travel-history Parzival is thus seen
against the background of wilderness. It is the setting which is
associated with him exclusively, for the background to the Gâwân-
story does not show wasteland of this kind. Moreover, we are
meant to imagine that Parzival's journey for the most part,
takes him through this type of landscape. For in Book IX, when
Parzival has already spent more than four years in search of
Munsalvaesche, Wolfram briefly characterizes the sort of country
which Parzival has most frequently explored, and significantly
calls him "waltmüede":

> 459.14 er moht wol waltmüede sîn:
> want er het der strâzen wênc geriten - -

In spite of this insistence on the wasteland scenery in Parzival's travels, settings of a different nature do occur as well.
Parzival is neither restricted in his experiences, nor is he
confined to one particular variety of background, but shares in
all. His parallel movement with Gâwân renders the exclusion of
other types of landscape impossible, but well before this sets
in, he is at times seen in a setting which bears no resemblance
to the wild aspect of Terre de Salvaesche.[97] By sheer force of
importance, however, the wilderness remains dominant in Parzival's background. He journeys here more frequently than elsewhere, it is the setting which is exclusively reserved for him,
and it forms the background to his most momentous experiences.
Its importance becomes evident through the consistency of its
character and the striking contrast in which it stands to the
scenery linked with the Gâwân-story.

The natural background to Gâwân's quest is dominated by motifs
of an entirely different nature. They too consistently point to
a specific variety of landscape. From the moment Gâwân sets out
from Arthur's court he is shown in pleasant, attractive surroundings. Before coming to Bêârosche he is seen riding along a valley

---

97 This occurs for example at Nantes, Grâharz and Pelrapeire.

and then halting on a hill. He has just passed through a forest:

> 339.15 sus reit der werde degen balt
> sîn rehte strâze ûz einem walt
> mit sîme gezog durch einen grunt.
> dâ wart im ûf dem bühel kunt
> ein dinc daz angest lêrte ---

Characteristically here as elsewhere, description begins when Gâwân emerges from the wood into open country. He is never portrayed in a forest-setting proper, of the kind that attaches itself to Parzival, in the wilderness, the lonely and deserted virgin landscape. A forest in the background of the Gâwân-narrative has none of the wild aspects, stressed so consistently when associated with Parzival. Gâwân, instead of wandering at random in its depth, finds his "rehte strâze" out of it. A similar treatment and conception of a forest-ride occurs when Gâwân approaches Ascalûn, and also before he reaches Schastel Marveile. At the end of Book VII he takes a road leading into a wood (387. 26: "Gâwâns strâze uf einen walt gienc..."), and at the beginning of Book VIII he is already before Ascalûn. Although the forest is said to be "lanc unde wît" (398.10), his journey through its depth has been omitted. Description begins when the wooded landscape, broken by large clearings, gradually merges with open country:

> 398.18 nu wart der walt gemenget,
> hie ein schache, dort ein velt,
> etslîchz sô breit daz ein gezelt
> vil kûme drûffe stüende.

In conclusion we are told that Gâwân has crossed many a high mountain-range and "manec muor" (398.26), but his travels in relation to this background are not portrayed; wilderness is avoided. In Book X Orgelûse takes Gâwân through a "grôzen walt" (534.12), but the forest-setting again is not treated in detail. Instead, the wood is left behind almost immediately, and Gâwân rides "anderhalp ûz in erbuwen lant" (534.19).

The only time Gâwân appears against a background sufficiently wild in its concrete features to be reminiscent of Parzival's

is at Li Gweiz Prelljûs. Here the description of torrents of
water between steep and rocky banks conjures up a natural scene
similar to that in which Parzival finds himself so frequently.
Nevertheless, Li Gweiz Prelljûs is far removed from being the
true wilderness into which Parzival is constantly drawn. It
lacks three most important traits - isolation from the inhabited
world, loneliness and the uncertainty of its expanse.[98]

While description of a virgin landscape in Gâwân's background is
deliberately avoided or at least subdued, another, its opposite
in character, is given great prominence. Gâwân appears predominantly in pleasant and pastoral scenery. After leaving the
Arthurian court he rides through a valley (339.17) and over a
hill (339.18), seeks out the shade of lime-tree and olive-tree
at Bêârosche (352.27-353.3), and crosses a wide meadow before
Schanpfanzûn (399.25/26). In the beginning of Book X he appears
once again on a meadow (504.8) by a lime-tree (505.9). With
Orgelûse, whom he discovered sitting by a spring (508.17), he
rides "ûf eine liehte heide" (516.22), and before Schastel Marveile fights a joust by the river on an "anger" (535.5), later
described as "blüemin velt" (544.11). Twice he is shown in a
garden-setting. At Lôgroys Orgelûse sends him to her luxuriant
orchard of southern trees:

> 508.9   alumben berc lac ein hac,
> des man mit edelen boumen pflac.
> vîgen boum, grânât,
> öle, wîn and ander rât,
> des wuohs dâ ganziu rîcheit.

At Plippalinôt's house he discovers the garden early in the
morning:

> 553.6   der venster eines offen was
> gein dem boumgarten:
> dar în gienc er durch warten,
> durch luft und durch der vogel sanc.

---

98 Li Gweiz Prelljûs lies in Terre Marveile, is within reach of
Rosche Sabbîns and Jôflanze, and not remote from the civilized
world. Its extent is not uncertain (601.22ff.). The quality
of loneliness does not apply either; Orgelûse and Gramoflanz
take part in the episode.

Once he appears in scenery even more luxurious than the orchard.
Accompanied by Orgelûse he rides to Clinschor's mixed wood of
exotic trees:

> 601.7   sus reit si mit ir gaste
> von der burc wol ein raste,
> ein strâzen wît unde sleht,
> für ein clârez fôreht.
> der art des boume muosen sîn,
> tämris unt prisîn.
> daz was der Clinschores walt.

The landscape linked with Gâwân is a pleasance; its main features
of meadows, trees, shade, southern flora, gentle breeze and birdsong, convey serenity and are designed to please. Compared with
Parzival's wilderness, it seems conventional, stereotyped even,
and it is indeed a literary convention whose roots reach back
into the classical past, which has furnished its major motifs.
Gâwân's characteristic setting is the ideal landscape of medieval rhetoric, appearing here in its varieties of the locus
amoenus, the viridarium and the mixed forest. The basic requirements of the locus amoenus, trees, shade, meadows, brook or
spring, birdsong, grass and flowers, and breeze,[99] all occur
in Gâwân's background, as has been seen. The 'viridarium', i.e.

---

99 Cf. H. Brinkmann, Zu Wesen und Form mittelalterlicher Dichtung, Halle, 1928, p. 83: "Die Ideallandschaft, nur geringen
Wandlungen unterworfen, steht seit dem Hellenismus fest, dem
Mittelalter über das Schrifttum Roms vererbt. Sie trägt alle
Züge südlicher Heimat: beblümte Aue, plauschendes Wässerlein,
strahlend blauen Himmel, Ölbaum, der gegen stechende Sonnen-
glut schattet, singende Vöglein im Baumgezweig, vielleicht
noch Blumenduft und kühlendes Lüftchen. Nur der Ölbaum hat
sich meist in die gute deutsche Linde verwandelt." E. R.
Curtius, op. cit., p. 195, "The locus amoenus (pleasance) ...
has not previously been recognized as possessing an independent rhetorico-poetical existence. Yet, from the Empire to
the sixteenth century, it forms the principal motif of all
nature description. It is ... a beautiful, shaded natural
site. Its minimum ingredients comprise a tree (or several
trees), a meadow, and a spring or brook. Birdsong and flowers
may be added. The most elaborate examples also add a breeze";
cf. also the whole chapter: The Ideal Landscape, pp. 183-202.
Leonid Arbusow, Colores Rhetorici, Göttingen, 1948. p. 112:
"Zu den langlebigsten der aus Antike und Spätantike stammen-
den, ins Mittelalter fertig übernommenen Rezepte und Klischees

the garden, more specifically the <u>boumgarte</u>, appears twice as
his setting in its unabridged form, and once reduced as shady
tree.[100] The mixed forest, also an established variation of the
ideal landscape,[101] is represented by Clinschor's copse of
brazilwood and tamarisks.

The use of traditional motifs in his background gives Gâwân
the stamp of a conventional figure. The association of the wild
forest with Parzival, on the other hand, a type of setting more
recently evolved in Western literature,[102] lends the hero an
aura of strangeness and marks him as an outsider.

---

gehört auch dasjenige für rhetorische unwirkliche Naturschil-
derung, wofür die Rhetorik einen "blumigen Stil" und die
Description einer zum Frohsinn stimmenden Örtlichkeit empfahl.
Bei Homer bildeten deren Kennzeichen: Hain Quelle, Au, Wiesen.
Von der Kaiserzeit an (Virgil, Aen. 7.30; Petronius, Appule-
jus, Met. 103.10) über Isidor (Etym. 14.8.33: "Amoena loca")
bis in das 16. Jahrhundert blieben hierfür in Geltung: ein
beschatteter Naturausschnitt mit Bäumen, Wiese, Bach oder
Quelle, Vogelgesang, Gras und Blumen, oft auch noch sanftem
Lufthauch (aura) - also sechs "Versatzstücke", von denen
einzelne dazwischen fortfielen, wieder andere, wie Bäume,
Vögel, Blumen, auch Anlaß zu umfangreichen, der Aufschwellung
des Dichtwerkes dienenden Aufzählungen gaben."

100 Leonid Arbusow, op. cit., p. 116: "Schließlich erscheint ne-
benher in der mittelalterlichen Epik und Literatur als stil-
geschichtliche Abbreviatur eines Locus amoenus das "Viridarium", der baumreiche Schattenort, Baumgarten (afrz. <u>verger</u>),
und selbst nur noch der schattenspendende Baum - ein <u>kaum</u>
mehr kenntliches Trümmerstück bukolischer Landschaftsschil-
derung als notwendiges episches Versatzstück, als Mittel epi-
scher Markierung der idealtypischen Landschaft, wozu auch
"Hügel, Berg und Tal" gehören, sowie die Andeutung einer
Ebene."

101 E. R. Curtius, op. cit., pp. 194/95.

102 E. R. Curtius, op. cit., p. 201: "Another indispensable piece
of epic stage setting is the orchard or plantation ("verger":
Song of Roland, II, 103, 501). But with the rise of the
courtly romance in verse, the primitive landscape requirements of the heroic epic are far exceeded. The new genre is
a creation of France and first appears about 1150. One of
its principal motifs is the wild forest - "una selva sel-
vaggia ed aspra e forte", as Dante will later put it.
Percival grows up in the forest. Arthur's knights often
pass through wild forest on their journeys."

Certain features of the two types of landscape which emerge,
provide an important allegorical commentary on the lives of
hero and counterpart, and on their meaning. While Gâwân is
seen against scenery which is tamed and civilized, Parzival's
background is untamed, remote from civilization, lonely and
inhospitable. While Parzival consistently explores wild, uninhabited country, Gâwân constantly appears in "erbûwen lant"
(398.23; 534.19). Parzival frequently suffers hardship through
his surroundings, Gâwân on the other hand experiences no difficulties of this kind. No natural obstacles impede his progress,
only once does he meet with difficult country, at Li Gweiz
Prelljûs. Parzival, however, is confronted with this problem
several times, in the first snow-scene, after his third meeting
with Sigûne, and before reaching Trevrizent. While many of Parzival's momentous encounters are with individual people in a
deserted landscape, Gâwân is drawn everywhere into a crowd or
else appears against a scenery with much human activity. Contrary to Parzival's background, that of Gâwân is alive with
people, lived in, built upon and essentially gregarious. Before
coming to Bêârosche he observes an enormous warlike crowd making
its way to the castle (339.21ff.). At Bêârosche he first rides
through the troops encamped there (350.24ff.), and settling
down by the castle-wall, is watched by the inhabitants of Bêârosche (352.5ff.). At Schanpfanzûn five hundred or more knights
ride up to greet him (399.25-30). At Barbigoel he appears for a
public combat (503.5-20). At Lôgroys he is surrounded by the
knights and ladies of Orgelûse's boumgarte (512.28-514.24). At
Schastel Marveile he performs his deeds of valour under the eyes
of over four hundred damsels and queens (534.27ff.), and at Jôflanze the Arthurian host, and his own and Orgelûse's following
are brought together expressly for his honour. Parzival appears
against a similarly crowded canvas only at Pelrapeire, the Grail
castle, and when drawn into the Arthurian setting. Even their
manner of travelling is differentiated. Parzival pursues his
travels alone, and is only seen four times moving along together
with others; he is led by the fisherman to Nantes, rides with

Orilus and Jeschûte to Fontâne la salvâtsche, takes Feirefîz to Jôflanze and is guided by Cundrîe to Munsalvaesche. For the remainder of his quest Parzival rides alone. Gâwân, on the other hand, appears almost always in company. His retinue escorts him to Bêârosche and Schanpfanzûn. From Lôgroys Orgelûse leads him to Schastel Marveile and from here to Li Gweiz Prelljûs and back again. To Jôflanze he proceeds together with her as well as with a great following of knights and ladies. He rides alone only to Barbigoel and Lôgroys and while in search of the Grail. The isolation and loneliness of the landscape stressed so consistently in the Parzival-story, are carefully eliminated where Gâwân is concerned. The regions which he visits are not isolated from the world of men but part of it, and the company of others prevents him from appearing as a figure in loneliness like Parzival.

It is important to keep in mind the implications of this contrast of inhabited land and wilderness to contemporary imagination. The natural world, including the land, presented an aspect exactly the reverse of that which it has to-day. While to modern man a large part of the earth's surface is either cultivated or built up and has at any rate, been tamed and controlled by human interference, to Wolfram's contemporaries the overwhelmingly greater part of the world was wild, chaotic and largely beyond human reach. While to modern man the civilized world dominates his earth, the conquest and exploration of those parts which are not wholly incorporated into it only being a matter of time, to medieval man the civilized world represented an oasis engulfed by a vast wilderness, unconquerable, mysterious, dangerous and remote.

In the contemplation of this chaos towering in superiority of size above the small portion of the earth which to Western Christendom was the civilized world, awe mingled with fear. For chivalrous society this feeling was accentuated, as existence in chaotic wilderness meant uncourtly living, a life cut off from the civilizing influence of chivalry, transgressing against its fundamental law of diu mâze. Thus Iwein's madness is played out against the background of wild and uninhabited country, Tristan's and Isôt's passion draws them into the wilderness, and Herzeloyde takes her immeasurable grief to the wasteland of Soltâne. Parzival's frequent appearance against this particular type of scenery, from the portrayal of his childhood onwards, singles him out as a being apart from the chivalrous norm.

This contrast of wilderness and inhabited land, however, also carries within itself a meaning it derives from that which the early anchorites found in it. Wilderness, if fear-inspiring and overawing, is also virginal and holy. The landscape of the wilds, untouched by human hands, is free from the polluting influence of civilization. It is a fit place for those who devote their lives to the contact with God.[103] In the manner of St. Antony[104] Trevrizent seeks out the wilderness of Terre de Salvaesche to atone for Anfortas's sins and Sigûne for perpetual prayer. In the midst of this impenetrable wilderness, at the holiest part of the holy landscape, stands Munsalvaesche.

The contrast in landscape in the romance is an extension of the contrast between its two leading figures. The difference in character and calling between Parzival and Gâwân is externalized, projected here into the background. Scenery is made to indicate emblematically the nature of the life enacted before it, the bent of each hero's temperament, the sphere of life allotted to him and his 'gradus'.

While Wolfram profited from guidance of genius in his establishment of a parallelism, he was no longer able to do so for its solution. Chrestien's work breaks off abruptly without a clue to

---

103 Cf. Hastings, op. cit., entry: "Monasticism".

104 Vita S. Antonii, ed. J. P. Migne, Patrologia Graeca, XXVI, 835-978; St. Athanasius, The Life of St. Antony, transl. and annotated by R. T. Meyer, Ancient Christian Writers, 10, London, 1950.

his intentions.[105] Wolfram was compelled to find the answers
to the questions raised by the parallelism without further inspiration from his source. The narrative which had kept hero
and counterpart in positions for constant comparison demanded
a solution of the problem as soon as one of them was settled
in his proper province.

How were hero and counterpart to be assessed within the scheme
of things? What were their contributions to the age of chivalry,
and how did they compare? What did they stand for and what was
their relationship to be? What was the verdict on their respective worth?

Wolfram had already answered some of these questions before being
forced to commit himself in final judgement. Within the scheme
of things Parzival and Gâwân appear primarily as knights. They
are part of chivalrous society; their bond with the Arthurian
world is never broken. Both represent modes of chivalrous existence at its highest level. But Parzival, the hero, is quite
obviously the more important, the more commanding figure of the
two. His lot is harder than Gâwân's, his experiences tragic and
moving, the demands upon him greater, the scope of his quest
more exacting. He claims a vast share of the author's compassion,
who handles Gâwân with respect, but frequently tends to see his
adventures in a humorous light, sometimes treating them as
uproarious fun.[106] Nevertheless, the purpose behind the portrayal of Gâwân is a deeply serious one; in him chivalry as a
manner of living is on trial. The serious dimension to the
character of Gâwân is often stressed and transpires clearly
whenever he is seen in relation to the hero. It reveals itself
in this manner in Book VI, in his patronage of Parzival, his
poise in a similar misfortune, his greater maturity at that
point and in his avowals of friendship and admiration later in

---

105 On the parallelism in Chrestien and its implications cf.
     Fierz-Monnier, op. cit., p. 67ff.

106 Cf. e.g. the episode of the Lît Marveile 566.27-567.30.

the narrative.[107]

The ultimate and vital question engendered by the parallelism
of hero and counterpart, really pivots around Gâwân. What is
to become of him? Is chivalry in its perfection to be ousted
by a yet higher form of chivalrous living, as symbolized by
Parzival? Will it be condemned, perhaps tolerated merely, or
will its worth be confirmed by Parzival?

Wolfram provides the answer by showing the two champions in
single combat. By doing so he uses a motif first introduced
into the Arthurian metrical romances by Chrestien. The hero's
duel with the most illustrious member of the Table Round in
order to establish his chivalrous excellence was first described by Chrestien in his 'Yvain'.[108] Wolfram most likely knew both
- the French 'Yvain' and its German adaptation by Hartmann, -
'Iwein'. His description of Parzival's joust with Gâwân is undoubtedly inspired by the similar scene in Hartmann's work.[109]

From the very beginning the emphasis lies heavily on the allegorical meaning of the episode. If Parzival and Gâwân are to
be shown in single combat, the only possible motivation for
this could be that they do so without recognizing one another,
as they are not conceived as rivals. This motivation Wolfram
uses without regard for the glaring inaccuracy on which it rests.

---

107   392.20-393.2; 619.20-24; 689.25-690.2.

108   Cf. Hildegard Emmel, Formprobleme des Artusromans und der
      Graldichtung, Berne, 1951, p. 137.

109   The following important features of the duel are common to
      the two scenes in 'Parzival' and 'Iwein': 1. Ignorance of
      opponent's identity (P. 688.19ff.; I. 6884-6906) - 2. Pre-
      diction of sense of grief and loss for victorious knight
      (P. 680.4-6.16/17; I. 6960-6964) - 3. Close friendship
      (P. 680.7-9.13/19; I. 6972-6976. 7011-7013. 7057-7060)
      - 4. Duel ended by circumstances (P. 688.8-10; I. 7349-7357).

      For other aspects of 'Parzival' directly inspired by 'Iwein'
      vid. H. Schneider, Parzival-Studien. A detailed comparison
      of the two scenes in Hartmann and Wolfram may be found in
      Wolfgang Harms, Der Kampf mit dem Freund oder Verwandten

Parzival still wears his brilliant, red mantle, and his horse is caparisoned in the same conspicuous colour:

> 679.10 noch roeter denn ein rubbîn
> was sîn kursît unt sînes orses kleit.

Since the slaying of Ithêr this colour has been associated with Parzival's appearance, and it is unlikely that Gâwân would fail to recognize its significance, in particular since he had responded to its meaning before.[110] However, the encounter is allegorical and considerations of realistic motivation do not enter. Gâwân recognizes the branch from Gramoflanz's tree, but not Parzival (679.14-17).[111]

In the beginning the similarities between them are stressed; both horses are from Munsalvaesche (679.23-25); for both Parzival and Gâwân the encounter is a misfortune (679.30; 680.12); both attack with skill (680.1: "Si tâtn ir poynder rehte"); their ancestry is the same (680.2/3); each has remained firm in friendship towards the other (680.7-9); for either, victory would mean disaster (680.16-17: "von swem der prîs dâ wirt genomen / des freude ist drumbe sorgen pfant"). The introductory paragraph, however, already suggests that Parzival is likely to be successful:

> 679.1 ob von dem werden Gâwân
> werlîche ein tjost dâ wirt getân,
> so gevorht ich sîner êre
> an strîte nie so sêre.
> ich solt ouch sandern angest hân:
> daz wil ich ûz den sorgen lân.

---

in der deutschen Literatur bis um 1300, Medium Aevum, Philologische Studien, hrsg. v. Friedrich Ohly, Kurt Ruh, Werner Schröder, vol. 1, Munich, 1963, pp. 159 and 160.

110 392.20-29.

111 Wolfgang Harms, op. cit., p. 156, draws attention to the misleading aspect of this branch for both Parzival and Gâwân: "Der Kranz stellt ... eine Verbindung zwischen Parzival und Gramoflanz her, denn Parzival brach den Kranz, um dadurch Gramoflanz zum Kampf aufzufordern, und glaubt jetzt, in Gawan, der sogleich den Kampf aufzunehmen bereit ist, Gramoflanz vor sich zu haben. Gawan und Parzival glauben also beide, jeder für sich, gegen Gramoflanz zu kämpfen."

After both have simultaneously unhorsed one another (680.18-21)
the description of the joust is interrupted for an episode with
Gramoflanz (681.2ff.). This does not represent an inconsequential
digression but serves on the one hand, to emphasize Gâwân's perfection in chivalrous skill, - Gramoflanz is prepared to fight
with Gâwân only, although he normally requires two opponents

> 685.4-8 wande mich des ie verdroz,
> strîtes gein einem man;
> wan daz der werde Gâwân
> den lîp hât gurboret sô,
> kampfes bin ich gein im vrô

- and on the other, to motivate the sudden end of the joust;
Arthur's messengers returning from Rosche Sabbîns recognize him,
and call out his name (688.4ff.).

The joust between Parzival and Gâwân thus ends by unexpected and
external intervention, rather in the manner of Parzival's combat
with Feirefîz. The outcome is undecided, but is distinctly not
a draw. Gâwân is not defeated and Parzival not victorious, but
he proves to be the stronger of the two:

> 688.11 ez was vil nâch alsô komn
> daz den sig hete aldâ genomn
> Gâwânes kampfgenoz.
> des kraft was über in so grôz,
> daz Gâwân der werde degen
> des siges hete nâch verpflegen,
> wan daz in klagende nanten
> kint diu in bekanten.

There is little doubt of what the ultimate result of the joust
would have been, but that is beside the point. The portrayal of
the conclusion is avoided for the sake of the allegory; showing
Gâwân in defeat would change its meaning entirely. Parzival takes
the palm in this struggle (694.26-695.7), not for victory but
for superior strength. Gâwân's exhaustion and Parzival's un-
impaired vigour are strikingly contrasted. Gâwân's strength is
spent:

> 690.3 dô disiu rede was getân
> done moht ouch mîn her Gâwân
> vor unkraft niht langer stên.

> er begunde al swindelde gên,
> wand imz houbt erschellet was:
> er strûchte nider an dez gras.

Parzival betrays no signs of fatigue:

> 693.1 Dô truoc der starke Parzivâl
> ninder müede lit noh erblichen mâl.

The allegorical meaning of the episode with its avoidance of the calamitous outcome is clear. Gâwân's sphere is subordinate to that of Parzival but is not to be condemned. Wolfram envisages and affirms a co-existence of two forms of elevated living in which Parzival represents the few and Gâwân the highest level of the many. The superiority of one of these two forms of existence does not imply a crushing verdict on the qualities of the other. Defeat is not portrayed. Wolfram indeed insists upon the positive relationship between them. The close bond which unites Parzival and Gâwân is nowhere so emphatically underlined as in the course of their combat. They are not only linked by blood relationship but also by the ties of friendship. They are of common lineage:

> 680.2 ûz der tjoste geslehte
> wârn si bêde samt erborn -

and are close in friendship:

> 680.7 gein ein ander stuont ir triwe,
> der enweder alt noch niwe
> dürkel scharten nie enpfinc.

They are not only 'mâge' but also 'gesellen' (680.19). In their joust "erkantiu sippe unt hôch gesellschaft" are at war (680.13-15). This twofold bond of kinship and friendship has created such proximity between them that Parzival can exclaim: "ich hân mich selben überstriten" (680.5). Gâwân gives expression to the same feeling, stressing the irrationality of their encounter:

> 689.25 Gâwân sprach: 'sô was ez reht:
> hie ist krumbiu tumpheit worden sleht.
> hie hânt zwei herzen einvalt
> mit hazze erzeiget ir gewalt.
> dîn hant uns bêde überstreit:
> nu lâ dirz durch uns bêde leit.
> du hâst dir selben an gesigt,
> ob dîn herze triwen phligt.'

Gâwân sees himself as inseparably joined to Parzival; he identifies Parzival with his own self. They are einvalt. A rivalry
between them, or a struggle against one another, is inconceiv-
able. In the terms of the allegory we must understand this to
mean that the two ways of life represented by hero and counterpart are inextricably interdependent. The triple reference:
"ich hân mich selben überstriten; dîn hant uns bêde überstreit;
du hâst dir selben an gesigt" - points to that same feature of
closeness to the point of identification. It moreover implies
that a victory of Parzival's exalted form of existence ending
in the opponent's overthrow, would mean a senseless defeat of
itself.

The allegory of Parzival's encounter with Gâwân thus answers
the main question raised by their parallelism. Worldly chivalry
in its perfection as symbolized by Gâwân, is not condemned and
not to be supplanted, but to be seen in new perspective, in
relationship to a nobility which equals it in its perfection,
yet adds a spiritual dimension by force of which it surpasses
the chivalrous world of Gâwân. Gâwân's chivalry of perfection
is by no means to be dismissed, on the contrary, the need for
its ideal and practice is confirmed by the intimate bond which
links it symbolically with Parzival's chivalry of greatness,
and by the very fact of its survival without defeat. Gâwân's
world appears reduced in stature, but only when seen from the
pinnacle of Parzival's achievement.[112]

Wolfram brings Chrestien's work to a triumphant conclusion,
altering the very nature of his model through manifold changes
and additions. Among the most important of these is the newly

---

112 Cf. on the other hand, Gottfried Weber's interpretation of
     the epic which insists that Wolfram's work exposes the
     "innere Bankrott des höfischen Rittertums" (Parzival. Rin-
     gen und Vollendung, Oberursel, 1948, p. 46); vid. also the
     account of the final duel p. 134. A different conclusion
     is reached by Wolfgang Mohr, Parzival und Gâwân, p. 16.

thought out, totally revised and brilliantly concluded relationship between the two leading figures of the epic. It is one of those major alterations which give the work a new dimension and help to add to its philosophical depth.

Wolfram's work has often been interpreted without much regard for the significance of Gâwân.[113] A vast amount of the poetic quality and its attendant magic is lost in this way; for to see Parzival without Gâwân is not to see him whole. Gâwân is the foil which sets off by contrast all the hero's qualities, experiences and achievements. The restraints imposed upon his life by destiny show the transcendence of these bounds in Parzival's fate. The aspect of flippancy in his adventures illuminates the extreme gravity of Parzival's experiences. His 'ordinariness' lights up Parzival's 'extraordinariness', and the constancy of his good fortune most movingly underlines the pathos of Parzival's suffering when laboriously learning about its mutability. At every point and from every aspect, Gâwân's career - and we must surely include here all those aspects described in other romances, French and German as well, for Gâwân after all arrived in Wolfram's narrative as a prefabricated figure, with his characteristics and symbolic capacity well fixed, - that career of perfect worldly chivalry is a vital stepping-stone towards the full understanding of the meaning of Parzival's quest and his transcendent goal.

---

113 As late as 1951 it was still possible to say "Es wäre sehr aufschlußreich, dem Schicksal Gâwâns im einzelnen nachzugehen...", Fr. Maurer, Leid. Studien z. Bedeutungs- u. Problemgesch., Berne, 1951, p. 121. Further comment on Wolfram's particular manner of handling the Gâwân-figure may be found in Xenja von Ertzdorff, Höfische Freundschaft, DU, 14 (1962), 35-51, passim; Marianne Wynn, Orgeluse. Persönlichkeitsgestaltung auf Chrestienschem Modell, German Life and Letters, 30 (1977), 127-37, passim; J. M. Clifton-Everest, 'ritter' as 'Rider' and as 'Knight'. A Contribution to the Parzival-Gawan Question, in: Wolfram-Studien, VI, ed. by Werner Schröder, 1980, pp. 151-166, and Neil Thomas, Sense and Structure in the Gawan adventures of Wolfram's 'Parzival', MLR, 76 (1981), 848-856.

IV. Transformation of a Narrative Unit –
Remodelling the Central Episode

Book IX is clearly the core of Wolfram's 'Parzival'. It shows
the hero at the chief pivotal point of his career; it contains
Wolfram's leading reflections on the fundamentals of life, his
probing of the relationship between man and God. It is the
intellectual focus of the work, its emotional centre, the narrative nerve of its poetic structure. No reader of 'Parzival'
would dispute this today, and it is unlikely that its contemporary listeners would have disagreed.

The significance which Wolfram himself attributed to this particular part of the romance is borne out by the change in his
attitude towards his source here. Elsewhere in 'Parzival' he
seems to have considered that Chrestien's narrative offered
reasonable scope for whatever he wished to express. Here, on
the other hand, at the point of the romance which we have come
to call Book IX, he appears to have found the range of poetic
potential inherent in his source-material to be wholly inadequate. His technique of adaptation markedly diverges for this
particular section from that brought to bear on the remainder
of 'Li Contes del Graal'. While the ratio of French source to
German text is normally 2:3 in 'Parzival', it changes radically
here to a proportion of 1:7. Wolfram has increased the narrative
substance sevenfold, the 302 lines devoted by Chrestien to the
description of events are expanded by Wolfram to 2100 verses.[1]

The raw material before him consisted of a description of the
hero's meeting with a group of pilgrims, and an account of an
episode with a recluse. Yet not only did Wolfram vastly expand
the searching dialogue between hero and hermit, and modify the

---

1 Jean Fourquet, Wolfram D'Eschenbach et le Conte del Graal.
 Les divergences de la tradition du Conte del Graal de Chrétien et leur importance pour l'explication du Parzival, Strasbourg, 1938, (Diss.), p. 97.

scene with the pilgrims, he found it necessary also to make major
additions. All of these he set into the narrative before the
great dialogue, none of them after, indicating by allotting this
particular place to them within the narrative network their function as preliminary, as stations on the road to the main burden
of his concern. He thus added a full introduction, interpolated
two new and freely invented episodes - another meeting of the
hero with his cousin Sigûne, and his duel with a border patrol
in Grail territory, - inserted the hero's challenge to Providence,
and included an elaborate reference to a fanciful source, and
to sources of this source. Six passages, of which five are new,
therefore precede the main episode of this narrative unit,
while Chrestien made do with one. That the centre of gravity
within this group of passages falls squarely on the dialogue
needs no especial argumentation. It represents the great dramatic climax of the hero's career, and of the work as a whole.
For it is here that at a crass emotional nadir he is subjected to the most gruelling test of his moral fibre yet experienced,
and that he wrestles with total despair, battling for spiritual
survival. It is the major crossroads of his life. In correspondence with the outstanding significance of the passage it has
attracted scholarly interest for nearly a century. Yet it is
not only the importance of the dialogue which has persistently
tempted critical attention, but also the difficulties of its
content. It is one of the most taxing passages in 'Parzival'.
Its substance stubbornly resists critical unravelling and the
uncovering of its levels of meanings. Thought appears close-
textured in detail, yet ramified overall; altogether the dialogue
ranges over a wide variety of topics. It is this range of themes
with an apparent lack of connection between them, and the seem-
ing absence of any particular links between the dialogue as a
whole and the scenes and passages which precede it in Book IX
that are so puzzling. On a first reading the whole of this narrative unit, the whole of Book IX, leaves a bewildering sensation of the disparateness of its component parts, a sensation
which even after many re-readings of it comes only to be partially

dispelled.

Wolfram at this juncture of the plot faced a complex problem of composition. The hero had reached a cul-de-sac in life, a stage which made appraisal of self essential. If the work was to transcend the limits of stereotyped portrayal as found in his French text at this point, and if it was to transmit an understanding of human distress, then the swift contrition and easy penance of Chrestien's hero had to be expanded into a grudging, slow, and agonizing psychological process. A description would have to be given of human vulnerability, of stress, of crisis, of the subtleties of the soul. Moreover, as faith, the loss of it and the lack of it, lay at the root of the hero's predicament, the Christian interpretation of it had to be explained, discussed, and stated. Both of these propositions would involve the author in the use of a high degree of abstraction, a problem which had not confronted him to this extent before. Furthermore the then current range of the vernacular barely equipped him for this task. Is it possible therefore that he found himself unable to cope with these demands? Did he flounder when it came to the presentation of abstracta? Was he perhaps not capable of intensive analysis, and of systematically treating thought? Not all poets after all are thinkers. Is it his inability which accounts for the opaqueness of the dialogue, and the rag-bag appearance of Book IX? - Yet, on the other hand, would so conscious an artist as Wolfram allow himself to enter deep water and attempt a task that lay beyond his powers? Would he not rather under such circumstances have kept closely to his source and abandoned projects of extension and innovation?

Or is the conglomerate look of the dialogue in itself, and of Book IX as a whole, due to the poet trusting his luck and composing at random? - Yet again, is it feasible to imagine that just here, at this most important point of the romance, he would leave so much to chance? Some of the subject-matter of the dialogue, as also some of its unexpected turns which in part

characterize it as spontaneous conversation, may indeed have
suggested themselves in the act of composition, but it is unthinkable that the poet had not considered in advance the direction which he intended the dialogue to take and the lines
along which he would steer it on this course. His gifts lay
very particularly in vision of design, capacity to execute it,
and power to create poetry by it.[2] His transformation of the
background to the work gives abundant evidence of these gifts.
It is hardly plausible to assume that they suddenly left him,
when it came to composing Book IX. The inevitable inference is
that the disjointed look of Book IX must lie in the eye of the
modern beholder, and not in the nature of the narrative unit.

The key to uncovering its form, and thereby to unlocking much
of its substance, lies in assessing Book IX as a poetic entity,
as a narrative unit of carefully co-ordinated parts. Everything
here which stands before the dialogue, is adjusted in its direction and points towards it. None of the additions and modi-
fications which precede it may in any way be considered haphazard. Quite the contrary, they were conceived, composed, and
introduced in relation to the narrative climax of Book IX. All
six passages, the five which are new, and the sixth through its
pattern of revision, tend towards the culmination of Book IX.
They govern the target-episode. There are links running between
them and the main scene, tenuous and firm, subtle and obvious,
intricate as well as simple. Invented and fashioned to perform
a variety of functions, they may fix emotive pitch or throw into
relief leading themes or even combine to give a cumulative
analysis of the hero's frame of mind. All of them, however,

---

2 His gift for design is exemplified also in an important
   feature of the work which is not discussed here, in the
   creation of a continuous time-scheme. Vid. Hermann J. Weigand, Narrative Time in the Grail Poems of Chrétien de Troyes and Wolfram von Eschenbach; in his: Wolfram's Parzival:
   Five Essays with an Introduction, ed. Ursula Hoffmann, 1969,
   pp. 18-74; originally published as Die epischen Zeiverhält-
   nisse in den Graldichtungen Chrestiens und Wolframs, PMLA,
   53, (1938), 917-950.

prepare for the target-scene, and all of them, except one, are
directly predictive of it. With them Wolfram provides an invaluable introduction to the dialogue, endeavouring to make it accessible, predominantly abstract as it is in its opening section,
and packed with information throughout. With them he moreover
gives guidance to his audience as to the correct reception of
the dialogue, and to the recognition of its major themes. The
means whereby he achieves this may be blatant, via surprise or
shock; they can also be discreet to the point of subliminal suggestion. The range of poetic articulateness which he displays
here is impressive. In presenting the six-part introduction to
the climax of Book IX Wolfram is seen to draw heavily on his
whole register of poetic accomplishments. The skill which he
expended here emphatically indicates, both by its variety and
volume, how important he considered this introduction to be.
Each one of its component parts was designed by him to fulfil
a particular role, always in relation to the dialogue, - giving
information relevant to it, accentuating a specific topic within
it, or evoking the mood with which to approach it. The analysis
of the content of these passages, and of the techniques whereby
this content is transmitted, affords important insights, not
only into the dialogue, but into the whole of the romance itself.[3]

---

3 For nearly a century now scholars have been trying to discover the 'logic' of the dialogue by way of isolating its
   structure of ideas. They have investigated its composition
   for the most part independently of the remainder of Book IX,
   or with passing reference only to some of its component
   sections. Criticism has been divided between the two extreme
   positions of accepting compositional flaws of the dialogue
   and/or Book IX, and of claiming an organized scheme for
   either or both. The consensus, however, seems to be uneasily
   biassed in favour of compositional defects. Gotthold Bötticher,
   in what appears to be the earliest detailed assessment of the
   narrative structure of Book IX (Das Hohelied vom Rittertum.
   Eine Beleuchtung des 'Parzival' nach Wolframs eigenen Andeutungen, Berlin, 1886; Excurs: Die Composition des IX. Buches,
   pp. 81-86.) stated emphatically that he considered the composition of the Kyôt-section and the dialogue to be extraordinarily crude. It was in fact its poor quality which prompted
   his investigation: "Die Composition des IX. Buches von 452.29

1. Literary Excursus I - The Lady Literature

The raison d'être for the opening passage of Book IX is clearly its function as a signpost. It marks off decisively the events which have gone before, against the scenes which are to bome.

---

an ist für unsere Begriffe so mangelhaft, dass sie verdient einmal kurz beleuchtet zu werden!" (p. 81). He specifically noted clumsiness (p. 81), lack of motivation (pp. 82, 84, 85), incoherence (pp. 81, 85), irritating repetitions (p. 84), and a series of irrelevant digressions (p. 82). The fundamental weaknesses of this section were proof to Bötticher that there was no justification for attributing central importance to it within 'Parzival'. Interestingly enough - although his excursus was entitled "Die Composition des IX. Buches", he confined his analysis to the dialogue and the reference to Kyôt. In a further article on the same subject (Noch einmal das IX. Buch des Parzival. Zu Zs. 44,241-248, ZfdA, 45 (1901), 149-152) he reiterated his earlier criticism and pointed to the basic blemishes of a lack of logic, an absence of causality, and the non-existence of any plan.

This early conviction, so forcibly expressed, of Wolfram's inadequate skill when it came to a major elaboration of a narrative unit, had a long echo. In 1924 Gustav Roethe characterized the dialogue as a collection of fragments on the grounds of its abrupt changes of theme: "Wolframs berühmtes neuntes Buch, die Unterredung mit Trevrizent, die sich strenger Disposition entzieht, hat zuweilen etwas von einer zusammengefassten Fragmentsammlung, so sprunghaft wechseln die Themata." (Der Dichter des Parzival. Rede zur Gedächtnisfeier des Stifters der Berliner Universität, König Friedr. Wilh. III, Berlin, 1924, p. 12). In 1947 H. Meyer drew attention to the lack of lucidity in the plan of the whole of Book IX: "Die Schwierigkeiten, die das neunte Buch des Parzival von jeher geboten hat, betreffen nicht zuletzt den wenig übersichtlichen Aufbau dieses Buches." (Zum Religionsgespräch im neunten Buch des Parzival, Neophil. 31 (1947), 18-26, here p. 18). In 1970 J. Bumke summarized the tenor of research with reference to Book IX as an awareness of long standing that the seams were showing in its structure: "Die Forschung ist schon lange auf Risse und Nähte in diesem Buch gestossen, ..." (Die Wolfram von Eschenbach-Forschung, p. 169). In all this, modern assessment curiously fell in with contemporary criticism. Gottfried von Strassburg had already alleged acidly that Wolfram possessed a penchant for suddenly and unpredictably changing direction ('Tristan', lls. 4638ff.).

Not long after the first statement regarding the jumble character of Book IX another interpretation was being developed which proposed the very opposite, namely that order, organization of subject-matter, could be detected here. In 1900, 1903 and 1906 three essays by Albert Nolte, Die Composition der

The poet enters the narrative, intervenes, and substitutes one
hero for another. Yet this is not its sole purpose. The change

---

Trevrizent-Scenen. Parz. IX 452.13-502, ZfdA, 44, N.F. 32
(1900) 241-248; A. B. Faust, A Defense and Interpretation
of the Ninth Book of Wolfram's Parzival, Modern Philology,
1 (1903/04, 275-293 and Joseph Austermann, Aufbau und Bedeutung der Trevrizentszene im neunten Buche des Parzival. (455.
23-502.30), Wissenschaftliche Beilage zum Jahresbericht des
Gymnasiums zu Attendorn, Siegen, 1906, pp. 3-32, endeavoured
to show it, but their attempts carried little conviction.
Their results consisted of no more than synopses with differing accentuations. All three of them, incidentally, restricted their enquiries to the dialogue.
In 1943 Bodo Mergell (Wolfram von Eschenbach, vol. II, pp.
165-245) suggested that Wolfram had had a symmetrical scheme
in mind when composing Book IX. He felt able to isolate a
blueprint in which eight sections precede a focal point, the
scene of recognition between hero and hermit, and another
eight sections follow. Like Nolte, Faust and Austermann
before him, he appended a synopsis (pp. 240 and 241). The
architectural rigidity of the plan as proposed by Mergell
found a critic in Walter Henzen who in the course of his
analysis (Das IX. Buch des 'Parzival'. Überlegungen zum Aufbau, in: Erbe der Vergangenheit. Germanistische Beiträge.
Festgabe für Karl Helm zum 80. Geburtstage, Tübingen, 1951,
pp. 189-217) came to be convinced of a different kind of
order immanent in Book IX. He too took the view that the narrative elements of Book IX were adjusted towards a particular
centre of gravity, but in his view that focus was the hero's
confession of his failure. When the essay was reprinted in
1966 (Wege der Forschung, 57, pp. 125-157) he still stood by
its main thesis: "Zur Hauptdarstellung: dass das IX. Buch ...
auf den Schwerpunkt von Parzivals Geständnis der unterlassenen
Frage ausgerichtet ist, glaube ich nach wie vor stehen zu kön-
nen" (p. 125, footnote). Similarly to Mergell he placed the
main weight of his investigation on the dialogue itself,
making brief mention only of the six preceding passages.
Blanka Horacek then in 1972 (Zur inneren Form des Trevrizentbuches, Sprachkunst, 3 (1972), 214-229) took up a position of
mediating between the interpretations of Mergell and Henzen
by joining them together, and proposing a symmetrical arrangement of narrative sections centred upon the hero's confession. Bernd Schirok in his examination of Book IX of 1976
(Trevrizent und Parzival. Beobachtungen zur Dialogführung
und zur Frage der figurativen Komposition, Amsterdamer Beiträge zur Älteren Germanistik, 10 (1976), 43-71) came to the
conclusion that Wolfram followed among other guidelines also
the principles of numerical composition: "dass Wolfram der
Trevrizentszene neben den Gesetzen logisch-psychologisch
stimmiger Personengestaltung und Dialogführung auch numerisch
bestimmte Kompositionsprinzipien zugrunde gelegt hat." (p. 70).

of hero alone would hardly have merited so elaborate an introduction. Chrestien managed it reasonably well, though unremarkably,
in a brief, if somewhat abrupt fashion (lls. 6211-6216). Wolfram,
it would appear, intended more; the signpost which he constructs
does not merely announce a change in the leading figure of the
romance, but it also discreetly signals a change in the emotional
level or direction of the narrative. He provides the passage with
an emotive twist which points straight to the seriousness which
is to come. What had gone before was farce. Gâwân's hilarious
erotic encounter with Antikônîe and its ludicrous aftermath. What
is to come is pathos and near-tragedy, Parzival's despair and
crisis, and his difficult and soul-searching meeting with Trevrizent. Wolfram prepares his audience for this change with a bridge-
passage which cleverly straddles the gap between frivolity and
gravity, gently turning the audience in the direction of the
latter.

The poet's banter with Frou Âventiure opens with a cliché familiar to the audience as a well-worn motif of contemporary love-
song: The Lady Literature demands to be allowed to enter the
poet's heart and to dwell in it: "ich wil inz herze hin ze dir"
(433.2).[4] Here as elsewhere in the romance Wolfram treats the

---

Others have contributed to the discussion, but not all can be
mentioned here. For supplementary information vid. Bernd
Schirok, op.cit.
Although the majority of publications on the problem of the
composition of Book IX now appears to be aligned on demonstrating a definitive plan for this narrative unit, the persistent
pursuit of the question would suggest a nagging discomfort
that such a plan is not immediately obvious. Despite the increasing volume of varying evidence of a programme for Book
IX, it is therefore still justified to see scholarly consensus
as slanted uncomfortably towards the suspicion of compositional
defects.
A wrong question is likely to elicit a wrong answer, or none
at all. The dialogue has no 'logic'. It was not composed as an
academic exercise based on a scheme of headings and sub-divi-
sions. Wolfram was not preparing an essay for a seminar. His
aim was to describe as realistically as possible a conversation
quasi discussion in which mistrust gradually gives way to trust,
and whose course is steered by emotion and not by logic.

motif as common coinage known to all, and raises laughter by
taking it literally. The poets answers the lady's plea to be
admitted to his heart with an obtuse refusal: "so gert ir zengem
rûme" (433.3) - you will not fit in.[5] The fact that the motif
is common poetic currency, evidently already slightly debased
through over-use, gives Wolfram an opportunity for creating
humour. The humorous effect of the motif misinterpreted is obvious and immediate. At the same time, however, he achieves an
additional effect with its use, less obvious, less immediate and
not humorous. Common coinage as it is, the motif automatically
and conveniently also points to a certain context, to the context
of love and lovers, and by virtue of its key phrase "ich wil inz
herze hin ze dir" to the framework of a genuine, close, and
emotional relationship. It is no ordinary lady who craves admit-
tance to the poet's heart, but âventiure, literature personified.
At this point of the narrative Literature suddenly takes possession of the poet's whole being. Poetry and poet come to be linked
in a lovers' union in which Poetry becomes the undisputed mistress.

---

4 For the history of this motif, as also for an interpretation
   of the introduction to Book IX which differs from the one
   above, vid. Friedrich Ohly, Cor amantis non angustum, Fs.
   William Foerste, Cologne/Vienna, 1970, pp. 454-476; reprinted
   in: Schriften zur mittelalterlichen Bedeutungsforschung, WBG,
   Darmstadt, 1977, pp. 128-155. The literary-historical background of the motif has been examined in detail by Xenja von
   Ertzdorff, Das 'Herz' in der lateinisch-theologischen und
   frühen volkssprachigen religiösen Literatur, PPB (Halle), 84
   (1962), 249-301, and Die Dame im Herzen und das Herz bei der
   Dame. Zur Verwendung des Begriffs 'Herz' in der höfischen
   Liebeslyrik des 11. und 12. Jahrhunderts, ZfdPh, 84 (1965),
   6-46.

5 By translating the motif into visual terms Wolfram adds a
   dimension of nonsense to it which he then exploits. He repeats
   the game in the Gâwân/Orgelûse love-story:
   > Orgelûse kom aldar
   > in Gâwâns herzen gedanc
   > der ie was zageheite kranc
   > unt gein dem wâren ellen starc.
   > wie kom daz sich dâ verbarc
   > sô grôz wîp in so kleiner stat?
   > si kom einen engen pfat
   > in Gâwânes herze, ...   (584,8-15).

The closeness between the poet and his art which is suggested
in this way, hints that the narrative juncture reached here is
undoubtedly important, and that in all likelihood events both
serious and moving will follow.

There is a similar ambivalence where humour and gravity are concerned in the comic pose which the poet adopts in this passage.
It too has serious undertones. Again, as in the case of the
motif, the immediate and primary effect of the pose is a humorous one. The poet overwhelms the Lady Literature with garrulous-
ness and with curiosity. The questions about Parzival tumble out
of him, eagerly and effusively as out of a child

> 433.17 ober an freuden sî verzagt,
> oder hât er hôhen prîs bejagt?
> oder ob sîn ganziu werdekeit
> sî beidiu lang unde breit,
> oder ist si kurz oder smal?

He wants to know about Anfortas "op der von jâmer sî erlôst"
(433.28), and more about Parzival,

> 434.6 ober liep od herzeleit
> sît habe bezalt an strîte.
> habt er sich an die wîte,
> oder hât er sider sich verlegn?

Like a child too he naïvely betrays a leading weakness with this
welter of questions, and openly reveals his ignorance on a subject with which he should be fully conversant. Clearly, Wolfram
is clowning; he has cast himself in the role of a jester. Yet
at the same time there is an underlying seriousness in this
pose of ignorance. The personified spirit of Literature is
treated here as the fund of poetic knowledge to which the poet
defers. Literature bestows the bounty of narrative detail, the
poet is its mere recipient. His direct and urgent appeal to this
font of knowledge suggests that he has reached an important and
complex point in the story which he has undertaken to tell, one
for which he must marshal all possible help.

But the most decisive pointer in the direction of seriousness
to come is the sudden change of tone with which this brief

introduction ends. The playful conversation with the imagined
lady with literature personified, comes to an abrupt end. The
poet now refers to âventiure not in its personification, but
as the actual story, as his authority, his source-material
which he is going to retell. He does so first at the beginning
of his summary of Parzival's immediate past: "nu tuot uns de
âventiure bekant,/ er habe erstrichen manec lant, ..." (435.11/
12) - and again at the beginning of his description of Parzival's present experiences:

> 435.1   diu âventiure uns kündet
>   daz Parzival der degen balt
>   kom geriten ûf einen walt,
>   ...

In both statements Wolfram uses verbal expressions which he
saves for important contexts. Bekant tuon in conjunction with
âventiure occurs on four other occasions when something fabulous
or miraculous is being described.[6] The verb künden is for him
an elevated term on which he relies when speaking of matters of
particular consequence.[7] Terminology suggestive of significance
thus introduces the description both of Parzival's past and of
his present. With the latter of the two emotive phrases, with
"diu âventiure uns kündet", the audience find themselves definitively launched on an atmosphere of seriousness - Parzival is
now being shown as travelling through the Grail forest.

---

6 Friedr. Ohly, op.cit., p. 152: "... daß sie /diu âventiure7
   uns tuot bekant oder uns tuot kunt, kommt sonst wie hier nur
   vor bei Erzählungen von Wunderbarem." Footnote 39: "Sie uns
   tuot bekant, daß Parzival am Tage weiter ritt als ein Vogel
   geflogen wäre (224.22), sie uns tuot kunt das Aussehen von
   Schastel marveile (565.6) und seiner Wundersäule (589.30)
   sowie daß Kondwiramurs zur Gralsburg bestimmt ist (734.10)...

7 Friedr. Ohly, op.cit., p. 152: "Anders als "künde hân" 'wissen,
   kennen' und "künde gewinnen" 'erfahren' steht "künden" im 'Parzival' nie ohne Gewicht. Seine Objekte sind schwere Leiden
   (footnote 35: Minnenot 810.21; Reue 448.25; Sünde 329.22;
   499.19), wichtige Lehren (footnote 36: Wesen der Minne 511.13;
   Gebot der Mitleidsfrage 477.28), der Gral (footnote 37: 453.
   21; 469.2) und an bedeutsamen Stellen die Dichtung. Im Prolog
   stellt Wolfram sein Werk als das hin, "daz ich iu eine künden
   wil" (4.7): viele andere schüfen es nicht gemeinsam. Vor dem

But more - seriousness forthcoming has been heralded also in
the paragraph dealing with Parzival's past by the mention of
a particular sword. At the end of his brief survey of Parzival's
career since his departure from the Arthurian court, Wolfram
reminds his audience of the sword which Anfortas had given him.
It had splintered in battle, so he says, and had then been
miraculously repaired by being steeped into the magic well near
Karnant (434.25-30). The story of the magic properties of this
sword and of its link with marvels as told by Sigûne (253.24ff.),
bears the stamp of a fairy-tale. The manner in which it is be-
stowed upon Parzival, the type of symbol which Sigûne sees in
it, the aura of fable which surrounds it and - last but not least -
its dangerous characteristic of splintering in the second thrust[8],
all combine to designate it as a sword destined not for ordinary
practical use in fighting, but as a symbol of investiture, as an
emblem of regal power.[9] With it Parzival is marked out by Anfortas as the ruler elect, as his successor.[10] He takes it with him

---

bedeutenden Tage der Taufe des Feirefiz sagt er: "ich wil iu
künden von dem tage" (816.8). Daß "diu âventiure uns kündet",
ist dem Eingang des IX. Buches vorbehalten, ..."

8 254.2: "daz swert gestêt ganz einen slac,/ am andern ez
zevellet gar".

9 That the sword given by Anfortas is an emblem of regal might
is argued convincingly by Werner Schröder, Parzivals Schwerter, ZfdA, 100 (1971), 111-132. After his analysis of what
Sigûne has to say with reference to this sword, he concludes
(p. 125): "... die in alle Geheimnisse der Gralsburg einge-
weihte Sigune sieht in dem Schwert des Anfortas nicht so
sehr ein Instrument zum Kämpfen, als vielmehr ein Herrschaftszeichen..."

10 W. Mersmann, Der Besitzwechsel und seine Bedeutung in den
Dichtungen Wolframs von Eschenbach und Gottfrieds von Straßburg, Medium Aevum, 22, (1971), says of the relevant scene
at the Grail castle (p. 136): "Der Vorgang ähnelt also einer
Abdankung, während Parzivals Beschenkung Züge einer Designation trägt!" Werner Schröder, op.cit., p. 126, comments:
"So konnte es - und sollte es wohl auch - dem mittelalterlichen Hörer oder Leser erscheinen, der um die Bedeutung des
Schwertes als Herrschaftszeichen wußte. Das Motiv klingt hier
jedenfalls an."

on leaving the Grail castle (246.1ff.), and it accompanies him
on his subsequent travels. It reappears in the introduction to
Book IX as a concrete reminder of the scene with Anfortas, and
with it of Parzival's tentative elevation and his simultaneous
failure.[11] It is highly appropriate, and at the same time deeply
serious, that Wolfram should display for his audience this symbol of the hero's possible destiny as king, and of his fundamental shortcoming as a human being, just before his gravest and
most exacting trial. The introduction of the sword at this point
calls to mind tangibly the huge gap between success and failure
as it relates to Parzival, the breathtaking height to which destiny has allowed him to aspire, and the (by comparison) shattering
fall to which he might condemn himself. It is a statement in
visual terms of what the issue of the forthcoming scenes is
going to be. Will Parzival show himself fit for this fate after
all, or will he fail its requirements entirely and finally? Will
he fail as he did at the Grail castle in the act of the presentation of this symbol, or will he overcome this failure, earn the
sword, prove himself worthy to bear the emblem and become king
of the Grail? The sword poses questions which relate to Parzival's emotional and spiritual survival or destruction. Its reappearance here suggests that the balance in which his life hangs
between failure and achievement, desolation and happiness, will
now be tipped. The visual motif of the sword could hardly point
to a complex of problems more vital and more serious.

A mood of gravity and suspense has now been fully established,
the abrupt change of tone, the judicious choice of terminology,
and the reintroduction of an object charged with symbolism all
combining to create it. Wolfram has successfully directed his
narrative into the seriousness which will mark the subsequent

---

11 Cf. Werner Schröder, op.cit., p. 126: "Das Gralsschwert in
    Parzivals Hand fungiert gleichsam als Dingsymbol verscherz-
    ter Königswürde und versäumter Menschlichkeit."

scenes, and he has persuaded his listeners into the correctly
perceptive frame of mind for them. Yet, having achieved the
right atmosphere he chooses momentarily to disrupt it for one
final flash of fun. He dispels it briefly and effectively just
before the last and irrevocable step into gravity, just before
his announcement: "diu âventiure uns kündet". He does this by
mocking the very instrument which he had used to bring it about.
The sword when assessed not as an emblem, but as a weapon, when
drawn from the context of symbolism into the confines of reality,
becomes an altogether improbable, even ludicrous object. The
lever for ridicule here its utter uselessness: it splinters at
the second thrust, thus leaving its owner defenceless. It had
splintered in Parzival's hands, Wolfram maintains, but had
nevertheless helped him in his quest for renown: "daz swert
gehalf im prîss bejac" (434.30). His concluding mock-serious
admonishment to his listeners - "swerz niht geloubt, der sündet"
(435.1) - believe it, or be damned! - strips the symbol of its
symbolism. [12] It focusses fleetingly on the sword through the
lens of realism and for a split second shows what remains of it
under realistic appraisal. It is a ridiculous weapon when seen
in this way, an absurd encumbrance rather than a tool of attack
and defence; and the idea that such a sword should help anyone
in a career based on fighting is a joke.

---

12 The interpretation above relates the sentence "swerz niht
    geloubt, der sündet" to the story of the sword, i.e. to the
    passage immediately preceding it. Leitzmann connects it with
    the preceding paragraph by a colon - ... 434.30: "daz swert
    gehalf im prîses bejac: swerz niht geloupt, der sündet".
    Lachmann puts a full-stop here instead of a colon, leaving
    it open whether the sentence is to be allotted to the pre-
    ceding or to the following section. Werner Schröder, op.cit.,
    p. 128, footnote 3, considering the sentence in relation to
    both these sections, concludes: "Erst der folgende Vers: diu
    âventiure uns kündet (435.2) leitet die dritte Begegnung mit
    Sigune ein. An ihr ist nichts, was vom Erzählablauf her un-
    glaubwürdig wäre. Die Salvierungsformel gegenüber skeptischen
    sachverständigen Hörern kann sich sinnvoll nur auf die dubio-
    se Geschichte von Anfortas' Schwert beziehen, und Leitzmanns
    Interpunktion erscheint mir als die einzig mögliche." He takes
    it to be a light-hearted wink at the audience (pp. 128/29).

The interplay of nonsense and emotionalism in the motif, the
mixture of silliness and solemnity in the pose, the firm and
carefully calculated lead into seriousness with yet a quick
step back into mischief at the end - all contribute towards
concocting a blend of humour and gravity which makes the introduction to Book IX into a very striking signpost indeed. The
underlying artistic intention, to ease the audience into a
serious mood, would presumably have been detected only by the
cognoscenti among them. Those who were less discerning would
merely have slipped into it. All of them, however, the discriminating and the indiscriminating alike, would have been alerted
to the particular importance of the events to follow by the
arresting character of this introduction. Wolfram had achieved
his objective - the path to momentous happenings was clear.

Friedr. Ohly, op.cit., p. 153ff., on the other hand, relates
the sentence to the passage immediately following: "diu
âventiure uns kündet/daz Parzival der degen balt/ kom ge-
riten ûf einen walt", (435.2-4) and takes it to be a solemn
declaration on the part of the poet.
The phrase in itself looks like a popular saying. Ernst
Martin saw it as such: "Der Satz ist formelhaft," (Kommentar, p. 339). It is unlikely that it would ever carry any
weight, but would rather be treated by everyone, including
Wolfram, as a frivolous quip.

2. Sigûne *inclusa*

The first scene of Book IX which involves the actual presence
of the hero shows him in Grail country, pinpointing unmistakably
by the choice of geographical background the serious nature of
the episode about to be depicted. It is the mention of Sigûne
in the very first passage of the scene which provides the clue
to its location: Parzival comes upon a newly built anchorage;
the anchoress enclosed in it, so the poet reveals, is Sigûne.
The reappearance of Sigûne and the ultimate re-emergence of the
Grail landscape here, together with the reintroduction of the
Grail sword in the opening passage, project the audience back
to the central event of Book V, to Parzival's visit to Munsalvaesche. Differing fundamentally here from Chrestien who describes neither sword, nor cousin, nor Grail setting at this
juncture, Wolfram goes back in the narrative, not to the point
where we had lost the hero from sight, not to his departure from
the Arthurian court in Book VI, but to the Grail castle. He
picks up the thread of the Parzival-plot at an earlier stage
in its chronology than might have been expected. His poetic
technique, so clearly deliberate on the basis of its discrepancy from the source, lays bare his thematic concern: Parzival
must retrace his steps back to the world of the Grail, to his
failure within it, in order to be able to progress. What was
left unfinished there, is to be taken up again now. The introduction of Sigûne here, apart from consolidating the tentative
mood of the opening passage to Book IX, thus achieves important
narrative connections for Wolfram. It points backwards to a
specific point in the chronology, and at the same time it points
forwards to the plot about to be unravelled.

This latter preparatory function of the Sigûne-scene in Book IX
has long been recognized. In various ways critics have commented
on the general predictive nature of the episode: Sigûne's task
is to condition Parzival for what is to come; the third meeting
with Sigûne is to make Parzival aware of his situation, and is

to rouse feelings of guilt in him; Sigûne prepares Parzival for
the events to follow by making him acutely conscious of the harm
done at the Grail castle; she points to God, thus expressing a
presentiment of Parzival's immediate needs; by commending him
to God she anticipates attitude and action of both Kahenîs and
Trevrizent, etc. etc.[13] The Sigûne-scene in Book IX indeed prepares the hero in many ways. A number of features in it, of
greater and of lesser importance, point to the near future, and
even beyond it.[14] The scene, however, does not only prepare the
hero for future events, but also the audience, and seen from
this particular vantage-point the dominant prefigurative quality
of the scene must logically be derived from that aspect which
the audience would consider to be its most striking feature.
- That feature is beyond doubt the incisive, dramatic, and
quite unexpected change that has overtaken Sigûne's personality
and the pattern of her life. Since her last meeting with Parzival
she has become - and has only recently become -[15] an inclusa, an
enclosed religiosa, an anchoress.

---

13 Thus e.g. Walter Henzen, op.cit., p. 135: "Parzivals dritte
    Begegnung mit der Base soll in ihm das Bewusstsein seiner
    Lage und Schuld wachrufen und ihn (- in unbestimmter Richtung
    noch -) auf den Weg zum Gral weisen;" and p. 136: "... (wir)
    möchten eine genügende Rechtfertigung für Sigunes Auftreten
    an dieser Stelle in ihrer vorbereitenden Rolle und im Vor-
    drängen einer Episode des Sigune-Schionatulandervorwurfs er-
    kennen, der Wolfram nebenher auch beschäftigt hat. Sigune
    bereitet vor, indem sie Parzival den Schaden der unterlas-
    senen Frage eindringlich erleben lässt." Cf. also Ursula
    Heise, Frauengestalten im Parzival Wolframs von Eschenbach,
    DU, 9 (1957), 37-62: "Obwohl sie keine Hoffnung sieht, ver-
    weist sie Parzival auf Gott, und wiederum ahnt sie damit
    das, was nun unmittelbar notwendig ist, voraus ..." (p. 51).

14 Aspects which point beyond Book IX are the themes of forgive-
    ness and of guidance to the Grail. Both are introduced at the
    end of the episode.

15 Enclosure had taken place not long ago; her anchorage is
    newly built (435.6: "aldâ sîn ougen funden/ ein klôsen niwes
    bûwes stên", ...).

Altogether Sigûne appears four times in Wolfram's work. Dif-
ferentiating between these four episodes on the basis of adaptation of source, or free invention, they neatly fall into two
categories. The first two - Sigûne grieving over Schîânatulander just killed in a joust with Orilus (Book III), and Sigûne
upbraiding Parzival after his visit to Munsalvaesche (Book V),
- are based on a single scene in the French romance. They are
splinter-episodes developed from one narrative block in 'Li
Contes del Graal', from Perceval's one and only meeting with
his kinswoman after his departure from the Grail castle (lls.
3428-3690). The last two, on the other hand, - Sigûne newly
enclosed in her anchorage (Book IX), and Sigûne dead at prayer
in her anchorage (Book XVI) - represent a freely invented sequel
to the earlier scenes. In these early scenes Sigûne is a worldly
figure, a girl weeping over her dead lover; in the sequel she
has been taken out of the context of worldliness, and has been
made into an _inclusa_. It is this change, freely developed by
Wolfram, precisely stated as both an outward and an inward
change, and first introduced in the Sigûne-episode here in Book
IX, which gives this particular scene its most memorable and
most momentous aspect. From it the episode derives its chief
predictive function within the composition of Book IX, revealing
at the same time the reason for its interpolation at this point.
- Sigûne as an _inclusa_ exemplifies faith. By her style of life,
on the _gradus_ to which the poet has now raised her, she exhibits
a selfless and wholly undemanding love of God which Parzival
has yet to understand and learn. Not only does she show herself
as reconciled to tragedy in life, and as at the same time constant in her faith, while Parzival has been manifestly unable
to do either, but she has even made fundamental sacrifices for
her faith. At the very beginning of the episode Wolfram describes
her as "ein klôsnaerinne,/ diu durch die gotes minne/ ir magetuom
unt ir freude gap (435.13-15), as an _inclusa_ who for the love of
God sacrificed the gift of her virginity and surrendered all
happiness.[16] Persistent in her loyalty to the dead Schîânatu-

lander she has not parted with his corpse. His coffin has been
walled up with her. (435.19-22). She thus has the tangible
proof of the central catastrophe of her life constantly before
her. Nevertheless she shows no rebellion, but rather typifies
humilitas, humility in the evident acceptance of her misery, and
in the steadfastness of her faith - her life is spent in prayer:
"ir leben was doch ein venje gar" (435.25). Sigûne now, when
compared with her former self, is portrayed as deliberately
having chosen near-martyrdom in order to serve God. In total
abnegation of self she has jailed herself, and by so doing demonstrates the depth, extent and purity of her faith. Sigûne is
at this moment everything Parzival is not. She is a reverse
mirror-image for him. She is selfless, humble, believing, while
he is self-centred, arrogant and unbelieving. She is a living
lesson to Parzival in his apostasy. Her life is an exemplum to
him of "triuwe". As such the Sigûne-episode foreshadows the leading theme of Trevrizent's religious instruction, and at the
same time glaringly isolates the central problem of Parzival's
life.

---

16 The notion expressed here by Wolfram is not easy to grasp
    for the modern reader - 'she offered up her chastity and
    along with it her happiness.' - The prerequisites for
    twelfth century dynastic marriage were the noblewoman's
    sexual innocence and her territorial and other material
    possessions. They were bargaining points without which a
    suitable marriage could not be negotiated. Under normal
    circumstances Sigûne would have contracted such a marriage
    in which society expected her to find fulfilment. By not
    using her virginity for the purpose of securing a marriage,
    but by offering it to faith instead, she forgoes voluntarily
    the contentment she would anticipate from marriage. In other
    words, she gives up both, chastity as a bargaining point,
    and the well-being which would follow the successful bargain.
    On marriage in the medieval centuries, vid. in particular
    Georges Duby, Medieval Marriage. Two Models from Twelfth-
    Century France, Baltimore and London, 1978; also R. H.
    Helmholtz, Marriage Litigation in Medieval England, Cam-
    bridge Studies in English Legal History, Cambridge, 1974.

"Triuwe", as is well known, is a key-concept in Wolfram's philosophy of life. It covers a wide spectrum of meanings[17], and many of his characters exhibit it in a variety of forms and in varying degrees. It is therefore notoriously difficult to define. Basically it may be described as a capacity for loving in total forgetfulness of self. It is an ability to feel for others in such a way that thoughts of ego are spontaneously forgotten. It can denote the bond between human beings, and it describes the bond between man and God.[18] "Triuwe" is the main theme of the romance: "ein maere wil i'u niuwen,/ daz seit von grôzen triuwen" (4.9/10) - stated at its beginning. Herzeloyde possesses this quality and shows it in the refraction of unbounded maternal love. She chooses life in the wilderness, and the poverty that goes with it, out of love for her child

> 116.15   genuoge sprechent, armuot,
> daz diu sî ze nihte guot.
> swer die durch triwe lîdet,
> hellefiwer die sêle mîdet.
> die dolte ein wîp durch triuwe.

The agony at parting from him kills her suddenly and dramatically the moment he leaves her (128.16-22). The tragic depth of her affection for her child, and her death prompted by it, grant her salvation (128.23: "ir vil getriulîcher tôt/ der frouwen wert die hellenôt./ ôwol si daz se ie muoter wart!"). This deep love of Parzival is seen as her chief and most in-

---

17 Cf. e.g. Joachim Bumke, Die Wolfram von Eschenbach Forschung, p. 105: "Wolframs triuwe-Begriff ist vieldeutig ..."

18 The most illuminating definition of "triuwe" in Wolfram is to be found in Marlis Schumacher, Die Auffassung der Ehe in den Dichtungen Wolframs von Eschenbach, Germanische Bibliothek, Heidelberg, 1967. Section: Wesensbestimmung der "triuwe", pp. 120ff. She distinguishes a "Grund-triuwe, die sich im Verhältnis des Menschen zu Gott und zu seinen Mitmenschen auswirkt", and continues: "Die triuwe ist im Unterschied zur staete, mit der sie den Charakter der Beständigkeit gemeinsam hat, eine Tugend, die nur in der Beziehung auf ein Du, in der Partnerschaft zu Gott oder dem Menschen bestehen kann. Sie kann sich in allen menschlichen Lebensbeziehungen äußern: in Freundschaft und Sippenverbundenheit,

cisively characterizing attribute by both Sigûne

> 140.16 deiswâr du heizest Parzivâl.
> der nam ist rehte enmitten durch.
> grôz liebe ier solch herzen furch
> mit dîner muoter triuwe.

and by Trevrizent

> 499.22 du solt ouch dîne muoter klagen.
> ir grôziu triwe daz geriet.
> dîn vart si vome leben schiet ...

This capacity for deep and selfless emotion in Herzeloyde, this "triuwe" descends to Parzival. It descends to him specifically from her (451.6: "sît Herzeloyd diu junge/ in het ûf gerbet triuwe, ..."). At the Grail castle, however, before Anfortas, he does not allow this inherited, inborn quality to guide him.

---

in Liebe und Ehe, in der Gefolgschaft und im Verhältnis des Herrschers zu seinen Untertanen, in der Gegnerschaft und in der flüchtigen Begegnung mit dem unbekannten Mitmenschen. Im Bereich des Menschlichen umspannt sie die speziellen Bedeutungen der Gerechtigkeit und Fairness, der tadelnden und zurechtweisenden Strenge, der Aufrichtigkeit und Zuverlässigkeit, der Treue und Beständigkeit, des Mitleides und der Hilfsbereitschaft, der selbstlosen Einsatzbereitschaft und der Opferwilligkeit. Diese menschliche triuwe ist (wie die wahre Minne) ein Analogon jener göttlichen triuwe, die das Urbild aller irdischen triuwe ist und den Menschen zur triuwe verpflichtet. Gott allein ist im Vollbesitz der triuwe (Pz. 462.19; 119.24) und der erbarmenden Liebe (Pz. 466.1ff.); dem Menschen ist nur eine graduelle Teilhabe an der triuwe (wie an den übrigen Tugenden) möglich." Vid. here also the bibliography with reference to "triuwe" in the footnotes to pp. 119 and 120, and in the Literaturverzeichnis.
Fundamental contributions to the exploration of "triuwe" in 'Parzival' have been made by Benedikt Mockenhaupt, Die Frömmigkeit im Parzival Ws. v. E. Grenzfragen zwischen Theologie und Philosophie, 20, Bonn, 1942; Reprint WBG, 1968; Julius Schwietering, Parzivals Schuld, ZfdA, 81 (1944), 44-68, reprinted in: Mystik und höfische Dichtung im Hochmittelalter, Tübingen, 1960, pp. 37-70; Gottfried Weber, Parzival. Ringen und Vollendung, Oberursel, 1948. On "triuwe" in Book IX vid. in particular Peter Wapnewski, Wolframs Parzival. Studien zur Religiosität und Form, Heidelberg, 1955, p. 191ff.: "triwe" im Parzival.

It comes to be stifled, overlaid by material, superficial concerns. Parzival is captivated by the splendour about him and
riveted by the marvel of the Grail (239.8: "wol gemarcte Par-
zivâl/ die rîcheit unt daz wunder grôz"), but the general atmosphere of grief and misery[19], the tears and lamentations at
court[20], and the suffering of his crippled host[21], pass him by.
Even the gift of the sword, this kingship by designation, in
which Anfortas so tragically tries to abdicate, even that does
not jolt his "triuwe" into action. Parzival, with his attention
engaged elsewhere, gives the ritual no thought, and consequently understands neither its pathos, nor the responsibilities in which it involves him. While indeed the poet may not
expect his hero to grasp the meaning of the ceremony, he
clearly <u>does</u> expect him to understand the gesture on another
level - namely that breathtaking gifts such as this sword (239.
20: "des palc was tûsent marke wert./ sîn gehilze was ein rubîn")
cannot but hide a demand, and that their acceptance automatically puts a recipient under inescapable obligation (240.5:
"wan do erz enpfienc in sîne hant,/ dô was er vrâgens mit
ermant".)[22] Parzival, however, does not even respond to the

---

19 227.7-16; 229.17

20 231.23-232.4

21 225.18; 230.18-20; 230.30-231.2; 237.7/8

22 Wolfram's audience, unlike Wolfram's hero, would have iden-
    tified the scene as a formal bestowal of kingship. The
    important clue to it is the dazzling monetary value which
    Wolfram puts on this sword. The scabbard alone, he says,
    was worth one thousand marks, so that the total value of
    the sword must be imagined as being at least twice that.
    During Wolfram's lifetime the mark was a monetary unit,
    not a coin, and the most reputable mark in Germany was the
    Cologne mark. It represented a standard of eight ounces of
    silver, i.e. approximately 233 grms (cf. Elisabeth Nau,
    Münzen und Geld in der Stauferzeit, Die Zeit der Staufer,
    vol. III, pp. 87-102; also Hedwig Heger, op.cit., pp. 192ff.).
    It is difficult to translate medieval sums into modern cur-
    rency, but an impression of the enormous value of the sword
    may be gained by relating its price to other well-known
    sums of the period. The most famous of these is the 150,000
    Cologne or silver marks paid to the Imperial crown as

gesture on its simple level; he does not sense the deeply personal bond with which he now links himself to Anfortas. He accepts the immensely costly sword which he moreover knows to be

---

ransom for Richard Lionheart in 1194. This was obviously a
huge amount. Its collection necessitated a general levy
throughout England. Moreover, the ransom was presumably
fixed with an eye to the fact that Richard, through his
mother, Eleanor of Poitou, was one of the richest monarchs
of his time. The Grail sword is thus assessed at nearly
1 1/2% of a truly breathtaking royal ransom. - The normal
fee for scutage in the twelfth century, (the fee paid to
the liegelord in lieu of war-service), was two marks. This
seems to have represented a knight's forty days' service
(Charles Oman, op.cit., vol. 1, p. 369). The monetary value
of the Grail sword could therefore have raised a force of
one thousand cavalry soldiers. - In July 1219 a representative of the Welf dynasty finally surrendered the Imperial
insignia to the emperor Frederick II at Goslar. He did so
in return for 11,000 marks and the office of imperial vicar
in the region bounded by the Weser and the Elbe (A. L. Poole,
Germany in the reign of Frederick II, in: Cambridge Medieval
History, vol. VI, 1929, chapter III, pp. 80-109, here pp.
82/83). If the office in question is reckoned at doubling
the price of the insignia, then the value of the Grail-sword
may be assessed at ca. 10% of one of the most important bar-
gains Frederick ever struck during the whole of his career.
The settlement sealed the peace between the Welf and Hohenstaufen families. - Nearer home, in Upper Germany, at Castle
Andechs above the Ammersee, a reputed 30,000 marks were given
in dowry to Hedwig of Andechs-Meran when she was married to
the first duke of Silesia and Poland at some time between
1186 and 1190. The dowry, one fifth of a king's ransom, and
probably apocryphal, would stamp Hedwig, a daughter of one
of the richest and most influential families in the Empire,
and the future patron saint of Silesia, into an outstanding
heiress of Wolfram's time. The normal dowry for Piast marriages in the thirteenth century was 3,000 marks. (Joseph
Gottschalk, op.cit., p. 93).
Thus the dazzling value of the Grail-sword clearly announced
to Wolfram's audience its character as part of the regalia.
At this stage of the description the earlier twofold reference to Parzival wearing Repanse's, the queen's, mantle
would also gain point (228.8-20; 235.25 - 236.15). The hero
is already clothed in the pallium, he now receives the sword
of kingship. That Repanse's cloak on Parzival's shoulders is
indeed the regal mantle, is corroborated later by Trevrizent:
"sine lêch dirs niht ze ruome:/ si wând du soltst dâ hêrre
sîn..." (500.28/29), 'she did not give it to you to swagger
in; she expected you to become king there.' On sword and
cloak as part of the regalia vid. Percy E. Schramm (mit Bei-

the king's own (239.25/26), without also acknowledging the obligation implicit in the startling value of the gift. He takes,
but he gives nothing in return. When finally in a last attempt
charged with pathos Anfortas tries to provoke the all-important
question by revealing the extent and nature of his affliction
- that God Himself has maimed him, "... daz mich got/ ame lîbe
hât geletzet" (239.26/27), Parzival still, incomprehensibly,
remains silent and unconcerned. His "triuwe" lies dormant, totally
and catastrophically. - Sigûne, outraged at his inhuman indifference, his frozen feeling, traces his failure to respond com-
passionately to the corruption of "triuwe" within him: "ir truogt
den eiterwolves zan,/ dâ diu galle in der triuwe/ an iu bekleip
sô niuwe." (255.14-16). Cundrîe identifies his lack of pity as
a complete lack of "triuwe": "ir vil ungetriuwer gast!/ sîn nôt
iuch solt erbarmet hân" (316.2/3). And Trevrizent in the end
interprets Parzival's silence before Anfortas as an irrational
lapse from "triuwe":

> 488.26 dô dir got fünf sinne lêch,
> die hânt ir rât dir vor bespart.
> wie was dîn triwe von in bewart
> an den selben stunden
> bî Anfortases wunden?

Parzival's innate capacity for deep and selfless emotion, for
compassion, love, loyalty, and for faith, thus failed to manifest
itself at a moment crucial for his future. This is how Sigûne,
Cundrîe and Trevrizent see it.[23] The failure of "triuwe" within

---

trägen verschiedener Verfasser), Herrschaftszeichen und Staats-
symbolik, Beiträge zu ihrer Geschichte vom dritten bis zum
sechzehnten Jahrhundert, Schriften der Monumenta Germaniae
historica, 13, 3 vols., Stuttgart, 1954-56, vol. I, p. 25ff.
and vol. II, p. 484ff.; also Percy E. Schramm/Florentine
Mütherich, Denkmale der deutschen Könige und Kaiser. Ein
Beitrag zur Herrschergeschichte von Karl dem Grossen bis
Friedrich II, 768-1250, Veröffentlichungen des Zentralinsti-
tuts für Kulturgeschichte in München, II, Munich, 1962,
p. 33ff., in particular pp. 50, 54 and 55.

23 Modern scholars have seen it less simply than Wolfram's three
    characters, and the explanations for Parzival's failure here
    have ranged over a wide area of possibilities; cf. Joachim
    Bumke, Die Wolfram von Eschenbach Forschung, chapter II,2:

him consigns him to a spiritual wilderness for years to come,
and at the same time sends the Grail kindred back to their misery.

Das religiöse Problem, pp. 150-176; also the bibliography
listed under Religiöse Problematik in his Wolfram von Eschenbach, pp. 90-92. The problem will continue to be debated, as
witness e.g. Ursula Hennig, Die Gurnemanzlehren und die unterlassene Frage Parzivals, PBB (Tübingen), 97 (1975), 312-
332. Entering into this controversy in detail lies beyond the
bounds of the present study. The "embarras de richesses" as
regards interpretations of why Parzival remains silent has
arisen, so it would seem, through jumping the poet's gun
when reading and rereading Book V. The modern reader, as
against the medieval listener, is almost always at a disadvantage in one particular respect: He is hampered by un-
authorised foreknowledge of the dénouement. The medieval
listener was either not preoccupied in this way at all, or
else he may have had foreknowledge of a similar dénouement
only in a different version of the tale. To either type of
listener, the story in hand was new, and their full attention would go to the step-by-step description by the poet.
Such step-by-step description in lls. 237.21-240.12 of Book
V carefully outlines two questions: the question which Parzival wants to ask, and the question which he should ask.
- At the Grail castle Parzival is received into a court of
elegance, sophistication and great luxury. The display of
riches culminates in the arrival of the court's dazzling
collection of gold plate on four trolleys. The golden sal-
vers, bowls and goblets are put out on the tables in order
to receive what is miraculously conjured up by the Grail.
The description of the golden treasures is introduced by
Wolfram with: "hoert mêr von rîchheite sagen" (237.21). The
description of the banquet spread by the Grail, which follows immediately, is prefixed by "nu hoert ein ander maere"
(238.2). Both, the fabulous riches and the marvel, make a
profound impression upon Parzival. He is fascinated by both:
"wol gemarcte Parzivâl/ die rîcheit unt daz wunder grôz"
(239.8/9). Yet though sorely tempted to ask questions, he
does not do so: "durch zuht in vrâgens doch verdrôz" (239.10),
manners restrain him from asking questions - as indeed they
might! Our code of etiquette has not changed in this respect
since the thirteenth century. We still do not enquire into
people's possessions and assets, nor do we pry into their
secrets. A man of breeding in the thirteenth century did
not do so either. Parzival would dearly like to know more,
but feels he cannot ask (239.13: "ich solte vil gevrâgen
niht"). Moreover, so he argues within himself, there may be
no need for it: "waz op mîn wesen hie geschiht/ die mâze als
dort pî im?" - I might stay here as long as I stayed with
Gurnemanz; "âne vrâge ich vernim/ wiez dirre massenîe stêt".

If Parzival is to be rescued from utter desolation, then he must
learn the overriding priority of "triuwe" in life, and must recover
"triuwe" in its essential form. In order for him to do so, it must
be reactivated. So withered is his capacity for selfless emotion,
and thus for true faith, so silted up its stream when years later
he finds himself in Grail country again, that it takes the powerful spectacle of the very personification of "triuwe" to bring it
back to life, and to make it flow again.

This does not mean that in the intervening period between leaving
the Grail castle (Book V), and returning to the Grail forest
(Book IX), Parzival is incapable of all kinds of "triuwe". Almost

---

- If so, I shall find out all about this court without asking any questions (239.14-17). While Parzival is pondering
the problem of the question which he wants to ask, the king's
sword is brought along (239.18: "in dem gedanke nâher gêt/
ein knappe, der truog ein swert".) Its value is such as to
be ominous when offered as a gift. Gifts such as this forge
a contract when accepted. They can pass with propriety, dignity and freedom only between the most intimately and closely
linked individuals, between members of a family, between
parent and child. A stranger who offers such a gift, hints
at a demand, and the one who accepts it, accepts this demand
with it. The attitude towards gifts of this kind in the
thirteenth century was clearly no different from what it is
in the twentieth; Wolfram considers that the moment Parzival
has accepted the gift, he has automatically put himself under
an obligation: "wan do erz enpfienc in sîne hant,/ dô was
er vrâgens mit ermant" (240.5/6). The demand which goes with
the costly gift is very nearly spelt out for Parzival; it is
the question which he should ask. Anfortas tries to prod him
into it:

> 239.25   hêrre, ich prâhtz in nôt
> in maneger stat,ê daz mich got
> ame lîbe hât geletzt,
> nu sît dermit ergetzet, ...

- take it, it is my own! I can no longer use it, for God has
crippled me. The automatic response to such tragic releva-
tions, - above all, if the gift which accompanies them, is
accepted - must be, then as now, an expression of sympathy,
an offer of comfort, - must be the all important question of
compassion. It does not come: "ôwê daz er niht vrâgte dô!"
(240.2).
The question which Parzival wants to ask therefore in no way
tallies with the question he should ask. The riches and curi-
osities of the court claim his attention, the suffering at
his side receives none.

immediately after leaving Munsalvaesche he even displays "triuwe"
again as compassion, though of a noticeably weaker brand than
before. He is moved, but obviously somewhat distantly, by
Sigûne's plight at their second meeting, and offers his services to her. His emotional distance expresses itself in his
formality

> 249.27 frouwe, mir ist vil leit
>   iwer senelîchiu arebeit.
>   bedurft ir mines dienstes iht,
>   in iwerem dienste man mich siht.

His detachment at this moment becomes clearer still when compared with his spontaneous compassion with her earlier, during their
first meeting

> 138.27 got halde iuch, sprach des knappen munt.
>   'ich hân hie jaemerlichen funt
>   in iwerm schôze funden.
>   wer gap iun ritter wunden?'
>   der knappe unverdrozzen
>   sprach 'wer hât in erschozzen?
>   geschahez mit eime gabylôt?
>   mich dunket, frouwe, er lige tôt.
>   welt ir mir dâ von iht sagn,
>   wer iu den rîter habe erslagn?
>   ob ich in müge errîten,
>   ich wil gerne mit im strîten.'

Nevertheless, though evidently governed by restraint and courtesy,
it is still "triuwe" as compassion of a kind, which manifests itself in Parzival's reaction to Sigûne, when he meets her for the
second time.

Shortly afterwards Parzival shows "triuwe" in the form of integrity. He swears Jeschûte's innocence on the relic, and Wolfram
comments "Parzival dô mit triwen fuor" (269.1); he acted honour-
ably. Just before rejoining the Arthurian court he manifests yet
another kind of "triuwe", "triuwe" as love-longing. He falls into a
love-trance as the drops of blood on the snow remind him of
Condwîrâmûrs. Wolfram explains: "von sînen triwen daz geschach"
(282.23) and again: "sîn triwe in lêrte daz er vant/ snêwec
bluotes zäher drî,/ die in vor witzen machten vrî." (296.2-4).

Parzival therefore displays a number of forms of "triuwe" to
varying degrees <u>after</u> his visit to the Grail castle and <u>before</u>
his third meeting with Sigûne. The essential "triuwe", however,
does not begin to break through again until <u>after</u> the Sigûne-
episode in Book IX.

Of all characters in the romance, the supreme expression of
"triuwe" is found in Sigûne. In Book IX she is presented as displaying it on an exalted <u>gradus</u> and in its highest form, as
faith. But within the total portrayal of Sigûne, within the
four episodes in which she is shown, "triuwe" as faith represents
only one form of "triuwe" among others, - albeit the most distinguished one, - of which she is capable. It represents the
final form of "triuwe", the culmination to which she attains.[24]
It begins as a minor dimension to her personality in the first

---

24 Marlis Schumacher, op.cit., observes that Sigûne is portrayed
as the very embodiment of "triuwe". Yet while distinguishing
a gradualism in the concept of "triuwe" in the romance itself,
she nevertheless does not isolate a progression of "triuwe" in
Sigûne: "Der Gradualismus im Bereich der triuwe läßt sich am
besten veranschaulichen anhand der Sigunengestalt, welche
der Dichter als den Inbegriff aller menschlichen triuwe darstellt: Pz. 249,24 al irdisch triuwe was ein wint,/ wan die
man an ir lîbe sach. An Sigunes triuwe gemessen, wird jede
irdische triuwe als flüchtig, unbeständig und nichtig bezeichnet. Sigunes triuwe bewährt sich in jeglicher Hinsicht:
1. gegen Gott, 2. gegen den toten Geliebten, 3. gegen Parzival und gegen ihre Mitmenschen. Inwiefern Sigune den übrigen
Gestalten an triuwe überlegen ist, soll durch einige Beispie-
le erläutert werden:
1. Im Unterschied zu Parzival (332.1ff.) ergibt sie sich
nach dem Tode Schionatulanders in den Willen Gottes, ohne
sich gegen ihr Schicksal aufzulehnen oder an Gottes Güte und
Gerechtigkeit zu verzagen.
2. Im Gegensatz zu Herzeloyde (triuwe: 140,19; 317,20;
499,23 u.ö.), die sich nach ihrer nicht-vollzogenen Ehe mit
Castis ein zweites Mal vermählt, bewahrt Sigune ihre Treue
über den Tod des Geliebten hinaus.
Im Unterschied zu Orgeluse (triuwe: 611,29; 616,28; 729,24)
723,4 der was ergetzens gewin/ komen nâch Cidegaste,/ den
si ê klaget sô vaste. (Vgl. 617,3) begehrt Sigune kein 'er-
getzen' für den unersetzlichen Verlust: 253,15 Sigûne gerte
ergetzens niht,/ als wîp die man bî wanke siht.
3. Auch hegt Sigune keinen Rachewillen, während Orgeluse
die ihr begegnenden Ritter als Werkzeug der Rache benützt

Sigûne-episode: it becomes a major one in the second, until in
the third, in Book IX, it has seized the whole person. In her
first meeting with Parzival she is shown as being acutely perceptive of "triuwe" in others, and intuitively recognizes it as
the essential emotional background to Parzival before she even
knows who he is: "du bist geborn von triuwen,/ daz er dich sus
kan riuwen" (140.1/2). She reveals her intrinsic grasp of "triuwe"
when she speaks of it as Herzeloyde's leading characteristic
the moment she has realized who Parzival is (140.16-19). She
mentions it in praise of Turkentâls, as feudal loyalty without
blemish which sent him to his death in the service of Parzival:
"dirre fürste wart durch dich erslagen,/ wand er dîn lant ie
werte:/ sine triwe er nie verscherte" (141.2-4). Finally, in
this episode, she declares her own "triuwe" in one of its important
permutations, as consideration, as concern for others. Although
the opportunity for immediate revenge on Orilus is before her,
and thus the possibility for at least some assuagement of her
suffering, she decides against it. Fearing that Parzival might
be killed in the joust he is so eager to fight for her, she deliberately sends him off in the wrong direction (141.29-142.2).[25]

In the next episode Sigûne is already the epitome of a much more
intense form of "triuwe" than was in evidence in her before, of
"triuwe" as loyalty in love. She has become "ein magt, der fuogte
ir triwe nôt" (249.15), a girl suffering for her faithfulness
in love. Shortly after leaving the Grail castle, Parzival finds
her clinging pitifully to the dead Schîânatulander from whom she

---

und gefährdet.
Auch die triuwe des Königs Artus (Pz. 150,26) steht, vergli-
chen mit Sigunes triuwe, auf einer geringeren Stufe der Wer-
teskala: In offenem Rechtsstreit mit Ither befangen, ent-
läßt er Parzival in den Kampf mit Ither, obgleich er befürch-
tet, daß der Unerfahrene erschlagen wird (150,24). Sigune
dagegen hatte den jungen Parzival, als er sich zum Rache-
kampf anbot (141.25ff.), in eine falsche Richtung gesandt,
denn: 142,1 si vorht daz er den lîp verlür." (pp. 121/122).

25 On Sigûne's curiously negative guidance which ultimately
    leads to the right road, vid. M. E. Gibbs, op.cit., pp.
    872-876.

cannot bring herself to part (249.11-17; 253.6-17). Wolfram
projects her now as the apotheosis of constancy in love: "al
irdisch triwe was ein wint,/ wan die man an ir lîbe sach" (249.
24/25) - no human loyalty in love could equal hers. Yet dominant though this particular "triuwe" may be in Sigûne in this
second encounter with Parzival, it has by no means displaced
another, and highly important form of "triuwe" which had been
adumbrated already in the first episode - "triuwe" as compassion.
Her consideration of others, shown first by her concern for the
young Parzival's safety, has grown and developed. It has become
deep compassion. She has such empathy with the anguish of Anfortas, that his release from it is the only happiness she can now
envisage for herself: "... sol mich iht gevröun,/ daz tuot ein
dinc, ob in sîn töun/ laezet, den vil trûrgen man" (253.19-21).
So important is this trait of profound pity in Sigûne that Wolfram specifically draws attention to it. After he has established
her "triuwe" as loyalty in love, and before she declares her "triuwe"
in the form of compassion, he calls to his audience to take note:
"hoert mêr Sigûnen triwe sagn" (253.18). Thus "triuwe" in Sigûne
from faint beginnings gathers momentum. Her considerate regard
for the needs of others has become a capacity for profound compassion. The dimension of "triuwe" latent in her, and glimpsed
through her intuitive recognition of "triuwe" in others, has become fully declared in her infinite devotion to the memory of
her love. Her progression in the ever increasing realization
of "triuwe" in the pattern of her life has been underlined by two
significant changes. Sigûne has moved from the country of Arthurian fable, from the forest of Brizljân, to the Grail forest.
Her appearance has changed startlingly, and almost beyond recognition, in the space of little more than a year. She is weak
and pallid, her mouth is colourless, her head is bald. Her beautiful and luxuriant hair has vanished (252.27-253.5). She has
torn it out by the roots in her immeasurable grief (138.16-19).
With the swathes of her fair hair gone and her red lips faded
she is no longer beautiful, no longer "minneclîch" as Parzival
says (253.2-5), no longer a possible object of love and desire.

The change in appearance and the shift in background herald a
growing spiritualization of Sigûne's life. Yet her immediate,
and clearly emblematic background in the Grail forest is still
the lime-tree, the tree of the worldly love-song, the tree with
its heart-shaped leaves (249.14/15)[26].

---

26 For Chrestien's "soz un chesne" (3431) - under an oak-tree,
    Wolfram has substituted "ûf einer linden" (249.14). The most
    likely explanation for this change is that Wolfram chose the
    lime-tree here for its well-known symbolic connotation. The
    change in prepositions is less easily explained. It could
    be based on the variant reading of this line: "sor un chesne".
    It could be a misreading of "sor" for "soz"; vid. Arthur B. Groos".
    "Sigune auf der Linde" and the turtledove in Parzival, JEGP,
    67 (1968), 631-646, for the relevant literature on these
    points. In either case the phrase need mean no more than -
    on a branch of a lime-tree, a lower one, of course, or - on
    a fallen lime-tree. Julius Schwietering, Sigune auf der Lin-
    de, ZfdA, 57 (1919/20), 140-143, took it to mean that Sigûne
    was sitting in the crown of a lime-tree. He had formed the
    impression moreover that Sigûne had sacrificed her hair: "...
    (sie) hat in trauernder askese den ehemaligen schmuck ihres
    langwallenden blonden haars von sich getan ..." (p. 141).
    The view is erroneous. There is no foundation for it in the
    text which is indeed quite explicit on this point: Sigûne
    tears out her hair in wild grief: "nu hoeret waz diu frouwe
    tuo./ dâ brach frou Sigûne/ ir langen zöpfe brûne/ vor jâmer
    ûzer swarten" (138.16-19). His notion of the sacrifice of
    her hair combined with the idea that Sigûne was sitting in
    the crown of the tree led Julius Schwietering to conclude
    that Sigûne was being characterized in Book V as a tree-
    dwelling saint: "so ligt die vermutung nahe, dass Wolfram
    auch in dieser scene eine ganz bestimmte form des eremiten-
    daseins vorschwebte, (namely that of the tree-dwelling saint)
    ... Wolfram schöpfte diese vorstellung, über deren einzel-
    heiten er keine rechenschaft gibt, (sic!) diesmal nicht aus
    der würklichkeit sondern aus der legende, von deren stimmung
    die erzählung von Sigune ganz durchdrungen ist." Arthur B.
    Groos, op.cit., following Julius Schwietering's idea that
    Sigûne is sitting in a lime-tree, suggests that the portrayal
    of her here echoes the motif of the turtle-dove on the dry
    branch. He sees additional proof for Julius Schwietering's
    assumption in the relevant illuminations of three 'Parzival'
    manuscripts of the fifteenth century. These, he says, "por-
    tray Sigune in a tree." (p. 632).
    The illuminators of the manuscripts in question are highly
    unreliable guides to Wolfram's 'Parzival'. They had at best
    a cursory acquaintance with the text. The artist of the
    Vienna Cod. 2914 does indeed show Sigûne as sitting in the
    fork of a tree, but without Schîânatulander (Fig. 7. fol.

In the third meeting in Book IX this symbol of profane love and
worldliness has gone. In a transformation which has extended
over more than four years[27] Sigûne has become an _inclusa_, and
her worldly love has come to be submerged in the love of God.
Her loyalty to Schîânatulander, her "alte triuwe" (435.16-18;
cf. also 436.23/24 and 440.13-15) is still agonizingly alive
in her, and her "triuwe" as compassion too reveals itself once
more, as she readily forgives Parzival in his wretchedness, for

---

160 r.; vid. Karl J. Benziger, Parzival in der deutschen Hand-
schriftenillustration des Mittelalters, Studien zur deutschen
Kunstgeschichte, 175, Strasbourg, 1914; Plate 39). Moreover
in the vignette with the rubric: "wie parcifal Sygunen in
der clusen vant" (Fig. 11. fol. 280 v. Benziger, op.cit.,
Plate 40) he portrays Sigûne as standing _outside_ her anchorage.
The illuminator of the Heidelberg Cod. Palat. Germ. 339 who
appears to have had grave difficulties with perspective, does
not show Sigûne in relation to a tree at all. Rudolf Kautzsch,
Diebolt Lauber und seine Werkstatt in Hagenau, Zentralblatt
für Bibliothekwesen, 12 (1895) as quoted by Karl Benziger,
op.cit., p. 32, gives the following assessment of him: "Man
kann dem Illustrator ein gewisses Raumgefühl nicht absprechen.
Innenräume begegnen noch nicht. Allermeist ist die Szene
ohne weiteres auf den grünen Bodenfleck verlegt. Oder es
tritt vereinzelt ein kapellenartiger, gewölbter, vorn offener
Raum auf. Die Aufgabe, Personen in dieser Welt unterzubringen,
führt zu den stärksten Mißverhältnissen, Unmöglichkeiten und
Gewaltsamkeiten. Die üblichen "Hügel", hinter denen Reiter
halb überschnitten auftauchen, die niedrigen Tische mit stei-
ler Platte sind noch nicht das Gröblichste. In Cod. Palat.
Germ. 339 finden sich z.B. Sigune und ihr toter Gemahl auf
dem Baum einfach als Brustbilder gezeichnet: das Uebrige
fehlt."
Neither this artist, nor the illuminator of the Dresden M 66,
seems to have had any real knowledge of the text. Karl Benziger comments on the Heidelberg Cod. Palat. Germ. 339 as
follows (op.cit., p. 28): "Wir besitzen hier ein typisches
Beispiel eines fabrikationsmäßig erstellten Buches, dessen
rohe Bilder nur wenig wirkliche Kenntnis des Gedichtes zei-
gen." He says of the artist of the Dresden M 66 (op.cit.,
p. 37): "... der Illustrator (kennt) auch hier seinen Stoff
noch sehr wenig."
The illuminators therefore, ignorant as they appear to have
been of the details of the text, can hardly be trusted as
commentators upon it. There is thus neither internal, nor
external evidence for Schwietering's theory of Sigûne as a
tree-dwelling saint.

his failure to release Anfortas (441.18-30). But dominant in
her now is another form of "triuwe", manifest in the stringent
asceticism which governs her life. Pallor characterizes her
appearance. She is a "juncfrouwe bleich gevar" (437.20). Her
one-time passionate lips have become ashen, proof that she has
put the world behind her: "ir dicker munt heiz rôt gevar/ was
dô erblichen unde bleich,/ sît werltlîch freude ir gar gesweich"
(435.26-28). She wears the grey habit of a _religiosa_ (437.25)
and a plain coif (438.9)[28]. Her chosen scourge is the hair-
shirt worn next to her skin (437.24/25).

Enclosed, as an anchoress, Sigûne has reached the most exalted
level of human "triuwe". Nevertheless, she hâs not left behind
other forms of "triuwe" which developed in her earlier. This new
and highest form of "triuwe" does not replace them, far from it,
it is added to them. Her loyalty in love and her compassion
towards her fellow-creatures have fused with her profound capacity for faith. "Triuwe" has now become her second nature, and
because of it she will in time come to be known as the very
embodiment of selflessness, as "rehter güete ein arke" (804.16).

The last Sigûne-episode in Book XV does not add substantially
to the image Wolfram had created of her in the first three
scenes. It merely completes and confirms it. Loyalty in love
has remained an important characteristic; she has continued to
grieve over Schîânatulander (804.14/15). More important, however, is and has been her unremitting and total immersion in
faith, indicated by the symbolic attitude in which she dies.
Death visits her as she kneels in prayer in her anchorage, and
Parzival and his companions find "Sigûnen an ir venje tôt"

---

27 Vid. pp. 126 and 129.

28 The description "senlîch was ir gebende" (438.9) could in-
    dicate a special coif of mourning. Whether is does or not,
    the adjective certainly characterizes the headdress as
    simple and unornamented. Cf. Ernst Martin on this line:
    "Gemeint ist wohl: keinen Kopfschmuck trug die Trauernde."

(804.23). Just as her life has been prayer without end (435.25:
"ir leben was doch ein venje gar"), so is her death.

Through being what she is now, here in Book IX, Sigûne pinpoints
the central problem of Parzival's life, the problem which must
be, and is about to be, tackled. At the same time the lesson of
Sigûne inclusa performs yet another equally vital function within
the poetic structure of Book IX: it anticipates the central lesson of Trevrizent's catechism. For while Sigûne as an inclusa
represents the finest, purest and truly perfect form of human
"triuwe", the highest manifestation of absolute "triuwe" is God Himself. The archetype of "triuwe", its great repository, is God.
"Triuwe" is the very nature of the Godhead: "Qui non diligit, non
novit Deum, quoniam Deus charitas est: - He that loveth not
knoweth not God; for God is love" (1. John 4:8); - "Sît getriwe
ân allez wenken./ sît got selbe ein triuwe ist" (462.18/19).
This is the dogma on which Trevrizent builds his initial instruction of Parzifal, it enshrines the doctrinal basis of the Christian faith, and it is the theme with which - in the opening part
of their long drawn-out discussion - he tries to win Parzival
back into believing.[29]

---

29 Cf. H. Meyer, op.cit., "Die auf Trevrizents zuversichtliche
    Beteuerung: er hilfet iu, wand er helfen sol (461.30) fol-
    gende Gotteslehre kreist um den zentralen Begriff der 'triu-
    we', deren Aktivierung eben Gottes "helfe" ist: sîn helfe
    ist immer unverzaget (462.10), den der staeten helfe nie
    verdrôz (462.16), ern kan an niemen wenken (462.28). Die
    dann folgende Darlegung der Heilsgeschichte im Sinne der
    Rekapitulationslehre ist gleichsam der konkrete Beweis der
    'triuwe' Gottes. Um seiner Menschheit die Treue zu halten,
    hat Gott, nach Adams Fall, selbst Menschengestalt angenom-
    men und den Sühnetod erlitten. Und dieselbe Treue, so darf
    erwartet werden, wird er auch Parzival beweisen! Die rich-
    tige Feststellung Ehrismanns: "Die Heilserzählung ist nichts
    anderes als die historische Offenbarung der Treue und Liebe
    Gottes" erhält so erst ihren vollsten Sinn." (pp. 24/25).

The compelling spectacle of "triuwe" presented by Sigûne _inclusa_
bears fruit. Some time after his visit to her anchorage, and
just before his meeting with Trevrizent, Parzival's own "triuwe"
begins to reappear in its essential form, in the form of a capacity for feeling deeply, - and he takes the first step in the
recovery of "triuwe" as faith. This innate and deep "triuwe" leads
him at last to consider once again the principle of a powerful
God, a tenet which he had vehemently rejected out of hand before
(332.1-4):

> 451.6 sît Herzeloyd diu junge
> in het ûf gerbet triuwe,
> sich huop sîns herzen riuwe.
> alrêrste er dô gedâhte,
> wer al die werlt volbrâhte,
> an sînen schepfaere,
> wie gewaltec der waere.[30]

Of the fundamental significance of the image of Sigûne _inclusa_
as "triuwe" within Parzival's spiritual regeneration there can
therefore be no doubt. It is vouchsafed further by the fact
that it is the Providential Will that guides him to it:

> 435.10 der junge degen unervorht
> reit durch âventiur suochen:
> sîn wolte got dô ruochen.
> er vant ein klôsnaerinne, ...

The Sigûne-episode thus forms an integral and indispensable link
in the narrative chain of Book IX. As an _exemplum_ of "triuwe" it
makes the audience aware of the nature of the hero's failing;
it outlines the problem with which he will have to grapple, thus
anticipating the substance of the events to follow; it reactiv-
ates his "triuwe" in preparation for what is to come" and it fi-

---

30 The quotation incorporates Lachmann's punctuation. This subordinates the "sît"-clause to the main clause which follows:
"sich huop sîns herzen riuwe". The "sît"-clause could also
be subordinate to the main clause which precedes it. Thus:
"dem (i.e. Parzival) riet sîn manlîchiu zuht/ kiusch und
erbarmunge,/ sît Herzeloyde diu junge/ in het ûf gerbet
triuwe./ Sich huop sîns herzen riuwe", etc. The different
grammatical connection of the subordinate clause does not
affect the main point of the interpretation of this passage
as given in the text above.

guratively predicts the initial content of the major scene of
the book.

The overriding importance of "triuwe" in the portrayal of Sigûne
is peculiar to Wolfram. When the description of Sigûne is compared with the depiction of her counterpart in the French romance, it becomes clear that a new conception governs the delineation of the figure in the German work. Its role has been
entirely recast. The chief function of Perceval's cousin is to
transmit Grail-lore to the hero, and half of the episode is
devoted to it (ca. 138 lls. out of 263 lls.). Yet it is easy
to see the seeds from which the aspect of "triuwe" proliferated.
Perceval's cousin grieves over her lover's headless body (3430-
3455), she shows pity for the Fisher King (3583-3590), and she
expressly denies any wish that Perceval should follow her lover's
killer (3644-3653).

That the image of an anchoress was here being used for the purpose of transmitting the notion of perfect faith would readily
be grasped and accepted by Wolfram's audience. Inclusae such as
Sigûne formed part of the common fund of experience of Wolfram
and his contemporaries. To them she was not an extravagant
idealization, an impression she might indeed make on the twentieth century reader, nor would they consider her portrait overdrawn. Her transformation from a figure of this world, from a
girl of rank and privilege, into an ascetic, who in the depth
and strength of her religious devotion had decided upon the most
austere, the most extreme form of self-denial, - on enclosure -,
such a transformation would to them have seemed realistically
conceived, plausibly motivated, and entirely credible. Within
the context of her own time Sigûne inclusa is not an abstraction,
but a portrait drawn from life.[31] The dominant feature of the

---

31 There is, of course, one important feature in the presentation of Sigûne which belongs to poetic utopia - the presence
   in her anchorhold of her lover's coffin. Nevertheless, the
   overriding idea which controls the portrayal is inspired by
   contemporary reality, namely that well-born women with the

new role in which Wolfram had cast her for Book IX, would instantly have crystallized itself for the poet's audience. Its
profound emotional impact upon them is not to be underestimated.
Certain features, both historical and social, of the time during
which 'Parzival' was being written (and before), make such in-
ferences regarding the reaction of the poet's listeners permis-
sible.

The practice of Christian solitaries, both men and women, to
submit to enclosure and to live in anchorholds, is widely attested for Western European countries. The custom appears to
have been known and followed throughout England, in Germany,
Austria and Switzerland, and also in France and other countries.[32] There is evidence for it in the German-speaking areas

---

expectation of standing at the apex of society might - and
not infrequently did - turn their back on the world of
power and riches and choose enclosure. In this sense the
portrait of Sigûne inclusa is drawn from life. Other features of description also indicate that she is entirely
realistically conceived: Her anchorage, like many contemporary anchorholds, is built across a brook (435.8) and
thus, as its counterparts in reality, has its natural water-
supply and waste-disposal system. A further touch of realism
is the servant who supplies her with food - Cundrîe (439.1-
5). Many anchorites and anchoresses, imprisoned as they
were through enclosure, had personal servants who ran essential errands for them. Finally, she is found reading the
psalter (438.1). Anchoresses were frequently highly literate
women, well versed in Latin.

32 Rotha Mary Clay, The Hermits and Anchorites of England, London, 1914, mentions the names of more than 650 hermits and
anchorites. The tables appended to her book give evidence
for approximately 750 cells. She claims "that there was not
a single county in England which had not at some time or
another a recluse's cell." (p. XVIII). Accounts of recluses
in France may be found in Francesca Maria Steele, Anchoresses
of the West, London, 1903; E. Sainte-Marie Perrin, Les reclusages en France au moyen âge, Revue hebdomadaire VIII,
No. 30, Paris, 1911, pp. 598-629 and Louis Gougaud, Ermites
et Reclus, Liguê, 1928. L.C. Pavy, Les recluseries, Lyons,
1875, was not accessible to me. Otmar Doerr, Das Institut
der Inclusen in Süddeutschland, Beitr. z. Gesch. des alten
Mönchtums und des Benediktinerordens, 18, Münster, 1934,
records widespread evidence for anchorholds in Southern
Germany. Ibid. also a general bibliography on the subject.

already from the eighth century onwards.[33] Recluses who resolved upon enclosure, were not treated as eccentrics. Neither society at large, nor the Church, looked upon them as outsiders;
nor was the decision to become enclosed theirs alone. At no
time was the desire for lifelong enclosure considered to be a
wish, which the individual ought to be permitted to gratify
without reference to anyone but himself. An order for enclosure
could not be given independently by anybody, but permission for
it had to be sought from some ecclesiastical authority, generally from the bishop of the relevant diocese.[34] Once enclosure had been approved, it was carried out with solemn rites
by a member of the clergy. The ceremony generally began with
the celebration of mass, after which the anchorite was taken
in full procession to his chosen dwelling. Here the officiat-
ing priest blessed the anchorhold, led the one to be enclosed
into it amid chanting and prayers, and finally, after leaving
him alone, allowed his cell to be made fast from outside.[35]
Once enclosed the anchorite was permitted to leave his dwelling
only when in mortal danger, or by order of his superior. Moreover, all anchorites were required to take vows, to recognize
an ecclesiastical authority above them, and to live according
to a regula.[36] Thus life in an anchorhold, voluntary solitary
confinement in the name of faith, bore the seal of acknowledg-
ment by the Church. In this way anchorites and anchoresses
were integrated into the social structure; they held a definitive place in the hierarchy of Western Christendom.

---

33 Otmar Doerr, op.cit., p. 71.

34 Otmar Doerr, op. cit., pp. 28/29; 32-34. Rotha Mary Clay,
    op. cit., p. XVII.

35 The ceremony for the enclosure of anchorites commonly con-
    sisted of five main parts: missa, processio, benedictio
    domus, introductio and obstructio. Other details of the
    ritual varied according to time and place. Otmar Doerr,
    op.cit., pp. 42-52; vid. also Rotha Mary Clay, op.cit.,
    p. 193ff. Appendix A: The Office for the enclosing of
    Anchorites according to the Use of Sarum.

36 Rotha Mary Clay, op.cit., pp. XVII/XVIII, also 90ff.;
    Otmar Doerr, op.cit., p. 2ff. Vid. Otmar Doerr also for a

This place was very high. The Liber Vitae of the Church of
Durham e.g. ranks anchorites above abbots, and only royal bene-
factors take precedence over them.[37] They were highly regarded
not only by those in Holy Orders, but also by the lay community,
by the nobility and the common people alike. The severity of
their style of life inspired awe. Their total rejection of self-
interest made them extraordinarily worthy of trust, while their
degree of self-denial vouchsafed an unusual clarity of the
spirit. For the ordinary mortal they had an aura of saintliness.
In consequence they were sought out by many who needed help. The
poor would come to beg for alms, the wretched to plead for comfort. Above all, however, the window of an anchorage came to be
looked upon in the Middle Ages as a place where counsel could be
had, spiritual guidance, and even the aristocracy, both temporal
and ecclesiastical, came to solicit it here.[38]

Throughout its history in Western Europe religious enclosure,
living as a captive of Christ, seems to have claimed far more
women than men. Records show that certainly in England, and very
likely also in the German-speaking areas, anchoresses outnumber-
ed anchorites at all times.[39] During a period lasting approximately one hundred years, however, their number rose particularly
steeply. From the beginning of the twelfth century to the early
decades of the thirteenth, - during the period which includes

list and a discussion of the rules for inclusi. Cf. Francis
D. S. Darwin, The English Mediaeval Recluse, London, n.d.
(probably 1938-1945). The most famous one among these rules
is the Middle English Ancren Riwle or Ancrene Wisse written
by an anonymous author for three sister recluses at the
beginning of the thirteenth century.

37 Liber Vitae Ecclessiae Dunelmensis, ed. by J. Stevens, Publications of the Surtees Society, 13, 1841, pp. XI and 6.

38 Otmar Doerr, op.cit., pp. 65-68; also Francesca M. Steele,
Anchoresses, p. 3.

39 Rotha Mary Clay, op.cit., p. 73. In the lists which Otmar
Doerr has compiled the names of women predominate over those
of men (pp. 74-119). His data refer to the German speaking
areas of the South only, but it would seem reasonable to

Wolfram's lifetime, - the number of anchoresses grew out of all
proportion to that of anchorites. The majority of these appear
to have been, like Sigûne, the daughters of the rich and powerful. Wherever there is evidence for their social origins it
points in the direction of an aristocratic background, or at
least of a Patrician one.[40] The reasons for this striking increase in the number of women seeking religious enclosure must
be sought in the temper of the age.

That the twelfth and early thirteenth centuries were a period
of religious fervour is a truism of history. It was the time
which saw the wildfire success of heresies that came to permeate
the whole fabric of society, especially in Southern France and
Italy. It organized a brutal war of religion to exterminate them
and to reaffirm the true faith. It mounted three crusades, one
of which claimed the life of an emperor - Barbarossa. It saw the
meteoric rise of the Cistercian Order which in the space of
forty years alone multiplied its original foundation threehun-
dredfold: Between 1112 when St. Bernard went to Cîteaux, and
1153, the year in which he died, three hundred dependancies of
Cîteaux were founded. It witnessed the spectacular career of
Thomas Becket (1118-1170) which spanned profane ambition and
worldly success, and which culminated in asceticism and martyr-
dom. For many others at a humbler level this may be said to have
been a typical career. Altogether the twelfth and early thirteenth centuries were a period of intense religious appraisal;
They were an age of faith. Whether faith was the cause of conflict, private and personal, or public and political, whether

---

assume a similar state of affairs for the North.
On anchoresses in the Middle Ages in general vid. Patricia
J. F. Rosof, Anchoresses in Twelfth and Thirteenth Century
Society, (Ph.D. diss. New York University), New York, 1978,
University Microfilms, no. HIN 78-18452.

40 Otmar Doerr, op.cit., pp. 30-36; cf. also Bernd Thum, Aufbruch und Verweigerung. Literatur und Geschichte am Oberrhein im hohen Mittelalter. Aspekte eines geschichtlichen
Kulturraums, 2 vols., (Literarische Gesellschaft Karlsruhe,
Scheffelbund), Waldkirch i. Br., 1979/80, vol. II, p. 351.

236

it was the target for intellectual probing, or the reason for
emotional surrender, - whatever part it played -, it clearly
stood at the core of life. One of the marked features of this
upsurge of religious sentiment and preoccupation, in particular
in Germany, was the ardent and widespread participation of women.
So many were involved in the northern regions of the Continent
that historians speak of this particular phenomenon as a religious movement among women.[41] It had been developing gradually
throughout the twelfth century and was gathering momentum towards its close. Large numbers of women in Northern France,
Belgium and Germany desired a _vita religiosa_ for themselves.

---

41 Herbert Grundmann, Religiöse Bewegungen im Mittelalter. Un-
    tersuchungen über die geschichtlichen Zusammenhänge zwischen
    der Ketzerei, den Bettelorden und der religiösen Frauenbe-
    wegung im 12. und 13. Jhrh. und über d. geschichtl. Grund-
    lagen der dtsch. Mystik. Anhang: Neue Beiträge zur Geschich-
    te der religiösen Bewegungen im Mittelalter (1955), Histor.
    Studien, 267, Berlin, 1935. Reprograf. Nachdr., WBG, 1977.
    Vid. in particular chapters IV and V: Die Anfänge der reli-
    giösen Frauenbewegung, and Die Eingliederung der religiösen
    Frauenbewegung in die Bettelorden. The outline above follows
    in the main Herbert Grundmann's analysis. It takes into ac-
    count also the description of the social situation relating
    to women as found in R. W. Southern, Western Society and the
    Church in the Middle Ages, The Pelican History of the Church,
    vol. 2, 1970.
    The earlier counterpart, or perhaps even background, to the
    religious movement among women in the twelfth century has
    been newly analyzed by K. J. Leyser in chapter II of his
    book, Rule and Conflict in an Early Medieval Society. Ot-
    tonian Saxony, London, 1979; The Women of the Saxon Aristo-
    cracy (5) Survival and Inheritance (pp. 49-62), and (6) The
    Saxon Nunneries (pp. 63-73). Further recent publications on
    the subject of women in the Middle Ages who found self-
    realization and fulfilment in a life devoted to religion
    include the following essays in: Medieval Women, ed. by
    Derek Baker, Dedicated and presented to Professor Rosalind
    M. T. Hill, Studies in Church History, Subsidia I, Oxford,
    1978: Christopher J. Holdsworth, Christina of Markyate,
    (pp. 185-204); Brenda Bolton, Vitae Matrum: a further aspect
    of the Frauenfrage, (pp. 253-274); Rosalind B. Brooke and
    Christopher N. L. Brooke, St. Clare (pp. 275-287). Vid. also
    Kaspar Elm, Die Stellung der Frau in Ordenswesen, Semireli-
    giosentum und Häresie zur Zeit der heiligen Elisabeth, in:
    Sankt Elisabeth. Fürstin Dienerin Heilige. Aufsätze Dokumen-
    tation Katalog, hrsg. v. d. Philipps-Universität Marburg in

They came from all strata of society, but prominent among them
were women of rank and social privilege, noblewomen and Patri-
cians, and in part at least their urge to dedicate their lives
to faith must be seen as a deliberate gesture of rejection of
the taint of riches. Nevertheless the dominant mood among them,
and also the mainspring of their action, were beyond doubt genuine
piety and religious idealism.[42] Nunneries in Germany more than
trebled between 1100 and 1250 in order to receive them. They
rose from 150 to 500, and still the demand for places in convents, certainly at the beginning of the thirteenth century,
vastly outran the supply.[43] There were only two solutions possible for those who could not be so accommodated: They could
apply for religious enclosure, and they could create their own
religious houses, their own nunneries. This they did, and they
spilt over into anchorages and into small independent communities.
Women living in anchorholds was, as has been seen, regular in

---

Verbindung mit dem Hessischen Landesamt für geschichtliche
Landeskunde, Sigmaringen, 1981, pp. 7-28. An important select bibliography of secondary literature is appended to
this last study.

42   There were other contributory factors, of course, to this
impetus towards a monastic life among women. For many of
them who were unmarried, widowed, or repudiated by their
husbands, a place in a convent offered the only chance of
shelter and decent livelihood. Others seem to have desired
it as an escape from unwanted wedlock, because of "disgust
at the recollection or prospect of marriage" (R. W. Southern,
op.cit., p. 311). Certainly there were features deeply off-
putting for the woman in medieval marriage - brutally early
childbirth, the loss of property beyond recall, the uncertainty of any benefit, material or otherwise, accruing
from it, (a dowry which had passed to the husband frequently
proved a poor investment for the woman), and - last but not
least - the fundamental requirement of submissiveness in
the ideal wife. This latter feature must have been peculiarly unpalatable to noblewomen who were born to command.
The prospect of one day perhaps becoming an abbess must have
held great appeal for them. The motive, among the highborn
at least, of wishing to avoid marriage, or remarriage, was
undoubtedly a potent one in the decision to take the veil.

43   Albert Hauck, Kirchengeschichte Deutschlands, vol. IV, Leipzig, [4]1913, p. 416.

the eyes of the Church. Women banding together in small groups,
however, and living without formal ties with any existing order,
was highly irregular. Yet they did it, and did so in increasing
numbers from the middle of the twelfth century onwards. The
astonishing proliferation of these independent convents presented the Church with grave problems of supervision, integra-
tion and control. In the end it was compelled to give way to
the pressure of numbers. In 1191 - a few years before Wolfram
embarked on the composition of his 'Parzival' - the records of
the Cistercian Order mention nuns for the first time. Up until
then the order had taken no official cognizance of the many
settlements of women professing to follow the Cistercian rule.
By 1191, however, they were too numerous to be ignored, and
their existence came at last to be officially acknowledged. In
the years following 1213 - when Wolfram was either still engaged on 'Parzival', or had recently completed it - the Cistercian
Order felt overwhelmed by feminine religious demand. Entries in
its records show that it tried to stem in every possible way the
flood of women wanting to become Cistercian nuns. Its efforts in
this direction, incidentally, proved a total failure.[44] Finally,
in the summer of 1216 - while, again, Wolfram was either still
working on his 'Parzival', or had recently finished it - the
Holy See gave way to the pressure exerted by the religious movement among women. Clearly there were now so many of them, in
particular in Northern France, Belgium and Germany, that they
could not all be intergrated into the existing orders. Yet here
was a genuine religious need, and accomodation had become essential. The Church was forced to accept the persistence and growth
of this movement as an unalterable fact. So in the summer of
1216 Pope Honorius III gave the devout women of the diocese of
Liège, and of the whole of France and Germany permission to found
religious communities of their own, non-affiliated with any

---

44 Cistercian hostility towards women in the Middle Ages has
    been examined by Sally Thompson, The Problem of the Cister-
    cian Nuns in the Twelfth and Early Thirteenth Centuries, in:
    Medieval Women, pp. 227-252. Vid. also R. W. Southern, op.
    cit., pp. 312-318.

existing order, and to instruct and preach within these communities. - These three bare facts of history: the grudging admission by the Cistercians in 1191 of the existence of Cistercian nuns, their subsequent attempts beginning in 1213 to shut
the flood-gates to women, and the Papal recognition in 1216 of
the necessity to let them be, and at the same time bring them
into the Church, are ample testimony of the force and size of
the religious movement among women. They are facts which strikingly illuminate the social scene in which Wolfram and his
audiences moved. The dates at which they occured - 1191, 1213
and 1216 - are directly relevant to the composition of 'Parzival' and stand in a meaningful relation to it.

'Parzival', as is now commonly accepted, was composed at some
time during the period of 1197 to 1222. However many, or however few, versions and instalments of the work are assumed, it
clearly took many years to write, not merely on account of its
length and its complexity, but chiefly because Wolfram was a
self-confessed part-time poet and a full-time soldier. Wherever
these years of composition may be placed within this period of
1197 to 1222 matters little within the present context. Any
place within this span of time would still indicate that 'Parzival' was being conceived, written and finalized at a time when
the religious movement among women was at its height, and when it
was about to be, or had already been, triumphantly vindicated.
It means that the work was in the making at a period when deeply
devout women, either as anchoresses, or as religiosae living in
independent communities, were part of contemporary experience.
It means that when Wolfram was rethinking and refashioning the
role of Sigûne within the romance he was handling a highly topical subject, and one which may indeed have closely concerned in
personal relationships the manor courts and families for whom
he composed his 'Parzival', or to whom he read it. For it is
for precisely those regions and their borderlands in which Wolfram lived, worked and travelled, and where he found his patrons
and audiences, that there is plentiful evidence of women living

in anchorholds in the twelfth and thirteenth centuries. Anchoresses are recorded among others for the dioceses of Würzburg, Eichstätt, Regensburg, Freising, Augsburg, Passau, Salzburg and Linz
- all areas which may be said to refer to Wolfram's immediate
geographical background. They are recorded also for the dioceses
of St. Pölten in Lower Austria and of Constance which are relevant as fringe localities.[45] Wolfram who spent part of his
life in Franconia, of which he mentions a number of places mostly
south of Nuremberg, also knew Styria well. He must in consequence have travelled through, and been familiar with, the country lying between Franconia and Styria, with Bavaria and Upper
Austria, i.e. with the stretch of countryside centred upon localities where anchoresses are known to have existed during his
lifetime. That he himself, and also the audiences he found in
these regions, had knowledge of anchoresses living in these
parts, is beyond doubt. Two details in particular link him quite
closely with such knowledge. For the year 1236 the enclosure of
a woman named Jutta is recorded as having taken place at Eschenbach in the diocese of Eichstätt.[46] Although the date of this
particular enclosure is no longer directly relevant to the composition of 'Parzival', it may still have a bearing upon it.

---

45 The list is based on the data in Otmar Doerr, op.cit., pp. 73-
    159. He relies chiefly on necrologies, but uses other evi-
    dence also. Necrologies generally record only the name of
    the deceased, and the day and the month of death, but not
    the year. Bearing in mind the extreme difficulties inherent
    in the dating of necrologies (ibid. pp. 16/17) and using the
    dates proposed by the author, it would seem reasonable to
    accept that there were anchoresses in the twelfth and thir-
    teenth centuries in or near the following places: Würzburg;
    Kastl, Eschenbach (Diocese of Eichstätt); Oberaltaich, Wind-
    berg, Obermünster/Regensburg (Diocese of Regensburg); Schäft-
    larn (Diocese of Freising); Augsburg, Dießen, Ottobeuren
    (Diocese of Augsburg); Niederaltaich (Diocese of Passau);
    Admont an der Ens, Salzburg (Diocese of Salzburg); Lambach,
    Mondsee (Diocese of Linz); Melk (Diocese of St. Pölten);
    Amtenhausen, Fischingen im Thurgau, St. Gall, Hermetschwil,
    Petershausen, Rheinau near Schaffhausen, Zwiefalten (Diocese
    of Constance).

46 Otmar Doerr, op.cit., p. 85.

Enclosure at Eschenbach in 1236 may indicate an established anchorhold here, one which had been occupied before. In 1210 another Jutha inclusa, anchoress of the Schottenkloster St. Jakob
in Würzburg, gifted a vineyard to the altar of St. James. That
vineyard was situated "im Sand", the locality north-east of Eschenbach which Wolfram mentions in 'Willehalm' 426.30.[47] Finally
a third event which is symptomatic of the atmosphere of religious
zeal among women, and which also illustrates the inevitable public awareness of it, deserves not only mention, but careful consideration, taking place as it did at a time when 'Parzival' was
being conceived and composed, or had just been completed, and in
circumstances which are strongly suggestive of links with its
author. - An embassy had been despatched by Landgrave Hermann of
Thuringia, Wolfram's one time, and again later patron, to the
court of Hungary. Its brief was to fetch the child princess Elizabeth, the future St. Elizabeth, for her betrothal to Hermann's
son. The betrothal had evidently been arranged to confirm a political alliance between the Ludovings of Thuringia, the Andechs-
Merans of Bavaria, and the court of Hungary. It was meant to
cement a common front against Otto IV.[48] In 1211 the glittering
train moved northwards from Hungary through Bavaria and Franconia,
through Wolfram-country, where it must have aroused enormous
popular interest. Elizabeth, through her mother Gertrude, the
queen of Hungary, was a member of that rich and powerful family,
the Andechs-Merans, whose territorial possessions extended
throughout Bavaria, Franconia and Styria, and even beyond, and

---

47 Ibid. p. 114.

48 Cf. Fred Schwind, Die Landgrafschaft Thüringen und der land-
    gräfliche Hof zur Zeit der Elisabeth, in: Sankt Elisabeth,
    pp. 29-44, in particular pp. 36 and 37. Also H. Patze, Die
    Entstehung der Landesherrschaft in Thüringen, 1. Teil, Mit-
    teldeutsche Forschungen, 22, Cologne/Graz, 1962, pp. 249-
    262.

49 J. Gottschalk, op.cit., Chapter 2: Die Andechser, das väter-
    liche Erbe, pp. 24-73.

who were at home not far from Eschenbach. Their family-seat
was Castle Andechs on the Ammersee.[49] It is more than likely
that they themselves, and also their vassals and serfs, followed the progress of the Hungarian princess, a granddaughter
of the lord of the manor of Andechs, with interest, offering
her hospitalitas wherever and whenever needed. The family connection alone, and the sense of a personal link with the princess which went far beyond the immediate family-circle of the
Andechs-Merans, would in themselves have assured Elizabeth's
journey of a great many participants and spectators, both actual and by hearsay. But there was yet another powerful stimulus to popular curiosity here - namely the abundant, extravagant
and eye-catching treasure which her ambitious mother had lavish-
ed on Elizabeth. Its centrepiece appears to have been a cradle,
wrought of silver, in which the four-year-old princess, wrapped
in silks, brocaded with gold and silver thread, had been handed
over to the Thuringian delegation.[50] By the time therefore that
the cortège had reached Nuremberg, a large number of people living in Bavaria and Franconia would beyond all doubt have come
into contact with it in one way or another. Then all of a sudden,
before the mission was completed, before they had reached the
court of Thuringia, Elizabeth lost a member of her immediate and
personal retinue - quite a prominent member it would appear - to
a life of religion. A girl called Alheit, a rote-player, remained behind in Nuremberg, severed her connections with the world

---

50 A description of the treasure sent with Elizabeth which in-
    cluded all manner of gold and silver plate, jewellery, silks,
    and even a silver bath tub, is given in her Vita by Dietrich
    of Apolda. Although this was written approximately eighty
    years after her journey from Hungary to Thuringia, and al-
    though allowance must be made for embellishments, there is
    little reason to doubt the basic veracity of Dietrich's
    account. His description is corroborated by the testimony
    of an eye-witness, Isentrud, one of Elizabeth's ladies-in-
    waiting. Historians are therefore inclined to accept it as
    in the main accurate. Cf. e.g. C. Polack, Die Landgrafen
    von Thüringen, p. 131; Allgemeine Deutsche Biographie, vol.
    9, pp. 72/73, entry: Gertrud von Meran. Königin von Ungarn;
    M. Werner, Bericht über die Überbringung Elisabeths von Un-
    garn nach Thüringen, Papierhandschrift, Koblenz, 1460/70,

of the court, and devoted herself to a _vita religiosa_. Her subsequent career makes it clear that she was no ordinary minstrel.
Not long after her conversion in 1211 she became the mistress
of a small band of independent _religiosae_ in Nuremberg who came
to be known - and widely known - as the _sorores Rottharinne_,
after her, the "rôtaerinne".[51] She was thus obviously a woman of
ability, with the qualities of leadership, and must therefore
have enjoyed a position of some consequence and trust within
Elizabeth's entourage. When she then betrayed this position in
order to embrace a life of religion, her decision - a defection
in a way - cannot but have attracted widespread attention and
caused much comment, associated as it was with an embassy of
considerable political importance and much human interest. -
The event in itself is an example of the powerful wave of feminine religious zeal as it swept through medieval society of the
closing decades of the twelfth century and the early ones of
the thirteenth.[52] The circumstances under which it occurred,

---

in: Sankt Elisabeth, pp. 338/339.

51   Herbert Grundmann, op.cit., p. 224ff.

52   The later life of Elizabeth of Hungary (1207-1231) is sympto-
     matic of the immense impetus towards total service of the
     Christian faith and its ideals, experienced by so many women
     of her own generation, and before. Fundamental for her bio-
     graphy is the work by A. Huyskens, Quellenstudien zur Ge-
     schichte der hl. Elisabeth, Landgräfin von Thüringen, Mar-
     burg, 1908, and: Der sog. Libellus de dictis quatuor ancil-
     larum s. Elisabeth confectus. Mit Benutzung aller bekannten
     Handschriften zum ersten Male vollständig und mit krit. Ein-
     führung hg. und erl., Kempten und München, 1911. A recent
     valuable contribution towards a fuller understanding of
     Elizabeth's personality and of her time, and thus of the
     women of that particular period who dedicated their lives
     to religion is represented by the volume: Sankt Elisabeth.
     Vid. in particular Paul Gerhard Schmidt, Die zeitgenössische
     Überlieferung zum Leben und zur Heiligsprechung der heiligen
     Elisabeth, pp. 1-6; Matthias Werner, Die heilige Elisabeth
     und Konrad von Marburg, pp. 45-69; Otto Gerhard Oexle, Armut
     und Armenfürsorge um 1200. Ein Beitrag zum Verständnis der
     freiwilligen Armut bei Elisabeth von Thüringen, pp. 78-100;
     as also the essays by Kaspar Elm and Fred Schwind already
     mentioned.

and the personalities linked with it, point to a wide audience
for it in Wolfram-country.

It may therefore be said that when Wolfram created Sigûne _in-
clusa_ expressly for Book IX, he used the raw material of
his own time. It is impossible to imagine that the urgency with
which the realization of a _vita religiosa_ was pursued by large
numbers of women, had not impinged profoundly on general awareness, and with it upon that of Wolfram and his audiences.[53] It
is equally impossible to imagine that the deep sincerity which
animated the religious movement among women had not left its
mark. Therefore when he introduced Sigûne in her new guise as
an _inclusa_ in Book IX, he was able to rely on the signal of this
sincerity. He drew in his re-portrayal of Sigûne on the established role of the anchoress in medieval society, and on
the generally accepted image of her. This image which the members of Wolfram's audience cannot have failed to have had in
their minds, allowed him to dispense with much explanation.
There was no need to explain what was familiar to all. He could
expect even listeners of only ordinary perceptiveness to respond
readily to the chief implication in a character cast as an anchoress. He could be certain that the dominant meaning of Sigûne in her new role in Book IX would be identified. What else
could an anchoress in a deeply serious context signify but the
ultimate degree of "triuwe" - faith!

The particular significance of the figure of Sigûne _inclusa_
within Book IX, demonstrated earlier on internal and comparative
evidence, thus finds further corroboration in reference to data
external and non-literary.

---

53 On the topicality of the subject of inclusae and the relev-
    ance of this theme to contemporary German literature vid.
    also Stephen L. Wailes, Immurement and religious experience
    in the Stricker's 'Eingemauerte Frau', PBB (Tübingen), 96
    (1974), 79-102 passim.

3. The Grail Charger

Like the formal introduction to Book IX, like the scene with
Sigûne _inclusa_, the episode in which Parzival takes possession
of a horse from the Grail stud is new. It owes nothing, not
even a suggestion, to Chrestien. - On leaving Sigûne, he follows the tracks of Cundrîe's mule which lead back to the Grail
castle, but loses them and is engulfeld by despondency (443.1:
"al sîner vröude er dô vergaz"). Clearly Providence considers
him far from ready to re-enter the world of the Grail. Yet he
has strayed close to it (443.16/17), for a cavalry soldier of
its garrison challenges him to mortal combat. The duel is ended
with a masterly thrust by Parzival which unhorses, and puts to
flight, his opponent. In pursuit of him, down a steep gorge,
Parzival's horse loses its foothold and plunges to its death.
He himself is saved miraculously by a branch of a cedar tree
at which he clutches in the fall. By an equally fortunate
chance the Grail charger, abandoned by the sentinel, has stepped
into its reins thus immobilizing itself. It stands as if waiting
for Parzival who makes himself into its new master.

The scene though brief, has important narrative repercussions
by virtue of its result: the ownership of the Grail charger.
The horse from the Grail stud comes to figure visibly in the
subsequent action. Parzival rides it when meeting the pilgrims;
it carries him to Fontâne la salvâtsche, and he is mounted on
it as he approaches Trevrizent. From the moment he wins it, until the time when he enters Trevrizent's cave, he is shown in
association with it. For the three episodes immediately following the acquisition of the Grail charger therefore, the audience
must picture the hero on horseback. There is no break in the
visual aspect of Parzival as rider, from his mounting of the
Grail charger after the joust with its owner, to dismounting
before Trevrizent. Because of this continuity, the audience
are likely to store in their memory the provenance of this particular horse belonging to the hero at this particular point in
time. Emblematic provenance has in any case been an important

feature of all the hero's horses. The wretched pony on which
he sets out as a boy, is a reminder of Herzeloyde's forlorn
hope that the ludicrous equipment which she gives him, will
send him back to her.[54] The Castilian charger which he takes
from Ithêr makes him into a knight outwardly, providing him
with the material and basic necessity of knighthood while at
the same time persistently calling to mind how this knighthood was won.[55] The Arab steed Inglîart which he claims as
part of his booty after the siege of Bêâroche, and which he
mounts himself, had belonged to Gâwân.[56] It exemplifies the
continued link between hero and counterpart and represents
one of many reminders to the audience that Parzival and Gâwân
are being measured one against the other. If provenance has
mattered in the case of all the hero's mounts,[57] it will matter again, unless the poet gives a counter indication. This he
does not do. Quite the contrary, apart from allowing no break
in the riding sequences, apart from fully demonstrating its
origin, he brings the Grail charger prominently to view in two
scenes which represent additions to his source material, in the
episode in which the hero challenges Providence, and in the one
in which Trevrizent insists on taking charge of it.

When after parting from the pilgrims Parzival suddenly resolves
to demand proof of God's omnipotence, he singles out the Grail
charger to bear the burden of that proof. Divine might, so he
decides, shall manifest itself in the proper guidance of his
horse. Providence responds, and the Grail charger becomes the
instrument of God. Spurred by Parzival, but led by God, it takes
the hero forthwith to the location of the main scene of Book IX,
to Fontâne la salvâtsche. The audience's attention towards the

---

54 126.19-29; 144.17ff.

55 157.25-30; 161.9-22; 163.19-30; 173.19ff.; 224.19-30; etc.

56 389.16-30; 398.1-17.

57 Parzival rides four horses until the main scene of Book IX,
    Perceval only two. On the importance of horses generally in
    'Parzival' vid. Walter Mersmann, op.cit., pp. 138-143.

end of this brief scene is thus firmly drawn to the Grail charger
as the concrete and visible agent of the mysterious and invisible
workings of the Divinity (452.1-14).

When Parzival then comes face to face with Trevrizent it is still
on horseback that he does so, and at the beginning of the main
scene of the book the charger claims some considerable share of
the foreground. Parzival remains on horseback as Trevrizent wel-
comes him; twice he is invited to dismount. Both these invita-
tions of Trevrizent are accompanied by formulas of courtesy, as
if to underline them: "nu ruocht erbeizen, hêrre, (ich waene iu
daz iht werre ..." (456.13/14) and "ruocht erbeizen, ob ichs
biten muoz" (456.22). Trevrizent's politeness then culminates
in a gesture of quite exceptional and eye-catching courtesy, a
gesture which Wolfram has added here to the description as he
found it in his source, and which centres all attention upon
the charger. The older, far more distinguished man of the two,
held in high esteem for the austerity of his life and the wisdom
of his counsel, humbles himself before his young visitor by playing groom to him. Trevrizent asks for the horse's bridle in order
to lead it to shelter. When Parzival predictably protests, Trevrizent claims the privilege of the host not to be crossed by his
guest, receives the bridle without further ado and stables the
horse himself (458.13-30).[58]

The Grail charger is thus distinctively brought to the fore, more
so even than the other horses which the hero has ridden. The implications of this provenance must be of noteworthy consequence.
What are they?

Until the scene in which Parzival comes to ride a Grail charger
only one other horse of the same provenance had been introduced
into the action. As almost every male figure in this vast roll
call of characters is mounted (and some female ones are as well),

---

58 Perceval's horse is of no particular importance in this
    scene. Perceval himself tethers it to a beech-tree and then
    enters the chapel to find the hermit (lls. 6340/41).

a large number of horses receives mention.[59] The unique origin
of these two lifts them out of the mass. Only twice does it occur
in the narrative that a horse is taken from a Grail sentry. Once
here by Parzival, and on an earlier occasion by Laehelîn, the
robber baron and enemy of the Angevin dynasty. But although the
provenance of both chargers is the same, the circumstances under
which they were obtained, are totally different. While Parzival
takes his charger as compensation for the loss of his own mount
in a fair fight of self-defence, Laehelîn steals his, after
having brutally murdered a sentry in an unprovoked raid into
the Grail demesne. While provenance is thus the same in both
cases, ownership is the result of different patterns of behaviour springing from different motives. These particular details
concerning Laehelîn's Grail charger are given already in Book
VII, where Trevrizent is specifically associated with knowledge
of them: "des sider Trevrizent verjach" (340.6). This first
Grail charger has thus, by the time Parzival wins his, already
a history, one with which Trevrizent is familiar. It has moreover been named, Gringuljete, and has changed hands twice, having been given by Laehelîn to his brother Orilus, and by Orilus
in turn to Gâwân[60]. Trevrizent knows of the loss of one Grail
charger, but the audience in a position of superiority over a
character within the narrative, know of the loss of two. It
would seem reasonable to assume that this knowledge would remain
active within the memory of the audience until this point in
Book IX, when Trevrizent stables the hero's horse. Gringuljete
has been shown as recently as the closing lines of Book VIII,
i.e. two episodes only before Parzival obtains his Grail charger.
Gâwân rides it here in pursuit of the Grail (432.25-30). An
additional guarantee that this other, first Grail charger would

59 Gertrud Jaron Lewis, Das Tier und seine Funktion in Erec,
    Iwein, Parzival und Tristan, Kanadische Studien zur deutschen
    Sprache und Literatur, 11, Bern/Frankfurt, 1974.

60 339.26ff.; also 261.27-30.

be remembered, is its association with Laehelîn. For Laehelîn's
existence though shadowy, is important in the threat it poses
to the house of Anschouwe and to the hero, and the audience are
not allowed to forget it.[61]

Provenance of the hero's horse in Book IX therefore has more
complex implications than the origin of the horses he owned previously. His Grail charger has a double. It will have one meaning
to Trevrizent, but quite another to the audience. As regards
Trevrizent it comes to represent a misleading clue. Stabling,
handling the horse, he recognizes its origin from its crest of
the turtle-dove, as he later explains (474.1-6) and thinks he
has identified the rider too. With reference to the audience
provenance recalls the other, first Grail charger of the narrative, enabling them to understand that Trevrizent may be committing an error. The error, a mere possibility at first, but
a definitive fact later, is for them a telling one. It leads to
the symbolism of mistaken identity, to the emblematic confusion
of the hero with his own enemy, which in retrospect colours the
first part of the dialogue. This first part comes to an end when
Trevrizent finally gives voice to his need to have his suspicion
confirmed. It ends abruptly with his question "hêrre, sît irz
Lähelîn?" (474.1), the very formulation of which indicates that
he has been treating the suspicion he has harboured as a near-
certainty: you _are_ Laehelîn, are you not?

Like the scene with Sigûne _inclusa_ then, that of the Grail
charger is used to structure the dialogue between the hero and
Trevrizent. Both episodes divide off a first part against its
sequel. While the episode with Sigûne _inclusa_ points to the
central theme of the first part, that of the Grail charger
supplies its conclusion and retrospectively sets the stamp of
a symbolic parallelism upon it. Once the false trail which has
been laid, has been exposed as false, the dialogue changes

---

61 For a character study of Laehelîn vid. L. P. Johnson, Lähe-
    lin and the Grail Horses, MLR, 63 (1968), 612-617.

radically in its orientation. While in its first part it was
geared to a stranger, to an anonymous sinner who could well be
Laehelîn, in its second part it is aimed at Parzival, a close
kinsman of Trevrizent, and the only heir to the Grail kingship.
At the same time once the mistake has been unmasked as such,
recollection of Part I of the dialogue is suddenly shot through
with remembrance of Laehelîn.

But the narrative functions of the scene with the Grail charger
do not end here. They are not exhausted with concluding and
colouring the first part of the main episode of Book IX. The
scene in addition gives impetus to Part II of the interchange
between the hero and Trevrizent. It ushers in with the Ithêr-
topic which is the direct result of the confusion to which it
had given rise, the overall theme of the second part, the theme
of Parzival within the family-nexus, of the hero and his kin,
of man vis-à-vis his fellow-men. So much for the primarily for-
mative effects of the scene introducing the hero's ownership of a
Grail charger. Its repercussions within the narrative, however,
reach out further, the characterization of the hero and the
assessment of his early behaviour come to be involved. By
doubling an occurrence in the plot, by making the hero repeat
an action of a fringe character, Wolfram evokes a symbolic congruence which qualifies the hero's personality and calls into
question the ethics of his chivalry. Trevrizent may have drawn
a wrong inference, but the trail he has followed proves false
only in part. Fundamentally and morally Trevrizent is unerringly
on the right track. Parzival's ownership of the Grail charger
proclaims to Trevrizent a deed of violence of a particular type
of which Parzival is indeed guilty. It misleads him only where
the identities of those involved are concerned. The crime to
which he has been alerted is the same, but killer and victim
are not. While Trevrizent is thinking of Laehelîn who killed
a Grail knight and then robbed him, the man before him is Parzival who murdered Ithêr and then stripped his corpse. Trevrizent's mistake ultimately brings out into the limelight the act

of brutality with which Parzival began his chivalric career,
and for which he has yet to atone. In emblematic confusion the
hero is momentarily placed on the level of a lawless thug, of
that self-same ruffian who had driven the hero's mother, widowed
and defenceless, from her estates, killing and capturing wherever he went (116.28-117.15; 128.3-10). The morals of his chivalry are as suspect as those of Laehelîn's. But there is worse
to come. Not only has Parzival incurred guilt in the same manner
as Laehelîn, but in his case this same act which is now remembered, will be seen to have been an even graver, more shattering
offence against society than with Laehelîn, and one of tragic
implications. For while Laehelîn's crimes are murder and theft,
Parzival's are murder and theft within the kin.

Thus again, like the two sections which precede it, the scene
with the Grail charger becomes effective within the target scene,
in relation to which it was conceived and composed.

4. Kahenîs peregrinus

The fourth passage in this series of six which introduce the
great dialogue of Book IX, occupies an exceptional position.
It is the only one of the sequence which is not of Wolfram's
invention. The episode in which the hero comes face to face
with a group of pilgrims on Good Friday forms Chrestien's introduction to the dialogue, and the German poet here follows the
plot of his French source, merely modifying the given material.
Already in Chrestien the scene is geared to the principle of
dramatic contrast.[62] Concrete and outward differentiation between the hero and those whom he meets is indicative of a fundamental, abstract and inward discrepancy between them: Perceval/
Parzival appears on horseback in full armour, thereby proclaiming his station within the social hierarchy and asserting his
identity as a knight. They as pilgrims, on the other hand, have
divested themselves of all socially distinguishing features and
have obliterated their rank by wearing the sclavin, the rough
cloak common to all pilgrims. While Perceval/Parzival is mounted
on a charger, they are on foot, and are barefoot moreover, thus
revealing themselves not just as ordinary pilgrims, but as exceptional penitents.[63] The manner in which they have humbled
themselves contrasts palpably with Perceval/Parzival's aggressive stance as a gentleman-at-arms. Their deliberate defence-
lessness and self-effacement stand out against the warlike
appearance and self-assertiveness of the hero. The tension between their humility and his pride is stated in visual terms,

---

62 This point and other parallel features of composition in
    the relevant scene in Chrestien are discussed by W. Henzen,
    Zur Vorprägung der Demut im Parzival durch Chrestien, PBB
    (Tübingen), 80 (1958), pp. 422-443, here pp. 432ff.

63 On the particular virtue of walking and of being barefoot
    when on pilgrimage vid. Jonathan Sumption, Pilgrimage. An
    Image of Mediaeval Religion, London, 1975, p. 127ff. For
    further information on pilgrimage in the Middle Ages vid.
    Margaret Wade Labarge, Medieval Travellers. The Rich and
    Restless, London, 1982, chapter 5: Noble Pilgrims, pp. 68-95.

and starkly isolates in Chrestien as in Wolfram the cardinal sin
with which the hero is burdened. Thus far the poets tally. Where,
however, the elucidation of the hero's thoughts and emotions is
concerned there is a decided parting of the ways.

From the very outset of the scene Chrestien's Perceval appears
as at least partially exonerated in his temporary godlessness.
He does not remember God because he has lost his memory (6217:
"Percevaus, ce conte l'estoire,/A si perdue sa memoire/Que de
Deu ne li sovient mes"). It is in consequence of this loss of
memory that he has neither worshipped nor entered a church (6221-
6223). The void in his heart has prevented him from taking note
of time, and when reprimanded by one of the pilgrims for bearing
arms, he indeed does not know what day of the year it is (6254-
6264). When told by the pilgrims that they have confessed their
sins to a nearby hermit and been counselled by him, contrition
in him follows immediately. He bursts into tears, and conscious
and repentant of his failings he sets out at once to seek that
same release which the pilgrims experienced (6310-6336). In
Chrestien's hero therefore godlessness and the loss of a sense
of time, of this principle of order within the universe of Christian interpretation, are involuntary. He has lost his memory
and remembers neither God, nor Time. Furthermore on being made
aware of his state of sin he does not persist in it. He neither
adduces reasons for his sinfulness, nor does he argue grounds
for prolonging it, but is overcome by feelings of guilt and
deplores his transgression instead. Perceval's attitude of _su-
perbia_ within the episode under discussion is thus seen as not
being deeply ingrained, and is shown as dissolving into _humili-
tas_ within a minimum of time. Parzival's _superbia_ by contrast
is both profound and stubborn. It is not speedily resolved, but
comes to be protracted by his own volition and continues beyond
this scene. Altogether Wolfram has dwelt more intensively and
extensively on the hero's sin, qualifying it as deep-seated,
radical, and deliberate, in this way throwing it into much sharper relief for his audience than Chrestien had done. _Superbia_

in the hero stands out blatantly in Wolfram's version of the
episode, unsentimentalized through the accentuation of his
wrong-headed courage, not softened through the portrayal of
emotional pliancy as in Chrestien. Superbia, this most heinous
of the seven cardinal sins,[64] comes to be the flaw which
Trevrizent identifies at first sight of the hero. After having
expounded the meaning of "triuwe", he will then turn to it as
the second great leading theme of his instruction, illustrating
it with the stories of Lucifer, Adam, and Cain. As in the Sigûne-episode an abstract theme which will play a dominant role
in the first part of the dialogue, is sharply profiled through
description, action and implication well in advance, the poet
here achieving the weight of his emphasis by subtle revision of
the French text.

Unlike Chrestien's hero Parzival, although he has lost his sense
of time, has not lost his memory. He remembers his extreme gesture of hubris only too well and redraws it aggressively for the
benefit of the pilgrims. His "ich diende eim der heizet got"
(447.23) harks back to his violent rejection of God at the
Arthurian court.[65] It restates succinctly his erroneous concept
of the man-God relationship as a feudal bond based on service
and reward. It declares now, as it did then, this link, and thus
any link, as null and void. The careful recapitulation of the
form in which superbia first declared itself in the hero, serves
not only to remind the audience of the dramatic moment of its
first public expression. The repetition brings home to them also
that the hero's superbia was by no means incurred involuntarily,
but emanated from, and is still fuelled by, rank self-will. The
earlier episode, non-existent in the French text, is used to
reinforce the impact of the present scene. Moreover the hero's

---

64 St. Augustine, Joannis Evangelium, tract. XXV, 16: "Caput
    omnium morborum superbia est, quia caput omnium peccatorum
    superbia", Migne, PL, 35, col. 1604.
    Vid. also supra p. 173, footnote 91.

65 Supra p. 173.

hostility, virulently stated then, is seen to have sharpened
in the passage of time and to have acquired an edge of bitterness. While in the grand denunciation then, God was still God
("wê waz ist got", etc., 332.1), he is now merely 'someone
called God', the formulation dwelling offensively on the ano-
nymity of a depersonalized Godhead with a haphazard name. Bitterness has been joined by cynicism. Mockery and disgrace have
come his way, so he says, by "sîn gunst" (447.27), by the particular favour of this being, of whom he had been promised
auxilium, ("von dem mir helfe was gesagt", 447.29). Social ruin
has come to him by His courtesy, as it were.[66] Coupled with
this restatement of his defiance, is the hero's sweeping acknowledgement that Time is of no consequence to him. His admission
that he is ignorant of the passage of years, weeks, and days
forms the prelude to his reaffirmation of his separation from
God. Joined together they amount to a declaration, to a high-
handed rejection of both, Time and God, to an avowal that he is
independent of either.[67] His attack, embittered and embattled,
calls forth an incredulous reaction on the part of Kahenîs. While
Chrestien's pilgrim is merely censorious with reference to Perceval's negligence, Kahenîs is startled into uncertainty by the
violence of Parzival's repudiation. He hints three times in the
course of his reply to him that he is reluctant to think of him
as a Christian: "Meint ir got den diu magt gebar?" (448.2) - 'do

---

66 Ernst Martin suggests for "gunst", 447.27: "hier 'zulassen,
    gestatten' ..." but gives no reason for this interpretation
    at this particular point. All other occurrences of "gunst" in
    'Parzival' (8.26; 58.2; 103.2; 123.13; and 643.22 -, this
    list is inclusive of variants) quite clearly have the meaning
    of 'favour'. There is no reason why the semantic content of
    "gunst" should be different here from elsewhere in 'Parzival'.
    Parzival clearly charges the term with irony. This view of
    his usage is expressed also by D. H. Green, Irony in the
    Medieval Romance, Cambridge, 1979, pp. 186/87 and 283.

67 On the importance of the hero being in harmony with Christian
    time, i.e. with the liturgical calendar and therefore with
    the divine plan of salvation vid. Arthur Groos, Time Refer-
    ence and the Liturgical Calendar in Wolfram von Eschenbach's
    Parzival, DVJ, 49 (1975), 43-65.

you have Christ in mind?'; "herre, pflegt ir toufes ..." (448.
13) - 'if indeed you are baptized'; and "ob ir niht ein heiden
sît" (448.19) - 'if you are not an infidel'. Parzival's blasphemous outburst suggests a pagan's attitude to Kahenîs who accordingly recommends to him immediate confession, and penance
with the hope of absolution (448.22-26). But Parzival, unlike
Perceval, feels no contrition. He remains obstinately locked in
superbia declaring once more, and now with the utmost clarity
in an inner soliloquy his very hatred of the being he will not
name: "sît ich gein dem trage haz,/den si von herzen minnent
..." (450.18/19). With the relentless logic of hate he finally
eliminates God from his formula of farewell. While Chrestien's
figures, including Perceval, commend one another to God, Parzival, when taking leave from the group of pilgrims, commends
them to "gelücke", to fortuna, to unpredictable, unreliable chance:
"gelücke iu heil gebe und freuden vollen teil" (450.25/26). He
thus remains unrepentant throughout the scene and to the very
last clings to his position of isolation in arrogance.

The reluctance on the part of the hero to accept counsel, the
staggering blasphemy of his utterance and thought, the repetition of his passionate disowning of God - all additions by Wolfram - have immeasurably increased the dramatic impact of the
episode. By portraying the hero as recalcitrant, and by moving
him into a position from which human effort is unlikely to be
able to retrieve him, Wolfram has also injected breathtaking
suspense into the scene. Impact and suspense combine to hold
the hero's superbia at the centre of concern. How will he be
purged of the worst of the deadly sins? The theme of the question points to the next episode, and beyond it to the target-
scene.

5. The Challenge

The next episode, once again freely invented by Wolfram, sees
the hero unchanged in his resistance and resentment, and in no
mood to heed the pilgrims' counsel and example. He makes no
attempt to retrace the pilgrims' tracks (448.21), but in yet
another, the third, vehement display of superbia he throws
down the gauntlet to God Himself, trying to force His hand,
willing Him, to put him, Parzival, on the right path.

Superbia in Parzival has escalated over the years. First, at
the king's court, in a violent reaction to shattering humilia-
tion and sense of loss, he takes refuge in pride, hiding his
suffering under the cloak of aggression. He not only queries
God's omnipotence, but denies it (323.1: "waer der gewaldec,
sölhen spot/het er uns peden niht gegebn,/kunde got mit kreften
lebn"). In the classic situation of "zwîvel" he doubts God, despairs of Him, and is engulfed by despair. His cry "wê waz ist
got?" hauntingly echoes his early question when still ignorant
of the world of Christendom: "ôwê muoter, waz ist got?" (119.17).
The genuine question has now become a rhetorical one, - 'what
after all is God?!' - and has thus taken on an air of arrogance
and superiority. Its tenor has changed, and at the same time
the congruence in formulation ominously insinuates that, where
knowledge of the nature of the Godhead is concerned, Parzival
has hardly progressed since his childhood days in the depth of
the wilds. With the utmost economy Wolfram has silhouetted the
disastrous ignorance in which Parzival has persisted. Parzival's
interpretation then of the relationship between man and God, as
the bond between vassal and overlord, is in keeping with his
lack of understanding. In unbridled anger he withdraws his vas-
salage from God: "nu wil i'm dienst widersagn" (323.7). Within
the context of feudal reality this deliberate cancellation of
the bond of allegiance by the vassal would be seen as an act of
awesome arrogance. It signified an independence of means and of
spirit that few could afford. Within the context of faith such

a gesture is _superbia_. _Superbia_, moreover, is the very application of the notion of feudal reciprocity to the link between man and God. The principle of mutuality according to which the feudal system functioned, placed obligation equally on liege as well as vassal. While the liegelord was entitled to service in a variety of forms, the vassal in his turn had the right to expect help and favours in return. In the feudal contract the overlord was thus under as much constraint as his vassal. By applying the pattern of automatic, mutual obligation to God and himself ("ich was im diens undertân,/sît ich genâden mich versan", 332.5,6), Parzival arrogates to himself a right which he does not have; he makes demands upon God to which he is not entitled, and he reduces the stature of God to one who must act under external compulsion. His _superbia_ manifests itself thus on two levels, in his denial of God's omnipotence, and in his application of feudal reciprocity to God and himself. It finally shows itself on another level, a third, which in brazenness and folly surpasses the other two: Parzival declares that he will willingly bear God's hatred - "hât er haz, den wil ich tragn" (328.8). Threefold though his _superbia_ here appears, it will yet climb and continue to remain on an upward curve, until Parzival reaches Trevrizent.

The second time that _superbia_ declares itself in the hero, during his meeting with the group of pilgrims, it is seen as having hardenend and having gained in complexity. While doubting and despondent, ignorant and foolhardy before, Parzival now expresses himself with bitterness and cynicism, taking on a stance of studied disrespect. Moreover, _superbia_ in him has progressed particularly where the ingredient of hatred in his relationship with God is concerned. Earlier on he had shrugged off the possible hatred issuing from God as inconsequential. Now, as he prepares to take his leave from the pilgrims, he concludes in his mind that it is _he_ who hates.

Still on its upward path, <u>superbia</u> in Parzival then drives him
to take on God Himself in open challenge. Paradoxically it is
his mother's heritage in him which leads to this still higher
degree of <u>superbia</u>. At the same time, this aspect of his nature
suddenly coming to the fore, suggests a flicker of hope in a
seemingly hopeless deadlock. All of a sudden he is characterized as 'Herzeloyde's offspring' ("Herzeloyde fruht", 451.2), and
as having inherited "triuwe" from her (451.7).[68] His capacity for
feeling deeply activates his suffering,[69] and he begins to ponder whether God after all might be able to give him the help he
craves, - "waz ob got helfe phligt,/diu mînem trûren an gesigt?"
(451.13/14). What he obdurately refused to believe before, he
is willing to consider now - that power resides in God. (451.9-
12). Parzival's emotional state now comes to be highly equivocal
and will continue to remain so for the better part of his meeting with Trevrizent. He falls prey to a welter of conflicting
emotions. The complex tug-of-war within him, mirrored in everything he will ultimately say to Trevrizent, is initiated here.
On the one hand modesty forces him to accept that he needs help
and cannot help himself, arrogance on the other goads him into
aggressively demanding this help: "ist hiut sîn helflîcher tac,
sô helfe er, ob er helfen mac" (451.21/22). His decision to put
the principle of a powerful God to the test, and his promise to
acknowledge the notion of divine omnipotence once he has proof
of it, but not before (452.1-4) is <u>superbia</u> which surpasses
through dogged intensity, inflexibility, and sheer impudence the
quality of <u>superbia</u> which he had shown before. It will rise
higher still and reach its apex in his obstinate, open, and
angry admission of his hatred of God. While before, when leaving the pilgrims he had confessed to this feeling privately to

68 Vid. supra p. 216, The aesthetic function of this type of
    circumlocution has been considered by D. H. Green, The Art
    of Namedropping in Wolfram's 'Parzival', Wolfram-Studien,
    VI, 1980, pp. 84-150, here pp. 135ff.

69 The term "riuwe", 'suffering', is applied to Parzival for the
    first time at this point: "sich huop sîns herzen riuwe"
    (451.8). Cf. Werner Schröder, Zum Wortgebrauch von 'Riuwe'

himself in an inner soliloguy, he later proclaims it defiantly
to Trevrizent justifying it with precision: "ouch trage ich
hazzes vil gein gote:/wand er ist mîner sorgen tote." (461.9/
10). This affirmation, uttered to another, marks the culmination
of <u>superbia</u> in Parzival.[70]

The scene here therefore, his challenge of God, like the preceding one, that of his meeting with the pilgrims, brings to the
narrative foreground the hero's cardinal sin and holds it there.
It underlines for the second time now before the target-episode
the fatal failing of <u>superbia</u> which will form one of the great
leitmotifs of the dialogue. Yet it leads into the central scene
of this narrative unit not only with the statement of a major
theme, but also with the adumbration of the new turmoil in the
hero's mind. The description of Parzival's thought-processes,
the portrayal of the type of conflict which is beginning to tear
him apart, succinctly foreshadows the emotional and intellectual
predicament from which Trevrizent will attempt to release him.
This double link of theme and description moves the scene close
to the dialogue and represents a vital preparation for it. In
addition Wolfram has stepped up the ingredient of suspense which
he had successfully introduced already into the previous scene.
In response to the hero's innate "triuwe" there is a sign of Grace,

---

bei Hartmann und Wolfram, GRM, 9 (1959), 228-234, p. 232.
Important within this context is also Friedrich Maurer's
observation that beginning with Book IX the term denotes
predominantly 'den tiefen Schmerz über das durch eigene
Handlungen oder Unterlassungen erlangte Leid'. (Leid. Studien zur Bedeutungs- und Problemgeschichte, p. 142).

70 Herbert Kolb, Schola Humilitatis. Ein Beitrag zur Interpretation der Gralerzählung Wolframs von Eschenbach, PBB (Tübingen), 78 (1956), 65-115, plots the course of the cardinal
sin in Parzival differently from the above interpretation.
In his view Parzival's <u>superbia</u> is linked and develops with
his pursuit of chivalry (p. 84ff.). He sees the apogee of
<u>superbia</u> in Parzival in his original rejection of God at
the Arthurian court: "Zum Höhepunkt der <u>superbia</u> aber ver-
steigt sich Parzival in der Auflehnung gegen Gott. Er tut
es in der Form einer regelrechten Aufkündigung eines ritter-
lich-lehnsmännischen Dienstverhältnisses und erniedrigt damit

God responds with His own "triuwe", and leads him to a new location, to a new stage in life.[71] The nature of the divinity
reveals itself here as infinite in its compassion, taking pity
upon man in his suffering even though he be burdened with the
worst of the cardinal sins. Despite protracted persistence in
transgression Parzival is being offered a chance to free himself
from its shadow, to rehabilitate himself morally, and to restore
himself to a state of grace. What will he make of it? - At this
point of utmost tension the narrative thread snaps, and Wolfram
introduces a wholly unexpected, and at this juncture totally
irrelevant subject - source criticism. He steps out of the matter
of the narrative and views the work from outside.

Gott in den Rang eines irdischen Lehnsherren, dessen Feind-
schaft dadurch herausgefordert zu haben seinem Selbstbewusst-
sein in keinerlei Weise Abbruch tut." (pp. 94/95).

71 Vid. supra p. 104.

6. Literary Excursus II. The Source

With the famous and infinitely debated passage on his source
Wolfram, in a move of breath-taking boldness, swings the mood
of the narrative back to that of the very first introductory
passage to Book IX, to that of the literary excursus. With the
violent change in his story's emotional level he risks his credibility as a poet. Will he be able to carry the audience with him,
or will they refuse to be ripped from their reverie on the hero's
intractable problems? Will they resent the sudden switch from
the depiction of vividly visual, live scenes to a discussion of
abstract notions? They might lag behind in mood, refuse to follow the poetic trail towards which they have been turned so
abruptly, and lose interest. They might resent this deliberate
form of alienation and begin to reflect negatively on his quality as a poet. Wolfram was gambling with high stakes in this
move, with his listeners' willingness to give him a continued
hearing, and with their regard for him as a poet. Evidently he
considered it essential. The analysis of the narrative fabric
of the passage will yield his motives for his action.

With the disclosure of the details of his sources Wolfram constructs a parallel passage to his earlier discourse on literature. The two discussions of literary problems frame the four
episodes involving Sigune, the Grail charger, the pilgrims, and
Providence, all four of them also showing the hero. This level
of narration, the portrayal of _concreta_ of visible _realitas_, is
abandoned for the framework which, though in parts descriptively
visualized, is predominantly cast in the form of disquisitions.
In the first literary excursus Wolfram dealt with problems of
literature in a twofold manner. In order to formulate a concept
of literature he personified it, thereby enquiring into a poet's
view of it. Then having dropped the personification he allotted
to it its ordinary, run-of-the-mill meaning of the received text,
the handed-down compound of story-elements, which provides the
poet with information. In the second literary excursus he extends

this latter part of his evaluation of literature, elaborating
it into a detailed account of his source-material. The first
literary excursus is thus continued in the second, Wolfram now
concentrating on the contemporary and widespread interpretation
of literature as a chain of chronologically transmitted and in-
terlinked texts.

Parallel with the first passage Wolfram once again uses in the
second the technique of personification within an imagined scene
in order to present a literary problem. And again, as in the
first excursus, he shows the agent of Literature in direct com-
munication with its personified spirit. In the first passage
Wolfram's paramount concern had been to lead the audience imper-
ceptibly from frivolity to pathos. In the second his objective
is the reverse; it is to blot out pathos momentarily and to
plunge them into frivolity for a brief space of time. His purpose here is to provide amusement before anxiety, to offer diversion, light-hearted trifling, before concentration on profoundly serious themes. In both cases suspense had shortly
before been strained in a specific direction, and in the second
case to an exceptionally high degree. In the first instance the
audience had been made to focus on Gâwân's Grail quest, and in
the second on Parzival's cardinal sin. Both digressions into
literary criticism relax the tension of an expectancy with a
particular orientation. But while the first leads into a total
reorientation of attention, the second only momentarily blurs
the poetic focus and allows the listeners' emotional energy to
become dispersed, so that it may be gathered again at a later
point with refuelled vigour.

Already with the first paragraph the audience are catapulted
into the land of absurd make-believe: The secrets of the Grail
have so far not been told, so Wolfram says, because Literature
herself had sworn Wolfram's colleague and authority to secrecy.
He in turn had enjoined Wolfram to silence. (453.5: "mich batez
helen Kyôt,/wand im diu aventiure gebôt/daz es immer man ge-

daehte ...")[72] The implication cannot but be that Wolfram knew
Kyôt who had extracted the promise from him, either in person
or by correspondence. Wolfram does not say which. It would seem,
however, that there had been little point in insisting on the
confidential treatment of these secrets, as there was nothing
much to be told. At the time of demanding sealed lips, Literature herself, so it appears, was still busily concocting those
very secrets and putting them into shape (453.6-10). They then
came to be finished and were ready for publication. Consumption,
however, was made difficult, at any rate, for Western Christendom, for the secrets of the Grail were written up in Arabic by
a Moslem called Flegetânîs. This Flegetânîs is characterized by
Wolfram as neither poet, nor even chronicler, but as a naturalist
("fisîôn", 453.25) whose interest in the stories surrounding the
Grail might legitimately be considered minimal. Nor indeed did
he search for them, but in his capacity as an astronomer happened
to discover them. When scanning the firmament he was able to make
out the name of the Grail, managed to read it from a constella-
tion of stars, and contrived in addition to learn of its mysteries
from the same source. After this astounding feat of perspicacity,
for clearly no other astronomer had lit upon this hidden information, he composed an account of his discovery in Arabic. So much
for Flegetânîs. A version of his work found its way to Toledo
where Kyôt unearthed it. Kyôt who in a previous reference had
been described as a minstrel from Provence (416.21ff.), appears
now as a magister (453.11: "meister"), as a man with clerical/
academic training, and as one, moreover, who is widely known
(453.11: der meister wol bekant") and of exceptional learning
(455.2: "der meister wîs"). This Kyôt then, adept, of course,

---

72 Although Literature here is not given the title "frou" as in
    the first literary excursus, the verb and phrase used in
    conjunction with the concept indicate personification ("ge-
    bôt, braehte mit worten an der maere gruoz"). There is
    marginal scribal support for this reading in that MSS D
    and G show a large initial: "diu Âventiure" in 453.8.
    It is not denied that another reading of the relevant lines
    is possible. They could be loosely interpreted as follows:
    "The demands of the story made it imperative for Kyôt that

in Latin (455.2-4) decided he would decipher his find and for
this purpose learnt Arabic (453.11-15). His researches concerning the Grail, however, did not end here. His interest now kind-
led by Flegetânîs's reference to the keepers of the Grail, and
to the qualities needed for its guardianship, he set about to
find the people, or dynasty, that would answer the description
(454.27ff.). His search for them necessitated wide reading, and
he consulted Latin sources, working his way steadily through
chronicles of Britain/Brittany, France and Ireland. It was finally in an Angevin chronicle that he found the information he
was seeking (455.2ff.). It contained a description of the Arthurian dynasty and of the Grail family. Thus far the second
literary excursus.

The two figures whom Wolfram introduces here, although not identifiable as individuals, are not entirely implausible as types.
Kyôt, referred to earlier as a minstrel and now as a learned
clerk, is conceivable as one of that band of wandering scholars
who with their learning combined a gift for music and song, and
who had taken to the road. As one of the restless vagantes he
might have roamed from Provence to Toledo and suddenly become
interested in an obscure manuscript. Nor is the character of
Flegetânîs necessarily to be seen as being beyond the realm of
contemporary possibility. Moslems were known for their accomplishments in the observation of natural phenomena. Their reputation as scientists had penetrated to the West, and they were
noted in particular for their knowledge of, and achievements
in, astronomy. So neither of these figures in so far as they
are depicted as types, can be assigned to the world of fantasy.
Yet acceptable though they may be as possible representatives
of the real world, two situations which are ascribed to them
make them into fictional characters with a decided slant towards

---

no one should get wind of it until the narrative was finalized." The excuse which Wolfram makes is ludicrous in either
reading. The device of personification, however, gives the
first reading a histrionic and spectacular and thus characteristically Wolframesque stamp.

the ludicrous. Kyôt put Wolfram under a vow of silence as regards the Grail narrative, because he himself was under one?
And Flegetânîs read the name 'Grail' in the stars? Absurd notions, both of them, and the more so because these features
are attributed to figures who are otherwise realistically typ-
ified. The unmistakeable pointer, however, to the intention that
Wolfram meant his account of his source-material to be a gigantic tall story is the mock-serious tone in which this whole
report is couched, a tone strikingly reminiscent of that of the
first literary excursus. What else could it be but clowning
when he speaks admiringly of Kyôt's ability to learn the Arabic
alphabet without calling in the aid of black magic, and yet
says in the same breath, that it was, of course, baptism that
got him there? Can his claim that he had not revealed more
about the Grail because Kyôt would not let him, be anything
else but a transparent white lie, destined to make the audience
laugh? Surely it is nothing but a sly admission that he had not
been prepared to give away the details of the Grail-story until
the present point in time! And would they not have been amused
at hearing someone paraded as a well-known _magister_ of whom no
one had ever heard before? When he then comes to Flegetânîs,
he introduces him grandly as a scientist of high repute, yet
immediately shakes his head sadly, clicking his tongue at the
sorry fact that all his intelligence could not save this man
from praying to a cow. The notion that the word 'Grail' was
spelt out in the sky is so preposterous and so outlandish that
no listener could have kept a straight face. Returning then to
Kyôt and his researches he may have thought that his audience
had had enough, for he cuts short the list of works and characters, gabbling off the hero's genealogy with tongue-twisting
swiftness, finally reaching the hero in person with an evident
sigh of relief:

> 455.13 er las von Mazadâne
> mit wârheit sunder wâne:
> umb allez sîn geslehte
> stuont dâ geschriben rehte,
> unt anderhalp wie Tyturel

> unt des sun Frimutel
> den grâl braeht ûf Amfortas,
> des swester Herzeloyde was,
> bî der Gahmuret ein kint
> gewan, des disiu maere sint.
> der rît nu ûf die niwen slâ,
> die gein im kom der rîter grâ.

The style of this last part of the literary excursus is one of
enumeration:"ze Britâne, ze Francrîche, ze Anschouwe; des sun
Frimutel, des swester Herzeloyde, bî der Gahmuret", etc. "des
disiu maere sint, der rît nu", etc. The list-character of this
final section, the deftness with which essentials are suddenly
picked out after a major detour into inessentials, marks this
part of the digression with the style of ad-libbing in performance. The poet suddenly takes on the pose of an ad-hoc performer,
casting himself in the role of a story-teller who with a hurried
report, factual and unadorned, but no doubt suitably accompanied
and underlined by gestures, states a conclusion and moves on.
Here as much as in the first literary excursus, poetic effect
and meaning yield themselves up with particular clarity when the
passage is projected into the situation of performance for which
after all the whole work was intended.

So the poet may be said to have entertained his audience at large
expertly. In the opening passage he flatters them into feeling
extraordinarily clever, as they see through the flimsiest of
white lies. He then amuses them with the paradox of a widely
renowned, yet unknown magister, makes them commiserate with him
over the sorry state of Moslem men of learning who for all their
knowledge still know no better than to address their prayers to
a beast, and startles them into laughter with the crowning impro-
bability of someone actually reading something in the sky. The
clowning continues with the quick recitation of Kyôt's source-
books. When he feels that the joke has gone on for long enough,
that the audience might be becoming restless, and that their
patience should not be tried any longer, he suddenly runs his
finger down the hero's genealogy. He quickly goes through his
chief antecedents in the male and female line - Mazadân and

Gahmuret on the one side, Titurel, Frimutel, and Herzeloyde on
the other, until quite out of breath, he reaches Parzival: 'Here
he is, on the new tracks!', and the story can take off again.

The manner of delivery, - facial expression, grimaces, and gestures - and the tone of recitation - the dominant note of mock-
seriousness, the change of key perhaps from high to low pitch,
and the alternation of speeds between slow and fast articulation
- would have given the contemporary audience an interpretation
of the substance of the second literary excursus which they
could not have mistaken. Elusive as these aspects of performance
may be to us now, there are still enough leads in the text itself to enable us to arrive at the same interpretation seven
centuries later.

While Wolfram amused his general audience on this level, he had
a particular treat for the lettered among them on yet another.
His source-ciriticism takes issue with prevailing attitudes. On
the face of it his account of his source-material bows to convention: He declares the origin of his narrative, thereby com-
plying with the contemporary demand that every author should
quote an authority. Yet the over-elaborate nature of this bow
to convention, and the enthusiastic thoroughness with which the
poet oversteps the limits of normal, literary practice here,
reveal this bow to be anything but the usual, respectful nod
to tradition it ought to be. The shower of details, their complex ramification, and the improbabilities blended with these
details, all combine to make what looks like an acceptance of
convention into a highly irreverent putting-down of it. The
very structure of the report cocks an outsize snook at the in-
sistance on the citation of a source, and ridicules at the same
time the pompous posturing of contemporary men-of-letters.

Wolfram in mock-serious stance goes far beyond the standard
requirements of the prevailing convention. He does not name one
source only, but gives also his source's sources, and in addition isolates the source of one of his source's sources. Kyôt's
version, the poet's immediate source, derives from two sources,

an Angevin chronicle, and the Arabic narrative of Flegetânîs.
This latter source has its own source, namely the stars. Far
from expecting his audience to be content with the mention of
his immediate source, Wolfram describes for them three layers
of his source-material, constructing for them what could only
be called - a stemma. Could anyone demand a more thoroughgoing
declaration of source-material? And to top it all he shows the
ultimate source of the Grail-story to be Heaven itself! Can
such a source be gainsaid? Does the veracity of his story need
to be vouchsafed any further? What more respectable authority
could there be? The guarantors for the accuracy of this account
are a renowned man of science from the East and a learned magister from the West, famous for his wide reading, and linguistic proficiency. It would be difficult to cap the overpowering
excellence of such a background to one's fiction!

The exaggerated style of the gesture points to its spuriousness.
The analysis of the source-material is so blatantly overdrawn
that its ludicrousness could scarcely have been overlooked by
the men and women of letters in Wolfram's audience. But there
is a point of serious criticism contained in the playful nonsense for all that - the absurdity of the wild claims pours
effective scorn on the continued observation of an outworn convention.

So Wolfram diverts his listeners, general public and intellectuals alike, with comedy, obvious yet subtle, cajoling them
into a carefree mood. Once again, as he had done in the first
digression, he creates for himself a vehicle of expression which
gives full scope to his histrionic gifts. As before, the actor
briefly takes over from the poet for highly controlled audience-
manipulation. When the merry-making then stops, his listeners
will be in a newly receptive frame of mind, revitalized after
the easing of tension, ready to face near-tragedy.[73]

─────────────────────

73 The literature on Kyôt, and on the problems surrounding this
    figure, is impressive in quantity. Generations of Parzival-

scholars have addressed themselves to the questions which
arise out of the Kyôt-material in 'Parzival'. Very roughly
these questions may be stranded into three categories: Did
Kyôt exist, i.e. did Wolfram use another extensive and coherent source apart from, or instead of, 'Li Contes del
Graal'? Is Kyôt a cover-name for other additional and minor
sources? Is Kyôt total fiction, a teasing disguise for Wolfram's own inventions? Contributions to the problem between
1945 and 1970 have been summarized and assessed by Joachim
Bumke, Die Wolfram von Eschenbach Forschung, chapter II,4:
Stoff und Quellen (pp. 198-250). Vid. also Ulrich Pretzel
and Wolfgang Bachofer, Bibliographie zu Wolfram von Eschenbach. Zweite, stark erweiterte Auflage unter Mitarbeit von
Wulf-Otto Dreessen, Herta Haas, Willy Krogmann, Elfriede
Neubuhr, Bibliographien zur deutschen Literatur des Mittelalters hrsg. v. U. Pretzel und W. Bachofer, vol. 2, Berlin,
1968, section: Quellenfrage und Kyotproblem, pp. 55-63. The
Kyôt-question has developed into a whole area of Parzival-
research which will no doubt continue to grow. The feature
which promotes this growth is the deliberate ambiguity of
Wolfram's Kyôt-references. This aspect has been emphasized
in a recent analysis of the Kyôt-material by Carl Lofmark,
Zur Interpretation der Kyotstellen im 'Parzival', Wolfram-
Studien, IV, Berlin, 1977, pp. 33-70. He shows that almost
every statement regarding Kyôt and Wolfram's source-material
may be read in a variety of ways, and that many references
cancel one another out. Vid. also Carl Lofmark, Wolfram's
Source References in 'Parzival', MLR, 67 (1972), 820-844,
and: The Authority of the Source in Middle High German Narrative Poetry, Bithell Series of Dissertations, vol. 5, Institute of Germanic Studies, University of London, 1981,
pp. 161 (London Ph.D. thesis submitted June 1973, revised
for publication), in particular chapter II: The Respect for
Written Authority (pp. 10-18) which outlines the reverence
for the 'book' and thus underlines Wolfram's waywardness,
and his stance as an outsider in flamboyantly flouting convention. Cf. also p. 59.
The intentional confusion, vagueness, and contradictory
character of Wolfram's account would seem further proof that
his report is meant to be a huge joke. On this point cf.
Arthur T. Hatto, On Chrétien and Wolfram, MLR, 44 (1949),
380-385, and: Y-a-t-il un Roman du Graal de Kyot le Provençal? in: Les Romans du Graal aux XIIe et XIIIe Siècles,
Paris, 1956, pp. 167-181. Even so, the present author is
under no delusion that the analysis given above will have
closed the discussion. It must be added, however, that to
her knowledge the interpretation here represents the first
attempt to understand the Kyôt-section within the context
of Book IX, to see it as an essential component of the
remodelled narrative unit, and to explain it in terms of a
counterpart to its introduction.

7. The Dialogue. Trevrizent eremita

The six introductory passages which Wolfram devised for the
target-scene, may all be said to have direct bearing on the
dialogue. Each one of them has prepared the listener in its
own particular way for the core-scene of the work. As the poet
unfolds it, their functions become operative and stand revealed
as essential. Through their poetic efficacy the dialogue achieves
form. Leading themes outline themselves with clarity, the nature
of the hero's problematic world of thought and emotion moves
sharply into focus as if of its own accord, and the requisite
temper of receptivity establishes itself with ease. For all this,
the organization of the dialogue around central concepts and
around the chaos in the hero's mind, as well as the correct mood
in which to approach and assess the dialogue, the ground has
been well laid in advance. Thus already the very first part of
this sixfold introduction struck a note of suspense and seriousness on a precise and distinctive level: It warned of the im-
peding crucial test of the hero. The Sigûne-episode then, continuing and deepening the tone of gravity, emblematically outlined the theme of the whole work, emphasizing its absolute
priority and permanent significance. It hammered home the fundamental importance of the quality of triuwe for the hero's
life, and by figurative presentation heralded the reappearance
of the theme in the dialogue. The scene also ushered in the
cumulative analysis of the hero's mind, showing through contrasting portrayal his moral defects and his extreme dilemma,
an analysis which would continue in the following episodes and
find its climax in the dialogue. The newly created encounter
with Sigûne moreover relentlessly sought out the hero's godlessness, probing into it and exposing it. Altogether the
Sigûne-scene through its poetic subtlety and intricate suggestiveness anticipates more features of the dialogue than any
of the other introductory passages. It may truly be called the
linchpin of the whole of the narrative unit.

The next episode, the duel with a border patrol of Grail country, laid the foundation for the symbolic parallelism of the hero with a murderer and thief, to be realized later in the dialogue. Its story-elements were to serve the division of the dialogue into two parts. The pilgrim-scene decisively pushed into the narrative foreground the hero's cardinal sin and further activated suspense by showing him in a seemingly irretrievable predicament, both problems which would be among the chief concerns of the dialogue. The challenge to God continued the description of the hero's frame of mind and portrayed the intensification of ˙superbia within him. The last passage alone, the second literary excursus, does not directly anticipate any aspect of the dialogue. Yet when the constantly increasing weight of gravity to which each of the previous five passages had contributed their share is taken into consideration, then its function as an interlude, as a breathing-space for the audience, is recognized as by no means superfluous, but as highly necessary. The hiatus of a change of subject, the introduction of a trifle to counterbalance substance, had become essential. Relief was needed after so much play on the emotions, after the creation of fear and pity. Apprehensiveness for self, the inevitable by-product here of self-identification with the hero, which the poet had so compellingly induced through pathos and drama, had to be permitted to slacken. So he momentarily releases the tension for the audience before plunging them ever more deeply into the spectacle of a human being in extremis.[74]

The listeners were well prepared, would recognize the accents on major concepts as accents, once they fell, and would identify the self-description of the hero as an extended echo of problems already isolated in preliminary portrayal. The dialogue therefore is far from haphazard in construction. Yet as conversation

---

74 Wolfram makes use of the same type of trigger, i.e. releasing the tension of tragedy with sudden trifling, in 'Willehalm'. Vid. Marianne Wynn, Book 1 of Wolfram von Eschenbach's 'Willehalm' and its Conclusion, Medium Aevum, 49 (1980), 57-65.

and discussion slowly culminating in confession, counsel and
comfort it is equally far removed from a rigid structure.

It is not only almost all of the introduction to the dialogue
which is new, but the dialogue itself, as the poet found it in
Chrestien, has been subjected by him to fundamental and extensive changes, necessitated by the new hero. Wolram's Parzival
by now hardly bears any resemblance to Chrestien's Perceval. A
murderer and thief, burdened with the worst of the cardinal
sins and in a state of stubborn apostasy, the hero is made to
face a stranger, a recluse, in the depth of a trackless forest
covered in snow. Sinner as well as criminal he seeks the counsel
of an unknown solitary in a comfortless wilderness. Chrestien's
Perceval by contrast was placed into a less forbidding situation, commensurate with the less complex nature of his character and his problems. - Riding along a proper path, carefully
marked and pointed out to him by the pilgrims, he reaches a
chapel in the woods where a hermit, together with a priest and
a sacristan are celebrating mass. Weeping bitter tears of contrition Perceval makes immediate confession of his lack of faith
and his failure to enquire into the mysteries of the Bleeding
Lance. The hermit accuses him of having been the cause of his
mother's death and as penance instructs him to attend mass
wherever possible. He counsels him to renew his belief in God,
to honour members of the clergy and to offer help to women. As
further penance he is to partake of the same austere food as
the hermit for two days. Perceval promises to do all he asks,
shows himself to be deeply penitent and is finally admitted to
Holy Communion. - The meeting of hermit and hero in Chrestien
is told in less than two hundred lines (lls. 6333-6513). There
is little elaboration of the leading facts and there is no commentary on Perceval's frame of mind beyond the obvious. He is
portrayed as the typical and ideal penitent, contrite and humble,
willing to accept counsel. It cannot be said that he is in any
way specifically individualized. This is the last time that he
appears in the unfinished work, and judging by the manner in

which Chrestien here handles the characterization of his hero
one might conclude that he was beginning to direct the greater
part of his attention to the mysteries in which the hero comes
to be involved, rather than to the hero himself. Apart from the
curious quality of the Bleeding Lance there is mention also of
a secret prayer which the hermit whispers into Perceval's ear.
The kinship pattern between hermit, hero, his mother and the
Fisher King is sketched in, but no further use is made of it.[75]

With his preoccupations oriented in a direction different from
those of Chrestien, Wolfram needed more than fourteen hundred
verses to portray his hero at this particular juncture of his
life and to lead his narrative back to the main concerns of the
work. His hero does not meet a hermit accompanied by others in
a chapel, in an island of civilization in the woods, but a
lonely man in a stark landscape, who shelters in caves. Trevrizent _eremita_ is as realistically conceived as Sigûne _inclusa_.
Like other hermits of his time and like his model in the French
romance, he is of aristocratic birth. Like many others he has
sought out an inhospitable landscape, a deep forest, in which
to lead his solitary life. He has chosen two caves for his re-
treat, in a particularly dark and rocky part of the forest
(458.27-28) by a waterfall (458.30). Like Sigûne he is lettered.[76]
His books and psalter are kept in a cave where he has also set
up an altar.[77] Another cave, because especially sheltered and
free from draughts, allows him to light a fire and a candle.

---

75 A recent detailed discussion of the Hermit scene in Chrestien, of the problem of its authenticity and of its placing
within the romance, is to be found in L. T. Topsfield, Chrétien de Troyes. A Study of the Arthurian Romances, Cambridge,
1981, p. 219ff.

76 462.11: "doch ich ein leie waere,/der wâren buoche maere/
kund ich lesen unde schrîben, ..."

77 459.21: "... zeiner andern gruft: dâ inne was/sîniu buoch
dar an der kiusche las./nâch des tages site ein alterstein/
dâ stuont al blôz." and 460.25: "ame salter laser im ...".

Its ground is covered with dried grass and bracken.[78] Here he
sleeps on straw (501.8-10). In all this and also in the poverty
which he has freely adopted,[79] Trevrizent does not distinguish
himself markedly from many others who in the twelfth and thirteenth centuries had chosen the vita eremitica. He is exceptional, however, in the extreme asceticism which he practises.
Not only has he given up meat and wine, but also fish, and even
bread.[80] All he will eat are the wild roots, plants and fruits
of the forest, always strictly observing the rule not to eat
before nones.[81] None of his food is cooked, all of it is left
raw.[82] He fasts frequently, sometimes involuntarily because
he cannot find again what he has gathered, more often deliberately so as an added chastisement and penance, and for the greater
glory of God. He perennially subjects himself to periods of
severe fasting.[83]

The emphatic indication given of Trevrizent's extreme austerity
makes him into a most impressive figure. Like Sigûne's extraordinary self-denial his outstanding self-discipline commands
the utmost respect. The poet's listeners would have been familiar with many who were in pursuit of the ideals of the vita
eremitica, for just as the anchoretic way of life had begun to

---

78 459.5: "... eine gruft,/dar selten kom des windes luft./dâ
    lâgen glüendige koln:/ ... ein kerzen zunde des wirtes
    hant:/ ... undr im lac ramschoup unde varm".

79 251.13/ "der vierde hât armuot,/durch got für sünde er daz
    tuot./der selbe heizet Trevrizent". Also 481. 1/2.

80 452.18: "er hete gar versprochen/môraz, wîn, und ouch dez
    prôt, sîn kiusche im dennoch mêr gebôt./der spîse het er
    keinen muot,/vische noch fleisch, swaz trüege bluot"; 480.16:
    "ich verswuor ouch fleisch, wîn unde brôt,/unt dar nâch al
    daz trüege bluot,/daz ichs nimmer mêr gewünne muot".

81 485.23: "der wirt sînr orden niht vergaz:/swie vil er gruop,
    decheine er az/der würze vor der none".

82 485.7: "mîn küche riuchet selten". Also 486.11: "dane was
    gesoten noch gebrâten, ..."

83 485.28: "durch die gotes êre/manegen tac ungâz er gienc,/
    so er vermiste dâ sîn spîse hienc". Cf. also 452.15-17 and
    452.27: "mit vaste er grôzen kumber leit".

be sought out by ever increasing numbers during the twelfth
century, so the eremitical pattern of existence seems to have
been followed by more and more.[84] They would therefore have
been able to recognize the exceptional austerity which governs
Trevrizent's bearing as a mark of uniqueness which sets him
apart from other recluses and lends him uncommon distinction.
Moreover, through the highly realistic description which Wolfram employs here, as he did with Sigûne, the figure of Trevrizent eremita would carry, and still does, as much compelling
conviction as that of Sigûne inclusa.[85] So the poet has first
of all sharpened aspects of the scene as he found it in the
French text. He has insisted on the harshness of the setting,
on the recluse's totally solitary existence and on his stringent asceticism. By so doing, by impressing upon the scene the
stamp of great severity, Wolfram has given it a dramatic under-
tow which the corresponding episode in Chrestien lacks and has
in this way heavily weighted its poetic impact.

---

84 Cf. e.g. H. Mayr-Harting, Functions of a Twelfth-Century
    Recluse, History, 60 (1975), 337-352, who speaks of the
    "great efflorescence of the hermit's way of life in twelfth-
    century England" (p. 338). Vid. also Dom Pierre Doyère,
    Ermites, in: Dictionnaire de Droit Canonique, vol. V, 1953,
    pp. 412-429, and Érémitisme en Occident, in: Dictionnaire
    de Spiritualité, vol. IV, 1960, columns 953-982; also L.
    Gougaud, La Vie érémitique au Moyen Âge, Revue d'ascétique
    et de mystique, 1 (1920), 209-240; 313-328. The pattern of
    eremitical life in medieval Germany has been discussed by
    Herbert Grundmann, Deutsche Eremiten, Einsiedler und Klaus-
    ner im Hochmittelalter (10.-12. Jahrhundert), Archiv für
    Kulturgeschichte, 45 (1963), 60-90. On German hermits through
    the centuries vid. Philipp Hofmeister, Eremiten in Deutsch-
    land, in: Fs. Michael Schmaus, vol. II, Munich, 1967, pp.
    1191-1214. Brief descriptions of men who had chosen to live
    as hermits in the Middle Ages, as also commentary on the
    vita eremitica may be found in Volker Mertens, Gregorius
    Eremita. Eine Lebensform des Adels bei Hartmann von Aue in
    ihrer Problematik und ihrer Wandlung in der Rezeption, Mün-
    chener Texte und Untersuchungen zur deutschen Literatur des
    Mittelalters, 67, Munich, 1978, p. 38ff.

85 Louise Gnädinger, Trevrizent - seine wüstenväterlichen Züge
    in Wolfram von Eschenbachs Parzival (Buch IX), in: Studi di
    Litteratura Religiosa Tedesca. In Memoria di Sergio Lupi,
    Florence, 1972, pp. 135-175, suggests that Wolfram's por-

The poet's other concern then was the elaboration of the hero's personality and his problem-laden attitudes, and the extension of the network of thoughts and emotions within him. The process which he had begun already long before Book IX and which he had accelerated and widened in the opening passages leading to the dialogue, that of adding new dimensions to the character of the hero, was now to find its climax by means of self-portrayal, authorial commentary and reaction by a major figure of the narrative.

Among these three forms of articulation authorial commentary plays the least part. Yet though kept to a minimum, it has not been restricted to peripheral features of the hero's personality and situation. Twice the poet draws attention to the physical hardship Parzival must endure and excites pity for him, forlorn as he appears. Near-frozen in his chain-mail he is shown standing on snowy ground in icy weather (459.1-4). Immediately afterwards Wolfram refers to his weary journey on horseback through wild country and his custom of sleeping rough (459.14-17). Twice he stresses Parzival's irreproachable manners (456.25, 458.20-26) and emphatically reminds the audience of his integrity (459. 25ff.). He underlines the hero's serious bearing (486.4) and shows him later as being deeply moved at the suffering of others (485.1) and suffering himself (487.17ff.). He finally comments on Parzival's moral fibre by briefly indicating the hero's ultimate achievement of composure (501.15-18). With all this Wolfram wins the audience for the hero and creates compassion and respect for him. Any misgivings his listeners may have had in giving such responses free rein, he undermines by declaring that the grace of God was with Parzival again (487.22). This is as far as direct portrayal of the hero in this episode goes. The space given to indirect description of him, in speech by himself and

---

trayal of Trevrizent derived from observation of contemporary reality, but in addition also, and according to her predominantly so, from the oral or literary tradition of the Lives of the Desert Fathers.

by another, is far greater. Through this unequal distribution
of the two types of style, through the overwhelming extension
of indirect description as against direct description, Wolfram
enhances the immediacy of the scene and with it increases the
involvement of the audience.

During the dialogue Parzival says considerably less than Trevrizent, but nevertheless reveals himself decisively, in particular
on five occasions. Three of these sharply profiled self-portrayals
occur in the first part of the dialogue and two in the second.[86]
These latter take the form of confessions (474.27-475.12 and
488.3-20). Three times during the first part of the dialogue
Parzival declares fundamental attitudes with a frankness so stark
and undisguised that Trevrizent is able instantly to identify
them and to adjust his guidance accordingly. The first instance
of these detailed disclosures of self, in which he proclaims his
hatred of God (460.28-461.26), is characterized by resentfulness
and anger, the second, in which he rejects God (467.11-18), by
bitterness and scepticism, and the third (472.1-11), in which
he attempts to put God under compulsion, by aggressiveness and
a pronounced sense of self-importance. <u>Superbia</u> marks them all.
Trevrizent's reaction is an extended homily on the cardinal sin
of pride and on divine <u>caritas</u>, God's "triuwe".

Parzival traces his misery to God. He sees his lack of happines
as deliberately being caused by God ("... er ist mîner sorgen
tote./die hât er alze hôhe erhabn ...", 461. 10/11) and also as
intentionally being prolonged by Him because of His refusal to
help, at the same time doubting God's very ability to help
("... des gihe ich dem ze schanden./der aller helfe hât gewalt,/
ist sîn helfe helfe balt,/daz er mir denne hilfet niht,/sô vil
man im der hilfe giht", (461.22-26). One again he queries His
omnipotence still looking for a cause external to his ego for
his wretchedness. - Wolfram here, as at the other four points of

---

86 For a discussion of the divisions of the dialogue into two
    parts vid. p. 249ff.

the hero's self-revelation, uses no qualifying adverbs or adjectives to indicate the tone or manner in which Parzival delivers himself of these statements. All he provides are the barest of introductions identifying the speaker. "Sprach Parzivâl" (461.1) serves for this first speech, "Parzivâl sprach zim dô" (467.11) for the hero's comment on Trevrizent's instruction, while the three further occasions of self-declaration are ushered in by "dô sprach aber Parzivâl" (471.30), "Parzivâl zem wirte sprach" (474.26) and "Parzivâl zem wirte sîn/sprach ..." (488.3/4) respectively. The poet's style during the dialogue moves close to that of drama. The personalities involved here are made to reveal themselves predominantly in verbal exchange. Nor indeed is there any need for comment on or detail of the hero's bearing at these points. Wolfram could afford to keep description sparse in relation to it. The preliminaries to the target-scene had outlined a logical and plausible progression in the hero's reasoning and feeling. The audience had witnessed the growing conflict within him, had seen him fall prey to anxiety, to feelings of helplessness and unhappiness and had watched him assert himself with anger, bitterness and resentment. The rising turmoil now bursts forth in contact with a confessor. - When Parzival first unburdens himself to Trevrizent, resentment and hostility are manifest in his words, and impatience and anger define their tone. It is this key-note of anger ("zorn", 462.5) on which Trevrizent fastens in his reply, suggesting with contrasting courtesy and reticence that he might enquire into the circumstances of its beginnings later. That Parzival's invective spills forth in a tone of high dudgeon is corroborated furthermore by Trevrizent's plea to moderate his speech ("sagt mir mit kiuschen witzen", 462.4) and also by his unwillingness to listen further for the moment. He is sensitive to the fiercely accusatory tone of Parzival's words and decides first of all to clear the accused and demonstrate his innocence - "vernemt von mir sîn unscholt,/ ê daz ir mir von im iht klagt" (462.8/9). So the dialogue begins with the would-be penitent bristling with anger, lacking insight into his failings, and totally unable to assess the causes of

his predicament. Trevrizent's sigh and close scrutiny of his
vis-à-vis - "der wirt ersiuft unt sah an in" (461.27) acknowledge his view of the near-hopelessness of the task which lies
before him. Trevrizent then formulates a homily, ostensibly on
the nature of the Godhead, but constantly returning to the
dilemma of the hero. He dwells in particular on divine caritas
(462.19; 465.9/10; 466.12 as "triuwe"; 465.29; 466.1-9 as "minne"),
but speaks at length also of divine omniscience (466.15-30).[87]
His first exhortation to the hero at the beginning of the homily
enshrines the principle of mutual "triuwe". As God is Love, man
must be unswerving in his faith - "sît getriwe ân allez wenken,/
sît got selbe ein triuwe ist" (462.18/19). He warns him in consequence of inconstancy - "hüet iuch gein im an wanke" (462.30),
solicits his forgiveness - "ir sult ûf in verkiesen" (465.11),
counsels him to observe restraint - "sît rede und werke niht sô
frî" (465.14) and finally exhorts him to force a change of heart
and to develop kindliness - "nu kêret iwer gemüete,/daz er iu
danke güete" (467.9/10). While the theme of faith is thus in the
foreground of the homily, the theme of pride is carefully inter-
woven with it. Trevrizent illustrates it with the example of
Lucifer, continuing with the stories of the disobedience of Adam
and Eve and of the murderous covetousness of Cain (463.4-465.6).

---

87 A vast number of critics have investigated and commented
    upon the religious concepts in 'Parzival'. Benedikt Mocken-
    haupt, Die Frömmigkeit im Parzival Wolframs von Eschenbach.
    Ein Beitrag zur Geschichte des religiösen Geistes in der
    Laienwelt der deutschen Mittelalters, Grenzfragen zwischen
    Theologie und Philosophie, 20, Bonn, 1942 (Reprint WBG 1968);
    Peter Wapnewski, Wolframs Parzival. Studien zur Religiosität
    und Form, Heidelberg, 1955 and Hans Joachim Koppitz, Wolframs
    Religiosität. Beobachtungen über das Verhältnis Wolframs von
    Eschenbach zur religiösen Tradition des Mittelalters, Bonn,
    1959, may be considered the seminal works in this field.
    For further references on this subject vid. Joachim Bumke,
    Die Wolfram-von-Eschenbach Forschung, II, 2: Das religiöse
    Problem, pp. 150-176. A recent contribution to this area of
    research is represented by David Duckworth, The Influence
    of Biblical Terminology and Thought on Wolfram's Parzival.
    With special reference to the epistle of St. James and the
    concept of zwîvel, Göppinger Arbeiten zur Germanistik, 273,
    1980.

On the face of it Trevrizent is primarily concerned with tracing
chronologically the progress of evil in the universe. He describes
to the hero how sin arose among mankind. Yet at the same time his
explanations have a particular application, namely to Parzival
himself. Parzival is in fact all three - Lucifer, Adam and Cain.
He has rebelled in pride like Lucifer, fallen from Grace like
Adam and murdered his kinsman like Cain. Nevertheless whatever
pains Trevrizent may have taken in anchoring his religious instruction in the personal situation of one individual,[88] through
a series of exhortations and through the specific relevance of
the lessons he has selected from the Bible, his homily misfires
disastrously. Parzival brushes aside Trevrizent's counsel and
his panegyric of the Christian God, expressing his contempt of
Him with acid mockery yet iron logic. He turns Trevrizent's lesson of a just God upside down, for he has contrary evidence -
his own case. The Christian concept of a God of Justice is a
falsehood; he can prove it from the experience of his own career.
As in the encounter with the pilgrims, his scepticism manifests
itself in his refusal to give God a name. The demonstrative pro-
noun, a derogatory usage in this context as much as in the
earlier one, must serve:

> 467.12 hêrre, ich bin des immer frô,
> daz ir mich von dem bescheiden hât,
> der nihtes ungelônet lât,
> der missewende noch der tugent.
> ich hân mit sorgen mîne jugent
> alsus brâht an disen tac,
> daz ich durch triwe kumbers pflac.

"I am so very grateful for your detailed explanation of the one
who leaves nothing unrequited, neither good nor evil. My portion
has been misery all through my young life until this very day,
misery in recompense for loyalty and love and faith." Parzival's

---

88 As far as Trevrizent is concerned that individual, that particular sinner, is Laehelîn. In an intricate double-take he
   will come to realize that the cap which fits Laehelîn fits
   Parzival as well.

sharp rejoinder cuts short the homily.[89] Trevrizent makes no
comment, but changes course. The formal teaching of the tenets
of the Christian faith is abandoned and Parzival's avowal of
his ambition to reach the Grail prompts the Grail-narration.

Trevrizent's description of the nature of the Grail and in particular his disclosure that only the one chosen by God may attain
the Grail kingship goads Parzival into yet another challenge of
God. In this third self-portrayal the bitterness and biting irony
of the previous one have disappeared, but the anger of the first
instance of self-revelation has returned in full force. Arro-
gantly he underlines his exceptional fighting skills - "ich

---

89 Parzival's comments here have traditionally been interpreted
    as being made in the spirit of mild acceptance. Cf. e.g.
    Benedikt Mockenhaupt, op.cit., on the effect of Trevrizent's
    homily: "Die Wirkung ist, wie man sie erwarten darf: im In-
    nersten getroffen, spricht Parzival sein neues Bekenntnis
    zu dem, der nihtes ungelônet lât, der missewende noch der
    tugent, und schließt mit einem letzten Abschiedsblick seine
    sorgenvolle, nunmehr zu Ende geführte Jugendentwicklung ab
    (467.11-18)" (p. 95). He sees at this point "beglückte Er-
    leichterung" in the hero and finds that he has achieved an
    "innere Umwandlung" here (p. 96). Walter Henzen, Das IX.
    Buch des Parzival, assesses Parzival's words in much the
    same way: "Die Ausführungen Trevrizents inmitten einer gün-
    stig abgestimmten Atmosphäre am wärmenden Feuer sind nicht
    auf steinigen Boden gefallen; sie haben den Zweifler wohl-
    tuend berührt: 'herre, ich bin des immer vrô etc.'" (p. 140).
    In a similar fashion Walter Blank takes Parzival's words to
    be a 'straight' utterance and not an ironical one: "... Par-
    zival /bedankt sich/ nach dem ersten Teil des Gesprächs für
    die erhaltene Gottes- und Heilslehre ausdrücklich ..." (Mit-
    telalterliche Dichtung oder Theologie? Zur Schuld Parzivals,
    ZfdA, 100 (1971), 133-148; here p. 147). Irony is notori-
    ously difficult to prove. (For a definition of irony as
    applicable to medieval texts vid. D. H. Green, Irony in the
    Medieval Romance, Cambridge, 1979, in particular p. 3ff.;
    also D. H. Green, Alieniloquium. Zur Begriffsbestimmung der
    mittelalterlichen Ironie, in: Fs. F. Ohly, Munich, 1975,
    vol. II, pp. 119-159). However, if someone expresses elabor-
    ate gratitude for information which he manifestly believes
    to be a falsehood on incontrovertible evidence, as here,
    what else could this gesture of gratitude represent but a
    stance of biting irony?

streit ie swâ ich strîten vant,/sô daz mîn werlîchiu hant/ sich
naehert dem prîse" (472.5-7) and impatiently demands of God to
call him to the office of the Grail on the testimony of his outstanding soldiering, if indeed God is qualified to judge: "ist
got an strîte wîse,/der sol mich dar benennen, ..." (472.8/9).
Angry and resentful, bitter and sceptical, aggressive and arrogant Parzival has remained unconvinced and unrepentant throughout
the first part of the dialogue. Trevrizent now decides to tackle
the glaring superbia in the man before him once more,[90] but this
time his example is not Lucifer, the remote and menacing figure
of religious allegory, but the weak and ailing king whom Parzival has met and whom he knows. That his shift in illustration
of superbia from the impersonal to the personal level is experienced as closely personal by Parzival is not known to Trevrizent.
It is known, however, to the audience.

The change, reinforced by the manifestation of Trevrizent's deep
emotional involvement ("... ieweder ouge im wiel,/dô er an diz
maere dâhte,/daz er dâ mit rede volbrâhte" (472.18-20), bears
fruit almost immediately. It leads to Parzival's first confession.

With Trevrizent's challenge to the hero to declare his identity
the first part of the dialogue comes to an end. Until now Trevrizent has been a distant stranger to Parzival, while Parzival has
been mistaken by him for a man dangerous and hostile to the Grail
dynasty.[91] With their discovery of the blood-relationship be-

---

90 He mentions "hôchvart" four times in his reply: 472.13; 472.17;
    472.26; 473.4.

91 The importance of the mistaken identity for this part of the
    dialogue has been recognized by a number of scholars. Cf.
    e.g. David Blamires, Characterization and Individuality in
    Wolfram's Parzival, Cambridge, 1966: "We see now the function
    that the Grail horse has that Parzival wins from the Grail
    knight earlier in Book IX. From here the confusion with
    Lähelîn occurs, and the fact that Lähelîn is guilty of rêroup
    leads Parzival to confess to his own rêroup and the killing
    of Ither, while at the same time informing Trevrizent of his
    penitent's identity." (p. 327); and Petrus W. Tax, Trevrizent.

tween them the dialogue undergoes a radical change in form, tone
and tenor, and in the roles of the participants. While Part I
of the dialogue was dominated by a homily, Part II becomes a
rambling family-history, of which the tragic biography of Anfortas forms the core. While distance and a degree of formality
governed the relationship between the speakers in the first
part of the dialogue, closeness, even intimacy, take over in
the second. An immediate signal of this is the change in Trevrizent's form of adress from "ir" to "du".[92] In Part I Trevrizent
had taken upon himself the function of a preacher delivering an
impromptu sermon. In Part II he acknowledges his role within the
hero's family as one of his chief kinsmen, as one of his mother's
brothers.[93] Parzival in his turn, who first saw himself as a
sinner seeking counsel from a stranger, now automatically slips
into the role of the ward. Finally, while the pivot problem of
Part I of the dialogue had been the hero's "triuwe" in relation to
God, in Part II this comes to be mutated to the hero's "triuwe" in
relation to his fellow men. Fundamental changes thus overtake the
dialogue midway, and its second part comes to present an entirely
new aspect. Along with it Parzival's bearing had changed course,
the difference in attitude manifesting itself in the speech which
ushers in this second part. In contrast with the three previous
self-portrayals this self-characterization is neither accusation

---

Die Verhüllungstechnik des Erzählers, in: Studien zur deutschen Literatur und Sprache des Mittelalters, Fs. Hugo Moser,
Berlin, 1974, 119-134, p. 122: "... /es/ muß betont werden,
daß alles, was Trevrizent an Unterweisung und Trost seinem
'Gegenüber' mit Worten mitteilt, gezielt, d.h. auf Lähelin
hin gesagt wird."

92 This occurs in 475.20.

93 The frequent occurrence of the uncle-nephew tie in the medie-
    val German romances and its origin have been examined by
    Clair Hayden Bell, The Sister's Son in the Medieval German
    Epic. A Study in the Survival of Matriliny, University of
    California Publications in Modern Philology, 10, 1920-1925
    (1922), pp. 67-182. Vid. in particular pp. 105-164. Accord-
    ing to her this bond has its roots in a matrilineal social
    structure. She comments: "The most tenacious and therefore
    the most common of these survivals /from a matrilineal so-

nor demand, but a confession. Declaring his lineage he adds a
plea for his father to be remembered in prayer and then confes-
ses to the crimes of murder and theft (474.27-475.12). His over-
bearing stance has given way to a display of feelings of guilt
and shame. Yet pride in his father's honourable death and in
his lineage, as also the excuse of early obtuseness and a boy's
lack of insight ("sô was ich an den witzen toup", 475.6) still
allow him some degree of confidence in himself. It is reflected
clearly in the measured, orderly and restrained fashion in which
he makes this first confession. In the second confession every
vestige of this self-confidence will be seen to have gone, as
his self-accusation agonizingly pours forth in fear, confusion
and despair.

The shock of Parzival's revelations leaves Trevrizent groping
for words - "waz râtes möht ich dir nu tuon?" (475.20). In Ithêr,
so he is compelled to disclose, Parzival has murdered a man of
exceptional integrity, and one widely admired, (475.28-476.11),
but worse still, he has committed the unspeakable crime of having killed someone linked with him by blood. He has repeated
the deed of Cain - "du hâst dîn eigen verch erslagn" (475.21).[94]

---

ciety_7 is the peculiar closeness of the relation between the
brother and his sister's children" (p. 68).

94 The blood-relationship is distant. It goes through Mazadân
and Terdelaschoye, Ithêr's great-grandparents and Gahmuret's
great-great-grandparents. (Vid. the family-tree: Gral- und
Artuskreis, in: Wolfram von Eschenbach, seventh edition, Karl
Lachmann/Eduard Hartl, Berlin 1952, and the relevant entries
in the Verzeichnis der Eigennamen by Friederike Weber, p. 421
ff. Cf. also the entries in the fully descriptive index of
names with lists of loci in: Die Namen im 'Parzival' und im
'Titurel' Wolframs von Eschenbach, bearbeitet von Werner
Schröder, Berlin, 1982). Distant though it may be, it is
nevertheless highly important. Parzival is shown here as
being related to both the Arthurian as well as the Grail
dynasties. The link between them is effected through Gahmuret. The murder within the kin thus has the widest possible
repercussions. Wolfgang Harms (Der Kampf mit dem Freund oder
Verwandten) comments illuminatingly on the significance of
the murder of Ither: "... die Tötung Ithers _/wiegt_7 wie ein
Brudermord. ... Die Verwandtschaft zwischen Ither und Parzi-

The Christian symbolism now vested in the act after Trevrizent's
explanations, would have communicated itself with ease to Wolfram's audience. They had not been left unprepared for such an
interpretation of the hero's early crime. Only shortly before
had Trevrizent told Parzival the story of Cain and had taught
him its significance. His deed had sown the seeds of hatred among
men: "dô huop sich êrst der menschen nît:/alsô wert er immer sît"
(464.21/22). The immense burden of guilt with which the hero is
now seen to be laden is underpinned still further by the gravity
of the offence being shown in yet another context, within the
vendetta code of conduct. According to the latter, and if mere
justice prevailed, his life would be forfeit (475.22-25). The
hero's crime is therefore a heinous one on all counts. A powerful poetic impact thus derives from a single feature, the blood-
bond, introduced into the work by Wolfram.[95] He had adumbrated
it already in the scene of the killing, where he refers to Ithêr
as being a member of the Arthurian family ("Artûses basen sun",
145.11), but the motif is left dormant at that point. It is not
brought to the fore until the dialogue, where through elucidation he makes it fully operative within the plot.

The revelation to Parzival of his kinship with Trevrizent and
Ithêr leads into the detailed family-history of the hero. The
story of the Grail family is a tragic one, marked by death and
marred by suffering. Its pathos culminates in the description
of the agony of Anfortas and of the anguished search for a cure
of his dreadful affliction. During the course of this narration

---

val ist ein Zeichen für die Brüderlichkeit aller Menschen
als Nachkommen Adams. Und da Gott durch Christus in diese
Menschen-Familie eingetreten ist, wird ein Verstoß gegen
die Brüderlichkeit der Menschen zugleich zu einem Verstoß
gegen die triuwe zu Gott. ... Die Unwissenheit, aus der
heraus die Tat geschehen ist, mindert das Ausmaß der of-
fenbarten Sündhaftigkeit nicht." (pp. 152/153). Vid. here
also the analysis of the scene in which the murder occurs:
pp. 147-154.

95   There is no blood-relationship in Chrestien between the hero
and the knight in red armour. This is Wolfram's invention.

Parzival will change fundamentally. Yet the poet chooses to
refrain from commenting either on the progress or on the nature
of the change. With the utmost economy he merely depicts its
beginning and its end. In order to be able to enter into the
suffering of others, Parzival must suffer himself. He is shown
to do so, deeply, for after Trevrizent has delivered his double
blow, his revelation of the kinship-murder coupled with the
sudden, brutally undisguised news of his mother's death and his
implication in it - "mîn swester lac ouch nâch dir tôt,/Herze-
loyd dîn muoter" (476.12/13) - he is stunned and cannot grasp
what he has heard (476.14-22).[96] After this the poet gives no
indication of what is happening in the hero's mind. It is not
until his second and final confession that the audience are given
to understand what has happened. His confession is proof of his
involvement in the story of Anfortas's suffering. His reaction
to the realization of the nature of his crime and of the manner
of his mother's death signals the point of his readiness to enter
upon that involvement.

A brief account of Sigûne's parents and her mother's death in
childbirth and of the sole surviving sister, Repanse, precedes
Trevrizent's moving description of Anfortas's tragic fate. In
the manner of his telling, the story of the life of Anfortas
becomes an exemplum of how superbia will provoke divine retalia-
tion. This is how he interprets the career of Anfortas to Parzival. The portrayal of its course eloquently illustrates to Par-

---

96 This idea that personal suffering is an essential stepping-
    stone to compassion finds parallel expression in the writing
    of St. Bernard, De gradibus humilitatis, cap. III, Migne,
    PL,182, col. 945 : "Sicut enim pura veritas non nisi puro
    corde videtur; sic miseria fratris verius misero corde senti-
    tur. Sed ut ob alienam miseriam miserum cor habeas, oportet
    ut tuam prius agnoscas: ut proximi mentem in tua invenias,
    et ex te noveris qualiter ille subvenias, exemplo scilicet
    Salvatoris nostri, qui pati voluit, ut compati sciret; miser
    fieri, ut misereri disceret." Herbert Kolb, op. cit., pp.
    111/112, draws attention to this congruence in thought.

zival the awesome quality of divine omnipotence and the implac-
able nature of divine wrath. It outlines for him glaringly the
peril which he had been courting and conjures up for him compellingly a terrifying vision of what the future might hold.
Already the first part of the dialogue had contained a statement
by Trevrizent in which he declared unequivocally that Anfortas
was guilty of superbia. His reference to "sîn herzebaere nôt,/
die hôchvart im ze lône bôt" (472.25/26) shows succinctly that
Trevrizent sees superbia as the root-cause of Anfortas's agony.
The reason for the mention of Anfortas's superbia at that point
had been the hero's own and final display during the dialogue
of his particular brand of superbia. Instantly recognized by
Trevrizent it drew a warning from him:

> 472.13 ir müest aldâ vor hôchvart
> mit senften willen sîn bewart.
> iuch verleit lîht iwer jugent
> daz ir der kiusche braechet tugent.
> hôchvart ie seic unde viel,...

This prior link between the cardinal sin of pride in Anfortas
and in Parzival ensures that the audience, during the second
part of the dialogue, will come to understand that the two stories
of superbia, that of the Grail king and that of the hero, are meant
to be compared.[97] They will come to discover a frightening discrepancy between the types and consequent weight, of the two
transgressions involved. They will hear that the Grail king's
superbia was an act of disobedience, reckless neglect of the
rule of his kingship that sexuality must be contained within
specifically permitted bounds, within those of dynastic marriage
(478.13-479.2).[98] The act, though culpable in its flouting of

---

97 The immense importance of the concept of superbia within
medieval thinking may be gauged from Wolfgang Hempel's
investigation: Übermuot Diu Alte ... Der Superbia-Gedanke
und seine Rolle in der deutschen Literatur des Mittelalters,
Studien zur Germanistik, Anglistik und Komparatistik, ed. by
Armin Arnold, vol. 1, Bonn, 1970. He enquires into the
history of thought which forms the background to the notion,
portrays the theory of superbia and then presents its history
beginning with the Old High German period. He shows con-

divine authority, is nevertheless presented as explicable on the grounds of his youth, and therefore as partially excusable (478. 8-12). They will remember, on the other hand, that the hero's superbia was not mere disobedience, prompted by an understandable inability, but considered, continued and open rebellion against God. At no time had the poet hinted that the inner circumstances from which it sprang had in part lessened the seriousness of the offence. Suspense generated through the contrast between these two stories, and fear and pity for the hero, will keep the audience attentive throughout the dialogue.

After having explained the details of Anfortas's superbia, Trevrizent describes the horrific and clearly emblematic punishment for his sin. Anfortas is effectively gelded by the thrust of a poisoned lance, deprived of his manhood and reduced to shame, paralyzed in his lower limbs, hopelessly and helplessly crippled, and condemned to living in constant racking pain and with the stench of a gangrenous wound. While Parzival had been told some

---

vincingly that the concept of superbia is central to the medieval assessment of human behaviour. Cf. e.g. p. 37: "Das wesentliche Merkmal der mittelalterlichen Superbia-Theorie ist also letztlich folgendes: Die Superbia, Egozentrik wie Egoismus umfassend, ist als Ursünde und Sündenwurzel Zentrum der kirchlichen Moraltheorie. In einem weit ausgearbeiteten Ableitungssystem werden sämtliche geistigen und tätlichen Verfehlungen auf dieses Zentrum als letzten Grund zurückgeführt. Die Reichweite des Begriffes superbia erstreckt sich also von der Ursünde bis zum geringsten konkreten Anzeichen von Egoismus und bis zur einfachsten Übertretung kirchlicher Moralvorschriften. Das bedeutet: Da in einem derart fest geknüpften Moralsystem auch das letzte Glied unlöslich dem Gesamtkomplex assoziiert ist, erscheint auch die konkreteste Derivation mit dem generellen Zentralbegriff im Kern identisch. Die Ursünde superbia ist in jeder Überheblichkeit, in jedem Ungehorsam, ja in jedem Vergehen überhaupt in ihrer ganzen Schwere gegenwärtig. Und in dieser assoziativen Wirkungsweise liegt der Grund für die außerordentliche Rolle, die der Superbia-Gedanke in der Praxis und im täglichen Leben des hohen Mittelalters spielt."

98 This point is taken up again later: "swer sich diens geim grâle hât bewegn,/gein wîben minne er muoz verpflegn./wan der künec sol haben eine/ze rehte ein konen reine," (495.7-10).

of these details before,[99] the whole horror of their totality
is now brought home to him. Nothing can help him, neither Trevrizent's supreme sacrifice, nor the countless remedies that his
family and his household obtain for him, reaching out in their
desperate attempts to find a cure beyond reality, into the world
of legend. Every kind of antidote is tried, every medical text-
book consulted (481.6-15). The waters of the four rivers of Para-
dise are sifted near their source and searched for medicinal herbs
(481.19-26). The branch which protected Aeneas in the underworld
is brought (481.30-482.10) and the pelican's heart-blood collect-
ed (482.12-22). The unicorn's heart is tried and also the car-
buncle-stone from underneath its antler (482.24-483.3).[100] The
herb which springs from a slain dragon's blood is gathered (483.
6-16) and every conceivable ointment is spread on the wound (484.
13-17). Yet Anfortas remains incurable and his pain unrelieved.
The catalogue of remedies is punctuated by a refrain expressing
in varied wording the notions of effort wasted and of total use-

---

99 Sigûne had already told him of Anfortas's paralysis in the
    lower half of his body (251.16-19). The gangrene is not
    specifically mentioned at this point, but may be taken to
    be implied. The wound is poisoned and open. Moreover, the
    feature is explained and elaborated later (491.6-8).

100 Ulrich Engelen, Die Edelsteine in der deutschen Dichtung
    des 12. und 13. Jahrhunderts, Münstersche Mittelalter-
    Schriften, 27, Munich, 1978; p. 56, comments on the sym-
    bolic meaning of the carbuncle and its relevance to the
    use of it in the treatment of Anfortas: "Für Wolfram wäre
    die Annahme eine Illusion, der Karfunkel könne die Wunde
    des Amfortas, die ihm seine Unkeuschheit schlug, heilen,
    da Gott die Heilung nicht will (Pz. 481.18). Die Wunde
    ist Strafe für ein Fehlverhalten gegenüber Gott, weshalb
    aller fîsiken liste (Pz. 481.15) wirkungslos bleiben müs-
    sen. Der Karfunkel kann umso weniger helfen, als er im
    Einhorn gefunden wird, das durchgehend auf Keuschheit und
    Reinheit gedeutet wird. Diese Bedeutung des Einhorns ist
    Wolfram bewußt; denn er betont, es schlafe ûf der meide
    schôz. Die Bedeutung des Tieres, in dem der Stein gefunden
    wird, prägt offenbar auch die des Karfunkels: Die Behand-
    lung des Amfortas soll Reinigung bewirken, nicht nur in
    einem medizinisch-antitoxinischen Sinn, sondern umfassend
    von der spezifischen Schuld und Krankheit des Gralkönigs."

lessness: "diene gâben keiner helfe lôn" (481.7); "der keinz
gehelfen kunde" (481.17); "daz was verlorniu arbeit" (481.27);
"dô was dem sper niht alsus" (482.11); "daz moht uns niht gehelfen sus" (482.23); "diu wunde was et lüppec var" (483.4);
"der /würze/ edel hôch geslehte/kom uns dâ für niht rehte" (483.
17/18); "im was et zallen zîten wê" (484.18). Monotony and repetition in the form of the account underline the hopelessness
which is expresses. Apart from being a harrowing evocation of
the hopelessness, grief and physical torture which govern Anfortas's existence the description also conveys most powerfully
man's puniness, the fruitlessness of human ingenuity and effort
in the face of the Divine Will. For Anfortas is incurable because God wills it so - "got selbe uns des verbunde" (481.18).
The deadlock of his dilemma can be released only by the miracle
of Grace (483.19ff.). After Parzival has learnt that he was to
have been the instrument of that instance of Grace and had failed, the dialogue is interrupted for a description of their search
for food (485.1ff.).

This sudden shift from the momentous to the mundane is expertly
timed. The interlude here does not represent an inconsequential
digression, but an essential hiatus in the action. After a long
and emotionally intensely demanding description, it provides
relief, a temporary slackening of tension. It offers the audience
a pause which enables them to absorb what has passed and to prepare for what is to come. Moreover, throughout the heart-rending
and ominous story of Anfortas not a single word has been said
about the hero. Only at its conclusion does the poet point out
that he too was moved ("Si bêde wârn mit herzen klage", 485.1).
So the question mark which relates to him remains for a while.
Suspense is given the necessary space of time in which to climb
to a climax. Have the lessons with which the life-story of Anfortas is packed, struck home? Has he suffered enough to have suffered with him? Will he confess? - And he does, immediately
after the trivia of daily living have been completed. The nature
of his confession declares abundantly his cumulative involvement

in the agony of another that has occurred during Trevrizent's
narration. It discharges itself now in a cry of despair from
which every trace of self-regard, even self-respect, has vanished. What is uppermost in his mind now is not thought of self,
but of another. His stumbling words are pervaded by an overpowering awareness of his failure in humanity, in "triuwe", which,
so he says, will crush him if he can find no solace:

> 488.9 ich hân sô sêre missetân,
> welt ir michs engelten lân.
> sô scheide ich von dem trôste
> und bin der unerlôste
> immer mêr von riuwe.

The poet brilliantly conveys the hero's agonizing sense of shame,
the hesitancy with which he wrings his admission from himself,
the fear in him of its consequences, and the confusion with
which he feels his way towards finally telling the truth. His
feeling of shame is expressed by the hero himself in the very
first sentence which he now addresses to Trevrizent - "getorst
ichz iu vor scham gesagn" (488.5). His hesitancy shows itself
in the form of his confession. Twice he speaks of his moral
failing, but it is not until he has reiterated it that he says
precisely what it is that he has done:

> 488.16 der ûf Munsalvaesche reit,
> und der den rehten kumber sach,
> unt der deheine vrâge sprach,
> daz bin ich unsaelec barn:
> sus hân ich, hêrre, missevarn.

His first mention of it is no more than a veiled allusion - "ich
hân sô sêre missetân" (488.9). His fear of what his admission
might do is again expressed by the hero in his plea for pity.
He asks for forgiveness: "daz verkiest durch iwer selbes zuht"
(488.7), urges affectionate understanding: "mîn triwe hât doch
gein iu fluht" (488.8), pleads not to punish him: "welt ir michs
engelten lân,/sô scheide ich von dem trôste/unt bin der unerlôste/
immer mêr von riuwe" (488.10-13) and begs for counsel and comfort: "ir sult mit râtes triuwe/klagen mîne tumpheit" (488.14/15).
His confusion, like his hesitancy, is mirrored in the style, in

the fourfold repetition of one and the same thought, the plea
not to reject him. A fundamental change is now seen to be manifest in the hero when his final confession is compared with his
opening harangue hurled at Trevrizent. The poet has taken him
through a development, rendered convincing through the indubitable impact of the homily, of the revelation to him of his
crimes, and of the story of Anfortas. The ground has been prepared for a total reversal of his fortunes, for a recapture of
a state of Grace.

Trevrizent responds to Parzival's desperate and impassioned plea
for help with kindliness and understanding. Severe strictures
would now crush Parzival; Trevrizent's reply therefore contains
no rebuke. In this way the poet comments indirectly and with
great subtlety on Trevrizent's tact, but also, and even more
importantly, on the hero's highly precarious frame of mind.
Trevrizent is made to avoid all forms of reprimand. His very
first words express pity for Parzival, pity for having been the
victim of his limitations in the hour of his destiny:

> 488.22 wir sulen bêde samt zuo
> herzenlîcher klage grîfen
> unt die freude lâzen slîfen,
> sît dîn kunst sich saelden sus
> verzêch.

After briefly exclaiming then at how it was possible that his
"triuwe", - his compassionate understanding, his humanity - should
have been in abeyance when he faced that melancholy king (488.26-
30), Trevrizent immediately tries to comfort him. By his injunc-
tion which follows, not to give way to inordinate grief (489.2-4),
the poet once again stresses his hero's extreme vulnerability at
this point. This same feature is emphasized further by Trevrizent's effort to infuse hope into Parzival's thoughts. Other
achievements are possible, so he points out, which could com-
pensate him for his loss (489.13-20). Finally and logically, -
the poet again throwing into relief the tenuous thread on which
the spiritual survival of his hero hangs - Trevrizent diverts

the direction of what he has to say. In order to prevent the
hero from brooding on his sense of defeat he abruptly changes
the subject from Parzival back to Anfortas, giving him no time
or opportunity for thoughts of self. His question: "nu sag mir,
saehe du daz sper/ze Munsalvaesche ûf dem hûs?" (489.22/23) is
designed to engage the hero's attention directly and to involve
him once more in the fate of another. The redirection of the
course of Trevrizent's reply is successful, for when Parzival
is heard to speak for the first time after his confession, he
is shown as participating in the further story of Anfortas and
as contributing to it eagerly ("al zehant", 491.19 and 491.20-
30). Throughout the dialogue the poet had employed the technique of portraying his main character via the reactions of
another. He lifts this method here on to a new level of sophistication. In a highly condensed form, in speech consisting of
just over sixteen couplets the audience are given a projection
of the hero's inward state which glosses and fully corroborates
the self-description of his second confession. Twice Trevrizent
is made to refer directly to Parzival's emotional prostration,
by his advice to eschew excessive sadness and by giving him hope.
Twice he is made to refer to it by implication, by avoiding a
reprimand and by diverting the course of his answer. The substance of this passage is intensively moving, yet technical
ingenuity and finesse of balance also contribute much to its
poetic effectiveness.

The last section of the dialogue is devoted to more family-history, more about Anfortas, and more details relating to the
rules governing the Grail community. Again it is Trevrizent who
speaks at length, some of his description being elicited by
Parzival's questions. There is no further self-revelation by
Parzival, but there is one brief and decisive authorial comment,
and one only, in which the poet declares that the hero has re-
gained his equilibrium:

> 501.15 Parzivâl die swaere
> truoc durch süeziu maere,
> wand in der wirt von sünden schiet
> unt im doch rîterlîchen riet.

Trevrizent's narrative ranges from further description of the
dreadful pain endured by Anfortas (489.24-491.5; 492.23-493.14),
and of his habit of having himself carried to the lake (491.6-
30) to an account of how his castle is defended (492.1-10) and
of how members of the Grail community conclude marriages (494.1-
495.12). He tells Parzival the story of his past life, of his
one-time impetuousness and illicit love, and describes for him
his restless travelling and insatiable love of soldiering (495.
13-496.18; 497.3-20; 498.21-27). His story includes a description of his meeting with Gahmuret in Seville, a mention of how
Gahmuret journeyed on to Outremer and how he gave Ithêr to
Trevrizent as squire (496.19-497.2; 497.21-498.20). The three
life-stories presented in the dialogue, of Anfortas, Trevrizent
and Gahmuret, all exhibit certain similarities on the level of
typicality. Each one of them exemplifies the typical career of
many a young nobleman at the turn of the twelfth and thirteenth
centuries. Animated by drive and physical courage, equipped
with first-rate horsemanship and skill at arms, motivated by a
desire to make a name for himself, each one of them sets out on
a fighting career that takes him far afield. The three lives
represent a realistic enough description for the poet to be able
to assume an automatic response of empathy in his listeners. It
also enables him to draw his hero's own fighting career into the
context of contemporary reality and to make certain of that
response of empathy on this particular plane for him as well.
This is not to say that Parzival had not been placed into this
specific context before. It had occurred many times, but the
renewed placing, the reminder of him in his capacity as a knight,
who had throughout the dialogue been predominantly sinner, criminal and individual, is of immense importance at this very point.
It suddenly throws into relief the question mark which hangs
over Parzival's career as a gentleman-at-arms. The three life-

stories recounted here have all shown a fighting career cut
short - one by untimely death, another by emasculating injury
and the third by sacrifice. Will the hero's career be cut short
also? Will he perhaps renounce it now, after this turning-point
in his life, despite the hope expressed by Trevrizent that he
will continue with it? (489.13-20). Or if he does not, where
will the pursuit of the profession of arms finally lead him?
Trevrizent tries to answer this last question. By defining for
him the form which his further chivalry should take he also sets
his goal for him: It should be the protection of the weak. Men
in holy orders and women do not bear arms; they must be protected. Defence of the defenceless is his proper aim (502.4-22). He
recommends a chivalry which is not self-serving, but serves
others, a chivalry of defence, not of aggression, of peace and
not of war.[101] And so he sends him on his way, still a knight,
absolves him: "gip mir dîn sünde her" (502.25) and formally
confirms what the audience already know, the fundamental change
that he has undergone: "vor gote ich bin dîn wandels wer" (502.
26). Before granting this absolution he had specified to Parzival the crimes for which he was to atone. He mentioned them
casually, without much emphasis, adding them as a rider to the
story of Gahmuret, yet clearly circumscribing their particular

---

101 Parzival does not follow Trevrizent's advice, as his sub-
    sequent career shows. He does not appear to devote himself
    to the defence of the defenceless after leaving Trevrizent.
    He continues to practise the profession of arms in the
    manner in which he had practised it before, i.e. fighting
    when the occasion requires it, or when the opportunity for
    it arises. Thus he fights at Lôgroys (559.9ff.; 618.19ff.),
    jousts with Gâwân near Jôflanze (679.1ff.), then with Gra-
    moflanz (703.29ff.) and Feirefîz (735.5ff.) and also visits
    tournaments. He mentions these when listing for the as-
    sembled Arthurian court the knights defeated by him: "diz
    ergienc dâ turnieren was,/die wîle ich nâch dem grâle reit"
    (772.24/25). On Parzival's fighting career vid. Martin H.
    Jones, Parzival's Fighting and his Election to the Grail,
    in: Wolfram-Studien, III, Schweinfurter Kolloquium 1972,
    Berlin, 1975, pp. 52-71; also Herta Zutt, Parzivals Kämpfe,
    in: Fs. Friedrich Maurer, Düsseldorf, 1968, pp. 178-198.

character and significance through grouping them together without any differentiation between them. There are three crimes
for which he must do penance - the murder of Ithêr, his involvement in his mother's death, and his neglect of Anfortas in his
agony. In each case Parzival had exhibited an extraordinary
callousness, an appalling disregard of pain as experienced by
others, a total inability to understand suffering. - When leaving Herzeloyde the boy never considered his mother's plight,
the loneliness to which he abandoned her. All his thought was
fixed on ambition for his own self (126.12-14; 128.13-15).
Despite his mother's deep and obvious distress at their parting
(126.15; 126.21; 126.30; 127.10), he rode off without even
looking back (128.16ff.).[102] When he challenged and killed
Ithêr, personal ambition motivated his action. His sole objective was to acquire Ithêr's possessions (148.15-18; 149.27-30;
153.28) which would bestow knighthood upon him as he saw it:

> 154.4   gip mir dâ du ûffe rîtes,
> unt dar zuo al dîn harnas:
> daz enpfieng ich ûf dem palas:
> dar inne ich ritter werden muoz.

and again:

> 154.21 gip her und lâz dîn lantreht:
> ine wil niht langer sîn ein kneht,
> ich sol schildes ambet hân.

The moment he had struck him down, he callously rolled the dead
man about trying to strip off his armour (155.19ff.). When he
had finally obtained all he wanted, he left without a thought
for his victim: "Ithêrn von Gaheviez/er jaemerlîche ligen liez"
(159.5/6). The pathos of death did not move him. Finally at the

---

102 Chrestien's hero here shows crass brutality. Perceval looks
back, sees his mother fall and whips his hunter so that he
gets away the faster (620ff.). Wolfram has reduced the
blatant cruelty here to a deplorable lack of perceptiveness.
In both portrayals the mainspring of behaviour is selfish-
ness. The difference between them is one of degree.

Grail castle he showed himself blind and deaf to all signs and
expressions of grief and suffering that were so unmistakably,
and even spectacularly, displayed.[103] - Parzival has failed
three times in humanity, and in each case an individual linked
with him in kinship has been involved. This is the dual common
denominator of his three transgressions. Through the recognition
and the tacit acknowledgement of the common root from which the
three guilty acts have sprung, Trevrizent sums up and underlines the dominant theme of Part II of the dialogue - the hero's
lack of "triuwe" towards his fellow-men.

The modern writer wishing to probe into his fictional character's
emotional and spiritual predicament, has at his disposal a subtly
differentiated vocabulary of immense range. It enables him to
portray minute aspects of individuality and the shades and nuances
of psychological change by direct description. It allows him moreover to transmit abstract thought with precision. Wolfram possessed nothing of the kind. The linguistic register available to
him was restricted, unsophisticated, and ambiguous where abstrac-
tions are concerned. Few words had to make do for many concepts.
Analysis of the mind by direct description, and the transmission
of ideas by detailed specifying, are methods of narration of
which he could not make use. He developed instead a technique
of portrayal by implication through visual impact. He added to
it at this core-scene of his romance the hero's self-revelation
in speech and also exploited to the full the narrative instrument of dialogue as a means of description. Every single component of the narrative unit represented by Book IX is vividly
visual. In all of them the poet presents people, individuals,
either introducing fictional characters or personification.

---

103 The poet gives ample indication of the crippling sadness
     that pervades the atmosphere at the Grail castle: 227.7-
     16; 228.26; 229.17; 230.18-20; 230.30; 231.1/2; 231.15ff.;
     239.25ff.; 242.1-7.

There thus appear in sequence, life-like and striking, the Lady
Literature, the author, the hero with Sigûne, with a border
patrol of Grail territory, with the pilgrims, the hero alone,
and finally with Trevrizent. Even his fictitious sources take
on human form. Kyôt comes to be fully characterized, and the
figure of Flegetânîs is clearly outlined. Three of the passages
preceding the great dialogue contain dialogue themselves, the
introduction, the scene with Sigûne and the encounter with the
pilgrims. The strong appeal to visual imagination which emanates
from the portrayal of figures is underpinned by the technique of
conversation and argument. Three of the scenes carry leading
ideas through their embodiment in human behaviour. The episode
with Sigûne conveys the principle of "triuwe" by the delineation
of her style of life. The scene of the challenge and that with
the pilgrims throw into relief the hero's superbia by the description of his bearing and by his utterances. The technique
of narration employed here, implication through visual impact,
proves a precise guide to ideas. The method of direct description which is able to draw on extensive vocabulary and specific
terminology could not have done better. By supplementing this
style of portrayal with the hero's self-declaration in speech
and extensive dialogue, the poet adds here a dramatic dimension
to his narrative, giving it in this way tense and tangible immediacy.

These three dominant methods of description in the narrative
unit of Book IX also go a long way towards meeting the particular
needs of the reception of poetry in the twelfth and thirteenth
centuries. They cannot but have been designed with certain difficulties inherent in the then situation of poetry in mind. The
modern writer aims his work at a reading public, a single reader
who can linger over the words chosen by the author, ponder their
meaning, and absorb it at an intellectual pace set by himself.
Wolfram, on the other hand, had predominantly a listening public,
dependent upon him and him alone for the pace of their reception of his work. They were unable to stop and muse, unable to

hurry on, if they wished. The only manner whereby a pace in common could be achieved was by intense involvement of the audience, by immediacy of portrayal. Forcing them to visualize, depicting for them individuals with distinctive characteristics, making them identify with the hero in his agonized self-revelations, and drawing them into the dialogue through suspense, ensured audience-participation to a high degree. While the modern reader in the course of reading establishes a relationship between himself and the work before him by himself, the medieval audience needed an intermediary, an extra link before they could relate to the work. They needed the poet/reciter himself. He would be guide and commentator for them through the style of his delivery and the accompanying gestures. Again the type of composition on which Wolfram relies in the remodelling here of Chrestien's episode takes cognizance of this requirement. Certainly three parts of Book IX, the introduction, the Kyôt-passage and the great dialogue itself give scope to the histrionic talents of a poet/reciter. Also the elements of drama are clearly discernible in the dialogue-structure of the first literary excursus and of the target-scene. - Wolfram indeed coped brilliantly, with matchless expertise, with the tasks he had set himself, with the portrayal of a new and fundamentally different hero and with the exploration of the meaning of faith within the context of Christianity.

V. Free Composition - Motivating the New Narrative

1. The Parents' Story

Chrestien's romance begins with the boyhood of his hero, a hero
who was to become in the course of the poet's telling the tale,
if not type-cast, at least much restricted in individualization,
when compared with his literary off-shoot, the German Parzival.
Chrestien's plan may have been to subordinate the characterization of his hero to the epic narration of events.[1] Introducing
the work he calls it the story of the Grail - "ce est li contes
del Graal" (1.66), and not the story of Perceval. Slight as this
pointer to the poet's conceptual approach to his material, and
to his expectations of its realization, may be, it nevertheless
becomes a telling one when compared with his adaptor's introduction to his version. Wolfram's declared interest is centred upon
the new theme which he has given Chrestien's story, upon the
principle of "triuwe" (4.9/10) and upon the hero (4.19), whose
career will exemplify its paramount importance in human life.
The hero, in the course of Wolfram's revision of the narrative,
will become the instrument whereby the significance of this new
theme is demonstrated to the audience. The hero therefore, his
personality, his destiny, will occupy the centre of the stage.
Events as they befall him will be seen as related to him. Lives
which run parallel to his, Gâwân's, Anfortas's, Laehelîn's and
Feirefîz's, will comment on him, on his character and on his fate.
His response to his quest, to the fact that there is and must be
a quest, and his growing awareness of the nature of this quest
will be analyzed and commented upon. His character in his reactions will show itself as being of a many-layered and many-
faceted complexity, despite his mono-linear drive, or perhaps
even because of it, an elaboration as against the poet's source
which is displayed in its most concentrated form in Book IX.
As the figure of the hero is thus kept in the poetic focus

---

1 A somewhat similar view is expressed by Stefan Hofer, Chrétien
  de Troyes. Leben und Werke des altfranzösischen Epikers, Graz
  - Cologne, 1954, pp. 214-222.

throughout, is not even lost sight of in the long and fully
detailed series of episodes which makes up the portrayal of
Gâwân's career, the poet's emphasis on it is self-evident.
To account for the motivation of the hero's behaviour, actions,
and destiny, as far as poetically possible, must have presented
itself as an essential and challenging need to the poet from the
moment he realized the intricacies and implications of the character as he was planning it, and had already partly projected
it. It is likely that this moment occurred after the composition
of Books III, IV, V and VI.[2] At any rate, however large or small
a portion of Chrestien's work Wolfram had already adapted, it
would seem that he had indeed begun by translating and recasting
'Li Contes del Graal' and then at some stage of this process had
turned to the composition of Books I and II. So Books I and II
were prompted by hindsight as well as foresight.

The obvious means for additional character-portrayal of the hero
was to extend description backwards, into his ancestry, his
parents, to the circumstances relating to them antecedent to his
birth, and to that birth itself. All this could then retrospectively explain the hero's character further and could also ultimately show itself as having been predictive of his fate and
mission. In order to achieve this extension of character description, the mere story of the hero's parents would have been enough.
Yet Wolfram goes further still, further backwards in time, and
adds an account of the father's life before his marriage to the
hero's mother, of the beginning of his adult, independent life,
and of an earlier marriage. The ultimate effect on the total
narrative of these additions to the received material, additions
which chronologically seek out the past, is far-reaching and
fundamental. They affect the whole of the biography of the hero
and radically transform the meanings implied in the story as
told by Chrestien. They lift the Parzival-story on to a level

---

2 Vid. p. 78.

never envisaged by the French author and give it an interpretation that most certainly can never have been part of his plan.
For none of this did Wolfram have even the barest of suggestions
by Chrestien beyond the basic and momentum-giving idea that there
could be a fully developed story of the hero's parents. Information about the parents in 'Li Contes del Graal' is highly condensed and given by the hero's mother in a single speech, not in an
independent authorial account as in the German work. This speech
comprises just over eighty lines and explains to the boy Perceval
the tragic world which his mother inhabits:[3] Following his
father's crippling injury the family fell into poverty. During
a period of decline and chaos after the king's death they fled
like many others and took refuge in their manor in the forest.
At the time of their flight Perceval was an infant still, and
no more than two years old. His two elder brothers remained in
the forest until it was time for them to seek their fortune. They
went out in pursuit of chivalry and almost immediately after their
accolade were both slain in combat. When their bodies were found,
it was discovered that birds had pecked out the eyes of the elder.
The grief-stricken father soon died, leaving his widow, whose own
family had perished, in misery and loneliness. Other details
about the hero's family which are revealed later in the narrative,
such as the existence of a cousin and two uncles, add nothing to
the story of his parents. There is no mention of the parents'
marriage, or of the father's life before that marriage. Not a
single one of the leading motifs as they appear here in the
mother's speech, is put to use in Books I and II. Those which
Wolfram might have taken up and elaborated, and which he could
have extended into the past, as for example the father's lingering sickness, their poverty due to his infirmity, the misfortune
that had befallen the whole country, and the existence of two
elder brothers, all these he drops.

---

3 lls. 407-488.

Neither do Books I and II bear the imprint of any striking
influence by the 'Bliocadran Prologue', if indeed Wolfram had
any knowledge of it. This eight hundred verse prologue extant
in two manuscripts of the thirteenth century which also contain
'Li Contes del Graal', tells the story of the hero's parents in
extenso. It is based in part on the ingredients of Chrestien's
narrative, yet alters some of these decisively. It may have
been composed before 1212, so that Wolfram might have known
it.[4] Its links with Chrestien's work are obvious, while with
Wolfram's work they would appear to be extraordinarily tenuous.
- Bliocadran, the sole survivor of twelve brothers, is prevented
from tourneying by his wife and friends. However, two years later, while his wife is expecting their first child, the news of
a particularly spectacular tournament proves irresistible, and
he leaves to join it. He comes to be mortally wounded and dies
within two days of the fatal encounter. Three days after his
departure for the tournament his wife gives birth to a son. She
sends a messenger to him, but he no longer finds him alive.
Bliocadran's death is at first concealed from his wife. Finally,
after elaborate arrangements an abbot breaks the news to her in
a carefully prepared speech. She is deeply distressed and mourns
her husband for a long time.

This point of the story represents approximately the half-way
mark of the fragmentary prologue. It marks off the section on
which Wolfram could have based himself at least for Book II, yet
it bears no resemblance to it in its major aspects. The author
does not portray how the marriage between the hero's parents is
contracted, whereas Wolfram does. Bliocadran dies in a tournament, while Gahmuret is killed on the battlefield in the Middle
East. His son is born <u>before</u> the message of his death reaches

---

4   Lenora D. Wolfgang, Bliocadran. A Prologue to the 'Perceval'
    of Chrétien de Troyes. Editions and Critical Study, Beihefte
    zur Zeitschrift für Romanische Philologie, 150, Tübingen,
    1976, pp. VII and 36.

his wife. In Wolfram, on the other hand, the hero is born <u>after</u>
his mother has been told of her husband's death. Both widows
grieve, but in Wolfram's version the hero's mother experiences
the news of death as so shattering a blow that both her life
and that of the unborn babe come to be threatened. The list of
differences between the two, between the 'Bliocadran Prologue'
and Book II, could clearly be prolonged, but these are perhaps
the most striking ones.

The remainder of the fragment shows close parallels with Chrestien's narrative. The author retells and elaborates story-elements of the beginning of Chrestien's romance. - In the Spring
following the disaster Bliocadran's widow decides to go and
live in the waste forest. She will bring up her only son in
isolation from the world and ignorance of chivalry. She does
not wish him to die in the manner of his father and his father's
brothers. She takes some of her people with her and they live
in the forest for many years. Her son learns to ride and use
the javelin, but remains a simpleton. She gives him some instruction warning him that men clad in metal are devils. Should he
ever see such men he is to cross himself, run away, and say his
creed. He promises to do this. Next morning he goes out hunting,
on his return he gives no details of his experiences. - This is
where the fragment breaks off. The series of motifs employed
here is found also in Chrestien. The mother's notion of rearing
the boy in isolation from the world and keeping knowledge of
soldiering from him, their life in the wilderness, the son's
naivety beyond his years, and the mother's attempt to give him
instruction are all features present already in Chrestien's narrative. Wolfram re-uses them for Book III, but they have no strict
relevance to the construction of his Books I and II.

Altogether there are three points of description only in the
fragment which may suggest possible contact between the 'Bliocadran Prologue' and Book II: the restlessness which characterizes the hero's father, the indication that Bliocadran's son is

an only son, and the timing of the mother's journey into the
wilderness <u>after</u> her husband's death.[5] Both Wolfram's version
of the parents' story and that found in the French fragment

---

5 Lenora D. Wolfgang, op.cit., makes much of the feature of
restlessness in Bliocadran and Gahmuret and concludes that
Wolfram based the delineation of Gahmuret's character on
Bliocadran. Discussing the two figures she says: "These
characters are independent of Chrétien, but are they independent of each other? Both illustrate a critique of worldly
chivalry. ... It is significant that Wolfram did not choose
to portray a sympathetic or tragic father in the manner of
Chrétien, but a compulsive knight in the manner of Bliocadran.
It may be that the Belakane episode was invented in order
to use Feirefiz later in the romance, but to show Gahmuret
repeating his folly would be absurd except as a critique of
the compulsive knight, i.e. except as illustrative of narrative theme. Both Bliocadran and Gahmuret die in mid-career and
cause great grief. ... My contention is that Wolfram was not
completely free to invent his character. He was attracted to
the possibilities suggested by the Bliocadran, a portrait of
a compulsive knight as yet unattached to the high purpose of
Arthurian knighthood and unacquainted with the companions of
the Grail. Gahmuret, invented after the model of a Bliocadran,
could not be a better contrast to his son, the loyal one of
loving devotion." (p. 37). Joachim Bumke too maintains that
there is considerable likelihood that Wolfram knew the French
fragment. He points to four parallels between the 'Bliocadran
Prologue' and Wolfram's version which are at variance with
Chrestien's account: "(1) Parzivals Vater fällt im Kampf, (2)
vor der Geburt seines Sohnes, (3) der sein einziger ist; (4)
erst nach seinem Tod zieht die Witwe in die Einöde..." (Wolfram von Eschenbach, op.cit., p. 42). Points one and two are
arguable. The hero's father is indeed killed in combat in
both versions, but Bliocadran dies from injuries he received
in a tournament, while Gahmuret falls on the field of battle.
Whether Bliocadran died before or after the birth of his son,
is not certain. The time references in the fragment do not
allow of any definitive conclusion. On his way to the tournament he lodges at a nearby castle for one night (lls. 161-170).
Then the tournament follows and he dies two days later (1.236).
Three days after his departure for the tournament his wife
had given birth to a son (lls.244-252). Birth and death could
have occurred on the same day. Mary A. Rachbauer also believes
that Wolfram knew and used the 'Bliocadran Prologue (op. cit.,
pp. VIII, 8, 13, 87, 253, 255, 257). Jean Fourquet, on the
other hand, comes to the conclusion that he did not know it
(Wolfram d'Eschenbach et le Conte del Graal, pp. 105-116).
R. S. Loomis, Arthurian Tradition and Chrétien de Troyes, New
York, 1949, pp. 347-355, and Otto Springer, Wolfram's Parzival,
in: Arthurian Literature in the Middle Ages. A Collaborative

tally here, and both diverge from Chrestien's description. In
Chrestien's work the father is briefly pictured as a figure of
pathos, leading a life of enforced passivity, he has three sons,
and the whole family are said to have fled together to the forest
before his death.

Wolfram may indeed have known the 'Bliocadran Prologue', but if
he did, he made such negligible use of it that its importance as
source-material may be discounted. In the composition of Books I
and II he was on his own. The assignment which he thus took on
here was very different from the task he set himself with Book
IX. There he had before him the segment of a plot provided by
Chrestien, the outlines of a narrative unit. He had the guidelines of a set action. Here he had nothing, no plot, no details,
only the leading idea, the suggestion of a story of the hero's
parents. Its tight summary in Chrestien satisfied him no more
than the enlargement in the 'Bliocadran Prologue', if he knew
it, and he struck out on his own. No doubt he plucked hints,
followed leads, and took cues, consciously, subconsciously, from
other works of literature and from the reality he knew, but in
all other respects Books I and II are free composition, as free
as literary composition can ever be said to be.[6]

Book II, concerned with the personalities of the hero's parents,
with the manner in which they contract their marriage, and with
the hero's birth, acts as part-explanation of the hero himself
and in part typifies his quest. Book I devoted to the father's
activities and a first marriage helps to place the events of

History, ed. by Roger Sherman Loomis, Oxford, 1959; pp. 218-
250; here p. 225, suggest a common source for the 'Bliocadran
Prologue' and Wolfram's version. For a further account of
scholarly opinions on the problem of Wolfram's knowledge or
ignorance of the 'Bliocadran Prologue' vid. Joachim Bumke,
Die Wolfram von Eschenbach Forschung, pp. 46, 201ff., 206 and
236.

6   Friedrich Panzer, Gahmuret. Quellenstudien zu Wolframs Parzival, Sb. der Heidelberger Akad. der Wissenschaften, philos.-
histor. Kl., Jg. 1939/40, Abh. 1, Heidelberg, 1940, analyzes
the suggestions which Wolfram may have received from other

Book II into precise focus and adds further dimensions of meaning to the Parzival-story. The analysis of Wolfram's use of factual geography and of his fusion of it with a geography of fiction has already shown part of the particular significance of this technique of focussing by contrast and of achieving new implications through the addition of new story-elements in relation to Gahmuret and to Book I. Gahmuret's restless travelling draws in the whole of the known world and also fabulous countries. The type of itinerary which the poet attributes to Gahmuret characterizes that figure, but it is also a means whereby he opens out the narrative at its very beginning and unfurls an enormous canvas for his main story. It helps to lend world-wide relevance to the hero's quest. Through it the allegory of the hero's search will be felt to reach out to all parts of the earth as known to man, and even beyond it. Its application has no limits. The description of Gahmuret's early travels, prior to the marriage with the hero's mother, thus affects the meaning and impact of the whole work. The same may be said of the poet's creation of the figure of Feirefîz in Book I. Here too, long-range planning seems to have been at work, for the introduction of that figure does not take proper effect until Book XV, until very nearly the end of the narrative. A vague hint of its special and ultimate function is given by the poet already in Book I, in his fleeting description of Feirefîz's appearance. The baby born to Belakâne is no ordinary half-caste. He is black, and has white marks, and his hair too is black and white (57.15-28). God has created an exception in him - "an dem got wunders wart enein" (57.17) -; Feirefîz will not fit into the category of other human beings as portrayed by Wolfram. He will have to be measured by a different yeardstick. Realistically described, yet put to allegorical use, interpreted as a serious figure by the author as well as by other characters in the work, yet given pronounced burlesque treatment at the same time, Feirefîz as a curiously hybrid creation will stand apart.[7]

---

works of literature and from contemporary reality.

7 A brief account of the portrayal of Saracens in the whole of

His importance is considerable, and so is by extension the significance of the marriage of his parents. The union of the hero's
father with a pagan queen, which precedes his Christian marriage
with the hero's mother, places a legitimate, elder, and pagan
brother alongside the hero. With this marriage between Christian
and infidel and its half-caste offspring the poet links the
world of Christendom to which his hero belongs, with the civilization of Outremer. The connection which he achieves in this way
with the world of heathendom broadens the narrative base at the
very moment of its being established, at the story's beginning,
just as the account of Gahmuret's early travels does. The breadth
of this base will make itself felt forcibly once again later on,
when the two brothers meet in allegorical combat. Yet the link
accomplishes still more. It does not simply secure the position
of the Parzival-story further in the context of universality,
for the poet charges it with innuendoes of a highly topical relevance for his contemporaries.

The hero's half-brother, like the hero, is of irreproachable
lineage. His mother, like the hero's, is a noblewoman and queen
in her own right. Both Christian hero and infidel half-brother
are conceived in wedlock. Both are legitimate and are of the same
patrilinear descent. Wolfram scrupulously dispels all possible
doubt that could be cast on their common paternity. Belakâne
when describing her predicament to Gahmuret, before their marriage, insists that she still has her maidenhead - "ih enwart
nie wîp decheines man" (28.9). Herzeloyde loses hers to Gahmuret
during their wedding-night - "frou Herzeloyd diu künegîn/ir
magettuom dâ âne wart", (100.14/15). Both Christian hero and
infidel half-brother have a father in common. They share a
heritage and may legitimately lay claim to it. With merely three
descriptive features - the identical social position of each

Wolfram's work is to be found in Siegfried Stein, Die Ungläubigen in der mittelhochdeutschen Literatur von 1050 bis 1250,
Diss. Heidelberg, 1933. (Reprint WBG, Darmstadt 1963; Libelli,
vol. 108), pp. 62-74.

mother, the conception of the children in wedlock, and the common
father - Wolfram defines a certain measure of equality between
Parzival and Feirefîz, between Christian and non-believer. The
plea for tolerance which lies in this equality is unmistakable.
The fact that he makes it not merely in allegorical terms, but
on the basis of the realistic portrayal of a situation that
cannot have been uncommon during the period of the crusades,
would give that plea more weight than it would otherwise have
had. A first marriage with a highborn woman, a non-believer, in
Outremer, a legitimate son born of that union, return to Europe
and to the realities of a second and Christian marriage entail-
ing territorial tenure - these must have been the ingredients
of experience of many a crusader. The lesson of tolerance, like
any lesson, was more easily learnt through personal involvement
invited by the realistic depiction of familiar cirumstances than
by any form of abstraction. Wolfram's conviction of the particular effectiveness of this type of descriptive technique manifests
itself here as it did in his extension of Book IX. In any one of
his audiences there would have been someone who had come into
contact with, or had at least heard of, the situation as told in
Book I and then continued in Book II.

To make a plea for tolerance at that time, and to be making it
in this particular form, was an act of intellectual independence
and moral courage. For while Wolfram was composing Book I, and
making plans for the delineation of Feirefîz and its future use,
the forces of _intolerance_ were gathering momentum, or had already
made their official mark. In 1215 at the Fourth Lateran Council
it was declared that both Saracens and Jews were to dress differently from Christians in future. Non-believers were ordered
to distinguish themselves from believers in dress, lest unawares
there might be carnal intercourse between them. The Fourth Lateran Council was one of the most important ecclesiastical as-
semblies of the Middle Ages, not only because many influential
decisions were passed in addition to the one legislating for the
segregation of non-Christians, but because the views and atti-

tudes embodied in these decisions gained wide currency, and the
decisions themselves came to be widely enforceable. The Council,
which had been called by Pope Innocent III, had a large number
of participants. It was attended by eight hundred abbots and
more than four hundred bishops, among other ecclesiastics. Many
crowned heads sent their representatives, as for example the
Byzantine emperor, the Emperor Frederick II, and the kings of
England, France, Hungary and Jerusalem. The Eastern patriarchs
attended as well. The social rejection of the non-believer thus
had every chance of becoming widespread and of affecting the
daily life of many. The decision to order Saracens and Jews to
dress differently from Christians was designed to prevent precisely such unions as Wolfram depicts in the marriage of Gahmuret and Belakâne.[8] As in the case of his portrayal of Sigûne
as an anchoress he draws into the narrative a highly topical
subject, the relation between Christian and non-believer, the
relation between Christian faith and civilization and their non-
Christian counterparts. However, while with his treatment of the
figure of Sigûne he remains with his interpretation within the
mainstream of approved opinion, here, with Gahmuret's first
marriage and the introduction of Feirefîz he takes an independent stand and distances himself from the authoritative view as
it was beginning to form itself, or had already been proclaimed.
Far from modifying this stand in the course of composition he
consolidates it later, remaining true to his convictions, his
vision, and his original poetic plan. The distinctive statement
of it to which Book I is the prelude and for which it laid the
basis, comes in the encounter between the two brothers.

---

8 Hasting's Encyclopaedia of Religion and Ethics, vol. 4; entry:
   Councils and Synods (Christian), p. 195ff.; H.J. Schroeder,
   Disciplinary Decrees of the General Councils. Text, Transla-
   tion, and Commentary, London, 1937, pp. 236-296; L. Elliott
   Binns, Innocent III, London, 1931, chapter VIII: The Lateran
   Council, pp. 164-184; Walter Ullmann, A Short History of the
   Papacy in the Middle Ages, London, 1972 (University Paperback,
   1974), p. 221ff.; Helene Tillmann, Pope Innocent III, Europe
   in the Middle Ages, Selected Studies, 12, Amsterdam/New York/
   Oxford 1980, passim.

Christian hero and non-Christian half-brother meet after the
hero's joust with Gâwân (678.18-680.30; 688.4-690.15), and
after superbia in him has been shown to have given way to humilitas (732.1-733.30). The brothers meet by chance and fight
without being aware of their respective identities. Before the
joust begins Wolfram underlines the difficulties the combat
will hold for the hero. All previous fighting experience was
child's play compared with what is to come now: "swaz sîn hant
ie gestreit, daz was mit kinden her getân" (734.18/19). He will
meet an opponent unsurpassed in martial skills: "in bestêt ob
allem strîte ein vogt" (734.30). The combat makes formidable
demands upon his fighting expertise; he finds himself in the
most perilous situation he has ever known - "in der groesten
nôt dier ie gewan" (740.22). However, his adversary too is more
hard pressed than ever before. He cannot manage to unhorse his
enemy, a failure which is new to him (739.7-10). The poet's
comments on the brothers' fighting ability are framed in such
a way as to suggest an even balance between them. This equality
between Christian hero and non-Christian half-brother is defined
in an even more pronounced manner by references to their close
kinship. Strangers according to appearances, yet intimates in
reality, their very hearts are interchangeable: "ieweder des
andern herze truoc:/ir vremde was heinlîch genuoc" (738.9/10).
They are the sons of one and the same father: "si wârn doch
bêde eins mannes kint" (740.5), and are one life and one blood
- "ein verch und ein bluot" (740.3). They are indeed one, as
brothers always are one flesh: "si wârn doch bêde niht wan ein./
mîn bruodr und ich daz ist ein lîp" (740.28/29). The all important quality of "triuwe" characterizes them both: "dâ streit der
triwen lûterheit:/grôz triwe aldâ mit triwen streit" (741.21/22).
The invitation to the audience to assess the two protagonists
in this fight as equals could hardly be more urgently or more
eloquently put.

Yet although the blood-relationship between them is thus stressed
heavily, they are nevertheless not presented in this scene pri-

marily as the two brothers Parzival and Feirefîz. Their individuality is deliberately blurred in the description for the sake
of the allegorical dimension of this encounter. Feirefîz is not
named until its conclusion, when he himself reveals his identity
(745.28). For the remainder the poet refers to him predominantly
as "the infidel" - "der heiden".[9] The hero is mentioned by name
during the fight eight times,[10] yet he is also described ten
times as "the baptized one" - "der getoufte".[11] So the contest
takes place between "der getoufte" and "der heiden", between Christian and non-Christian, between a representative of the Christian
faith and that of another religion.

The contest does not run its normal course. It does not end in
the usual manner. Neither of the figures is shown in the act of
having won. The poet consciously avoids the depiction of victory
and defeat. God Himself intervenes in the struggle and causes
the hero's sword to splinter (744.10-18). This leaves the hero
at the mercy of his opponent, who in his magnanimity, however,
spares his life (747.1-18).[12]

---

9   735.11; 736.4; 738.11; 739.7 and 23; 740.7, 13, 18 and 23;
     741.1; 742.1 and 16; 743.1; 744.8, 11, 20 and 25; 745.13
     and 25.

10   734.15; 735.5; 737.13; 740.25; 742.27; 743.14; 744.2 and 15.

11   738.12; 739.23 and 27; 740.14; 741.1 and 26; 742.16; 743.9
     and 23; 745.13.

12   The conception and structure of this scene and the narrative
     technique employed for its description show some striking
     parallels with the portrayal of the Parzival/Gâwân encounter.
     Both fights are conceived as allegorical duels. Both break
     off through external intervention. In both descriptions the
     poet insists on the equal standing of the protagonists and
     stresses their closeness to one another. In neither of them
     does he depict a final triumph, but leaves the scene open-
     ended instead.
     The joust with Feirefîz is the last of the hero's three
     momentous encounters with men who are linked with him in
     blood relationship. Each one is charged with special meanings;
     each in its own way demonstrates man's dependance on Grace.
     The fight with Ithêr ends catastrophically with murder, which
     brands the hero with a stigma that he bears for the better
     part of his career. The duel with Gâwân very nearly takes the

This allegorical encounter between Christian hero and non-Christian half-brother, as freely invented by the poet as the figure of that half-brother itself, can only be interpreted as an unambiguous plea for tolerance. The dominant features of the description are trained unequivocally in this direction. The poet's insistence by various means on the equal standing of the two brothers, his particular emphasis of the blood-bond between them and his persistent use of the contrasting designations Christian/non-Christian, all point this way. So does his avoidance of the portrayal of conqueror and vanquished. With such delineation the poet urges his listeners to give an alien civilization with an alien belief its due, to acknowledge its positive qualities and to respect them, and to consider the possibility, indeed to grasp the rationality, of a conciliatory attitude. Feirefîz's subsequent conversion undoes nothing of all this. It is a declaration on the part of the poet that the Christian faith is and remains the premier one, an affirmation fully to be expected and one which in no way undermines the position which he takes up here. The views and sentiments which he so powerfully expresses here to

---

same course, but is ended by chance intervention. The combat with Feirefîz breaks off through the merciful intervention of God Himself. A distinct progression connects the three scenes. Cf. Wolfgang Harms, Der Kampf mit dem Freund oder Verwandten, p. 167: "Auf dem an potentiell tragischen Situationen des Scheins reichen Weg Parzivals, der sich darin vom Weg eines Artusritters abhebt, ist das Erkennen der Verwandten-"triuwe", an der die Analogie zu der Verwandtschaft der Menschen untereinander in Gott mitzuverstehen ist, nicht aus menschlicher Kraft allein möglich, sondern nur durch göttliche Gnade. ... Dem Erkennen Gawans folgte zunächst nur die Klage, daß er, Parzival, im Begriff war, die Ither-Tat zu wiederholen, und für das weitere Geschehen um Parzival blieb die Verwandtschaft zu Gawan nur eins unter mehreren Motiven. Jetzt (i.e. after the fight with Feirefîz) ist das Erkennen Schluß eines großen, den ganzen Weg Parzivals umfassenden Zusammenhangs: dem Mord an Ither folgt, von der bestürzenden Erkenntnis nach dem Kampf mit Gawan vorbereitet, die gnädige Bewahrung vor neuem Verwandtenmord und zugleich die demütige Einsicht Parzivals, auf Gottes Gnade angewiesen zu sein."

his audience in a vividly projected scene had formed themselves
already in the poet's mind during the composition of Book I.
His description of the marriage between the hero's father and
a non-Christian woman alone could bear witness to this. However,
the appearance of Feirefîz at this point of the narrative does
so too. The character of Feirefîz cannot have been introduced
into Book I for any other reason but to serve ultimately as a
vehicle for the distinct formulation of these convictions and
feelings. As the poet makes no extensive use of the figure of
Feirefîz in Book I, but merely hints at its significance, it
is obvious that he was planning for a future function of this
figure in which a full explanation of this significance would
be given.

The first marriage of the hero's father and the child of that
union are thus employed by the poet to transmit a message of
tolerance and understanding, a message which qualifies the hero's
mission and enlarges its scope. It adds a further dimension to
his quest and links it with the ideological conflict which dominated the contemporary reality of the poet and his audiences.
Immensely important as these effects of Book I are where the
main story is concerned, its repercussions do not end here. The
portrayal of the first marriage, in particular the manner in
which it is contracted typifies the second, and through this,
through the clear-cut character of the second marriage thus won,
the hero's role within society comes to be circumscribed. Taken
together Books I and II are the story of Gahmuret, but they are
also, and predominantly so, the story of two marriages.[13]

---

13 Petrus W. Tax, Gahmuret zwischen Äneas und Parzival. Zur
    Struktur der Vorgeschichte von Wolframs 'Parzival', Zeit-
    schrift f. dtsch. Philologie, 92 (1973), 24-37, has consi-
    dered the two stories of marriage with Belakâne and marriage
    with Herzeloyde from the viewpoint of narrative structure.
    He suggests that Gahmuret's repeat action in Books I and II,
    one marriage after another, foreshadows the structure of the
    hero's quest, his two journeys to the Grail castle.
    Siegfried Richard Christoph in his dissertation, Wolfram von
    Eschenbach's Couples, Amsterdamer Publikationen zur Sprache
    und Literatur, 44, Amsterdam, 1981, devotes two chapters to

In this sequence of two marriages, the marriage-patterns differ, and in their difference comment upon one another, the first marriage upon the second and vice versa. Once again, as for many other levels and components of his narrative, the poet here applies the chiaroscuro technique which is so striking a characteristic of his craftsmanship. The contrast in the nature of the two marriage-patterns gives each its distinctive profile. While the marriage with Belakâne bears the decided marks of a love-match, that with Herzeloyde is shown predominantly as a union prompted by rational considerations. Yet although there is a palpable difference in the content of the two marriages, the framework in which they are conceived and presented is the same. Both marriages are given the character of dynastic arrangements. Both are illustrations of a form of aristocratic marriage that was accepted, practised, and often pursued as policy in contemporary society. That a champion fighter of gentle birth with little prospect of inheritance should succeed to vast estates and property through marriage, as here, was by no means uncommon. Power and riches for the exceptional male through marriage is not a theme introduced from fiction, but taken from reality. Territories that had through lack of legitimate sons, or through widowhood, descended to a woman, and which were thus in need of military protection and feudal leadership, might be offered to a man of outstanding soldierly proficiency as here. The contract, i.e. the conveyance of property to the chosen male and his consequential elevation to the position of liegelord, would be effected through marriage. So it is possible to recognize a blueprint in the leading practical details of both Gahmuret's marital alliances, a framework that corresponds closely to a type of marriage of which the noble families of medieval Europe approved and which they accepted as nothing out of the ordinary.[14] The basic fea-

Gahmuret's two marriages (pp. 33-62) concentrating on Wolfram's treatment of love.

14 Herbert Ernst Wiegand, Studien zur Minne und Ehe in Wolframs Parzival und Hartmanns Artusepik, Quellen und Forschungen

tures in which both marriages tally give them an outward congruence. Yet the respective chains of development which lead
to each marriage, and the differing manner in which each comes
to be contracted, make an inward contrast apparent.[15]

The poet's interest in the subject of marriage, the importance
which he attached to it, his awareness of its permutations, and
possibly even of its problems, is vouchsafed by the fact that he
introduces into the narrative fourteen betrothals and marriage-

zur Sprach- und Kulturgeschichte der germanischen Völker,
Neue Folge, 49 (173), Berlin/New York, 1972, gives numerous
examples of feudal marriages in which the woman represents
the instrument whereby power and riches were transferred
to the male (pp. 14-15). Cf. also Volker Mertens, Laudine.
Soziale Problematik im 'Iwein' Hartmanns von Aue, Beihefte
zur Zeitschrift für deutsche Philologie, 3, Berlin, 1978,
p. 22f.

15 The present changes in the pattern of marriage and the
changes in Family Law have sparked off innumerable descriptions and discussions of marriage in print. The current
interest in the subject has brought marriage in the middle
centuries into focus also. Publications to be mentioned under
this head are R.H. Helmholz, Marriage Litigation in Medieval
England, Cambridge Studies in English Legal History, ed. by
D.E.C. Yale, Cambridge, 1974; Georges Duby, Medieval Marriage. Two Models from Twelfth-Century France. (Translated
by Elborg Forster), The Johns Hopkins Symposia in Comparative History, 11, Baltimore and London, 1978; Love and
Marriage in the Twelfth Century, edited by Willy Van Hoecke
and Andries Welkenhuysen, Mediaevalia Lovaniensia, Series 1/
Studia VIII, Leuven/Louvain, 1981; Marriage in the Middle
Ages, Viator. Medieval and Renaissance Studies, vol. 4, 1973
pp. 413-501, containing: John Leyerle, Introduction. The
Substance of this Panel, pp. 413-418; John T. Noonan, Jr.,
Power to Choose, pp. 419-434; Henry Ansgar Kelly, Clandes-
tine Marriage and Chaucer's 'Troilus', pp. 435-457; Ann S.
Haskell, The Paston Women on Marriage in Fifteenth-Century
England, pp. 459-471; Roberta Frank, Marriage in Twelfth- and
Thirteenth-Century Iceland, pp. 473-484; Vern L. Bullough,
Medieval Medical and Scientific Views of Women, pp. 485-501.
Further essays concerned with the subject under discussion
are: David Herlihy, Land, Family and Women in Continental
Europe. 701-1200, Traditio, 18 (1962), 89-120 and The Me-
dieval Marriage Market, Medieval and Renaissance Studies, 6
(1976), 3-27; Michael M. Sheehan, C.S.B., Choice of Marriage
Partner in the Middle Ages: Development and Mode of Applica-
tion of a Theory of Marriage, Studies in Medieval and Re-

arrangements, as against the French text which has none.[16]
Eight of these he mentions in passing, giving brief detail of
some of them,[17] two he treats at greater length,[18] but to
four he gives considerable prominence. This group of four comprises the marriage between the hero and Condwîrâmûrs, that
between the secondary hero and Orgelûse, and the two marriages
of Gahmuret. The marriage with Belakâne opens the series of
these leading four alliances.

When Gahmuret is presented to Belakâne she falls in love at
first sight. The moment she sees him she is in love, captivated
by his handsome looks. Although she had been devoted to her
first suitor (26.30-27.3), the encounter with Gahmuret is a new
love-experience for her. Never before had her heart opened in
this manner:

> 23.22 der küneginne rîche
> ir ougen fuogten hôhen pîn,
> dô si gesach den Anschevîn.
> der was sô minneclîche gevar,
> daz er entslôz ir herze gar,
> ez waere ir liep oder leit:
> daz beslôz dâ vor ir wîpheit.

---

naissance History, 11 (1978), 3-33; and Constance B. Bouchard, Consanguinity and Noble Marriages in the Tenth and
Eleventh Centuries, Speculum, 56 (1981), 268-287.

16 While there may be no descriptions of weddings in 'Li Contes
del Graal' there are detailed analyses of marriage and much
commentary on it in Chrestien's other works. Cf. the recent
assessment of his treatment of marriage by Peter S. Noble,
Love and Marriage in Chrétien de Troyes, Cardiff, 1982.

17 These are the marriages between the Duke of Brabant and the
Princess of Gascony, Lämbekîn and Alîze (67.23-28 and 89.7-
20), between Gurzgrî, the third son of Gurnemanz and Mahaute,
sister to Schôette and thus Parzival's great-aunt (178.15-26),
between Clâmidê and Cunnewâre, sister to Orilus and Laehelîn
(326.30-327.30), between Castis, King of Wâleis and Norgâls,
and Herzeloyde (494.15-30), between Gramoflanz and Itonjê,
one of Gâwân's sisters (729.27-30), between Lischoys and
Cundrîe, another sister of Gâwân (730.1-5), between Flôrant
and Sangîve, Gâwân's mother and sister of King Arthur (730.6-
10), and between Loherangrîn, one of Parzival's sons, and
the Princess of Brabant (824.1-826.28).

Gahmuret, on the other hand, who finds the dark-skinned women unattractive (20.4-6; 20.19-26), does not react to the negro-queen in a similar fashion. It needs the revelation of her nature with its keynotes of warmth, compassion and capacity for suffering to engage his emotions. Once he has perceived the gentleness which illuminates her account of her suitor's death and of her involvement in it, he too comes to be captivated. The qualities of generosity and candour which govern this account and the troubled self-accusation which forms its core (26.9-28.8) make him forget that she is a non-believer. Her loving nature ("triuwe"), her sweetness ("wîplîcher sin") and her unpretentiousness ("kiusche") win him:

> 28.10 Gahmureten dûhte sân,
> swie si waere ein heidenin,
> mit triwen wîplîcher sin
> in wîbes herze nie geslouf.
> ir kiusche was ein reiner touf,
> und ouch der regen der sie begôz,
> der wâc der von ir ougen flôz ...

Now they are both in love - "aldâ wart undr in beiden/ein vil getriulîchiu ger:/si sach dar, und er sach her" (29.6-8) - and they have fallen in love with one another very nearly simultaneously. The reciprocity of the sentiment which links them is underlined by the poet: "des herze truoc ir minnen last./daz selbe ouch ir von im geschach" (34.16/17). Gahmuret begins to long for her (35.2-4 and 35.20-25). Their union then follows swiftly, after the fighting has ceased and the siege has been raised. The wedding-night precedes the proclamation of their marriage (44.18-30 and 45.20-28). After this Gahmuret is accepted as liegelord and enfeoffs his vassals (51.27ff.).[19] Love of Belakâne continues to dominate Gahmuret's thoughts. He openly

---

18 The marriages between Meljanz and Obîe (345.27-347.18; 365.1-366.1; 396.10-397.11) and between Feirefîz and Repanse, Herzeloyde's sister (810.10ff.).

19 An analysis of Gahmuret's relationship with Belakâne and of their marriage may be found in Herbert Ernst Wiegand, op.cit., p. 245ff.

admits to his devotion to her (49.22/23) and is plunged into a
conflict between his deep love of her and his inborn need of
roaming and campaigning. The born soldier and the tender lover
in Gahmuret cannot be reconciled with one another:

> 54.17 dâ was der stolze küene man,
> unz er sich vaste senen began.
> daz er niht rîterschefte vant,
> des was sîn freude sorgen phant.
> Doch was im daz swarze wîp
> lieber dan sîn selbes lîp.

When he then gives way to the exigencies of his nature, the manner in which he leaves her underlines the love he bears her.
Unable to face her he leaves by stealth (54.27-55.12) thus con-
fronting her with a fait accompli. The parting letter which he
writes her dwells insistently on his deep emotional involvement
with her. He refers to himself as one who loves her ("Hie enbiu-
tet liep ein ander liep", 55.21), insists that his deception and
secrecy were essential in order to assuage the agony of parting
("ich pin dirre verte ein diep:/die muose ich dir durch jâmer
steln", 55.22/23) and assures her of his continued longing for
her ("und hân doch immer nâch dir pîn", 55.27). His interpretation of the strength and durability of the bond between them will
prove to be correct. Remembrance of Belakâne continues to haunt
him. Long after he has left Africa and returned to Europe, in the
midst of fighting and sport, he finds himself reminded of her and
is overcome by a yearning for her (80.30-81.4). Within the
dazzling blaze of military triumph and amid laughter and banter
among men the compulsion of this yearning returns and with deep
seriousness, courage, and sincerity he openly declares his love
and tenderness for her at length. He speaks of his misery, his
grief at having left her, his longing for her, his sense of guilt
and shame at having abandoned her, and of his boundless admiration of her:

> 90.17 ... ich muoz bî riwen sîn:
> ich sen mich nâch der künegîn.
> ich liez ze Pâtelamunt
> dâ von mir ist mîn herze wunt,
> in reiner art ein süeze wîp.

> ir werdiu kiusche mir den lîp
> nâch ir minne jâmers mant.
> ...
> mich tuot frô Belakâne
> manlîcher freuden âne:
> es ist doch vil manlich,
> swer minnen wankes schamet sich.
> ...
> die sach ich für die sunnen ane.
> ir wîplich prîs mir füeget leit:
> si ist /ein/ bukel ob der werdekeit.

Finally, when a second marriage is about to be forced on him,
he unhesitatingly asserts that he is linked to her in valid
wedlock, adding moreover that he loves her more than his very
life: "... frouwe, ich hân ein wîp:/diu ist mir lieber danne
der lîp" (94.5/6). The fact that he says this to Herzeloyde,
his prospective second marriage-partner, and also that he uses
it as a first defence against unwanted second wedlock, give
added point to the strength of the bond between himself and
Belakâne, a strength to which he so often testifies.

So the sentiment of love, genuine and deep, dominates the relationship between Gahmuret and Belakâne. Feudal union though
their marriage may be, the poet dwells emphatically on the in-
wardness of this marriage. It begins as a love-match and remains
one.

Gahmuret's second marriage with Herzeloyde, with the hero's
mother, on the other hand, will be seen to be of a totally different character. Given no less serious a treatment by the poet
than the first marriage, as an alliance of considerable consequence between a man and a woman, its aspect of seriousness
will nevertheless show itself as being of a different quality.
Herzeloyde has decided on marriage before she sets eyes on Gahmuret. The circumstances in which she finds herself compel her
to marry. In possession of the lordship over two territories she
must provide country and people with a liegelord, and ultimately
with an heir. Such would be the realistic background to her
situation here in fiction. The conveyance of property and the

installation of its overlord are to be effected through a marriage-
contract. Her two territories and her own person are on offer to
the finest champion that can be found. He is to reveal himself
by self-selection in a tournament (60.15- 7). Herzeloyde has
therefore resolved up n marriage as an obligation, out of a
sense of duty and an awareness of her social responsibility. Once
that champion has declared himself, she will marry him, regardless
of whether his personal qualities appeal to her. In total acceptance of her social role she is prepared to subordinate her personal desires to the needs of others.[20] Her conduct is stamped
by altruism, recognition of the demands of privilege, and disregard of self. Gahmuret's bearing in relation to this marriage
is initially not marked by these characteristics, but comes to
exhibit them in the end. He stumbles into her strategy. Love of
adventure, of travelling, fighting and tourneying has made him
stop in a place where there is likelihood of armed combat. (59.21-
60.8). When he then emerges as the undisputed victor and finds
himself in Herzeloyde's trap, he uses every argument at his
disposal to free himself.

The approach to this second marriage by both prospective partners
is therefore very different from the attitudes that Gahmuret and
Belakâne displayed towards their marriage. While it clearly served the public good, it was also welcomed and wanted by both. With
the greatest good fortune personal desire and public purpose)
proved to be congruent; here, in the Gahmuret/Herzeloyde combination, they are not. As regards Herzeloyde personal desire had been
discounted in any case in advance, as regards Gahmuret it is
pulling in the wrong direction, away from the projected marriage
and back to the first one. Emotional distance between the future
partners comes to stand out as a marked feature of the second
marriage when considered against the emotional closeness portrayed in the first. This distance which the poet establishes between

---

20 Herbert Ernst Wiegand, op.cit., pp. 33/34 also stresses this
    particular point.

them by the use of specific motifs and by clear self-delineation
through its juxtaposition against its opposite principle, closeness, in a parallel occurrence, is not employed by him to imply
a criticism of the second marriage, far from it. It ultimately
becomes the backdrop against which Gahmuret's move to Herzeloyde's
position is silhouetted, the move to the position of dedication
to the common good, to compliance with the demands exacted by
exceptional status, to self-denial. In recognition of the superior claims pronounced by his peers, of service, leadership,
public accountability, Gahmuret in the end subordinates personal
desire to his social role. Characteristically for Wolfram, for
his humour and his humaneness, this is not accomplished without
the help of love of a kind.

From the moment it becomes clear, already during the Vespers,
the exercises preliminary to the tournament, that Gahmuret's
fighting ability outstrips that of all other knights, Herzeloyde
goes to call on him (82.3-83.4). There is abundant evidence of
his superiority in the field over all other would-be participants
in the tournament (85.12-86.4). He has in fact wrought such havoc
among them that the tournament can no longer take place (86.21-
23). In the face of such overwhelming proof Herzeloyde claims
him in marriage. She sees her claim as an irrevocable right upon
him: "swaz mînes rehtes an iu sî,/dâ sult ir mich lâzen bî" (87.
1/2). When a counter-claim is brought by the recently widowed
Ampflîse (87.6-88.6), she decides to take her case to court:
"... lât ze rehte mînen lîp./sît hie unz ich mîn reht genem"
(88.28/29). So far Gahmuret has made no comment. It is not until
Herzeloyde stakes her claim for the second time, this time supported by a court decision and the majority opinion of her legal
counsellors, that he speaks out (94.1-4)[21]. The very first

---

21 diu volge in 94.4 would seem to have a clear legal signifi-
    cance, as in 96.6. In both cases a court of law comes to be
    involved. Once a decision has to be made whether Ampflîse's
    challenge invalidates Herzeloyde's marriage-claim, and once
    the court has to consider Gahmuret's objection. Each time
    the court finds for Herzeloyde; she has diu volge on her

defence against this new unwanted wedlock which springs to his
mind is Belakâne, his marriage to her and his love for her.
(94.5/6). To Herzeloyde's argument that a Christian marriage
supersedes the vows exchanged with a non-believer, he can find
no answer (94.11-16). On her mention of Ampflîse therefore he
switches tactics, and instead of pressing his marriage as an
impediment to a new alliance he now fastens on his long-standing
obligations to Ampflîse as the real obstacle:

> 94.21 ja diu ist mîn wâriu frouwe.
> ich brâht in Anschouwe
> ir rât und mîner zühte site:
> mir wont noch hiute ir helfe mite,
> dâ von daz mich mîn frouwe zôch,
> ... mir gap diu gehiure
> vom lande de besten stiure:
> (ich was dô ermer denne nuo)
> dâ greif ich willeclîchen zuo.

And just in case this dialectic should be found unconvincing,
Gahmuret appeals to Herzeloyde's sense of propriety. He is in
mourning, marriage should not be urged on those who are bereaved:
"mir ist mîn werder bruoder tôt./durch iwer zuht lât mich ân nôt./
kêrt minne dâ diu freude sî" (95.7-9). Herzeloyde impatiently
brushes aside all three of Gahmuret's reasons for not being able
to contract another marriage - "lât mich den lîp niht langer
zern" (95.11) - and demands a valid refutation of her claim:
"sagt an, wâ mite welt ir iuch wern?" (95.12).[22] Gahmuret then
with considerable ingenuity raises a technical objection to it
which could constitute a just cause in law. The marriage-clause
had been linked to participation in a tournament, yet no tournament had taken place, and there are many witnesses to this: "ez
wart ein turney dâ her/gesprochen: des enwart hie niht./manec

---

side. The verdict is achieved by majority vote. Cf. Matthias
Lexer under volge, "...bei- zustimmung, bes. die rechtl. bei-
abstimmung zur fassung eines urteils ..."

22 The specifically legal connotation of wern within this context was recognized already by Ernst Martin, Kommentar, on
95.12; "wern 'verteidigen' hier im juristischen Sinne 'An-
sprüche zurückweisen'".

geziuc mir des giht" (95.14-16). He asks her not to compel him
to make his defence in a court of law - "ir sult mich nôtrede
erlân" (95.22)[23] - and declares that she has no legal claim on
him - "iwer reht ist gein mir laz" (95.24). As neither will give
way, the matter is referred to court: "dô nam der ritter und diu
magt/einen rihtaere übr der frouwen klage" (95.28/29). Judgement
is then passed with a majority vote and pronounced in favour of
Herzeloyde (96.1-6). As soon as this has occurred she asserts
her rights with lightning speed and triumphantly proclaims her
ownerwhip of him: "dô sprach si 'hêr, nu sît ir mîn" (95.7).
Gahmuret bows to the judgement as he must. He shortly afterwards
declares his realization that there is no other way; he is bound
to abide by the verdict of his peers: "ich werdes trûric oder
geil,/mich behabt hie rîters urteil" (98.1/2).

So it can hardly be said that Gahmuret and Herzeloyde enter
eagerly upon matrimony, as lovers, in the manner in which Gahmuret and Belakâne did. Far from showing them as deeply engaged
emotionally with one another, the poet presents them in the roles
of plaintiff and defendant in relation to the projected marriage
between them. Gahmuret does not wish to be joined to Herzeloyde
in wedlock and vigorously tries to fend off the pressure brought
on him. He cites four obstacles that in his view stand in the way
of this marriage. His dogged resistance to it finally sends the
matter to a court of law. Herzeloyde fights the issue with equal
determination and detachment. Nothing will deflect her from having
the husband that the tournament was to have selected for her. She
readily takes her plea to court not once, but twice, utterly in-
sistent to her rights. In the end the marriage between them comes

---

23 Ernst Martin on 95.22: "nôtrede 'Zwangsrede, erzwungene Rede';
    juristischer Ausdruck: 'Verpflichtung zu gerichtlicher Ver-
    teidigung, dann diese selbst'; s. Haltaus Glossarium medii
    aevi 1428: Notrede excusatio forensis ad quam jure adigimur,
    causae dictio, defensio in jure, litis contestatio. ...
    Vid. also Matthias Lexer under "nôtrede" "... rede, die man
    notgedrungen tut, erzwungene rede bes. die rede vor gericht,
    ..."

to be decided in a court of law. Underlining in this way Herzeloyde's tenacity and Gahmuret's opposition, the poet builds up
the marriage project into a public issue. While he depicted
Gahmuret and Belakâne as seeing the union with one another as
an endorsement of their love, he portrays Gahmuret and Herzeloyde
as accepting it predominantly as a transaction. Where Herzeloyde
is concerned it is a foregone conclusion. In the case of Gahmuret
it takes on the aspect of an inevitability from which he cannot
escape and to which he submits with reluctance. Whereas the poet
thus emphasized the emotional content of the first marriage over
and above its public significance, he here shifts the weight of
his portrayal to precisely this public significance by making
no mention of emotional content and by drawing attention to its
public aspect through giving the marriage-proceedings the striking
form of a legal wrangle. Gahmuret and Herzeloyde, in the approach
to their marriage, are made to appear as primarily acknowledging
their public role. The union between them is prompted by social
considerations. Herzeloyde is motivated by her status and function
as liegelady, Gahmuret by his membership of a fraternity to whose
code of ethics, principles, and concepts of justice he must adhere
(97.25-30).

A marriage such as this, a dynastic alliance which involves conscious and deliberate self-sacrifice on both sides, must be seen
as an ideal within medieval marriage-practice. It would be an
anachronism of interpretation to try and apply to the poet's
projection of it notions of nineteenth-century sentimentality.
The marriage between the hero's parents as he portrays it, exhibits a large number of positive features when examined within
the context of marriage-custom among the European nobility during
the poet's own time. It is in the first place no cradle-marriage.
The partners are not being forced into the contract by their respective families, into a contract settled already in their
babyhood. The marriage is not contracted over a distance, but
each partner has met the other. The alliance has not been arranged, and is not being enforced, by a liegelord. Within the restric-

tions which the prospective partners have prescribed for themselves, they act as free agents, making their decisions themselves. No pressure is brought on the weaker party, the woman.
There is in the end <u>consensus</u> on both sides. As both show willingness to sacrifice personal inclination, a certain measure of
equality prevails between them. It is a marriage between two
consenting adults of Christian faith, who have set their own
rules of conduct and have of their own free will decided to abide
by them. A union of this type would not merely command the utmost
respect among the poet's audience, but would be seen as wholly
admirable, highly desirable, and as near perfect as poetic imagination could devise it. The modern reader, unlike the medieval
listener, will here look for and miss, an ingredient of paramount
importance to him - the emotional content. He may be tempted to
conclude that this second marriage, through its comparison with
the first, is being shown by the poet as devalued, because of
this missing feature. Such an assessment brings to bear post-
medieval concepts of marriage on medieval marriage-description.
It does not, indeed cannot, coincide with that of the poet and
his audience. The fact that the marriage of the hero's parents
is no love-match would in no way lower it in their estimation.
The reverse is nearer the truth. The partners forgo the possibility of a love-match. Their marriage in consequence bears the
stamp of service, of a sense of public obligation, of an awareness of the individual's role within society, and as such forms
a most fitting prelude to the hero's career.

Yet with wit and kindliness the poet softens the severity of
this model and introduces into it love of a kind. The type which
he allots to it allows him to treat it as a fringe-element. He,
moreover, keeps it firmly in its place as a subordinate ingredient among its more important qualities by mere brief and spas-
modic reference to it. - An amorousness springs up between Gahmuret and Herzeloyde early on. Each senses the erotic appeal of
the other. Gahmuret, when catching his first glimpse of Herzeloyde, is startled by her attractiveness. He immediately reacts

to the physical appeal which emanates from her with an involuntary gesture that brings his whole body into play:

> 64.4 von dem liehten schîne,
> der von der künegîn erschein,
> derzuct im neben sich sîn bein:
> ûf rihte sich der degen wert,
> als ein vederspil,
> daz gert.

When first they meet, Herzeloyde is instantly sexually aroused
by him, and like him reacts with a gesture. Reaching out for him
she pulls him close to her and presses her whole body against
him:

> 84.2 si twanc iedoch sîn minne.
> er sâz für si sô nâhe nidr,
> daz sin begreif und zôch in widr
> Anderhalp vast an ir lîp.

The poet specifically draws the audience's attention to the
astonishing nature of such a gesture by an inexperienced girl:
"si was ein magt und niht ein wîp,/diu in sô nâhen sitzen liez"
(84.6/7). Gahmuret, so the poet comments, would have responded
with alacrity, had he not been in mourning (84.16-18). This sadness of his, however, is finally dispelled by springtime and its
delights. The newly green countryside, the trees in blossom, and
the fragrant air of May awaken Gahmuret's senses:

> 96.11 Er het iedoch von jâmer pîn.
> dô was des abrillen schîn
> zergangen, dar nâch komen was
> kurz kleine grüene gras.
> daz velt was gar vergrüenet;
> daz ploediu herzen küenet
> und in gît hôchgemüete.
> vil boume stuont in blüete
> von dem süezen luft des meien.

Descended as he is from the fairy Terdelaschoye the blood of these
fabled creatures which runs in his veins, now makes itself felt.
Traditionally pictured in myth and folklore as seductive and las-
civious the fairies of his remote ancestry now send their influence down to him. They reactivate his amorousness: "sîn

art von der feien/muose minnen oder minne gern" (96.20/21). This
recovery of vigour and virility is made by the poet to occur at
a most opportune moment, namely when wedlock is inevitably upon
Gahmuret, and when a prospective sweetheart is ready and waiting:
"des wolt in friundîn dâ gewern" (96.22).

The love which develops between Gahmuret and Herzeloyde before
the consummation of their marriage is therefore pictured by the
poet as being of a different kind from that which had evolved
between Gahmuret and Belakâne. Its nature is erotic. They kindle
a sensous response in one another. Since at no point of the description is mention made of an involvement of deeper feelings,
the sexuality of this love remains stressed throughout.[24] It is
by this means, by the introduction of the motif of plausible
eroticism into the confrontation of a man and a woman facing a
dynastic alliance, that Wolfram rescues the marriage of the
hero's parents from representing a totally impersonal transaction
and a pattern of cruel claims upon two individuals. Moreover he
takes care to show that there is mutuality in this erotic response. Both partners are involved equally. Neither will be
forced to submit to a distasteful physical demand. On the level
of sexuality each is seen to meet the other halfway. The poet's
handling of this aspect of their relationship is frankly humorous,
and the partial intent of the description was clearly to cause

---

24 Marlies Schumacher, op.cit., does not differentiate adequate-
    ly between the various kinds of "Liebe/Minne". She speaks of
    "voll entfaltete(r) Liebe" in relation to Herzeloyde, and
    claims, "daß auch diese Ehe letztlich aus persönlicher Zunei-
    gung erwächst". With reference to Gahmuret she says that he
    consents to the marriage "aus freier Neigung". (p. 18). The
    passages which she cites 62.25; 64.11f.; 69.24ff.; 81.27-82.4;
    86.29-87.6; 88.25-30; 94.11-96.10; 83.11; 84.2ff.; 94.16;
    96.20 and 96.19 do not support her thesis. Most of these
    have been analyzed above. L. 101.20 which she also quotes,
    is not applicable within this context as it refers to Gahmu-
    ret's and Herzeloyde's situation after their marriage and
    not before.
    The analysis of the Gahmuret/Herzeloyde marriage by Herbert
    Ernst Wiegand, op.cit., pp. 261-271, concerns itself chiefly
    with the conflict of "minne" and "strît" in Gahmuret and not

amusement. Yet the distinct and subtle modification of the motif of eroticism into one of reciprocity in desire suggests serious thinking on his part on contemporary marriage-practice. It signifies a humaneness all too uncommon at the turn of the twelfth and thirteenth centuries and one which would unerringly have sent out a powerful emotive appeal to his audience, in particular to the female listeners among them.[25] This humaneness also prompts him briefly to point out that the initial physical attraction to one another mercifully managed to engender a bond between the partners in the end: "ir zweier minne triwen jach" (101.20). After the consummation of their marriage, and after they have been together for some time, the poet shows them not only as having become adjusted to the circumstances which tie them together, but also as having established a relationship of deeper meaning between one another.

Yet the act of marriage, through their respective attitudes towards it, and through their behaviour and actions prior to it, is made to be seen as signifying not emotional self-fulfilment, but self-denial. It involves sacrifice on both sides. Where Herzeloyde is concerned implicit disregard of self has prompted marriage-plans. Consideration of self does not enter her marriage-negotiations; consideration of her needs and rights as liegelady does. She has made her sacrifice before any prospective partner even appeared. Gahmuret finally puts aside his own

---

with the aspects treated above.
It is important also to take into consideration the wide semantic spectrum of the terms "minne" and "minnen". Vid. Dorothea Wiercinski, Minne. Herkunft und Anwendungsschichten eines Wortes, Niederdeutsche Studien, 11, Cologne, 1964. She adduces eight different mainstream categories of meaning. More could undoubtedly be isolated. Herzeloyde for example uses the term "minnen" at one point in a manner in which it could hardly refer to anything else but to the marriage-contract: "... minnet mich nâch unser ê" (94.15) - 'marry me in accordance with our faith'.

25 The brutality and disregard of the individual in the marriage-practice among the medieval nobility is graphically described by Georges Duby, op.cit., chapter III: A Noble House: The Counts of Guines, pp. 83-110.

clamorous needs and stifles his genuine and deeply felt wishes.
Not only does he leave Belakâne, but by formally consenting to
a second marriage he assigns her to that melancholy group of
medieval women, the repudiated wives, of whom there were many.[26]
He makes a personal sacrifice of astonishing magnitude in order
to conform to the standards exacted by the social group to which
he belongs and in order to comply with their demands. So there
is implicit in the marriage of the hero's parents a subordination
of self rather than a prime consideration of it, an acknowledgement of their existence within a community, and a certain measure
of humility in allowing the claims of their social role to override those of self. The character of their marriage points for-
ward to the hero's quest, and once this quest has been accomplished, comments and elucidates it in retrospect. On levels in life
different from those of his parents' example, the hero will have
to forget assertion of ego, will have to learn not to seek self-
fulfilment, but to practise self-denial, will have to show an
awareness of the needs of his fellow-men, and above all will have
to grasp the meaning of humilitas as a governing principle of
life.

The marriage of the hero's parents is therefore made to have, and
seen to have, a predictive function within the narrative. This,
however, by no means exhausts the subsequent significance of
Gahmuret and Herzeloyde. Highly individualized as they are, they
remain memorable in their own right. Moreover, the remaining part
of the work carries numerous reminders of them.[27] In addition,

---

26 On the dissolution of this marriage and on the contemporary
   view of the Church of such marriages vid. Marlis Schumacher,
   op.cit., pp. 26-30, in particular pp. 29/30.

27 Vid. the list of references under "Gahmuret" and "Herzeloyde"
   in Werner Schröder, Die Namen im 'Parzival'.
   Wolfram's individualizing technique of portrayal in relation
   to Gahmuret and Herzeloyde has been analyzed by D. M. Blamires, Characterization and Individuality in Wolfram's 'Parzival', Cambridge, 1965, in the chapters: "Gahmuret" (pp. 14-65)
   and "Herzeloyde" (pp. 66-104).

however, the poet specifically continues to link them with the
hero, and the personalities of his parents are made to enter
into his destiny. Certain qualities of his parents descend to
him. When he displays a natural talent for fighting, is quick
to learn its proper pursuit, and achieves immediate mastery in
it at the court of Gurnemanz, the poet attributes it to the
heritage derived from Gahmuret ("Gahmuretes art", 174.24). This
nature of Gahmuret in him also makes him prone to fall in love.
When he feels dejected at having left Lîâze and cannot forget
her, then, so the poet points out, this is due to the blood of
Gahmuret flowing in his veins (179.24/25). The expertise with
which he fights off Keie's assault as he approaches the royal
court, is also made to appear as being reminiscent of Gahmuret
(293.22/23). Similarly, the poet sees him primarily as "Gahmuretes kint" when he underlines his undiminished strength during
the joust with Clâmidê (212.2/3) and when he claims after the
fight with Gramoflanz, that victory lies in the hero's very nature (717.21-23). The hero's immense martial gifts, his apti-
tude for fighting, his strength, his endurance, his skill in
horsemanship and at arms, are all seen to derive from his father.
It is to Herzeloyde, however, that the poet quite explicitly
traces that key-quality of "triuwe", that capacity for deep emotion, which will prove to be of paramount importance in his life.
When this maternal heritage, as the poet calls it himself, finally becomes dominant in him once again, it does so not in Parzival, but in "Herzeloyde fruht" (451.3-7). Moreover, that other
vital quality which will be the key to his re-achievement of
Grace and which will ultimately send him to the Grail, the quality of humilitas, is also traced back by the poet to the hero's
mother. Here, however, his technique of indicating heredity is
implicit (113.15/16; 128.23-28), while in the instance of triuwe
he insists on undisguised and detailed declaration. The mother's
role in the hero's life is given fundamental, far-reaching and
permanent importance. She provides the link with the Grail dynasty and through handing on to him the kinship with the Grail
family, makes him heir to the Grail Crown. (333.27-30.[28] The

prospective king of the Grail is the one "den Herzeloyde bar"
(333.29), and as "Herzeloyden kint" he reaches the Grail (827.
6/7). Wolfram makes particular qualities of the parents reappear
in their son, the hero, by explicit statement and implicit description. Both parents contribute to his individuality. At
certain times the paternal heritage is seen to come to the fore,
at others the maternal share claims the foreground. Sometimes the
natures of both parents are seen as active in the hero simultaneously, and he comes to be presented as the confluence of their
personalities. When love and longing for Condwîrâmûrs have him
in their grip, then this ability to love deeply comes to him from
both parents equally, "von vater und von muoter art" (300.19).
Before facing the most severe ordeal of his life, the revelations
of Trevrizent and his own near-collapse, the poet refers to him
as "der süezen Herzeloyden barn", and as "Gahmurets sun" in immediate and unbroken sequence (434.3/4). Vindicated by a fundamental moral change and received back into Grace, his proclamation
as Grail king is not addressed to him by name but to "Gahmuretes
suon" and to the one "den Herzeloyde bar" (781.3 and 5).[29]

---

28   Through his father the hero is related also to the Arthurian
     family. However, the connection is far more remote than the
     one with the Grail dynasty. While the Grail king Anfortas is
     one of his maternal uncles, his mother's brother, he is related
     lated to King Arthur through his paternal great-great-grand-
     father Lazaliez whose brother Brickus was Arthur's grand-
     father. Nevertheless, this dual blood relationship is a point
     of symbolic importance and must be taken into account. It is
     stressed e.g. by Gunhild and Uwe Pörksen, Die 'Geburt' des
     Helden in mittelhochdeutschen Epen und epischen Stoffen des
     Mittelalters, Euphorion, 74 (1980), 257-286: "Die auf recht
     ungewöhnliche Weise zustande gekommene Verbindung der Eltern
     - sie wird von Herzeloyde erzwungen, Gahmuret wird buchstäb-
     lich zur Ehe mit ihr verurteilt - hat einen genealogischen
     Sinn: sie führt die beiden Geschlechterlinien der Artussippe
     und der Gralssippe zusammen; diese doppelseitige Herkunft
     Parzivals ist für Wolfram von grosser Bedeutung." (p. 286).

29   The narrative continuity which links the parents' biography
     with the Parzival-story is stressed for different levels of
     the work by Christa Ortmann, Ritterschaft. Zur Frage nach
     der Bedeutung der Gahmuret-Geschichte im 'Parzival' Wolframs
     von Eschenbach, DVJ, 47 (1973), 664-710. Commenting on 112.16
     -20: "nû wizzet wâ von iu sî komn/diss maeres sachewalte/ und

The careful early portrayal of the parents, a portrayal which
is extended later in the work, but for which he lays the definitive foundation in Books I and II, enables the poet to characterize the hero with precision. He makes use of it with subtlety
and sophistication as a means to elucidate the hero's nature
and to motivate his achievement. These ultimate narrative results
lay bare the original reasons why the poet felt moved to invent
a prelude to the received narrative.

Commensurate with her important subsequent role the hero's mother
is given great prominence in Book II, and her delineation not as
type, but as individual, and as an individual of unique qualities,
continues after the father's death. Her imperious nature and

---

wie man den behalte./man barg in vor ritterschaft,/ê er koeme
an sîner witze kraft", she says: "Die epische Ansage des Dichters enthält also eine authentische Verhältnisbestimmung, nach
der die beiden Geschichten in mehrfacher Hinsicht aufeinander
verwiesen und miteinander verbunden sind, d.h. die Dichteran-
sage bezeichnet an dieser entscheidenden Stelle die Funktion
der Gahmuret-Geschichte und ihre fundamentale Bedeutung für
die Möglichkeit einer Parzival-Geschichte überhaupt: Die Hörer sollen wissen, dass diese Parzival-Geschichte, die in dem
Augenblick expressis verbis begonnen hat, in dem "des maeres
sachewalde" geboren ist, auf dem Boden der Gahmuret-Geschichte
steht. Es wird nicht möglich sein, dieses maere zu verstehen,
ohne zu wissen, woher sein "sachewalde" kommt, denn (1) es ist
von der Geschichte dieser Herkunft thematisch wie strukturell
vorherbestimmt, in ihr vorgebildet, präfiguriert, und (2) es
ist selbst die Fortsetzung dieser Geschichte, die genealogi-
sche Verbindung ist Träger einer thematischen Kontinuität
(Parzival wird Ritter sein, wie sein Vater Gahmuret Ritter
war), aber (3) es ist dieser Geschichte exegetisch nach- und
übergeordnet (Parzival wird "aller ritter bluome"), d.h. es
ist als Fortsetzung die Steigerung der Gahmuret-Geschichte
..." (p. 698).
This continuity between Books I and II and the remainder of
the work forms the subject also of an article by Eleanor
Kutz, The Story of the Parents in Wolfram von Eschenbach's
'Parzival', Monatshefte, 70 (1978), 364-374. She sees the
opening books as "providing a guidepost" and adds that "their
careful examination in relation to the whole gives much information as to Wolfram's structural and thematic design for
his work." (p. 364).

masterful manner had already been made manifest in her public
insistence on her rights, her perseverance in her demands, and
her total lack of reluctance to pursue them to the end. This,
as has been shown, underlines a social awareness, her understanding of herself as liegelady. The moment she has reached
her goal, however, she slips easily and automatically, and with
complete equanimity into acceptance of yet another role that
society requires of her, namely that of the obedient wife. With
the finality of authority she lays claim to Gahmuret - "hêr,
nu sît ir mîn" (96.7) - and in the same breath acknowledges her
inferior status in marriage - "ich tuon iu dienst nâch hulden
schîn" (96.8). She sees her function in marriage as one of service. Once this marriage is over, however, once she is on her
own again, thrown back on her own resources, the poet straightway accords her the stature of liegelady again, and shows her
as re-assuming it in a manner both authoritative and profoundly
impressive. She is seen to rise to the sudden reversal of status,
to the return of her former function that is now unexpectedly
being thrust upon her, with dignity, courage, breath-taking
presence of mind and circumspection. - The news of Gahmuret's
death reaches her at midday, and just when her women have woken
her from a terrifying nightmare. Into the lingering panic of
her dream falls the dreadful blow of his death, and she faints
(103.25-105.7). During the squire's long narration of how Gahmuret met his death fighting in Outremer, and how he was buried,
she is left unattended. Although a crowd has gathered to listen
to the account (104.29; 105.1-3; 105.9; 108.30; 109.8; 109.13-
17), no one takes any note of her. Heavily pregnant as she is,
she hovers on the brink of death (109.2-15). At last she is remembered and brought round (109.16-18). No sooner has she re-
gained consciousness that she decides to address her people.
Surrounded by her ladies-in-waiting (104.29), knights (105.8),
squires and pages (105.1-3; 106.27/28) she delivers a dirge for
their dead lord, a dirge of a very particular kind, one which
enshrines the proclamation of his rightful successor. - She
begins with a cry of woe, calling for her lost love: "... ôwê

war kom mîn trût?" (109.19) and lets her lamentations ring out:
"diu frouwe in klagete über lût" (109.20). She pays tribute to
the dead lord's memory and at the same time salutes the new lord.
She first recalls Gahmuret's distinction for those who are watching and listening and immediately thereafter announces the coming
of his heir. This proclamation of the liegelord's legal successor
to whom automatic allegiance will be due is underlined by her
with striking gestures. Stressing the blood-bond between husband,
herself, and the child about to be born, she points to her body
- "alhie" - , as bearing the dead man's continuing life - "ich
trage alhie doch sînen lîp" (109.26) - , his seed which she received in wedlock - "sînes verhes sâmen" (109.27). She then appeals to God to allow this seed to come to fruition (109.30-
110.1), laments her fate (110.2/3) and apostrophizes death (110.4).
Finally she draws attention to the dead lord's gentleness with
women which she cites as proof of his honourable nature (110.5-9).

The first part of the dirge completed she now concentrates predominantly on the proclamation of his successor, emphasizing her
words tangibly by gesture. So important are these gestures, performed in public for all to see, that the poet alerts his audience
to them, telling them to follow his description carefully: "nu
hoert ein ander maere,/waz diu frouwe dô begienc" (110.10/11).
Herzeloyde then encircles her belly and the child within it with
both hands and arms and begins the second part of her dirge with a
prayer. She pleads with God to make her survive and let her give
birth (110.14-22). Following this she tears her shift and exposes
her breasts - "daz hemde von der brust si brach" (110.24). The
milk which she will now make flow, will serve as evidence that
the child within her will not be stillborn, but is alive. She
describes her breasts as holding a living child's nourishment:
"du bist kaste eins kindes spîse;/die hât ez vor im her gesant,/
sît ichz lebende im lîbe vant" (110.30-111.2). At this point the
poet refers to her as "diu wîse" (110.29), the woman knowledge-
able, gifted with insight, maturity and understanding.[30] In order

to activate the milk she sucks her breast - "ir brüstel linde
unde wîz,/dar an kêrte si ir vlîz,/si dructes an ir rôten munt"
(110.25-27) - and shows how women do it - "si tet wîplîche fuore
kunt" (110.28). Then with a queenly gesture she presses out
the milk, while with a parallelizing reference to baptism she
stresses the ritual nature of what she is performing:

> 111.5   diu milch in ir tüttelîn:
> die dructe drûz diu künegîn,
> sie sprach 'du bist von triwen komn.
> het ich des toufes niht genomn,
> du waerest wol mîns toufes zil.

Wolfram who throughout this scene has described her as "diu vrouwe"
(109.20; 110.11; 110.23; 111.3), the liegelady, ·and once as "diu
wîse" (110.29), here throws into relief her regal bearing and
calls her "diu künegîn" (111.6). Tears and milk, so Herzeloyde
concludes her remarkable dirge, will mingle in her lament for
Gahmuret. (111.10-13).

Herzeloyde's speech of mourning is no mere cry of pain, no maud-
lin display of self-pity, no expression of purely personal grief.
It does not bear the marks of the disorientation of hysteria, but,
on the contrary, shows control, clear vision, and grasp of the
emergency which has arisen. It is a desperate, yet courageous
bid for power. By blending the obligatory dirge with the proclamation of the rightful heir she tries to secure the succession
for her son thereby keeping the feudal network intact. It is an
attempt to prevent the inevitable chaos which occurs when the

---

30   It is likely that the notion of women as especially well-
informed and skilled in medicine, in particular in matters
of childbirth, enters this concept of Herzeloyde as "diu
wîse" also. Midwifery in the Middle Ages was chiefly performed by women. Cf. e.g. Aus der Zeit der Verzweiflung.
Zur Genese und Aktualität des Hexenbildes, Beiträge von
Gabriele Becker, Silvia Bovenschen, Helmut Brackert, Sigrid
Brauner, Ines Brenner, Gisela Morgenthal, Klaus Schneller,
Angelika Tümmler, I: Zur Situation der Frau im Mittelalter
und in der frühen Neuzeit, pp. 11-128; in particular p. 79ff.,
Frankfurt, 1977, and Beryl Rowland, Medieval Woman's Guide
to Health. The First English Gynecological Handbook, London,
1981.

liegelord dies and leaves no living, legitimate, male heir. Her
extraordinary address is an appeal to her people not to upset
the balance of feudal order, but to wait for the new lord, and
to acknowledge him even before his birth. Her appeal through its
fusion of plaint and proclamation has a compelling eloquence.
She gives it added impact by accompanying it with vividly dramatic, almost self-sacrificial gestures. Far from mourning
privately and selfishly, she mourns publicly and altruistically,
making herself in her moment of peril and tragedy into a rallying
point for her people.[31]

The poet thus allots to the hero's mother a quite outstanding
role. He endows her with qualities that the hero will need and
will develop and show in later life. He adds here in this grandiose scene of his own invention the quality of leadership to
the spectrum of hereditary characteristics derived from the
mother. He makes her manifest it in such a form and to such a

31 The unique character of Herzeloyde's speech of mourning is
    perhaps best appreciated when compared with the words and
    behaviour of other heroines in medieval fiction. Hartmann
    e.g. describes Laudîne's reaction to her husband's death in
    considerable detail and also Ênite's behaviour when she pre-
    sumes Erec dead ('Iwein', 1305ff.; 'Erec', 5743ff.).
    Peter Wapnewski, Herzeloydes Klage und das Leid der Blanche-
    flur. Zur Frage der agonalen Beziehungen zwischen den Kunst-
    auffassungen Gottfrieds von Strassburg und Wolframs von
    Eschenbach, in: Festgabe für Ulrich Pretzel, ed. by Werner
    Simon, Wolfgang Bachofer, Wolfgang Dittmann, Berlin, 1963,
    pp. 173-184, seems to see this scene as a mad scene: "Das
    Verhalten dieser Frau in ihrer kreatürlichen Verlorenheit,
    der Einsamkeit ihres Schmerzes ist von Wolfram mit derarti-
    ger Gewalt wiedergegeben, dass man sich geradezu scheut,
    Zeuge zu sein: Dies gehört nur ihr, da sind in der letzten
    Verlassenheit Gebärde und Verhalten nicht mehr zu messen an
    Gesetzen der Form und Ordnung, der Mensch wird eingehüllt
    vom rettenden Wahnsinn, der ihn von den andern entrückt (und
    zugleich die Erkenntnis dieser Tatsache verhindert)" (p. 181).
    The problems of the widowed queen and her involvement in
    succession politics in the early centuries have been de-
    scribed by Pauline Stafford, Queens, Concubines and Dowagers.
    The King's Wife in the early Middle Ages, London, 1983, vid.
    chapter VI: Queen Mother, pp. 143-174, in particular pp. 151/
    152 and pp. 166-174.

degree that she becomes a figure unforgettable and unique. The
mould into which this episode has been cast, and the manner in
which the account of it has been handled, succinctly show a
characteristic brilliance of the poet's craft. It exhibits his
facility for conjuring up the vividly visual scene, for the description of the loaded gesture, and for the evocation of the
drama as it can suddenly erupt in human life.[32]

In his brief mention of the hero's birth the poet singles out
the size of the baby's bones, implying strength and capacity
for survival (112.6-8).[33] A little later he also speaks of the
fighting spirit which will ultimately develop in him, and of
his future success in the field (112.28-30), thus taking up the
themes with which he originally greeted the hero as yet unborn,
long before his parent's marriage (4.14-19). This is all the
information in the form of direct description of the future hero
which the audience will have received during this prelude to the
main story. The only other features about him which the poet
divulges early on in this way are that he will be "traeclîche
wîs" (4.18) - slow to reach maturity -, and that the pursuits
of chivalry will remain hidden from him during his childhood
(112.19/20). He gives away no more explicitly. Other facets of
the hero's personality and the particular brand of destiny that
awaits him, have to be inferred from the expectations which he
raises through the portrayal of his parents. This indirect,
predictive method of description gives the poet a vehicle for
creating suspense in his listeners. With it he makes suggestions,
gives hints, lays trails, and raises questions. Few members of
his audience, if any, would willingly have missed the sequel to

---

32 'Willehalm' offers an excellent example of this. Vid.
    Marianne Wynn, Hagen's Defiance of Kriemhilt, in: Mediaeval
    German Studies. Presented to Frederick Norman, London, 1965,
    pp. 104-114.

33 Infant mortality in the Middle Ages was high. Powers of
    survival in a newborn child was therefore a point worth
    mentioning. Cf. e.g. J. C. Russell, Population in Europe
    500-1500.

this introduction, so carefully planned and so brilliantly executed.

In the last part of his prelude to the Parzival-story the poet establishes the hero's mother as a figure embodying humilitas. She is presented as achieving an astonishing degree of humility, as the allusion here to the Holy Virgin implies. Contrary to contemporary custom, and with deliberate parallelism with the Virgin Mary, Herzeloyde decides not to hand her newborn child over to a wet-nurse, but to suckle the babe herself (113.5-19).[34] The startling nature of her action, the vivid image of the child at her breast, the reference to the Virgin, and the brief, explanatory comment by the poet - "diemuot was ir bereit" (113.16) - all combine to ensure that this quality of Herzeloyde will remain in the collective memory of the audience. The judicious placing of the portrayal of this quality, at the conclusion of the parents' story, cannot but support its narrative continuance further.

Despite her valiant bid for survival and feudal leadership and despite her admirable characteristics Herzeloyde's fate will be cruel. The poet had already cryptically adumbrated her future in the pattern of an allegory, in her prophetic dream while still carrying the child. The hero appears here both as serpent and as dragon who on leaving her forever, destroy her. Both creatures feed on her like suckling babes. The serpent tears open her womb, while the dragon breaks her heart out of her body. (103.25-104.30).[35] The last line of Book II strikes a similarly

---

34 Having children reared by wet-nurses was the established practice among the nobility in the Middle Ages. Later it became customary among all who could afford it, and also among those whose economic circumstances forced them to farm out their children. The custom continued until well into the nineteenth century. Cf. Shulamith Shahar, Die Frau im Mittelalter, Königstein/Ts., 1981, p. 132; also Elisabeth Badinter, The Myth of Motherhood. An Historical View of the Maternal Instinct, London, 1981. Originally published under the title: L'Amour en Plus, Paris, 1980.

ominous note: "ir schimph ertranc in riwen furt" (114.4), and
Wolfram releases his audience into a mood in which fears and
hopes are mingled.[36]

Wolfram's achievement in this freely invented and freely composed prelude to the received narrative is truly dazzling. The
poetic effects which he manages to create, reverberate down the
vistas of the main story. Tearing open the restricted boundaries
of Chrestien's text he adds new dimensions to the work by introducing another world, the world of Outremer and its pagan civilization. Through it he gives the Parzival-story a sudden topicality relating it in this way to the ideological conflict of
his time. It allows him to transmit the urgent message of tolerance. Yet the poetic gains go further still. This third world
of Outremer and the non-believer is added to the other two, to
the world of Arthurian utopia and to that of the Grail. The
relevance of his hero's quest will reach out to every man everywhere. Its universality is infinite.

The hero's future and role within society is foreshadowed by
the actions of his parents, his character is forecast through
the description of their personalities. They in their turn,
through complex contrastive and layered composition are characterized in part via the depiction of past events. Thus the hero
comes to be portrayed in advance through the portrayal of his

---

35 A. T. Hatto, Herzeloyde's Dragon-Dream, GLL, 22 (1968),
    16-31, pursues the question why the hero should here be
    presented as a dragon.

36 There has been much commentary on the figure of Herzeloyde,
    all of it very different from the above analysis and con-
    clusions. Cf. e.g. the contribution by D. M. Blamires al-
    ready mentioned, also S. M. Johnson, Herzeloyde and the
    Grail, Neophilologus, 52 (1968), 148-156; M. E. Gibbs,
    Wîplîchez Wîbes Reht. A Study of the Women Characters in
    the Works of Wolfram von Eschenbach, Duquesne, 1972, pp. 3-
    21; G. J. Lewis, Die unheilige Herzeloyde. Ein ikonoklasti-
    scher Versuch, JEGP, 74 (1975), pp. 465-485; David N. Yeandle,
    Herzeloyde: Problems of Characterization in Book III of
    Wolfram's 'Parzival', Euphorion, 75 (1981), Abhandlungen,
    pp. 1-28. Vid. also S. M. Johnson and David N. Yeandle for
    further references on the subject.

parents. Yet his image at this stage is still purposely kept
shadowy. It remains implicit in them - a most subtle technique
of predictive narration. Explicit statements relating to the
hero are kept minimal and brief, for overt description at this
point would destroy suspense. It will not be until the conclusion
of the work, until everyone has heard all, that the hero's character and motivation, and his function in society will elucidate
themselves through the early story of his parents.

Poetic continuity, a vital concern of the poet at all stages of
the composition of his work, is kept over the whole stretch of
this massive narrative. Buttressed by references to the parents,
and the appearance of the hero's elder half-brother towards the
close of the work, its mainstay is the hero himself. His character and fate are rooted in the personalities and lives of his
parents. Heredity and inheritance link him indissolubly with
them. His future is firmly anchored in the past, a past which he
himself did not witness, but which lives on in him. By adding
the biography of the parents the poet has given himself scope
for the motivation of a reconceived hero. It has enabled him to
extend and confirm the hero's individuality, to increase his
credibility, and to reinforce his impact as the bearer of the
new theme which he has given Chrestien's story.

VI. Conclusion

Wolfram at work on 'Li Contes del Graal' reveals a bewildering
abundance of gifts and consciously applied skills. Their range,
variety, and poetic effectiveness leave the critic spellbound.
The features of his craftsmanship which have come to be isolated
in the course of this study would furnish any poet with an impressive manual of guidelines. Even so, the long list of narrative devices that has been brought to light here, represents
only a fragment of his poetic craft. Only one of his works has
been examined here, and only selected parts of this work have
been subjected to scrutiny. The register thus obtained can therefore by no means be considered complete. No more than a small,
possibly even infinitesimal segment of the ultimate and total
profusion of gifts and skills that were his, has been laid bare
and portrayed here. Some of the techniques which Wolfram employs
in 'Parzival' must have been learnt from observation, derived
from other works of literature which he made it his business to
know intimately, and which he then quarried for suggestions.
Others he may have invented, and even if they did exist, may
have initiated independently and coincidentally. How his poetic
expertise is to be divided into these two categories is impossible to say. The patterns of gradation and a fictional character's self-revelation in speech were to be found already in
'Li Contes del Gral' and in Chrestien's other works. Banter with
the audience, the use of personification, and the allegorizing
of key scenes could have been gleaned from Hartmann. He might
have watched the deployment of suspense and the hinting at peril
in the work of that master craftsman of both, the poet of the
'Nibelungenlied'. Portrayal of fictional figures via dialogue,
the strategy of authorial comment, and the use of symbolism he
might have learnt from anyone. Yet from wherever he may have
taken such techniques, in the process of adoption he made them
peculiarly and inimitably his own, through the deftness with
which he handled and mastered them, and through the consistency
with which he saw them through. Some features of his narrative

art stand out as characteristic of the style and form of 'Parzival': the scheme of place-names joining reality with fantasy, the parallelism of heroes, the creation of a coherent fictional landscape, the chiaroscuro technique, prominently in evidence in the travel-histories, in landscape description, and in the portrayal of the two marriages in Books I and II, the method of implication by visual impact as in the case of Sigûne, the sudden switch from one emotional level to another, seen frequently throughout the work, and in particular in Book IX, and the unexpected injection of humour. These are the eye-catching forms of expression in 'Parzival'. Striking too is Wolfram's pronounced gift for the portrayal of the escalation of emotion and for the staging of the grandiose scene weighted with pathos and drama, as in Anfortas's would-be abdication, Parzival's rejection of faith, and Herzeloyde's public lament and proclamation.

Yet the brilliance of Wolfram's poetic craftsmanship alone would have never raised his 'Parzival' to the level of uniqueness which it so justly occupies. Paul Valery's famous dictum: "C'est l'exécution du poème qui est le poème" is only half the truth. For were it not for the compelling depth of thought and emotion which informs the work, Wolfram's version of the Parzival-story would be no more than a vehicle for the display of virtuosity.

Abbreviations

DVJ	Deutsche Vierteljahrsschrift für Literaturwissenschaft und Geistesgeschichte
DU	Der Deutschunterricht
Euph.	Euphorion. Zeitschrift für Literaturgeschichte
Fs.	Festschrift
GLL	German Life and Letters
GRM	Germanisch-romanische Monatsschrift
JEGP	Journal of English and Germanic Philology
MLR	Modern Language Review
Neophil.	Neophilologus
PBB	Pauls und Braunes Beiträge zur Geschichte der deutschen Sprache und Literatur
PMLA	Publications of the Modern Language Association of America
Spec.	Speculum
WdF	Wege der Forschung, Darmstadt
WW	Wirkendes Wort
WBG	Wissenschaftliche Buchgesellschaft, Darmstadt
ZfdA	Zeitschrift für deutsches Altertum
ZfdPh	Zeitschrift für deutsche Philologie

Wolfram is quoted according to Karl Lachmann, Wolfram von Eschenbach, 6th edition (Eduard Hartl), Berlin/Leipzig, 1926. Chrestien is quoted according to Alfons Hilka, Der Percevalroman (Li Contes Del Graal), herausgegeben unter Benutzung des von Gottfried Baist nachgelassenen handschriftlichen Materials, Halle (Saale), 1932.

Select Bibliography

ABEL, OTTO, König Philipp der Hohenstaufe, Berlin, 1852.
ACKERMANN, ROBERT W., The Knighting Ceremonies in the Middle
English Romances, Speculum, 19 (1944), 285-313.
ADAMS, JEREMY DU QUESNEY, Patterns of Medieval Society, Engle-
wood Cliffs, 1969.
ADOLF, HELEN, On Medieval Laughter, Speculum, 22 (1947), 251-
253.
Der altfranzösische höfische Roman, ed. by ERICH KÖHLER, WdF,
425, 1978.
ALTIERI, MARCELLE, Les Romans de Chrétien de Troyes, Leur per-
spective proverbiale et gnomique, Paris, 1976.
ANDERSON, WILLIAM, Castles of Europe. From Charlemagne to the
Renaissance, London, 1970.
ARBUSOW, LEONID, Colores rhetorici. Eine Auswahl rhetorischer
Figuren und Gemeinplätze als Hilfsmittel für akademische
Übungen an mittelalterlichen Texten, Göttingen, [2]1963.
ARENS, FRITZ, Die staufischen Königspfalzen, in: Die Zeit der
Staufer, III, 129-142.
Arthurian Literature in the Middle Ages. A collaborative History,
ed. by R. S. LOOMIS, Oxford, 1959.
Der arthurische Roman, ed. by KURT WAIS, WdF, 157, 1970.
ASCHBACH, JOSEPH, Geschichte der Grafen von Wertheim von den
ältesten Zeiten bis zu ihrem Erlöschen im Mannesstamme im
Jahre 1556, 2 vols., Frankfurt a.M., 1843.
ASCHE, SIGFRIED, Die Wartburg und ihre Kunstwerke, Eisenach,
1954.
ATKINS, J.W.H., English Literary Criticism: The Medieval Phase,
London, [2]1952.
AUBIN, HERMANN, and ZORN, WOLFGANG (eds.), Handbuch der deutschen
Wirtschafts- und Sozialgeschichte, 2 vols., Stuttgart, 1971/
1976, 1: Von der Frühzeit bis zum Ende des 18. Jahrhunderts.
AUERBACH, ERICH, Mimesis. Dargestellte Wirklichkeit in der abend-
ländischen Literatur, Berne, 1946.
- , Literatursprache und Publikum in der lateinischen Spätantike
und im Mittelalter, Berne, 1958.
Aus der Zeit der Verzweiflung. Zur Genese und Aktualität des
Hexenbildes. Beiträge von Gabriele Becker, Silvia Bovenschen,
u.a., Frankfurt a.M., 1977.
AUSTERMANN, JOSEF, Aufbau und Bedeutung der Trevrizentszene im
neunten Buche des Parzival 455.23-502.30, Wissenschaftliche
Beilage zum Jahresbericht des Gymnasiums zu Attendorn, Siegen,
1906, 3-32.

BADINTER, ELISABETH, The Myth of Motherhood. An Historical View
of the Maternal Instinct, London, 1981.
BALDWIN, C.S., Medieval Rhetoric and Poetic, New York, 1928.
BARRACLOUGH, GEOFFREY, The Origins of Modern Germany, Oxford,
[2]1947.
- , The Medieval Empire, Idea and Reality, The Historical
Association, Pamphlet 17, London, 1950.

BÄUML, FRANZ H., Medieval Civilization in Germany 800-1273, London, 1969.

BEAZLEY, C.R., The Dawn of Modern Geography, 3 vols., London, 1897-1906.

BECHTEL, HEINRICH, Wirtschaftsgeschichte Deutschlands, I: Von der Vorzeit bis zum Ende des Mittelalters, Munich, [2]1951.

BEDNAR, JOHN, La Spiritualité et le Symbolisme dans les Oeuvres de Chrétien de Troyes, Paris, 1974.

BEELER, JOHN, Warfare in Feudal Europe 730-1200, Ithaca, 1971.

BEHAGHEL, OTTO, Zur Technik der mittelhochdeutschen Dichtung, PBB, 30 (1905), 431-564.

BELL, CLAIR HAYDEN, The Sister's Son in the Medieval German Epic. A Study in the Survival of Matriliny, University of California Publications in Modern Philology, 10, 1920-1925 (1922), 67-182.

BENTON, JOHN F., The Court of Champagne as a literary centre, Speculum, 36 (1961), 551-591.

BENZIGER, KARL J., Parzival in der deutschen Handschriften-illustration des Mittelalters, Studien zur deutschen Kunstgeschichte, 175, Strassburg, 1914.

BERNARDS, MATTHÄUS, Geistigkeit und Seelenleben der Frau im Hochmittelalter, Beihefte zum Archiv für Kulturgeschichte, 16, Cologne/Graz, [2]1981.

BERTAU, KARL, Neidharts "bayrische" Lieder und Wolframs "Willehalm", ZfdA, 100 (1971), 296-324.

- , Deutsche Literatur im europäischen Mittelalter, vol. I: 800-1197, vol. II: 1195-1220, Munich, 1972/73.

BEZZOLA, RETO R., Les origines et la formation de la littérature courtoise en occident, 3 vols., Paris, 1944-1963.

- , Le sens de l'aventure et de l'amour (Chrétien de Troyes), Paris, 1947.

- , Zur künstlerischen Persönlichkeit Chrétiens, Archiv f. d. Studium der neueren Sprachen und Literaturen, 167 (1935), 42-54.

BIESE, ALFRED, Die Entwicklung des Naturgefühls im Mittelalter und in der Neuzeit, Leipzig, 1888.

BINNS, L. ELLIOTT, Innocent III, London, 1931.

BLAMIRES, DAVID, Characterization and Individuality in Wolfram's Parzival, Cambridge, 1966.

BLANK, WALTER, Mittelalterliche Dichtung oder Theologie? Zur Schuld Parzivals, ZfdA, 100 (1971), 133-148.

BLOCH, MARC, Feudal Society, 2 vols., London, 1965, (Reprint 1975. Translation from: La Société Féodale, 2 vols., Paris, 1939/40).

- , Land and Work in Medieval Europe, Selected Papers, London, 1967 (Translated and extracted from Mélanges Historiques, École Pratique des Hautes Études, 1966).

- , A problem in comparative history: the administrative classes in France and in Germany, Ibid., 82-123.

BLOCH, R. HOWARD, Medieval French Literature and Law, Berkeley/ Los Angeles/London, 1977.

BÖCKMANN, PAUL, Formgeschichte der deutschen Dichtung, Hamburg, 1949.

BOEHEIM, WENDELIN, Handbuch der Waffenkunde, Seemanns Kunstgewerbliche Handbücher, 7, Leipzig, 1890.

BOESCH, BRUNO, Die Kunstanschauung in der mittelhochdeutschen Dichtung von der Blütezeit bis zum Meistergesang, Berne/Leipzig, 1936.

BOLTON, BRENDA, Vitae Matrum: a further aspect of the Frauenfrage, in: Medieval Women, 253-274.

BONATH, GESA, Untersuchungen zur Überlieferung des Parzival Wolframs von Eschenbach, Germanische Studien, 238/239, Lübeck/Hamburg, 1970/1971.

DE BOOR, HELMUT, Geschichte der deutschen Literatur von den Anfängen bis zur Gegenwart, II, Die Höfische Literatur. Vorbereitung, Blüte, Ausklang, 1170-1250, Munich, [10]1979.

BORODINE, MYRRHA, La femme et l'amour au XIIe siècle d'après les poèmes de Chrétien de Troyes, Paris, 1909.

BORST, ARNO, Das Rittertum im Hochmittelalter. Idee und Wirklichkeit, Speculum, 10 (1959), 213-231, (Reprinted in: Das Rittertum im Mittelalter, WdF, 349 (1976), 212-246).

- , Lebensformen im Mittelalter, Frankfurt a.M., 1973.

BOSL, KARL, Frühformen der Gesellschaft im mittelalterlichen Europa. Ausgewählte Beiträge zu einer Strukturanalyse der mittelalterlichen Welt, Munich/Vienna, 1964.

- , Die Reichsministerialität der Salier und Staufer, Ein Beitrag zur Geschichte des hochmittelalterlichen deutschen Volkes, Reiches und Staates, 2 vols., Schriften der Monumenta Germaniae Historica, 10, Stuttgart, [2]1968/69.

- , Die Grundlagen der modernen Gesellschaft im Mittelalter. Eine deutsche Gesellschaftsgeschichte des Mittelalters, 2 vols., Stuttgart, 1972.

- , Das Problem der Armut in der hochmittelalterlichen Gesellschaft, Österreichische Akademie der Wissenschaften, philosophisch-historische Klasse, Sitzungsberichte, 294, Vienna, 1974.

- , Die Gesellschaft in der Geschichte des Mittelalters, Göttingen, [3]1975.

BOSSERT, GUSTAV, Die Ministerialen der Staufer in ihrer schwäbischen Heimat und in Franken, Württembergische Vierteljahreshefte für Landesgeschichte, 13 (1890), 76-80.

BÖTTICHER, GOTTHOLD, Das Hohelied vom Rittertum. Eine Beleuchtung des "Parzival" nach Wolframs eigenen Andeutungen, Berlin, 1886.

- , Noch einmal das IX. Buch des Parzival, ZfdA, 45 (1901), 149-152.

BOUCHARD, CONSTANCE B., Consanguinity and Noble Marriages in the Tenth and Eleventh Centuries, Speculum, 55 (1981), 268-287.

BOWRA, C.M., Inspiration and Poetry, London, 1955.

BRACKERT, HELMUT, Rudolf von Ems: Dichtung und Geschichte, Heidelberg, 1968.

BRAND, WOLFGANG, Chrétien de Troyes, Zur Dichtungstechnik seiner Romane, Freiburger Schriften zur romanischen Philologie, Munich, 1972.

BREUER, TILMANN, Kunst, in: Handbuch der bayerischen Geschichte, vol. III, Part 2, Munich, [2]1979, 896-899.
BRINKMANN, HENNIG, Zu Wesen und Form mittelalterlicher Dichtung, Halle, 1928.
- , Diesseitsstimmung im Mittelalter, DVJ, 2 (1924), 721-752.
- , Schönheitsauffassung und Dichtung vom Mittelalter bis zum Rokoko, DVJ, 11 (1933), 230-250.
- , Mittelalterliche Hermeneutik, Darmstadt 1980.
BROGSITTER, KARL OTTO, Artusepik, Stuttgart, [3]1980.
- , Chrétien de Troyes, in: Enzyklopädie des Märchens. Handwörterbuch zur historischen und vergleichenden Erzählforschung, vol. II, Berlin/New York 1979, col. 1366-1379.
BROOKE, CHRISTOPHER, The Twelfth Century Renaissance, London, 1969.
BROOKE, ROSALIND B. and BROOKE, CHRISTOPHER, N.L., St. Clare, in: Medieval Women, 275-287.
BRUCE, JAMES DOUGLAS, The Evolution of Arthurian Romance. From the Beginnings down to the Year 1300, 2 vols., Hesperia, Ergänzungsreihe: Schriften zur englischen Philologie, Baltimore/ Göttingen, [2]1928.
BRÜCKL, OTTO, Betrachtungen über das Bild des Weges in der höfischen Epik, Acta Germanica, 1 (1966), 1-14.
BRUFORD, W.H., Der Beruf des Schriftstellers, in: Wege der Literatursoziologie, 266-286.
BRUNDAGE, JAMES A., Richard Lion Heart, New York, 1974.
BRUNNER, HEINRICH, Deutsche Rechtsgeschichte, 2 vols., Munich, [2]1928.
BRUNNER, OTTO, Sozialgeschichte Europas im Mittelalter, Göttingen, 1978 (First published as: Inneres Gefüge des Abendlandes, Historia Mundi, 6 (1958)).
BRUYNE, EDGAR DE, L'Ésthétique du moyen âge, 3 vols., Louvain, 1947.
BUCHNER, FRANZ XAVER, Das Bistum Eichstätt. Historisch-statistische Beschreibung auf Grund der Literatur der Registratur des Bischöflichen Ordinariats Eichstätt sowie der pfarramtlichen Berichte, 2 vols., Eichstätt, 1937/38.
BULLOUGH, D.A., Early medieval social groupings. The terminology of kinship, Past and Present, 45 (1969-70), 3-18.
BUMKE, JOACHIM, Parzivals "Schwertleite", in: Fs. Taylor Starck, Den Haag, 1964, 235-245.
- , Die romanisch-deutschen Literaturbeziehungen, Heidelberg, 1967.
- , Die Wolfram von Eschenbach-Forschung seit 1945. Bericht und Bibliographie, Munich, 1970.
- , Ministerialität und Ritterdichtung. Umrisse der Forschung, Munich, 1976.
- , Wolfram von Eschenbach, Stuttgart, [4]1976.
- , Studien zum Ritterbegriff im 12. und 13. Jahrhundert, mit einem Anhang: Zum Stand der Ritterforschung 1976, Beihefte zum Euphorion, 1, Heidelberg, [2]1977.
- , Mäzene im Mittelalter. Die Gönner und Auftraggeber der höfischen Literatur in Deutschland 1150-1300, Munich, 1979.

BUSBY, KEITH, Gauvain in Old French Literature, Amsterdam, 1980.
Butler's Lives of the Saints, ed. by HERBERT THURSTON and DONALD
ATTWATER, 4 vols., London, ²1956.

The Cambridge Economic History of Europe, I: The Agrarian Life
of the Middle Ages, ed. by M.M. POSTAN, ²1966, II: Trade and
Industry in the Middle Ages, ed. by M.M. POSTAN and E.E. RICH,
1952.
The Cambridge Medieval History, planned by J.B. BURY. General
Editors: J.R. TANNER, C.W. Prévité-Orton, Z.N. BROOKE, 8 vols.,
1911-1939.
CAMPBELL, J.K., Honour, family and patronage, Oxford, 1964.
CHAMBERS, E.K., The Medieval Stage, 2 vols., Oxford, 1903.
CHAYTOR, H.J., From Script to Print: An Introduction to Medieval
Vernacular Literature, London, ²1966.
Chivalry, A series of studies to illustrate its historical signi-
ficance and civilizing influence, ed. by EDGAR PRESTAGE, London,
1928.
CHRISTOPH, SIEGFRIED RICHARD, Wolfram von Eschenbach's Couples,
Amsterdamer Publikationen zur Sprache und Literatur, 44, Am-
sterdam, 1981.
Die Chronik von Stederburg, übersetzt von EDUARD WINKELMANN,
Die Geschichtsschreiber der deutschen Vorzeit. XII. Jahrhun-
dert, 11, Berlin, 1866.
CLANCHY, M.T., From Memory to Written Record, England 1066-1307,
London, 1979.
CLAY, ROTHA MARY, The Hermits and Anchorites of England, London,
1914 (Reissue Detroit, 1968).
- , Further Studies on Medieval Recluses, The Journal of the
British Archaeological Association (3rd series), 6 (1953),
74-86.
CLIFTON-EVEREST, J.M., "ritter" as "Rider" and as "Knight". A
contribution to the Parzival-Gawan Question, Wolfram-Studien,
6 (1980), 151-166.
COLBY, ALICE M., The Portrait in twelfth-century French Litera-
ture. An Example of the stylistic Originality of Chrétien de
Troyes, Geneva, 1965.
COMFORT, WILLIAM W., The Literary Rôle of the Saracens in the
French Epic, PMLA, 55 (1940), 628-659.
COULTON, G.G., The Medieval Scene. An informal introduction to
the Middle Ages, Cambridge, 1960.
CROSBY, RUTH, Oral Delivery in the Middle Ages, Speculum, 2 (1936),
88-110.
CUCUEL, ERNST, Die Eingangsbücher des Parzival und das Gesamtwerk,
Deutsche Forschungen, 30, Frankfurt a.M., 1937.
CURSCHMANN, FRITZ, Hungersnöte im Mittelalter, Ein Beitrag zur
deutschen Wirtschaftsgeschichte des 8. bis 13. Jahrhunderts,
Leipziger Studien aus dem Gebiet der Geschichte, 6, Leipzig,
1900 (Reprint 1970).
CURSCHMANN, MICHAEL, Das Abenteuer des Erzählens. Über den Erzäh-
ler in Wolframs "Parzival", DVJ, 45 (1971), 627-667.

CURSCHMANN, MICHAEL, Waltherus cantor, Oxford German Studies, 6
(1972), 5-17.
- , The French, the Audience and the Narrator in Wolfram's Wille-
halm, Neophilologus, 59 (1975), 548-562.
CURTIUS, ERNST ROBERT, European Literature and the Latin Middle
Ages (Translated from the German: Europäische Literatur und
Lateinisches Mittelalter, Berne, 1948, by William R. Trask),
London, 1953.

DARWIN, FRANCIS D.S., The English Medieval Recluse. London, n.d.
DAVIS, HORTON and MARIE-HÉLÈNE, Holy Days and Holidays, The Medieval Pilgrimage to Compostela, London/Toronto, 1982.
DAVIS, R.H.C., A History of Medieval Europe. From Constantine to
Saint Louis, London, ²1970.
DEINERT, WILHELM, Ritter und Kosmos im Parzival. Eine Untersuchung der Sternkunde Wolframs von Eschenbach, Münchner Texte
und Untersuchungen zur deutschen Literatur des Mittelalters,
2, Munich, 1960.
DELBRÜCK, HANS, Geschichte der Kriegskunst im Rahmen der politi-
schen Geschichte, III: Das Mittelalter, Berlin, ²1923 (Re-
print Berlin, 1964).
Deutsches Städtebuch, Handbuch für städtische Geschichte, ed.
by ERICH KEYSER, 5 vols. (10 parts), Stuttgart, 1939-74;
vol. V: Bayerisches Städtebuch, ed. by ERICH KEYSER and HEINZ
STOOB, Part 1 (1971); Part 2 (1974).
DICK, ERNST, S., Katabasis and the Grail Epic: Wolfram von
Eschenbach's Parzival, Res Publica Litterarum, 1 (1978), 57-87.
DILTHEY, WILHELM, Die ritterliche Dichtung und das nationale
Epos. Von deutscher Dichtung und Musik, Berlin, 1933.
DOERR, Otmar, Das Institut der Inclusen in Süddeutschland, Bei-
träge zur Geschichte des alten Mönchtums und des Benediktiner-
ordens, 18, Münster, 1934.
DOYÈRE, DOM PIERRE, Ermites, Dictionnaire de Droit Canonique,
vol. V (1953), 412-429.
- , Erémitisme en Occident, Dictionnaire de Spiritualité, vol. IV
(1960), 953-982.
DUBY, Georges, Rural Economy and Country Life in the Medieval
West, London, 1968 (Translated from L'Économie Rurale et la
Vie des Campagnes dans l'Occident Médiévale, Paris, 1962).
- , Le dimanche de Bouvines, 27 juillet 1214, Paris, 1973.
- , The chivalrous society, London, 1977.
- , Medieval Marriage. Two Models from Twelfth-Century France,
(translated by Elborg Forster), The Johns Hopkins Symposia
in Comparative History, 11, Baltimore/London, 1978.
DUCKWORTH, DAVID, The Influence of Biblical Terminology and
Thought on Wolfram's Parzival. With special reference to
the epistle of St. James and the concept of "zwivel", Göp-
pinger Arbeiten zur Germanistik, 273, Göppingen, 1980.
DUNGERN, OTTO VON, Adelsherrschaft im Mittelalter, Munich, 1927,
(Reprint Darmstadt, 1967).

ECKENSTEIN, LINA, Woman under Monasticism: chapters on saint-
lore and convent life between A.D. 500 and A.D. 1500,
Cambridge, 1897 (Reprint 1963).
EGGERS, HANS, Literarische Beziehungen des "Parzival" zum 'Tri-
strant' Eilharts von Oberg, PBB (Tübingen), 72 (1950), 39-51.
- , Strukturprobleme mittelalterlicher Epik dargestellt am Parzi-
val Wolframs von Eschenbach, Euphorion, 47 (1953), 260-270.
- , Non cognovi litteraturam. Zu Parzival 115.27, in: Fs. Ulrich
Pretzel, Berlin, 1963, 162-172. (Reprinted in: Wolfram von
Eschenbach, WdF, 57, 533-548).
EHRISMANN, GUSTAV, Geschichte der deutschen Literatur bis zum
Ausgang des Mittelalters, Munich, 1932 (^{2}I); 1922 (II,1);
1927 (II,2); 1935 (II,3).
Eichstätt, Stadt, bearbeitet von FELIX MADER. Mit einer histori-
schen Einleitung von FRANZ HEIDINGSFELDER, Die Kunstdenkmäler
von Bayern, 5, Heft 1, Munich, 1924.
Eichstätt, Bezirksamt, Ibid., Heft 2, Munich, 1928.
EIS, GERHARD, Zur Datierung des Nibelungenliedes, Forschungen
und Fortschritte, 27 (1953), 48-51.
ELIAS, NORBERT, Die höfische Gesellschaft. Untersuchungen zur
Soziologie des Königstums und der höfischen Aristokratie,
Soziologische Texte, 54, Neuwied, 1969.
ELM, KASPAR, Die Stellung der Frau in Ordenswesen, Semireligiö-
sentum und Häresie zur Zeit der Heiligen Elisabeth, in:
Sankt Elisabeth. Fürstin, Dienerin, Heilige, 7-28.
EMMEL, HILDEGARD, Formprobleme des Artusromans und der Graldich-
tung. Die Bedeutung des Artuskreises für das Gefüge des Romans
im 12. und 13. Jahrhundert in Frankreich, Deutschland und den
Niederlanden, Berne, 1951.
ENGELEN, ULRICH, Die Edelsteine in der deutschen Dichtung des
12. und 13. Jahrhunderts, Münstersche Mittelalter-Schriften,
27, Munich, 1978.
ERBEN, WILHELM, Kriegsgeschichte des Mittelalters, Munich/Berlin,
1929.
ERDMANN, CARL, Entstehung des Kreuzzugsgedankens, Stuttgart, 1935
(Reprint Darmstadt, 1955).
Études sur l'Histoire de la Pauvreté (Moyen Age - XVIe siècle)
sous la direction de MICHEL MOLLAT, Publications de la Sorbonne,
Série "Etudes", 8, Paris, 1974.
ERTZDORFF, XENJA VON, Höfische Freundschaft, DU, 14 (1962), 35-51.
- , Das "Herz" in der lateinisch-theologischen und frühen volks-
sprachigen religiösen Literatur, PBB (Halle), 84 (1962), 249-
301.
- , Die Dame im Herzen und das Herz bei der Dame. Zur Verwendung
des Begriffs "Herz" in der höfischen Liebeslyrik des 11. und
12. Jahrhunderts, ZfdPh, 84 (1965), 6-46.
ETZLER, GERWIN, Die Komposition des Gahmuret-Teiles von Wolframs
Parzival und seine Funktion im Gesamtwerk, Diss. Kiel, 1950
(Typescript).
EVANS, JOAN, Life in Medieval France, London, ^{2}1957.

353

FALK, WALTER, Das Nibelungenlied in seiner Epoche, Revision eines romantischen Mythos, Heidelberg, 1974.
FARAL, EDMOND, Les Jongleurs en France au Moyen Âge, Bibliothèque
de l'École des Hautes Études, Paris, 1910.
- , Recherches sur les sources latines des contes et romans cour-
tois au moyen âge, Paris, 1913 (Reprint, 1967).
- , Les arts poétiques du XIIe et du XIIIe siècle. Recherches et
documents sur la technique littéraire du moyen âge, Biblio-
thèque de l'École des Hautes Études, Paris, 1923 (Reprint
1962).
- , La Légende Arthurienne; Études et Documents, Bibliothèque
de l'École des Hautes Études, 3 vols., Paris, 1929.
FAUST, A.B., A Defense and Interpretation of the Ninth Book of
Wolfram's Parzival, Modern Philology, 1 (1903/04), 275-293.
FECHTER, WERNER, Das Publikum der mittelhochdeutschen Dichtung,
Deutsche Forschungen, 28, Frankfurt a.M., 1935 (Reprint, 1972).
- , Lateinische Dichtkunst und deutsches Mittelalter, Philologi-
sche Studien und Quellen, 23, Berlin, 1964.
FERRANTE, JOAN M., Woman as image in medieval literature from
the twelfth century to Dante, New York, 1975.
FIERZ-MONNIER, ANTOINETTE, Initiation und Wandlung. Zur Geschich-
te des altfranzösischen Romans im zwölften Jahrhundert von
Chrétien de Troys zu Renau de Beaujeu, Diss. Berne 1951.
FILLITZ, HERMANN, Nicolaus von Verdun, Die Zeit der Staufer, V,
279-290.
FINK, GONTHIER-LOUIS, L'érémite dans la littérature allemande,
Études Germaniques, 18 (1963), 167-199.
FISCHER, HANNS, Die mittelhochdeutsche Literatur, Handbuch der
bayrischen Geschichte, vol. I (31975), 521-536.
FISCHER, RUDOLF, Zu den Kunstformen des mittelalterlichen Epos,
Wiener Beiträge zur englischen Philologie, 9, Vienna/Leipzig,
1899.
FLECKENSTEIN, JOSEF, Friedrich Barbarossa und das Rittertum, Zur
Bedeutung der grossen Mainzer Hoftage von 1184 und 1188, in:
Fs. Hermann Heimpel, Göttingen, 2 (1972), 1023-1041.
- , Review of HANS GEORG REUTER, Die Lehre vom Ritterstand. Zum
Ritterbegriff in Historiographie und Dichtung vom 11. bis zum
13. Jahrhundert (Neue Wirtschaftsgeschichte, 4, Cologne/Vienna,
1971), Blätter für deutsche Landesgeschichte, 108 (1972), 524-
528.
- , Das Rittertum der Stauferzeit, in: Die Zeit der Staufer, III,
103-112.
FLOHRSCHÜTZ, GÜNTER, Der Adel des Wartenberger Raums im 12. Jahr-
hundert, Zeitschrift für bayerische Landesgeschichte, 34 (1971),
85-164 and 462-511.
The Flowering of the Middle Ages, ed. by JOAN EVANS, London, 1966.
FOLDA, J., The Fourth Crusade, Some Reconsiderations, Byzantinoslavica, 26 (1967), 277-290.
Fontes rerum Germanicarum. Geschichtsquellen Deutschlands, ed. by
JOHANN F. BOEHMER, 4 vols., Stuttgart, 1843-68.
FOURQUET, JEAN, Wolfram d'Eschenbach et le Conte del Graal. Les
Divergences de la tradition du Conte del Graal de Chrétien
et leur importance pour l'explication du Parzival, Strasbourg,
1938.

FOURQUET, JEAN, Les Noms propres du "Parzival". Mélanges de
    Philologie Romane et de Littérature Médiévale offerts à
    Ernst Hoepffner, Strasbourg, 1949, 245-260.
- , La Structure du Parzival, in: Les Romans du Gral aux XIIe
    et XIIIe siècles, Colloques Internationaux, CNRS, III, Paris,
    1956, 199-211.
- , Die Entstehung des "Parzival", Wolfram-Studien, III (1975),
    20-27.
FRAPPIER, JEAN, Chrétien de Troyes. L'homme et l'oeuvre, Paris,
    [6]1969.
FRAUENHOLZ, EUGEN VON, Das Heerwesen der germanischen Frühzeit,
    des Frankenreiches und des ritterlichen Zeitalters, Munich,
    1935.
FREED, J.B., The origins of the European nobility: the problem
    of the ministeriales, Viator, 7 (1976), 211-242.
FRIEDEMANN, KÄTE, Die Rolle des Erzählers in der Epik, Berlin,
    1910 (Reprint Darmstadt, 1965).
FROMM, HANS, Komik und Humor in der Dichtung des deutschen Mit-
    telalters, DVJ, 36 (1962), 321-339.
FUHRMANN, HORST, Deutsche Geschichte im hohen Mittelalter. Von
    der Mitte des 11. bis zum Ende des 12. Jahrhunderts, Göttin-
    gen, 1978. (Deutsche Geschichte, 2, ed. by JOACHIM LEUSCHNER).

GANSHOF, F.L., Feudalism, London, 1952, [3]1964 (Translated from:
    Qu'est-ce que la féodalité, Brussels, [2]1947; all English edi-
    tions revised by the author).
GANZ, PETER, Polemisiert Gottfried gegen Wolfram? Zu Tristan
    Z. 4638f., PBB (Tübingen), 88 (1967), 68-85.
- , Der Begriff des "Höfischen" bei den Germanisten, Wolfram-
    Studien, IV (1977), 16-32.
GANZENMÜLLER, WILHELM, Das Naturgefühl im Mittelalter, Beiträge
    zur Kulturgeschichte des Mittelalters und der Renaissance,
    18, Leipzig/Berlin, 1914.
GEBHARDT, BRUNO, Handbuch der deutschen Geschichte, 9, neu be-
    arbeitete Auflage, ed. by HERBERT GRUNDMANN, Stuttgart, 1970-
    1976.
- , Vol. I: Frühzeit und Mittelalter, bearbeitet von Friedrich
    Baethgen, Karl Bosl, u.a.
GEIL, GERHILD, Gottfried und Wolfram als literarische Antipoden.
    Zur Genese eines literaturgeschichtlichen Topos, Cologne, 1973.
GENICOT, LEOPOLD, Contours of the Middle Ages, London, 1967
    (Translated from the French "Les Lignes De Faîte Du Moyen
    Âge", 1961).
GERNENTZ, HANS JOACHIM, Die gesellschaftliche Stellung des Künst-
    lers in Deutschland um 1200, Wissenschaftliche Zeitschrift
    der Universität Rostock, Gesellschafts- und Sprachwissenschaft-
    liche Reihe, 9 (1959/60), 121-125.
GERZ, ALFRED, Rolle und Funktion der epischen Vorausdeutung im
    mittelhochdeutschen Epos, Germanische Studien, 97, Berlin,
    1930.
GIBBS, MARION E., Wrong paths in "Parzival", MLR, 63 (1968), 872-
    876.

GIBBS, MARION E., Wîplîchez Wîbes Reht. A Study of the Women
    Characters in the Works of Wolfram von Eschenbach, Duquesne
    Studies, Philological Series, 15, Duquesne, 1972.
GILLINGHAM, J.B., The Kingdom of Germany in the High Middle Ages,
    (900-1200), Historical Association, Pamphlet 77, London, 1971.
- , Richard the Lionheart, London, 1978.
GIESEBRECHT, WILHELM VON, Geschichte der deutschen Kaiserzeit,
    6 vols., Leipzig, ^{4}1873-95.
GIRVAN, RITCHIE, The Medieval Poet and his Public, English
    Studies To-day, Oxford, 1951, 85-97.
GLUNZ, HANS H., Die Literarästhetik des europäischen Mittelalters,
    Frankfurt a.M., ^{2}1963.
GNÄDINGER, LOUISE, Trevrizent - seine wüstenväterlichen Züge in
    Wolframs von Eschenbach Parzival (Buch IX), Studi di Lettera-
    tura religiosa tedesca in Memoria di Sergio Lupi, Biblioteca
    della Rivista di Storia e Letteratura Religiosa. Studi e
    Testi, 4, Florence, 1972, 135-175.
- , Rois Peschière/Anfortas. Der Fischerkönig in Chrétiens und
    Wolframs Graldichtung, in: Orbis Mediaevalis. Mélanges de langue
    et de littérature médiévales offerts à R. R. Bezzola, Berne,
    1978, 127-148.
GOTTLIEB, THEODOR, Über mittelalterliche Bibliotheken, Leipzig,
    1890.
GOTTSCHALK, JOSEF, St. Hedwig. Herzogin von Schlesien, Forschun-
    gen und Quellen zur Kirchen- und Kulturgeschichte Ostdeutsch-
    lands, 2, Cologne/Graz, 1964.
GOUGAUD, DOM LOUIS, La vie érémitique au Moyen âge, Rev. d'ascéti-
    que et de mystique, 1, (1920), 209-240 and 313-328.
- , Ermites et reclus: Etudes sur d'anciennes formes de vie re-
    ligieuse, Ligugé, 1928.
GREEN, DENNIS H., Der Auszug Gahmurets, Wolfram-Studien, (1970),
    62-86.
- , Der Weg zum Abenteuer im höfischen Roman des deutschen Mittel-
    alters, Veröffentlichung der Joachim Jungius-Gesellschaft der
    Wissenschaften, Göttingen, 1974 (Extended version: The Pathway
    to Adventure, Viator, Medieval and Renaissance Studies, 8 (1977),
    145-188).
- , Alieniloquium. Zur Begriffsbestimmung der mittelalterlichen
    Ironie, in: Fs. F. Ohly, Munich, 1975, II, 119-159.
- , Irony in the Medieval Romance, Cambridge, 1979.
- , The Art of Namedropping in Wolfram's "Parzival", Wolfram-
    Studien, 6 (1980), 84-150.
- , The Art of Recognition in Wolfram's Parzival, Cambridge, 1982.
GREEN, DENNIS H., and JOHNSON, LESLIE PETER, Approaches to Wolf-
    ram von Eschenbach. Five essays, Mikrokosmos, 5, Berne/Frank-
    furt a.M./Las Vegas, 1978.
GREEN, V.H.H., Medieval Civilization in Western Europe, London,
    1971.
GRÉGOIRE, HENRI, The Question of the Diversion of the Fourth Cru-
    sade. An old Controversy solved by a Latin Adverb, Byzantion,
    15 (1940), 158-166.

GROOS, ARTHUR B., "Sigune auf der Linde" and the turtledove in Parzival, JEGP, 67 (1968), 631-646.
- , Wolfram's Lament for Herzeloyde. (Parzival 128.23ff.), Modern Language Notes, 89 (1974), 361-366.
- , Time Reference and the Liturgical Calender in Wolfram von Eschenbach's Parzival, DVJ, 49 (1975), 43-65.
- , Parzival's "swertleite", Germanic Review, 50 (1975), 245-259.
- , Trevrizent's "Retraction": Interpolation or Narrative Strategy?, DVJ, 55 (1981), 44-63.
GRUENTER, RAINER, Landschaft. Bemerkungen zur Wort- und Bedeutungsgeschichte, GRM, 34 (1953), 110-120, (Reprinted in: ALEXANDER RITTER (ed.), Landschaft und Raum in der Erzählkunst, WdF, 418 (1975), 192-207).
- , Das "wunnecliche tal", Euphorion, 55 (1961), 341-404.
- , Zum Problem der Landschaftsdarstellung im höfischen Versroman, Euphorion, 56 (1962), 248-278, (Reprinted in: ALEXANDER RITTER (ed.), Landschaft und Raum in der Erzählkunst, WdF, 418, 293-335).
GRUNDMANN, HERBERT, Religiöse Bewegungen im Mittelalter. Untersuchungen über die geschichtlichen Zusammenhänge zwischen der Ketzerei, den Bettelorden und der religiösen Frauenbewegung im 12. und 13. Jahrhundert und über die geschichtlichen Grundlagen der deutschen Mystik, Anhang: Neue Beiträge zur Geschichte der religiösen Bewegungen im Mittelalter (1955), Historische Studien, 267, Berlin, 1935 (Reprint Darmstadt, 1977).
- , Die Frauen und die Literatur im Mittelalter, Archiv für Kulturgeschichte, 26 (1936), 129-161.
- , Litteratus - illitteratus, Der Wandel einer Bildungsnorm vom Altertum zum Mittelalter, Archiv für Kulturgeschichte, 40 (1958), 1-65.
- , Deutsche Eremiten, Einsiedler und Klausner im Hochmittelalter (10.-12. Jahrhundert), Archiv für Kulturgeschichte, 45 (1963), 60-90.
- , Dichtete Wolfram von Eschenbach am Schreibtisch?, Archiv für Kulturgeschichte, 49 (1967), 391-405.
GSTEIGER, MANFRED, Die Landschaftsschilderungen in den Romanen Chrestiens de Troyes, Literarische Tradition und künstlerische Gestaltung, Berne, 1958.
GÜRTTLER, KARIN, Künec Artûs der guote: eine Untersuchung zum Artusbild der höfischen Epik des 12. und 13. Jahrhunderts, Studien zur Germanistik, Anglistik und Komparatistik, 52, Bonn, 1976.

HAHN, INGRID, Raum und Landschaft in Gottfrieds "Tristan", Medium Aevum, Philologische Studien, 3, Munich, 1963.
HAMILTON, BERNARD, The Albigensian Crusade, Historical Association, Pamphlet, 85, London, 1974.
HAMILTON, JEAN, Landschaftsverwertung im Bau höfischer Epen, Diss. Bonn, 1932.
HAMPE, KARL, Germany under the Salian and Hohenstaufen Emperors, Oxford, 1973 (Translated from the twelfth German edition of "Deutsche Kaisergeschichte in der Zeit der Salier und Staufer", ed. by FRIEDRICH BAETHGEN, Heidelberg, 1968).

Handbuch der bayerischen Geschichte, ed. by MAX SPINDLER, 4 vols.,
Munich, 1969-75.

HARDING, ROSAMOND E.M., An Anatomy of Inspiration and an essay
on the creative mood, with an Appendix on The Birth of a Poem
by Robert Nichols, Cambridge, [3]1948.

HARMS, WOLFGANG, Der Kampf mit dem Freund oder Verwandten in der
deutschen Literatur bis um 1300, Medium Aevum, Philologische
Studien, 1, Munich, 1963.

- , Homo viator in bivio, Studien zur Bildlichkeit des Weges,
Medium Aevum, Philologische Studien, 21, Munich, 1970.

HARROFF, STEPHEN C., Wolfram and his Audience, A Study of the
Themes of Quest and of Recognition of Kinship Identity, Göppinger Arbeiten zur Germanistik, 120, Göppingen, 1974.

HARVEY, RUTH, Moriz von Craun and the Chivalric World, Oxford,
1961.

HARVEY, SALLY, The Knight and the Knight's Fee in England, Past
and Present, 49 (1970), 3-43.

HASKINS, Charles Homer, The Renaissance of the Twelfth Century,
Cambridge (Mass.)/London, 1927.

Hastings' Encyclopaedia of Religion and Ethics, 12 vols., Edin-
burgh, 1908-1921.

HATTO, ARTHUR T., On Chrétien and Wolfram, MLR, 44 (1949), 380-
385.

- , Zur Entstehung des Eingangs und der Bücher I und II des Parzival, ZfdA, 84 (1952/53), 232-240.

- , Y-a-t-il un Roman du Graal de Kyot le Provençal?, Les Romans
du Graal aux XIIe et XIIIe Siècles, 167-181.

- , Herzeloyde's Dragon-Dream, German Life and Letters, 22 (1968),
16-31.

HAUCK, ALBERT, Kirchengeschichte Deutschlands, vol. IV, Leipzig,
[4]1913.

HAUSER, ARNOLD, The Social History of Art, 4 vols., London, [2]1962
(Translated in collaboration with the author by Stanley Godman),
vol. I: From prehistoric times to the Middle Ages.

- , Sozialgeschichte der Kunst und Literatur, 2 vols., Munich,
[2]1967.

HAY, DENYS, The Medieval Centuries, London, 1964 (First published
1953 under the title: From Roman Empire to Renaissance Europe).

HEER, FRIEDRICH, Die Tragödie des Heiligen Reiches, 2 vols., Stuttgart, 1952/53.

HEGER, HEDWIG, Das Lebenszeugnis Walthers von der Vogelweide. Die
Reiserechnungen des Passauer Bischofs Wolfger von Erla, Vienna,
1970.

HEINZLE, JOACHIM, Gralkonzeption und Quellenmischung. Forschungskritische Anmerkungen zur Entstehungsgeschichte von Wolframs
"Parzival" und "Titurel", Wolfram Studien, 3 (1975), 28-39.

HEISE, URSULA, Frauengestalten im Parzival Wolframs von Eschenbach, DU, 9 (1957), 37-62.

HELLER, EDMUND KURT, Studies on the Story of Gawain in Chrestien
and Wolfram, JEGP, 24 (1925), 463-503.

HELMHOLTZ, R.H., Marriage Litigation in Medieval England, Cambridge
Studies in English Legal History, Cambridge, 1974.

HEMPEL, HEINRICH, Französischer und deutscher Stil im höfischen Epos, GRM, 23 (1935), 1-24 (Reprinted in: Kleine Schriften, Heidelberg, 1966, 240-260).

HEMPEL, WOLFGANG, Übermuot Diu Alte... Der Superbia-Gedanke und seine Rolle in der deutschen Literatur des Mittelalters, Studien zur Germanistik, Anglistik und Komparatistik, 1, Bonn, 1970.

HENNIG, URSULA, Die Gurnemanzlehren und die unterlassene Frage Parzivals, PBB (Tübingen), 97 (1975), 312-332.

HENZEN, WALTER, Das IX. Buch des "Parzival". Überlegungen zum Aufbau, in: Fs. Karl Helm, Tübingen, 1951, 189-217 (Reprinted in: WdF, 57 (1966), 125-157.)

- , Zur Vorprägung der Demut im Parzival durch Chrestien, PBB (Tübingen), 80 (1958), 422-443.

HERLIHY, DAVID, Land, Family and Women in Continental Europe, 701-1200, Traditio, 18 (1962), 89-120.

- , Life Expectancies for Women in Medieval Society, in: The Role of Woman, 1-20.

- , The Medieval Marriage Market, Medieval and Renaissance Studies, 6 (1976), 3-27.

HESSE, HANS R., Herzeloydens Traum (Zu Parzival 103.25-104.30), GRM, 43 (1962), 306-309.

HILKA, ALFONS, Die direkte Rede als stilistisches Kunstmittel in den Romanen des Chrestien de Troyes, Halle, 1903.

HIRSCHBERG, DAGMAR, Untersuchungen zur Erzählstruktur von Wolframs Parzival. Die Funktion von erzählter Szene und Station für den doppelten Kursus, Göppinger Arbeiten zur Germanistik, 139, Göppingen, 1976.

History of the Crusaders, A, ed. by KENNETH M. SETTON, Medieval Academy of America, Philadelphia, 1955 - then Wisconsin, 1969. I: The First Hundred Years (1955), [2]1969; II: The Later Crusades 1189-1311 (1962), [2]1969; III: The Fourteenth and Fifteenth Centuries (1975); IV: The Art and Architecture of the Crusader States (1976).

HODGETT, GERALD A.J., A Social and Economic History of Medieval Europe, London, 1972.

HOFER, STEFAN, Chrétien de Troyes. Leben und Werke des altfranzösischen Epikers, Graz/Cologne, 1954.

- , La Structure du Conte del Graal, in: Les Romans du Graal aux XIIe et XIIIe siècles, 15-26.

HOFMEISTER, PHILIPP, Eremiten in Deutschland, in: Fs. Michael Schmaus, Munich/Paderborn/Vienna, 1967, II, 1191-1214.

HOLDSWORTH, CHRISTOPHER J., Christina of Markyate, in: Medieval Women, 185-204.

HOLMES, URBAN TIGNER, Daily Living in the Twelfth Century. Based on the Observations of Alexander Neckam in London and Paris, Wisconsin, 1952.

HOLZKNECHT, Karl J., Literary Patronage in the Middle Ages, London, 1966.

HORACEK, BLANKA, "Ichne kan deheinen buochstap", in: Fs. Dietrich Kralik, Horn, N.-Ö., 1954, 129-145.

HORACEK, BLANKA, Zur inneren Form des Trevrizentbuches, Sprach-
    kunst, 3 (1972), 214-229.
HORTZSCHANSKY, ADALBERT, Gahmurets Wappen, ZfdPh, 12 (1881),
    73-77.
HOTZ, WALTER, Burg Wildenberg im Odenwald. Ein Herrensitz der
    Hohenstaufenzeit, Amorbach, 1963.
HUBY MICHEL, Wolframs Bearbeitungstechnik im "Parzival" (Buch III),
    Wolfram-Studien, III (1975), 40-51.
HUYSKENS, A., Quellenstudien zur Geschichte der heiligen Elisabeth,
    Landgräfin von Thüringen, Marburg, 1908.

IWAND, KÄTHE, Die Schlüsse der mittelhochdeutschen Epen, Germ.
    Studien, 16, Berlin, 1922.

JENKINS, R.J.H., The Byzantine Empire on the Eve of the Crusades,
    Historical Association, Pamphlet, 24, London, 1953.
JOHNSON, LESLIE PETER, Lähelin and the Grail Horses, MLR, 63 (1968),
    612-617.
JOHNSON, SIDNEY M., Herzeloyde and the Grail, Neophilologus, 52
    (1968), 148-156.
JONES, MARTIN H., Parzival's Fighting and his Election to the
    Grail, Wolfram Studien, 3 (1975), 52-71.
JORDAN, LEO, Wie man sich im Mittelalter die Heiden des Orients
    vorstellte, GRM, 5 (1913), 391-400.

Kaiser Friedrich II. in Briefen und Berichten seiner Zeit, ed.
    and translated by KLAUS J. HEINISCH, Darmstadt, 1977.
KAISER, GERT, Textauslegung und gesellschaftliche Selbstdeutung,
    Die Artusromane Hartmanns von Aue, Wiesbaden, [2]1978.
KANT, KARL, Scherz und Humor in Wolframs von Eschenbach Dichtun-
    gen, Heilbronn, 1878.
KAMP, NORBERT, Moneta Regis. Beiträge zur Geschichte der königli-
    chen Münzstätten und der königlichen Münzpolitik in der Stau-
    ferzeit, Diss. Göttingen, 1957 (Typescript).
KANTOROWICZ, ERNST, Kaiser Friedrich der Zweite, Berlin, [4]1936.
- , Kaiser Friedrich der Zweite. Ergänzungsband, Quellennachwei-
    se und Exkurse, Berlin, 1931.
KARG-GASTERSTÄDT, ELISABETH, Zur Entstehungsgeschichte des "Par-
    zival", Sächsische Forschungsinstitute in Leipzig, Forschungs-
    institut für neuere Philologie, I, Altgermanistische Abteilung,
    H. 2, Halle, 1925.
KAYSER, WOLFGANG, Das sprachliche Kunstwerk, Eine Einführung in
    die Literaturwissenschaft, Berne, 1948.
KEEN, MAURICE, A History of Medieval Europe, London, 1968.
KEFERSTEIN, GEORG, Die Gawanhandlung in Wolframs Parzival, GRM,
    25 (1937), 256-274.
KEHRER, HUGO, Die Heiligen Drei Könige in Literatur und Kunst,
    2 vols., Leipzig, 1908/09.
KELLERMANN, WILHELM, Wege und Ziele der neuen Chrestien de
    Troyes-Forschung, GRM, 23 (1935), 204-228.
- , Aufbaustil und Weltbild Chrestiens von Troyes im Parzival-
    roman, Zeitschr. f. roman. Philologie, Beihefte, 88, Halle,
    1936.

KELLY, DOUGLAS, Chrétien de Troyes. An analytic Bibliography, London, 1976.

KENNEDY, ANGUS J., The Hermit's Role in French Arthurian Romance (1170 - c.1530), Romania, 95 (1974), 54-83.

- , The Portrayal of the Hermit-Saint in French Arthurian Romance: The Remoulding of a Stock-Character, in: An Arthurian Tapestry. Essays in memory of Lewis Thorpe, ed. by KENNETH VARTY, Glasgow, 1981, 69-82.

KER, W.P., Epic and Romance. Essays on Medieval Literature, London, [2]1908.

KEUTGEN, FRIEDRICH, Die Entstehung der deutschen Ministerialität, Vierteljahrsschrift f. Sozial- und Wirtschaftsgeschichte, 8 (1910), 1-16; 169-195; 481-547.

- , Bürgertum und Ministerialität im 11. Jahrhundert, Ibid., 18 (1925), 394-396.

KEYSER, ERICH, Bevölkerungsgeschichte Deutschlands, Leipzig, [3]1945.

KIMBLE, G.H.T., Geography in the Middle Ages, London, 1938.

KNAPP, FRITZ PETER, Der Lautstand der Eigennamen im "Willehalm" und das Problem von Wolframs Schriftlosigkeit, Wolfram-Studien, 2 (1974), 193-218.

KNOCHENHAUER, THEODOR, Geschichte Thüringens zur Zeit des ersten Landgrafenhauses (1039-1247), Gotha, 1871.

KNOWLES, DAVID, Archbishop Thomas Becket. A Character Study, The Raleigh Lecture on History 1949, Proceedings of the British Academy, 35, London 1970.

- , Thomas Becket, London 1970.

KOBEL, ERWIN, Untersuchungen zum gelebten Raum in der mittelhochdeutschen Dichtung, Zürcher Beiträge zur deutschen Sprach- und Stilgeschichte, 4, Zürich, 1951.

KÖHLER, ERICH, Ideal und Wirklichkeit in der höfischen Epik. Studien zur Form der frühen Artus- und Graldichtung, Zeitschrift für romanische Philologie, Beihefte, 97, Tübingen, 1956.

- , Zur Selbstauffassung des höfischen Dichters, in: Wege der Literatursoziologie, 245-265.

KÖHLER, GUSTAV, Die Entwicklung des Kriegswesens und der Kriegsführung in der Ritterzeit, 6 vols., Breslau, 1886-93.

KOLB, HERBERT, Schola Humilitatis, Ein Beitrag zur Interpretation der Gralerzählung Wolframs von Eschenbach, PBB (Tübingen), 78 (1956), 65-115.

- , Munsalvaesche. Studien zum Kyotproblem, Munich, 1963.

KOPPITZ, HANS-JOACHIM, Wolframs Religiosität. Beobachtungen über das Verhältnis Wolframs von Eschenbach zur religiösen Tradition des Mittelalters, Bonn, 1959.

KRAPPE, ALEXANDER H., The Fisher King, MLR, 39 (1944), 18-23.

Die Kreuzzüge aus arabischer Sicht, Aus den arabischen Quellen ausgewählt und übersetzt von FRANCESCO GABRIELI, Munich, 1975 (First published in Italian, 1957).

KÜHNEL, HARRY, Die materielle Kultur Österreichs zur Babenbergerzeit, in: 1000 Jahre Babenberger, 90-109.

KULISCHER, JOSEF, Allgemeine Wirtschaftsgeschichte des Mittelalters und der Neuzeit, I: Das Mittelalter, Darmstadt, [4]1971.

KURZ, Johann B., Wolfram von Eschenbach und seine Beziehungen zum Hochstift Eichstätt, Historische Blätter für Stadt und Landkreis Eichstätt (Beilage zum Donau-Kurier), Jg. 3, 10 (1954).
KUTZ, ELEANOR, The story of the Parents in Wolfram von Eschenbach's Parzival, Monatshefte, 70 (1978), 364-374.

LABARGE, MARGARET WADE, A Baronial Household of the Thirteenth Century, London, 1965.
- , Medieval Travellers. The Rich and Restless, London, 1982.
LADURIE, EMMANUEL LE ROY, Montaillou. Cathars and Catholics in a French village 1294-1324, London, 1978, (Translated from: Montaillou: village occitan de 1294 à 1324, Paris, 1978).
Landschaft und Raum in der Erzählkunst, ed. by ALEXANDER RITTER, WdF, 417, (1975).
LANGLOIS, CHARLES-VICTOR, La connaissance de la Nature et du Monde au Moyen Âge. (D'après quelques écrits français à l'usage des laïcs), Paris, 1911.
LAUSBERG, HEINRICH, Handbuch der literarischen Rhetorik, 2 vols., Munich, 1960.
Laʒamon: Brut, ed. by G.L. BROOK and R.F. LESLIE, vol. I: Text (Lines 1-8020), Early English Text Society, 250, Oxford, 1963.
LECLERCQ, JEAN, "Eremus" et "Eremita". Pour l'Histoire du Vocabulaire de la Vie Solitaire, Collectanea Ordinis cisterciensium, 17 (1963), 8-30.
- , Bernard of Clairvaux and the Cistercian Spirit, Cistercian Studies Series, 16, Michigan, 1976 (Originally published in French as: S. Bernard et l'esprit cistercien, Paris, 1966).
The Legacy of the Middle Ages, ed. by C.G. CRUMP and E.F. JACOB, Oxford, 1926.
LE GOFF, JACQUES, Das Hochmittelalter, Fischer Weltgeschichte, 11, Frankfurt, 1965.
- , Time, Work, and Culture in the Middle Ages, (Transl. by Arthur Goldhammer from: Pour un autre Moyen Age: temps, travail et culture en Occident.), Chicago/London, 1980.
LEHMANN, EDGAR, Die Bibliotheksräume der deutschen Klöster im Mittelalter, Berlin, 1957.
LERNER, LUISE, Studien zur Komposition des höfischen Romans im 13. Jahrhundert, Diss. Frankfurt a.M., 1936.
LEWIS, GERTRUD J., Das Tier und seine Funktion in Erec, Iwein, Parzival und Tristan, Kanadische Studien zur deutschen Sprache und Literatur, 11, Berne/Frankfurt a.M., 1974.
- , Die unheilige Herzeloyde. Ein ikonoklastischer Versuch, JEGP, 74 (1975), 465-485.
Lexikon für Theologie und Kirche, ed. by JOSEF HÖFER and KARL RAHNER, Freiburg, ²1957 - .
LEYSER, KARL, The German aristocracy from the ninth to the early twelfth century: a historical and cultural sketch, Past and Present, 41 (1968), 25-53.
- , Rule and Conflict in an Early Medieval Society. Ottonian Saxony, London, 1979.

Libellus de dictis quatuor ancillarum S. Elisabeth confectus, Der sogenannte, Mit Benutzung aller bekannten Handschriften zum ersten Male vollständig und mit kritischer Einführung herausgegeben und erläutert von A. HUYSKENS, Kempten/Munich, 1911.

Liber Vitae Ecclesiae Dunelmensis, ed. by J. STEVENS, Publications of the Surtees Society, 13, London, 1841.

Life in the Middle Ages, selected, translated and annotated by G.G. COULTON, 4 vols., Cambridge, ²1928-30.

LINTZEL, MARTIN, Die Mäzene der deutschen Literatur im 12. und 13. Jahrhundert, Thüringisch-Sächsische Zeitschrift für Geschichte und Kunst, 22 (1933), 47-77.

LOFMARK, CARL, Wolfram's Source References in "Parzival", MLR, 67 (1972), 820-844.

- , Zur Interpretation der Kyotstellen im "Parzival", Wolfram-Studien, IV (1977), 33-70.

- , The Authority of the Source in Middle High German Narrative Poetry, Bithell Series of Dissertations, 5, Institute of Germanic Studies, University of London, 1981.

LOOMIS, ROGER SHERMAN, Arthurian Tradition and Chrétien de Troyes, New York, 1949.

LORD, WILLIAM JACKSON, Die finanzielle Lage der amerikanischen Schriftsteller, in: Wege der Literatursoziologie, 287-314.

Lordship and Community in Medieval Europe, ed. by F.L. CHEYETTE, New York, 1968.

LOT, FERDINAND, L'Art Militaire et les Armées Au Moyen Âge en Europe et dans le Proche Orient, 2 vols., Paris, 1946.

Love and Marriage in the Twelfth Century, Mediaevalia, Lovaniensia, Series 1, Studia VIII, Leuven/Louvain, 1981.

LUCAE, KARL, Über den Traum der Herzeloyde im Parzival, ZfdPh, 9 (1878), 129-135.

LUDWIG, FRIEDRICH, Untersuchungen über die Reise- und Marschgeschwindigkeit im XII. und XIII. Jahrhundert, Berlin, 1877.

LÜNING, OTTO, Die Natur. Ihre Auffassung und poetische Verwendung in der altgermanischen und mittelhochdeutschen Epik bis zum Abschluß der Blütezeit, Zürich, 1889.

LÜTGE, FRIEDRICH, Deutsche Sozial- und Wirtschaftsgeschichte, Berlin/Heidelberg/New York, ³1966.

McDONALD, WILLIAM C. and ULRICH GOEBEL, German Medieval Literary Patronage from Charlemagne to Maximilian I: a Critical Commentary with Special Emphasis on Imperial Promotion of Literature, Amsterdamer Publikationen zur Sprache und Literatur, 10, Amsterdam, 1973.

Marriage in the Middle Ages, Viator. Medieval and Renaissance Studies, 4 (1973), 413-501, containing: JOHN LEYERLE, Introduction. The Substance of this Panel, 413-418. 1. JOHN T. NOONAN, Jr, Power to Choose 419-434, 2. HENRY ANSGAR KELLY, Clandestine Marriage and Chaucer's "Troilus", 435-457, 3. ANN S. HASKELL, The Paston Women on Marriage in Fifteenth-Century England, 459-471. 4. ROBERTA FRANK, Marriage in Twelfth- and Thirteenth-Century Iceland, 473-484, 5. VERN L. BULLOUGH, Medieval Medical and Scientific Views of Women, 485-501.

Mappae mundi, Die ältesten Weltkarten, hrsg. und erläutert v.
KONRAD MILLER, Stuttgart, 1895/98.

MAURER, FRIEDRICH, Parzivals Sünden. Erwägungen zur Frage nach
Parzivals Schuld, DVJ, 24 (1950), 304-346 (Repr. in WdF,
17, 49-103).

- , Leid. Studien zur Bedeutungs- und Problemgeschichte, beson-
ders in den grossen Epen der staufischen Zeit, Berne, 1951.

- , Wolfram und die zeitgenössischen Dichter, in: Typologia
litterarum, Fs. Max Wehrli, Zürich, 1969, 197-204 (Reprinted
in: Friedrich Maurer, Dichtung und Sprache des Mittelalters,
Berne, [2]1971, 447-453).

MAURER, HANS-MARTIN, Burgen, in: Die Zeit der Staufer, III, 119-
128.

MAYER, HANS EBERHARD, The Crusades, Oxford, 1972 (Translated
from: Geschichte der Kreuzzüge, Stuttgart, 1965).

- , Bibliographie zur Geschichte der Kreuzzüge, Hannover, [2]1965.

MAYR-HARTING, H., Functions of a Twelfth-Century Recluse, History,
60 (1975), 337-352.

Medieval Contributions to Modern Civilization. A Series of Lectures delivered at King's College, University of London, ed. by
F.J.C. HEARNSHAW, London, 1921 (Reprint 1967).

Medieval Culture and Society, ed. by DAVID HERLIHY, London, 1968.

The Medieval Nobility, Studies on the ruling classes of France
and Germany from the sixth to the twelfth century, edited and
translated by TIMOTHY REUTER, Europe in the Middle Ages,
Selected Studies, 14, Amsterdam/New York/Oxford, 1979.

Medieval Women, ed. by DEREK BAKER, Dedicated and presented to
Professor Rosalind M.T. Hill, Studies in Church History, Sub-
sidia, 1, Oxford, 1978.

MELLER, WALTER C., A Knight's Life in the Days of Chivalry, London, 1924.

MENDELS, JUDY, and LINUS SPULER, Landgraf Hermann von Thüringen
und seine Dichterschule, DVJ, 33 (1959), 361-388.

MERGELL, BODO, Wolfram von Eschenbach und seine französischen
Quellen, I. Teil: Wolframs Willehalm, II. Teil: Wolframs
Parzival, Forschungen zur deutschen Sprache und Dichtung, 6
and 11, Münster, 1936 and 1943.

- , Der Gral in Wolframs Parzival. Entstehung und Ausbildung
der Gralssage im Hochmittelalter, PBB, 73 (1951), 1-94 and
PBB, 74 (1952), 77-159.

- , Les livres de Gahmuret dans le Parzival de Wolfram d'Eschenbach, in: Les romans du Graal aux XIIe et XIIIe siècles, 185-
195.

MERSMANN, WALTER, Der Besitzwechsel und seine Bedeutung in den
Dichtungen Wolframs von Eschenbach und Gottfrieds von Straßburg, Medium Aevum, Philologische Studien, 22, Munich, 1971.

MERTENS, VOLKER, Laudine. Soziale Problematik im "Iwein" Hartmanns von Aue, Zeitschrift für deutsche Philologie, Beihefte,
3, Berlin, 1978.

- , Gregorius Eremita. Eine Lebensform des Adels bei Hartmann
von Aue in ihrer Problematik und ihrer Wandlung in der Rezeption, Münchener Texte und Untersuchungen zur deutschen Literatur des Mittelalters, 67, Munich, 1978.

MEYER, H., Zum Religionsgespräch im neunten Buch des Parzival, Neophilologus, 31 (1947), 18-26.

The Middle Ages 1000-1500, The Fontana Economic History of Europe, ed. by CARLO M. CIPOLLA, vol. I, London and Glasgow, 1972.

MILLER, EDWARD/JOHN HATCHER, Medieval England - Rural society and economic change 1086-1348, Social and economic history of England, 2, London, 1978.

MILLER, KONRAD, Kurze Erklärung der Weltkarte des Frauenklosters Ebstorf, Cologne, 1896.

- , Itineraria Romana. Römische Reisewege an der Hand der Tabula Peutingeriana dargestellt von Konrad Miller, Stuttgart, 1916.

Mittelalterliche Bibliothekskataloge Deutschlands und der Schweiz. Herausgegeben von der Bayerischen Akademie der Wissenschaften in München. I: Die Bistümer Konstanz und Chur, bearb. v. PAUL LEHMANN, 1918; II: Bistum Mainz, Erfurt, bearb. v. PAUL LEHMANN, 1928; III: 1. Teil: Bistum Augsburg, bearb. v. PAUL RUF, 1932, 2. Teil: Bistum Eichstätt, bearb. v. PAUL RUF, 1933, 3. Teil: Bistum Bamberg, bearb. v. PAUL RUF, 1939.

MITTELBACH, HILDE, Natur und Landschaft im klassisch-höfischen Epos, Diss. Bonn, 1941.

MOCKENHAUPT, BENEDIKT, Die Frömmigkeit im Parzival Wolframs von Eschenbach. Ein Beitrag zur Geschichte des religiösen Geistes in der Laienwelt des deutschen Mittelalters, Grenzfragen zwischen Theologie und Philosophie, 20, Bonn, 1942 (Reprint Darmstadt, 1968).

MOHR, WOLFGANG, Parzivals ritterliche Schuld, Wirkendes Wort, 2 (1951/52), 148-160 (Also in: Der arthurische Roman, 332-354).

- , Hilfe und Rat in Wolframs Parzival, in: Fs. Jost Trier, Meisenheim Glan, 1954, 173-197.

- , Parzival und Gâwân, Euphorion, 52 (1958), 1-22 (Also in: Wolfram von Eschenbach, WdF, 17, 287-318).

- , Wolframs Kyot und Guiot de Provins, in: Fs. Helmut de Boor, Tübingen, 1966, 48-70.

MOLLAT, MICHEL, Les Pauvres au Moyen Âge, Étude sociale. (Le Temps et les Hommes), Paris, 1978.

MUIR, EDWIN, The Structure of the Novel, London, 1928.

MÜLLER, KARL FRIEDRICH, Die literarische Kritik in der mittelhochdeutschen Dichtung und ihr Wesen, Deutsche Forschungen 26, Frankfurt a.M., 1933.

MUNDY, JOHN H., Europe in the High Middle Ages 1150-1309, London, 1973.

MUNZ, PETER, Frederick Barbarossa: a study in medieval politics, London, 1969.

MÜSSENER, A., Der Eremit in der altfranzösischen nationalen und höfischen Epik, Rostock, 1930.

Die Namen im "Parzival" und im "Titurel" Wolframs von Eschenbach, bearbeitet von WERNER SCHRÖDER, Berlin, New York, 1982.

NAUMANN, HANS, Doch ich ein leie waere, Archiv f. d. Studium der neueren Sprachen, 187 (1950), 116-117.

NAU, ELISABETH, Münzen und Geld in der Stauferzeit, Die Zeit der Staufer, III, 87-102.

NELLMANN, EBERHARD, Wolframs Erzähltechnik, Untersuchungen zur
Funktion des Erzählers, Wiesbaden, 1973.
NEUMANN, FRIEDRICH, Wolfram auf der Burg zu Wertheim, in: Fs.
Helmut de Boor, Munich, 1971, 365-378.
- , Wolfram von Eschenbach auf dem Wildenberg, ZfdA, 100 (1971),
94-110.
NOBLE, PETER S., Love and Marriage in Chrétien de Troyes, Cardiff,
1982.
La Noblesse au Moyen âge, XIe-XVe siècle. Essais à la mémoire de
Robert Boutruche, ed. by P. Contamine, Paris, 1976.
NOLTE, ALBERT, Die Composition der Trevrizent-Scenen. Parzival IX
452.13-502, ZfdA, 44, NF. 32 (1900), 241-248.
NOSSACK, HANS ERICH, Die schwache Position der Literatur, in: Die
schwache Position der Literatur, Reden und Aufsätze, Frankfurt,
1967, 7-27.

OEXLE, OTTO GERHARD, Armut und Armenfürsorge um 1200. Ein Beitrag
zum Verständnis der freiwilligen Armut bei Elisabeth von Thüringen, in: Sankt Elisabeth, 78-100.
OHLY, FRIEDRICH, Vom geistigen Sinn des Wortes im Mittelalter,
ZfdA, 89 (1958-59), 1-23 (Also in: F. Ohly, Schriften zur mittelalterlichen Bedeutungsforschung, Darmstadt, 1977, 1-31).
- , Wolframs Gebet an den Heiligen Geist im Eingang des "Wille-
halm", ZfdA, 91 (1961/62), 1-37, reprinted with Nachtrag 1965
in: Wolfram von Eschenbach, WdF, 57, 455-518.
- , Die Suche in Dichtungen des Mittelalters, ZfdA, 94 (1965),
171-184.
- , Cor Amantis non angustum, in: Fs. William Foerste, Cologne/
Vienna, 1970, 454-476, (Also in: Schriften zur mittelalterli-
chen Bedeutungsforschung, 128-155).
OMAN, CHARLES W.C., A History of the Art of War in the Middle
Ages, 2 vols., London, ²1924.
- , The Art of War in the Middle Ages A.D. 378-1515, revised and
edited by John H. Beeler, Ithaca/New York, 1953.
ORTMANN, CHRISTA, Ritterschaft, Zur Frage nach der Bedeutung der
Gahmuret-Geschichte im "Parzival" Wolframs von Eschenbach,
DVJ, 47 (1973), 664-710.

PAETZEL, MARTIN ROBERT, Wolfram von Eschenbach und Crestien von
Troyes. Parzival,Buch 7-13 und seine Quelle, Diss. Berlin,
1931.
PAINTER, SIDNEY, French Chivalry, Chivalric Ideas and Practices
in Medieval France, Baltimore, 1940.
- , Medieval Society, Ithaca/New York, 1951.
PANZER, FRIEDRICH, Gahmuret. Quellenstudien zu Wolframs Parzival,
Sb. der Heidelberger Akademie der Wissenschaften philosophisch-
historische Kl. 1939/40, Abh. 1, Heidelberg, 1940.
- , Vom mittelalterlichen Zitieren, Ibid. 1950, Abh. 2, Heidelberg,
1950.
PARSHALL, LINDA B., The Art of Narration in Wolfram's Parzival and
Albrecht's "Jüngerer Titurel", Anglica Germanica, series 2,
Cambridge, 1981.

PATZE, HANS, Die Entstehung der Landesherrschaft in Thüringen,
1. Teil, Mitteldeutsche Forschungen, 22, Cologne/Graz, 1962.

PAVY, L'ABBÉ, Les Recluseries, Lyon, 1875.

PEIL, DIETMAR, Die Gebärde bei Chrétien, Hartmann und Wolfram.
Erec - Iwein - Parzival, Medium Aevum, Philologische Studien,
28, Munich, 1975.

PERRIN, E. SAINTE-MARIE, Les reclusages en France au moyen âge,
Revue hebdomadaire, VIII, No. 30, Paris, 1907/1911, 598-629.

PESCHEL, OSCAR, Geschichte der Erdkunde bis auf Alexander von
Humboldt und Carl Ritter, Geschichte der Wissenschaften in
Deutschland, Neuere Zeit, 4, Munich, 1865.

PHILPOTTS, BERTHA S., Kindred and Clan in the Middle Ages,
Cambridge, 1913.

PIPER, OTTO, Burgenkunde. Bauwesen und Geschichte der Burgen
zunächst innerhalb des deutschen Sprachgebietes, Munich,
³1912.

PIRENNE, HENRI, Medieval Cities, Their Origins and the Revival
of Trade, Princeton, 1925.

- , Economic and Social History of Medieval Europe, London,
1936 (Translated from the French).

PITZ, ERNST, Wirtschafts- und Sozialgeschichte Deutschlands im
Mittelalter, Wissenschaftliche Paperbacks, 15, Sozial- und
Wirtschaftsgeschichte, Wiesbaden, 1979.

PLANITZ, HANS, Die deutsche Stadt im Mittelalter. Von der Römerzeit bis zu den Zunftkämpfen, Vienna - Cologne - Graz, ⁴1975.

PLOSS, EMIL, Die Datierung des Nibelungenliedes, PBB (Tübingen),
80 (1958), 72-106.

POAG, JAMES F., Heinrich von Veldeke's minne: Wolfram von Eschenbach's liebe und triuwe, JEGP, 61 (1962), 721-735.

- , Wolfram von Eschenbach's Metamorphosis of the Ovidian Tradition, Monatshefte für deutschen Unterricht, deutsche Sprache
und Literatur, 57 (1965), 69-76.

POLACK, C., Die Landgrafen von Thüringen. Zur Geschichte der
Wartburg, Gotha, 1865.

POOLE, A.L., Germany in the reign of Frederick II, in: Cambridge
Medieval History, vol. VI (1929), 80-109.

PÖRKSEN, UWE, Der Erzähler im mittelhochdeutschen Epos. Formen
seines Hervortretens bei Lamprecht, Konrad, Hartmann, in
Wolframs Willehalm und in den Spielmannsepen, Philologische
Studien und Quellen, 58, Berlin, 1971.

PÖRKSEN, GUNHILD, and PÖRKSEN, UWE, Die "Geburt" des Helden in
mittelhochdeutschen Epen und epischen Stoffen des Mittelalters,
Euphorion, 74 (1980), 257-286.

POUNDS, NORMAN J.G., An Economic History of Medieval Europe,
London, 1974.

- , An Historical Geography of Europe 450 BC-AD 1330, London,
1976.

POWER, EILEEN, Medieval People, London, 1924.

- , Medieval Women, ed. by M.M. Postan, Cambridge, 1975.

PRETZEL, ULRICH, and BACHOFER, WOLFGANG, Bibliographie zu Wolfram von Eschenbach, 2., stark erweiterte Auflage unter Mitarbeit von WULF-OTTO DREESSEN, HERTA HAAS, WILLY KROGMANN
und ELFRIEDE NEUBUHR, Berlin, 1968.

PRETZEL, ULRICH, Gahmuret im Kampf der Pflichten, in: Fs. H. de Boor, 1971, 379-395.
Probleme mittelhochdeutscher Erzählformen, ed. by PETER GANZ and WERNER SCHRÖDER, Berlin, 1972.

QUELLER, DONALD E., The Fourth Crusade. The Conquest of Constantinople, 1201-1204, Leicester, 1978.
QUELLER, DONALD E., and S.J. STRATTON, A Century of Controversy on the Fourth Crusade, Studies in Medieval and Renaissance History, 6 (1969), 235-277.

RACHBAUER, MARY A., Wolfram von Eschenbach. A Study of the Relation of the Content of Books III-VI and IX of the Parzival to the Crestien Manuscripts, The Catholic University of America, Studies in German, IV, New York, 1934 (Reprint 1970).
RAGOTZKY, HEDDA, Studien zur Wolfram-Rezeption. Die Entstehung und Verwandlung der Wolfram-Rolle in der deutschen Literatur des 13. Jahrhunderts, Studien zur Poetik und Geschichte der Literatur, 20, Stuttgart, 1971.
RANKE, FRIEDRICH, Zur Symbolik des Grals bei Wolfram von Eschenbach, Trivium, 4 (1946), 20-30 (Also in: Der arthurische Roman, WdF, 157, 321-331).
REID, T.W., Chrétien de Troyes and the Scribe Guiot, Medium Aevum, 45 (1976), 1-17.
RENOIR, ALAIN, Gawain and Parzival, Studia neophilologica, 31 (1959), 155-158.
REUTER, HANS GEORG, Die Lehre vom Ritterstand. Zum Ritterbegriff in Historiographie und Dichtung vom 11. bis 13. Jahrhundert, Neue Wirtschaftsgeschichte, 4, Vienna, [2]1975.
RICHEY, MARGARET F., Gahmuret Anschevin. A contribution to the study of Wolfram von Eschenbach, Oxford, 1923.
- , Ither von Gaheviez, MLR, 26 (1931), 315-329.
- , The Independence of Wolfram von Eschenbach in Relation to Chrestien de Troyes as shown in "Parzival" Books III-VI, MLR, 47 (1952), 350-361.
- , Schionatulander and Sigune, London, n.d.
Ritterliches Tugendsystem, ed. by GÜNTER EIFLER, WdF, 56, 1970.
Das Rittertum im Mittelalter, ed. by ARNO BORST, WdF, 349, 1976.
ROEHL, RICHARD, Patterns and Structure of Demand 1000-1500, in: The Fontana Economic History of Europe, 1, 107-142.
ROETHE, GUSTAV, Der Dichter des Parzival. Rede zur Gedächtnisfeier des Stifters der Berliner Universität, König Friedrich Wilhelm III, Berlin, 1924.
The Role of Woman in the Middle Ages, Papers of the sixth annual conference of the Center for Medieval and Early Renaissance Studies, State University of New York at Binghamton, 6-7 May 1972, ed. by ROSMARIE THEE MOREWEDGE, London, 1975.
Les Romans du Graal aux XIIe et XIIIe siècles, Colloques Internationaux, CNRS, III, Paris, 1956.
ROSCHER, H., Papst Innozenz III und die Kreuzzüge, Göttingen, 1969.
ROSSKOPF, RUDOLF, Der Traum Herzeloydes und der rote Ritter. Erwägungen über die Bedeutung des staufisch-welfischen Thronstreites für Wolframs "Parzival", Göppinger Arbeiten zur Germanistik, 89, Göppingen, 1972.

ROSOF, PATRICIA JANE FREEMAN, Anchoresses in Twelfth and Thirteenth Century Society, Ph. D., New York University, 1978, 183 pp., University Microfilms, No.: HIN 78-18452.

ROWLAND, BERYL, Medieval Woman's Guide to Health. The First English Gynecological Handbook, London, 1981.

RUH, KURT, Höfische Epik des deutschen Mittelalters, I: Von den Anfängen bis zu Hartmann von Aue, II: 'Reinhart Fuchs', Lanzelet, Wolfram von Eschenbach, Gottfried von Strassburg, Berlin, 1967 and 1980.

RÜHRMUND, F.W., Wolframs von Eschenbach Beschreibung von Terre Marveile, ein poetisches Landschaftsgemälde, Germania, 9 (1850), 12-35.

RUNCIMAN, STEVEN, A History of the Crusades, 3 vols., Cambridge, 1951 (Reprint 1971).

RUSSELL, JOSIAH COX, Medieval Regions and their Cities, Studies in Historical Geography, Newton Abbot, 1972.

- , Population in Europe 500-1500, Length and Expectation of Life, in: The Fontana Economic History, I, 25-70.

St. Athanasius, The Life of St. Anthony, translated and annotated by R.T. MEYER, Ancient Christian Writers, 10, London, 1950.

Sankt Elisabeth, Fürstin, Dienerin, Heilige. Aufsätze, Dokumentation. Katalog, hrsg. v. der Philipps-Universität Marburg in Verbindung mit dem Hessischen Landesamt für geschichtliche Landeskunde, Sigmaringen, 1981.

SALZMAN, L.F., English Life in the Middle Ages, London, 1926.

SAUERLÄNDER, WILLIBALD, Die bildende Kunst der Stauferzeit, in: Die Zeit der Staufer, III, 205-229.

SAX, JULIUS, Versuch einer Geschichte des Hochstiftes und der Stadt Eichstätt, Nuremberg, 1858.

- , Die Bischöfe und Reichsfürsten von Eichstätt 745-1806, Versuch einer Deutung ihres Waltens und Wirkens, 2 vols., Landshut, 1884.

SCHADENDORF, WULF, Zu Pferde, im Wagen, zu Fuß. Tausend Jahre Reisen, Bibl. d. German. National-Museums Nürnberg, vol. II, Munich, [2]1961.

SCHALLER, HANS MARTIN, Die Kanzlei Kaiser Friedrichs II., ihr Personal und ihr Sprachstil, Archiv f. Diplomatik, Schriftgeschichte, Siegel- und Waffenkunde, 3 (1957), 202-286, and 4 (1958), 264-327.

SCHILDT, JOACHIM, Gestaltung und Funktion der Landschaft in der deutschen Epik des Mittelalters (1050-1250), Diss. Berlin, 1960.

- , Zur Gestaltung und Funktion der Landschaft in der deutschen Epik des Mittelalters, PBB (Halle), 86 (1964), 279-307.

SCHIROK, BERND, Der Aufbau von Wolframs "Parzival". Untersuchungen zur Handschriftengliederung, zur Handlungsführung und Erzähltechnik, sowie zur Zahlenkomposition, Diss. Freiburg i. Br., 1972.

- , Trevrizent und Parzival. Beobachtungen zur Dialogführung und zur Frage der figurativen Komposition, Amsterdamer Beiträge zur älteren Germanistik, 10 (1976), 43-71.

SCHIROK, BERND, Parzivalrezeption im Mittelalter, Erträge der
    Forschung 174, Darmstadt, 1982.
SCHMID, KARL, Zur Problematik von Familie, Sippe und Geschlecht,
    Haus und Dynastie beim mittelalterlichen Adel, Zeitschrift
    für die Geschichte des Oberrheins, 105 (1957), 1-62.
SCHMIDT, PAUL GERHARD, Die zeitgenössische Überlieferung zum
    Leben und zur Heiligsprechung der heiligen Elisabeth, in:
    Sankt Elisabeth, 1-6.
SCHNEIDER, HERMANN, Parzival-Studien. Sitzungsberichte der Aka-
    demie der Wissenschaften, Phil.-hist. Klasse, 4 (1944/46),
    Munich, 1947.
SCHNITZLER, HERMANN, Der Dreikönigsschrein, Bonn, 1939.
SCHOLZ, MANFRED G., Walther von der Vogelweide und Wolfram von
    Eschenbach. Literarische Beziehungen und persönliches Verhält-
    nis, Diss. Tübingen, 1966.
- , Hören und Lesen. Studien zur primären Rezeption der Litera-
    tur im 12. und 13. Jahrhundert, Wiesbaden, 1980.
SCHRAMM, PERCY ERNST, (mit Beiträgen verschiedener Verfasser),
    Herrschaftszeichen und Staatssymbolik. Beiträge zu ihrer
    Geschichte vom dritten bis zum sechzehnten Jahrhundert, Schrif-
    ten der Monumenta Germaniae historica, 13/I/II/III, Stuttgart,
    1954-1956.
SCHRAMM, PERCY E., and MÜTHERICH, FLORENTINE, Denkmale der deut-
    schen Könige und Kaiser. Ein Beitrag zur Herrschergeschichte
    von Karl dem Grossen bis Friedrich II., 768-1250, Veröffent-
    lichungen des Zentralinstituts für Kulturgeschichte in Mün-
    chen, vol. II, Munich, 1962.
SCHREIBER, ALBERT, Neue Bausteine zu einer Lebensgeschichte Wolf-
    rams von Eschenbach, Deutsche Forschungen, 7, Frankfurt a.M.,
    1922.
- , Die Vollendung und Widmung des Wolframschen "Parzival",
    ZfdPh, 56 (1931), 14-37.
SCHREIER-HORNUNG, ANTONIE, Spielleute, Fahrende, Aussenseiter:
    Künstler der mittelalterlichen Welt, Göppinger Arbeiten zur
    Germanistik, 328, Göppingen, 1981.
SCHRÖDER, E., Der Anteil Thüringens an der Literatur des deut-
    schen Mittelalters, Zeitschrift des Vereins für thüringische
    Geschichte und Altertumskunde, 39, N.F. 31 (1934/35), 1-19.
SCHRÖDER, H.J., Disciplinary Decrees of the General Councils.
    Text, Translation and Commentary, London, 1937.
SCHRÖDER, WERNER, Zur Chronologie der drei großen mittelhochdeut-
    schen Epiker, DVJ, 31 (1975), 264-302.
- , Zum Wortgebrauch von "Riuwe" bei Hartmann und Wolfram, GRM,
    9 (1959), 228-234.
- , Parzivals Schwerter, ZfdA, 100 (1971), 111-132.
SCHRÖDER, WALTER JOHANNES, Der dichterische Plan des Parzival-
    romans, PBB (Halle), 74 (1952), 160-92; 409-53.
SCHRODT, RICHARD, Anfortas' Leiden, in: Fs. Otto Höfler, Vienna/
    Stuttgart, 1976, 589-626.
SCHÜCKING, LEVIN, Soziologie der literarischen Geschmacksbildung,
    Berne, ³1961.
SCHULTZ, JAMES A., The Shape of the Round Table. Structures of
    Middle High German Arthurian Romance, Toronto/Buffalo/London,
    1983.

370

SCHULZ, HANNA, Die Landschaft im mittelhochdeutschen Epos,
    Diss. Freiburg i. Br., 1924 (Typescript).
SCHUMACHER, MARLIES, Die Auffassung der Ehe in den Dichtungen
    Wolframs von Eschenbach, Germanische Bibliothek, Heidelberg,
    1967.
SCHWARTZ, DIETRICH W.H., Sachgüter und Lebensformen. Einführung
    in die materielle Kulturgeschichte des Mittelalters und der
    Neuzeit, Grundlagen der Germanistik, II, Berlin, 1970.
SCHWEIKLE, GÜNTHER (ed.), Dichter über Dichter in mittelhoch-
    deutscher Literatur, Tübingen, 1970.
SCHWIETERING, JULIUS, Sigune auf der Linde, ZfdA, 57 (1919/20),
    140-143.
- , Der Fischer vom See Brumbane (Parzival 225.2ff.), ZfdA, 60
    (1923), 259-264.
- , Die deutsche Dichtung des Mittelalters, Potsdam, 1941.
- , Parzivals Schuld, ZfdA, 81 (1944), 44-68 (Also in: Julius
    Schwietering, Mystik und höfische Dichtung im Hochmittelalter,
    Tübingen, 1960, 37-70).
SCHWIND, FRED, Die Landgrafschaft Thüringen und der landgräfliche
    Hof zur Zeit der Elisabeth, in: Sankt Elisabeth, 29-44.
SHAHAR, SHULAMITH, Die Frau im Mittelalter, Königstein/Ts., 1981.
SHEEHAN, MICHAEL M., Choice of Marriage Partner in the Middle
    Ages: Development and Mode of Application of a Theory of
    Marriage, Studies in Medieval and Renaissance History, 11
    (1978), 3-33.
SMAIL, R.C., Crusading Warfare 1097-1193, Cambridge, 1956.
SNELLEMAN, W. Das Haus Anjou und der Orient in Wolframs Parzival,
    Diss. Amsterdam, 1941.
SOUTHERN, R.W., The Making of the Middle Ages, London, 1953.
- , Western Society and the Church in the Middle Ages, The Peli-
    can History of the Church, 2, Harmondsworth, Middlesex, 1970.
SPRINGER, OTTO, Wolfram's Parzival, in: Arthurian Literature in
    the Middle Ages, Oxford, 1959, 218-250.
SPROEDT, KRIEMHILD, Gahmuret und Belakâne. Verbindung von Hei-
    dentum und Christentum in einem menschlichen Schicksal, Diss.
    Hamburg, 1964.
Die Stadt des Mittelalters, 3 vols., ed. by CARL HAASE, WdF,
    243-245, 1969-1973.
STAFFORD, PAULINE, Queens, Concubines and Dowagers. The King's
    Wife in the Early Middle Ages, London, 1983.
STAIGER, EMIL, Die Zeit als Einbildungskraft des Dichters, Zürich,
    1939.
- , Grundbegriffe der Poetik, Zürich, 1946.
- , Zu einem Vers von Mörike. Ein Briefwechsel mit Martin Heideg-
    ger, Zürich, 1951.
- , Die Kunst der Interpretation, Djakarta, 1951.
STARCK, CHRISTIAN, Die Darstellungsmittel des Wolframschen Humors,
    Diss. Schwerin, 1879.
STAUFFER, MARIANNE, Der Wald. Zur Darstellung und Deutung der
    Natur im Mittelalter, Berne, 1959.
STEELE, FRANCISCA MARIA, Anchoresses of the West, London, 1902.
STEIN, SIEGFRIED, Die Ungläubigen in der mittelhochdeutschen
    Literatur von 1050-1250, Diss. Heidelberg, 1933 (Reprint
    Libelli, 108, Darmstadt, 1963).

STEINEN, WOLFRAM VON DEN, Der Kosmos des Mittelalters von Karl
   dem Grossen zu Bernhard von Clairvaux, Berne/Munich, [2]1967.
STEINGER, HANS, Fahrende Dichter im deutschen Mittelalter, DVJ,
   8 (1930), 61-80.
STEINHOFF, HANS-HUGO, Die Darstellung gleichzeitiger Gescheh-
   nisse im mittelhochdeutschen Epos, Studien zur Entfaltung
   der poetischen Technik vom Rolandslied bis zum "Willehalm",
   Medium Aevum, Philologische Studien, 4, Munich, 1964.
STEPHENSON, CARL, Medieval Feudalism, Cornell, 1942 (Great Seal
   Books, 1956).
STOCKMAYER, GERTRUD, Über das Naturgefühl in Deutschland im 10.
   und 11. Jahrhundert, Beiträge zur Kulturgeschichte des Mit-
   telalters und der Renaissance, 4, Leipzig, 1910.
STOLTE, HEINZ, Eilhard und Gottfried: Studien über Motivreim
   und Aufbaustil, Halle, 1941.
STOREY, R.L., Chronology of the Medieval World 800-1491, London,
   1973.
STROTHMANN, DIETRICH, Die Regie des Autoreneinsatzes, in: Wege
   der Literatursoziologie, 315-331.
SUHLE, ARTHUR, Deutsche Münz- und Geldgeschichte von den Anfän-
   gen bis zum 15. Jahrhundert, Berlin, [2]1964.
SUMPTION, JONATHAN, Pilgrimage. An Image of Medieval Religion,
   London, 1975.
SWINBURNE, HILDA, Gahmuret und Feirefiz in Wolfram's Parzival,
   MLR, 51 (1956), 195-202.

TATLOCK, J.S.P., Medieval Laughter, Speculum, 21 (1946), 289-
   294.
1000 Jahre Babenberger in Österreich, Stift Lilienfeld, Katalog
   der Ausstellung (Niederösterreichische Landesregierung),
   Vienna, [3]1976.
TAX, PETRUS W., Gahmuret zwischen Äneas und Parzival. Zur Struk-
   tur der Vorgeschichte von Wolframs "Parzival", ZfdPh, 92
   (1973), 24-37.
- , Trevrizent. Die Verhüllungstechnik des Erzählers, in: Fs.
   Hugo Moser, Berlin, 1974, 119-134.
THOMAS, NEIL, Sense and Structure in the Gawan adventures of
   Wolfram's "Parzival", MLR, 76 (1981), 848-856.
THOMPSON, JAMES W., Feudal Germany, Chicago, 1928.
- , Economic and Social History of the Middle Ages (300-1300),
   London, 1928.
- , The Literacy of the Laity in the Middle Ages, New York, 1960.
THOMPSON, SALLY, The Problem of the Cistercian Nuns in the
   Twelfth and Thirteenth Centuries, in: Medieval Women, 227-252.
THROOP, PALMER A., Criticism of the Crusade, A Study of Public
   Opinion and Crusade Propaganda, Amsterdam, 1940 (Reprint
   Philadelphia, 1975).
TILLMANN, CURT, Lexikon der deutschen Burgen und Schlösser, 4
   vols., Stuttgart, 1958-1961.
TILLMANN, HELENE, Pope Innocent III, Europe in the Middle Ages,
   Selected Studies, 12, Amsterdam/New York/Oxford, 1980.
THUM, BERND, Aufbruch und Verweigerung. Literatur und Geschichte
   am Oberrhein im hohen Mittelalter. Aspekte eines geschichtli-
   chen Kulturraums, 2 vols., Waldkirch i. Br., 1979/80.

TOECHE, THEODOR, Kaiser Heinrich VI., Jahrbücher der deutschen Geschichte, Leipzig, 1867.

TOPSFIELD, L.T., Troubadours and Love, Cambridge, 1975.

– , Chrétien de Troyes. A Study of the Arthurian Romances, Cambridge, 1981.

TRACHSLER, ERNST, Der Weg im mittelhochdeutschen Artusroman, Studien zur Germanistik und Komparatistik, 50, Bonn, 1979.

TREIS, KARL, Die Formalitäten des Ritterschlags in der altfranzösischen Epik, Diss. Berlin, 1887.

TRIER, Jost, Architekturphantasien in der mittelalterlichen Dichtung, GRM, 17 (1929), 11-24.

– , Der deutsche Wortschatz im Sinnbezirk des Verstandes, 1. Von den Anfängen bis zum Beginn des 13. Jahrhunderts, Heidelberg, 1931.

TSCHIRCH, FRITZ, Das Selbstverständnis des mittelalterlichen deutschen Dichters, Miscellanea Mediaevalia, Veröffentlichungen des Thomas-Instituts an der Universität Köln, 3, Beiträge zum Berufsbewußtsein des mittelalterlichen Menschen, Berlin, 1964, 239-285.

TÜCHLE, HERMANN, Die Kirche der Christenheit, in: Die Zeit der Staufer, III, 165-175.

UNGER, OTTO, Die Natur bei Wolfram von Eschenbach, Diss. Greifswald, 1912.

ULLMANN, WALTER, Medieval Political Thought, Penguin Books, 1975 (First published as: A History of Political Thought: The Middle Ages, 1965).

– , A Short History of the Papacy in the Middle Ages, London, 1972 (Reprint 1974).

URBACH, THEODOR, Zur Geschichte des Naturgefühls bei den Deutschen, Dresden, 1885.

URRY, WILLIAM, Canterbury under the Angevin Kings, University of London Historical Studies, 19, London, 1967.

VERBRUGGEN, J.F., The Art of Warfare in Western Europe during the Middle Ages. From the Eighth Century to 1340, Europe in the Middle Ages, Selected Studies, 1, Amsterdam/New York/ Oxford, 1977 (Transl. from: De Krijgskunst in West-Europa in de Middeleeuwen, IXe tot begin XIVe eeuw, Verhandelingen van de Koninklijke Vlaamse Academie voor Wetenschappen, Letteren en schone Kunsten van België, Klasse der Letteren, 20, Brussels, 1954. Revised by the author for the English edition.)

VIËTOR, KARL, Die Kunstanschauung der höfischen Epigonen, PBB, 46 (1922), 85-124.

VINAVER, EUGÉNE, Form and Meaning in Medieval Romance, The Presidential Address of the Modern Humanities Research Ass., Leeds, 1966.

Vita, S. Antonii, ed. by J.P. MIGNE, Patrologia Graeca, 26, 835-978.

WAAS, ADOLF, Geschichte der Kreuzzüge, 2 vols., Freiburg, 1956.

– , Der Mensch im deutschen Mittelalter, Graz, [2]1966.

WAILES, STEPHEN L., Immurement and religious experience in the
Stricker's "Eingemauerte Frau", PBB (Tübingen), 96 (1974), 79-
102.
WAKEFIELD, WALTER L., Heresy, Crusade and Inquisition in Southern
France 1100-1250, 1974.
WALSHE, MAURICE, O'C, Travel-Descriptions in Middle High German
Arthurian Epics, Diss. London, 1935 (Typescript).
- , The Fabulous Geography of Lanzelet, London Medieval Studies,
1 (1937-39), 93-106.
- , Der Künic von Kukumerlant, Ibid., 280-284.
- , Notes on Parzival, BK. V., Ibid., 340-353.
WAPNEWSKI, PETER, Wolframs Parzival. Studien zur Religiosität und
Form, Heidelberg, 1955.
- , Herzeloydes Klage und das Leid der Blancheflur. Zur Frage
der agonalen Beziehungen zwischen den Kunstauffassungen Gott-
frieds von Straßburg und Wolframs von Eschenbach, in: Fs.
Ulrich Pretzel, Berlin, 1963, 173-184.
WARLOP, ERNEST, The Flemish nobility before 1300, 4 vols.,
Kortrijk, 1975/76.
WARNER, PHILIP, Sieges of the Middle Ages, London, 1968.
WATTENBACH, WILHELM, Deutschlands Geschichtsquellen im Mittel-
alter. WILHELM WATTENBACH/WILHELM LEVISON, Vorzeit und Karo-
linger, 5 vols., Weimar, 1952-1963, vols. II-IV revised by
HEINZ LÖWE, Beiheft: Die Rechtsquellen by RUDOLF BUCHNER.
- , Deutschlands Geschichtsquellen im Mittelalter, WILHELM
WATTENBACH/ROBERT HOLTZMANN, Die Zeit der Sachsen und Salier,
3 vols., ed. by FRANZ JOSEF SCHMALE, Darmstadt, 1967-1971.
- , Deutschlands Geschichtsquellen im Mittelalter, WILHELM
WATTENBACH/FRANZ JOSEF SCHMALE, Vom Tode Kaiser Heinrichs V.
bis zum Ende des Interregnum by FRANZ JOSEF SCHMALE unter der
Mitarbeit von IRENE SCHMALE-OTT und DIETER BERG, Darmstadt,
1976.
WEBER, GOTTFRIED, Wolfram von Eschenbach. Seine dichterische und
geistesgeschichtliche Bedeutung, Deutsche Forschungen, 18,
Frankfurt, 1928.
- , Parzival. Ringen und Vollendung. Eine dichtungs- und reli-
gionsgeschichtliche Untersuchung, Oberursel, 1948.
- , Wolframs von Eschenbach Antwort auf Gottfrids von Straßburg
"Tristan", Zur Grundstruktur des "Willehalm", Sitzungsberichte
der Wiss. Gesellschaft an der Johann Wolfgang Goethe-Universi-
tät, 12, Frankfurt a.M., 1975.
Wege der Literatursoziologie, ed. by HANS NORBERT FÜGEN, Berlin,
1968.
WEHRLI, MAX, Strukturprobleme des mittelalterlichen Romans, WW,
10 (1960), 334-345.
WEIGAND, HERMANN J., Trevrizent as Parzival's Rival? Modern
Language Notes, 69 (1954), 348-357.
- , Narrative Time in the Grail Poems of Chrétien de Troyes and
Wolfram von Eschenbach, in: Wolfram's Parzival: Five Essays
with an Introduction, ed. Ursula Hoffmann (1969), 18-74 (Ori-
ginally published as: Die epischen Zeitverhältnisse in den
Graldichtungen Chrestiens und Wolframs, PMLA, 53 (1938),
917-950).

374

WEISS, J., Gandîne, ZfdA, 28 (1884), 136-139.
WERNER, KARL FERDINAND, Adel, in: Lexikon des Mittelalters, 1.1
    (118-128), Munich, 1977.
WERNER, M., Bericht über die Überbringung Elisabeths von Ungarn
    nach Thüringen, Papierhandschrift, Koblenz, 1460/70, in: Sankt
    Elisabeth, 338-339.
- , Die heilige Elisabeth und Konrad von Marburg, Ibid., 46-69.
WESSELS, PAULUS BERNARDUS, Die Landschaft im jüngeren Minnesang,
    Vroenhoven, 1945.
WESTON, JESSIE L., The Legend of Sir Perceval, 2 vols., London,
    1906.
WHITE, LYNN Jr., Medieval Technology and Social Change, Oxford,
    1962 (Reprint 1979).
WIEGAND, HERBERT ERNST, Studien zur Minne und Ehe in Wolframs
    Parzival und Hartmanns Artusepik, Quellen und Forschungen
    zur Sprach- und Kulturgeschichte der germanischen Völker,
    Neue Folge, 49 (173), Berlin/New York, 1972.
WIERCINSKI, DOROTHEA, Minne. Herkunft und Anwendungsschichten
    eines Wortes, Niederdeutsche Studien, 11, Cologne, 1964.
WILLSON, H. BERNARD, The Symbolism of Belakâne and Feirefîz in
    Wolfram's Parzival, GLL, 13 (1959/60), 94-105.
- , The Grail King in Wolfram's Parzival, MLR, 55 (1960), 553-
    563.
- , Literacy and Wolfram von Eschenbach, Nottingham Medieval
    Studies, 14 (1970), 27-40.
WILMS, P. HIERONYMUS, Geschichte der deutschen Dominikanerinnen
    1206-1916, Dülmen i. W., 1920.
WINKELMANN, EDUARD, Philipp von Schwaben und Otto IV. von Braun-
    schweig, 2 vols., Jahrbücher d. dtsch. Geschichte, Leipzig,
    1873-1876 (Reprint Darmstadt, 1968).
- , Kaiser Friedrich II., 2 vols., Jahrbücher der deutschen Ge-
    schichte, Leipzig, 1889 and 1897 (Reprint Darmstadt, 1967).
WINTER, J. M. VAN, Rittertum. Ideal und Wirklichkeit, Munich,
    1969.
WOLF, WERNER, Die Wundersäule in Wolframs Schastel Marveile,
    in: Fs. Emil Öhmann, Helsinki, 1954, 275-314.
WOLFF, LUDWIG, Wolframs Schionatulander und Sigune, in: Fs.
    Friedrich Panzer, Heidelberg, 1950, 116-130 (Also in: Wolf-
    ram von Eschenbach, WdF, 17, 549-569).
WOLFGANG, LENORA D., Bliocadran. A Prologue to the "Perceval"
    of Chrétien de Troyes, Edition and Critical Study. Beihefte
    zur Zeitschrift für romanische Philologie, 150, Tübingen,
    1976.
Wolfram-Jahrbuch, ed. by WOLFGANG STAMMLER, 5 vols., Miltenberg/
    Amorbach, 1952-1956.
Wolfram Studien, ed. by WERNER SCHRÖDER, Berlin 1970 - .
Wolfram von Eschenbach, ed. by HEINZ RUPP, WdF, 57, 1966.
Wolfram von Eschenbach. Parzival und Titurel, hrsg. und erklärt
    von ERNST MARTIN, 2 vols., Halle 1900-1903.
Women in Medieval Society, ed. by SUSAN MOSHER STUARD, University
    of Pennsylvania, 1976.
WRIGHT, J.K., The Geographical Lore of the Time of the Crusades,
    American Geographical Society, Research Series, 15, New York,
    1925.

Writers at Work, The Paris Review Interviews. 1st Series ed. and
  with an introduction by MALCOLM COWLEY; 2nd series ed. by
  GEORGE PLIMPTON and introduced by VAN WYCK BROOKS; 3rd series
  ed. by GEORGE PLIMPTON and introduced by ALFRED KAZIN; 4th
  series ed. by GEORGE PLIMPTON, introduced by WILFRID SHEED,
  London, 1958-1977.
WÜHRER, KARL, Romantik im Mittelalter. Beitrag zur Geschichte
  des Naturgefühls im besonderen des 10. und 11. Jahrhunderts,
  Veröffentlichungen des Seminars für Wirtschafts- und Kulturge-
  schichte an der Universität Wien, 6, Baden/Vienna/Leipzig/
  Brünn, 1930.
WYNN, MARIANNE, Hagen's Defiance of Kriemhilt, Medieval German
  Studies, Presented to Frederick Norman, London, 1965, 104-114.
- , Orgeluse. Persönlichkeitsgestaltung auf Chrestienschem Modell,
  GLL, 30 (1977), 127-137.
- , Book I of Wolfram von Eschenbach's "Willehalm" and its Con-
  clusion, Medium Aevum, 49 (1980), 57-65.

YEANDLE, David N., Herzeloyde: Problems of Characterization in
  Book III of Wolfram's Parzival, Euphorion, 75 (1981), 1-28.

Die Zeit der Staufer, Geschichte-Kunst-Kultur. Katalog der Ausstellung, 5 vols., Stuttgart 1977-1979, I: Katalog; II: Ab-
  bildungen; III: Aufsätze; IV: Karten und Stammtafeln; V:
  Supplement: Vorträge und Forschungen.
ZEYDEL, EDWIN H., Wolfram von Eschenbach und diu buoch, Eupho-
  rion, 48 (1954), 210-215.
ZIMMERMANN, HORST, Zu Parzivals Gralsweg. Die "verschobenen Prä-
  missen" in Wolframs Parzival. (Zu dem scheinbaren Widerspruch
  zwischen Parzival 798.1ff. und den Worten Trevrizents im 9.
  Buch), Diss. Tübingen, 1961.
ZIOLKOWSKI, THEODORE, Der Karfunkelstein, Euphorion, 55 (1961),
  297-326.
ZUTT, HERTA, Parzivals Kämpfe, in: Fs. Friedrich Maurer, Düssel-
  dorf, 1968, 178-198.
ZWIERZINA, KONRAD, Beobachtungen zum Reimgebrauch Hartmanns und
  Wolframs, in: Fs. Richard Heinzel, Halle, 1898, 437-511.